D1878959

AMERICA'S AFGHANISTAN WAR

The success that failed

AMERICA'S AFGHANISTAN WAR

Tha Success That Failed

jagmohan meher

KALPAZ

Published by

Gyan Publishing House
5, Ansari Road
New Delhi-110002

Distribution Network
gyanbooks.com
India, USA, Canada, UK, Australia, France

© Publisher

All rights reserved. No part of this work may be reproduced, stored, adapted, or transmitted in any form or by any means, electronic, mechanical, photocopying, micro-filming, recording or otherwise, or translated in any language, without the prior written permission of the copyright owner and the publisher.

ISBN: 97887-83-526-26 (HB)

15 impression 2019

Printed at: G. Print Process, Delhi

The book is sold subject to the condition that it shall not, by way of trade or otherwise, be lent, resold, hired out, or otherwise circulated without the prior publisher's written consent.

Contents

Foreword

Afghanistan has had a turbulant history, a landlocked country that had traditionally been a kind of a buffer between the British Indian empire and the Russian eastward expansion. Afghanistan has remained fiercely independent with equally fierce tribal loyalties. Modern day turbulance in Afghanistan begins with the deposition of Zahir Shah in a military coup that brought Daud into power. What began as a 'socialist' experiment went into a series of ups and downs that ended with the Soviet intervention through Babrak Karmal in 1979. Therein begins the next phase of the Afghan crisis. This saw the entry of American interests, initially within the cold war framework, and later on in an attempt to utilize the region as a point of access to the resource rich Central Asia. American backing to the Mujahiddin began as an anti Soviet Struggle. Eventually with the exit of the Soviets from Afghanistan under Gorbachev's initiatives American interests in the region came to be spelt out more clearly. The American linkage with Pakistan and its Afghanistan policy has been a matter of debate amongst the students of this region. Dr. Jagmohan Meher's book is yet another attempts to understand the complexities of this relationship.

The central argument that the author seeks to make revolves around the American interests in Afghanistan and their implications to the politics of the region. He focuses on the American policy during the days of the Soviet intervention and analyses American policies therein. he then moves on to understand the post-Soviet phase and the American connections with the Taliban. The post September Eleven phase brings in a new dimension to the American policy that now comes to focus on problem of terrorism. Operation Enduring Freedom represents the American military intervention in the region.

The September Eleven attacks brought the concept of postmodern terrorism into the forefront. It also raised questions about strategies designed to counter this new form of terrorism. At one level are the several initiatives taken by the United States that have global implications of this new American strategy. American actions in the context of Afghanistan have now demonstrated a crafting of a well-articulated strategy to fight terrorism. This strategy appears to have the following key elements:

(i) The building up an international front against terrorism. This front would have several layers, ranging from those that would be providing a principled support to those who would commit human and material resources to fight terrorism. This front would involve both, a political level action and an economic level action. This latter is being attempted by freezing the monetary assets of various terrorist organisations across the world. The willingness of the G-8 and the Organisation of Islamic Conference to pursue economic restraints reflects the success at this end.

(ii) Initiating a strike against the terrorist networks by use of the modern sophisticated weaponry. Ever since the Gulf War of 1991 the revolution in military affairs (RMA) has been a matter of constant debate. The ability to use high precision weapons, combined with automated control systems and an almost total transparence of the battlefield has enabled the Americans to conduct preemptive destruction of targets at the very outset of a war. The technologies of seeing, aiming, and intelligence mapping of the deep battlefield have altered the traditional ways of conducting a war.

(iii) The third element of the American strategic response emerged as the strike against Afghanistan came to be initiated. The element was an attempt to 'quarantine' the United States. The concerns about the use of biological weapons by terrorists, especially the anthrax case, have led to rising of barriers that the Americans have traditioanlly been unaccustomed to.

In a sense the Americans have, symbolically, laid out their 'battlefield.' The central element of this battlefield is the scientific and technological capability to fight a sustained battle against terrorism. The current history of Afghanistan, in a sense, begins from the American strikes against the Osama bin Laden camps in 1998 and continues with the present American resolve to carry forward the fight against terrorism. The launching of Operation Enduring freedom was the logical culmination of this struggle. Today, the second phase of this war against terrorism has centred Iraq. American efforts to establish 'order' in the region have taken it into Iraq. This perhaps, is a matter of subsequent work that the author may consider planning.

Dr. Jagmohan Meher needs to be complemented for providing an excellent piece of research to the students of international politics, which would be of immense benefit to them in their study and understanding of an important area of concern in matters of security. This is a serious study of an important country, which is under siege and may yet have the ability to reassert its sense of independence in the world at large. This is an area that needs to be studied with both, urgency and care.

26 August 2003

Dr. Shrikant Paranpe
Professor and Head, Dept. of Defence
and Strategic Studies,
University of Pune, Pune—411 007
India

Preface

Afghanistan had never been a high priority area in the U.S. global strategy to contain communism until the Soviets invaded that country in late December 1979. But at the same time, Washington had never written it off as a land of no strategic value or a Soviet sphere of influence. What the U.S. policy sought was a "visible presence" in Kabul and, over the years, Washington continued in its efforts to maintain Afghanistan's traditional buffer status between the Soviets and the Pakistanis. The United States had periodically warned Kabul not to rely too much on the Soviets because the latter could be a threat to Afghanistan's sovereignty. By contrast, Washington was also not prepared to provide "too much" economic and military aid to this land-locked country partly because Kabul refused to join in the Western-sponsored military alliance, and also because neither country wanted to bring the cold war into Afghanistan. It seems that Washington was satisfied with its limited leverage in Afghanistan up to the Soviet invasion.

But the invasion led to a sharp and unambiguous reaction from the United States as Washington clearly drew a line in Southwest Asia and the Persian Gulf to contain the Soviet threat. Superpower antagonism ushered in the New Cold War era, and the policy of seeking détente was severely jolted. For the United States it was a challenge of great magnitude and Washington sought to demonstrate its political will and military superiority over Moscow by invoking several punitive measures against the Soviet Union besides demarcating a clear security zone in Southwest Asia stipulating that in case of any eventual Soviet push towards the region, the United States would use military force to protect its vital interests. Also, as a part of its policy, Washington made a deliberate effort to supply arms and financial assistance to the rebels who were fighting the Soviet supported regime in Afghanistan.

Over the years, the United States policy was to increase the military, political, and economic costs to Moscow of its invasion of Afghanistan. From the beginning, there appeared two tracks of opinion in Washington with some believing that the Soviets would never leave Afghanistan. Afghanistan in this view was doomed to become a Soviet satellite, no matter whatever pressure Washington exerted against Moscow at bilateral level or through aid to the Afghan resistance. The other view was premised on the belief that military pressure could drive them out or, even, "a little covert military and financial support to the Afghan mujahiddin could transform Afghanistan into a Soviet Vietnam." Those who believed in the former were known as "doves," where as the believers of the later hypothesis became popular as "hawks." In 1985-86, the hawks won out, and their view prevailed. The American supplies of arms to the mujahiddin increased in both quality and quantity paving the way for a political settlement to the problem, and ultimately the withdrawal of Soviet troops from a "no win situation" inside Afghanistan.

So the Geneva Accords of April 14, 1988 between Pakistan and Afghanistan as two signatories, and the United States and the Soviet Union as two guarantors was only a "face-saving escape" for the Soviets. The accord had only provided a venue to withdraw its troops from Afghanistan. In fact, the mainstay of the U.S. approach towards Afghanistan had not been negotiations as much as the arms supply to the anti-government resistance forces.

With the withdrawal of the Soviet troops from Afghanistan, a major question for the U.S. policy was how much the United States should seek to shape the political outcome of the Afghan conflict. Now that from the strategic point of view, the Soviet troop withdrawal transformed the nature of the Afghan problem, though it did not completely resolve it. It also meant, for the Americans, an end to the threat to Pakistan and the Persian Gulf posed by the Red Army's thrust (if it had one) in 1979. So, within a very short period after the Soviet withdrawal, Afghanistan reduced to a low priority area in the American thinking and Washington did not pay much attention to either the political situation of the country, or to the issues like the return and rehabilitation of about five million refugees who lived in Pakistan and Iran for a decade, or to the much needed reconstruction of the country. The United States virtually left Afghanistan to anarchy and civil war that led to an uncertain situation and the country became a breeding ground for international terrorism.

Amidst this situation, the United States did not hesitate to support an ultra-fundamentalist force called Taliban in the mid 1990s. In fact, a popular perception emerged in the whole region that the United States was allied with Pakistan and Saudi Arabia in this effort, as in channeling aid and arms to the mujahiddin during the 1980's war against the Soviets. America discovered some kind of benefit in supporting the Taliban, which obviously led to a realignment of forces within the country and the region. However, the Americans soon realized their folly of supporting an Islamic fundamentalist regime, and withdrew their support although internally through Pakistan, they continued to look for a moderate leadership in the existing Taliban set up. But it was already too late to check the "warriors of Allah" from exporting terror to different corners of the world, including the United States.

September 11, 2001 attacks on the U.S. come in this background and Washington decides to retaliate against its own creation in Afghanistan. The United States successfully overthrew the Taliban regime, but failed to bring about reconciliation among the warring factions and to initiate a nation-building process. The indefinite American presence in Afghanistan in the name of "war against terrorism" may ultimately lead to ethnic and geo-political entanglement of Washington and invite large-scale Afghan resentment against the "occupying forces." It seems that Americans have won the war but lost the peace. After a phase of protracted war,

Americans might be painfully learning the hard way that it was one way to bomb a country and conduct ground operations to oust an unacceptable regime, but it was quite another thing to fight the force that created and sustained that regime.

The present study surveys and evaluates how the United States viewed Afghanistan between 1945 to 1979, and how its policy takes a turn after the Soviet invasion, and how it evolves into a concrete winning strategy towards the mid-1980's that ultimately compels the Soviets to withdraw its troops from Afghanistan. It also looks at the nature of U.S. policy in the post-Soviet Afghanistan and the Taliban era, and the phase of "war on terrorism." The study seeks to demonstrate that Washington, trying to develop a realistic policy had never accepted Kabul as a Soviet satellite. Moreover, it finds that whenever Afghanistan moved close to the U.S., it led to a negative Soviet response. Mostly, the study focuses on U.S. policy towards the Afghan resistance in the 1980's. It attempts to show that in spite of many other sources of arms and aid, the U.S. assistance was the primary factor, which not only sustained the mujahiddin for about nine years, but also enabled them to put up a fierce and effective resistance against a superpower. It was American arms and aid, which made the Afghan war costly for the Soviets, and the Russian economy was strained to the point of collapse. After this American "victory," Washington failed to develop a tangible policy to contain the spread of terrorism that leads to attack on the U.S. and counter attacks on Afghanistan.

The present study addresses these hypotheses.

In the words of a friend, my research work went through like my own adventure from "Kalahandi to (K)alifornia." From purely a rural, remotest and most backward background, it has been quite a stupendous task to generate and develop interests in a subject like international relations, especially American foreign policy. At a time when this work was initiated for a university degree, my part of the country was literally totally cut off from the rest of the world; I used to travel 80/90 kilometres to make a telephone call to outside, not to think of fax, internet, etc. While travelling to Delhi in a rainy season to face the Fulbright Fellowship interview, I had to start by a bicycle for 28 kilometres crossing the whole mountainous terrains (where I myself had once come across a Royal Bengal Tiger) through *kachha* road, and three flooded rivers by a small local-made boat in order to get to the "nearest" bus station from where to again travel more than 40/60 kilometres for the "nearest" railway station to catch a train for Delhi. In course of this "adventure," I have run into many people and institutions who have been very encouraging, inspiring, and supportive in my work and it is to them that I would like to acknowledge. But at the same time I would like to mention that the views expressed in this book are entirely those of my own and do not necessarily reflect the opinions of anybody else or any institution.

In the department of political science and public administration, Sambalpur University, Orissa, my beloved teachers Prof. A.P. Padhi, Prof. B. Patel, Prof. S, Nanda, Prof. R.G. Pradhan, and Prof. S.P. Guru have been encouraging throughout the course of my work. I wish to thank all of them.

During the period of my work, I have visited American Studies Research Centre (ASRC), Hyderabad; Indian Council of World Affairs (Sapru House Library), Institute for Defence Studies and Analysis (IDSA), and Jawaharlal Nehru University Library, all in New Delhi; and American Centre Libraries of Delhi, Calcutta and Bombay. I extend my hearty thanks to all the staff of these libraries. Also I wish to express my thanks to ASRC Hyderabad, and Indian Council of Social Science Research (ICSSR) branches of Delhi, Calcutta, Bambay and Hyderabad for their financial supports in the shape of "study grants." During my stay in Hyderabad, I have been benefited by academic guidance of Prof. B. Ramesh Babu, Prof. P.M. Kamath, Prof. Kausar J. Azam, and in New Delhi, I have been guided by Prof. M.S. Venkataramani (formerly of SIS, JNU). To all these noble people, I will ever remain indebted.

I believe that the quality of this work would have been seriously undermined had I not been granted a pre-doctoral Fulbright Fellowship to visit the United States. In this connection, I would like to thank the United States Educational Foundation in India (USEFI) for its financial support during my yearlong fruitful stay in the US. I am especially thankful to Dr. Uma Das Gupta, former Regional Officer, USEFI Calcutta for her timely encouragement and help on the eve of my US trip.

During my tenure as a Fulbright Scholar in the University of Illinois at Urbana-Champaign in the academic year 1994-95, I have been greatly benefited from Prof. Marvin G. Weinbaum, Director, Program in South and West Asian Studies, who was my 'official' (American) academic supervisor, and Prof Stephen P. Cohen, Director, Program in Arms Control, Disarmament and International Security (ACDIS). Both of them equally loved me, shared their notes, files, research materials, and memories with me, and both of them gave comments on an earlier draft of a major portion of this book. In fact, Marvin and Steve made my life much easier and comfortable in all respect during my stay with them. I will never forget their loving impression, and help and encouragement. Many thanks to both of them.

Dr. Amit Gupta was a constant source of inspiration behind my own emotion and homesickness at Illinois. He not only entertained me in several ways, and tried to keep me happy, he also assisted me in my research in many occasions. Many thanks to you Amit.

From the former officials of the US government, I wish to thank Dr. Zbigniew Brzezinski, President Jimmy Carter's National Security Advisor; Prof. Elie Krakowski, formerly an aide at the Pentagon under President Reagan, and presently a professor at Harvard; and Ms Robin Raphel, Assistant Secretary of State for South Asia in the first four years of the Clinton administration. Brzezinski provided me with some rare documents on US policy towards South Asia and Afghanistan, Krakowski allowed me an hour-long interview with him at Boston, and Raphel also allowed me an interview. Also, I am thankful to some officials in the State Department who allowed me to use Freedom of Information Act to obtain documents relating to my research. I have also worked at the University of Illinois Library at Urbana, and the

Library of Congress, Washington D.C. I wish to extent my hearty thanks to the staff of these libraries who assisted me in finding materials.

Finally, I would like to express my deep sense of gratitude to my teacher and supervisor of the Ph.D. dissertation Prof. L.N. Misra of the Department of Political Science and Public Administration, Sambalpur University, Orissa. It is his constant guidance, love, encouragement, and inspiration, which showed me the way to embark on this adventure. I hope that he will continue to be my guide throughout my life, and I will ever remain grateful to him.

Family acknowledgements come last. I take this opportunity to express my gratitude and feelings to my father Shri Raghunath Meher and mother Smt. Labani Meher who have sacrificed everything to see me stand on my own feet. In fact it is their love, support, encouragement and inspiration, which gave me freedom and impetus to pursue this career. Also, I wish to thank all my family members, relatives and friends who helped me in some way or the other during the course of my work.

Lastly, I wish to say that I feel flattered, and greatly inspired by the constant encouragement of my loving wife and life-long friend Nivedita (means dedicated).

National Defence Academy, Khadakwasla, Pune, India
The 20th June 2003

Jagmohan Meher

Note on Sources of Research Materials

Primary Sources

1. Two rare documents had been obtained from former President Jimmy Carter's National Security Advisor, Zbigniew Brzezinski that deals with the White House decision on Afghanistan in the early 1980's.
2. Personal correspondence with a couple of former US officials who had provided very insightful information on the subject.
3. Correspondence from the US State Department to its various embassies in the region and vice versa. These documents were obtained under Freedom of Information Act.
4. Some White House, State Department, and National Security Council documents were obtained from Jimmy Carter Library, Atlanta, Georgia, and Ronald Reagan Library, Simi Valley, California.
5. Testimony and statements of official witnesses in the US Congressional Hearings that had dealt with US policy towards South and Southwest Asian region in general and Afghanistan in particular, before various Committees and Sub-committees of both the Senate and the House of Representatives during the period under investigation.
6. US Congressional debates on the various aspects of its policies towards the region in general, and Afghanistan in particular.
7. Public Papers of the US Presidents.
8. Department of State Bulletin documents of the period.
9. US embassy press releases from Kabul, Islamabad, Tehran, New Delhi and London.
10. Notes borrowed from various seminars and workshops attended to by many former US government officials who had evinced significant interest on the issue or who had directly been involved in the decision-making process.
11. Memoirs of former US Presidents and government officials.
12. US Department of State Press Release, Dispatch, Background Reports, and Special Report Series etc.
13. Personal interview with a couple of former US government officials who were involved in the Afghanistan problem.

14. Some relevant documents especially, the United Nations documents which were available in the US libraries.
15. A few Afghan Government documents those were available in the US libraries.

Secondary Sources

16. Research articles and books related to the subject under investigation.
17. Reports and Issue Briefs on the subject, published by the US Congressional Research Service as well as by a few US-based professional and public interests groups.
18. Reports, news items and editorials of major newspapers and periodicals from Afghanistan, the United States, U.K., India, and Pakistan.
19. Reports, Monographs and other research works on the subject as were available in various Indian and American libraries.

Introduction

. . . I want to emphasize that no where in the world where I have been, among people so different from my own, have I met those whom I esteem more highly than the Afghans, or those with whom I would rather work again. Their honor is their bond, their hospitality is full and generous; and their toleration is more honest than our own . . .

—Ernest F. Fox,
Travels in Afghanistan, 1943.[1]

For centuries before the down of the Westphalia nation-state system, today's Afghanistan was at the junction of overland trade routes linking South, East, and West Asia and beyond the Mediterranean and Europe. These routes were not only the sources of art, culture, polity and economy for the Afghans for a long time but also helped brought in Greek armies and art, Indian Buddhism, Mongol conquest, and Arab Islam, all of which helped shaped and enriched the country's heritage. During the colonial era, this land-locked landmass remained sandwiched between the British-Indian Empire and the Tsarist Empire (later Soviet Union) who aimed at penetrating each other's "spheres of influence" until the mid-twentieth century, which is popularly known as the "Great Game."[2] After the British withdrawal from the Indian sub-continent, Americans assumed the "western responsibility" of competing with the Soviets over Afghanistan and the country emerged as a "strategic storm center" during the cold war years. The traditional buffer status of the country, its direct access to the legendary tactical land routes through which invaders and conquerors marched through out history, and its strategic location as the "cross-road of Asia" continued to invite the focus of superpower rivalry that later leads to war, rebellion, ethnic crisis, jihad (holy war), terrorism and finally, America's "war against terrorism."

The present study is significant as it deals with the political and strategic dimensions of relationships between the most powerful country (the United States) and one of the poorest countries (Afghanistan). This book is an attempt at a paradoxical perception where the Americans never accepted Afghanistan as a Soviet satellite, and that whenever the land-locked country moved closer to Washington, it had led to a negative Soviet response. The Soviet invasion of Afghanistan in December 1979 was not outside the scope of this perception as it was already clear to the leadership in Kremlin that the Afghan leaders were in the verge of striking deals with Washington.[3] The subsequent American reaction along with the decade long western involvement in the guerrilla war vindicated this fear, which ultimately turned out to be a big enragement for Moscow. Even after the end of the cold war and disintegration of the Soviet Union, the study reveals, some strategic and political ambition of the United States and its obsession with the regional actors continued to be the causes of concern for Moscow as well as the present Afghan tragedy. The study professes that the United States aims at a long-term presence in the country to further its geo-political and strategic interests in the region. However, it concludes, the only surviving superpower would end up in a no-win situation, and even face a very rough weather before this otherwise fiercely independent and freedom loving people of Afghanistan.

What American policy, and strategic interests were involved in Afghanistan before the Soviet invasion of that country in December 1979? What made the United States to invest so much money and prestige in this land locked landmass during the cold war years? What "forced" the Carter administration take a hard-line on the Afghanistan question? What were the factors that motivated Washington to declare a "doctrine," in the format of the Truman Doctrine of an earlier geo-political era, which was enunciated in 1947 to aid Greece and Turkey? How did Washington move from a low label aid program to the unorganized and frenzied Afghan fundamentalists to one of the largest covert operation of the world, involving billions of dollar, hundreds of thousands of Islamic zealots, and a clear cut winning strategy against a superpower, the Soviet Union? How did Washington formulate a policy that changed the course of history in a strategically important part of the world? What was American approach and attitude on United Nations peace negotiation? How was US policy towards the post-Soviet Afghanistan and beyond? How did Washington 'coddle' against the Taliban regime and how its policy takes a turn after the terrorist attacks in the US? What is America's present strategic interests in Afghanistan and the region and how it is going to get a dose of what the British and the Russians had had enough of it during their turn?

To understand these questions with any sophistication, it is necessary to have a glance of history of the country, its people, and more significantly, its geopolitical location, which attracted so many outside powers, including the United States.

This introductory chapter has been divided into four sections. Section one briefs Afghanistan's "Land and the People," section two is entitled "A Record of Conquests" and deals with a short history of the country, section three highlights the "Great Game," and section four discusses about "The Early American Contacts with Afghanistan." Also the last section intends to dwell upon the early governmental interests of the United States on this otherwise backward country.

Land and the People

Afghanistan is a small and landlocked country, with frontiers that were mostly demarcated towards the end of the nineteenth century. Situated in the strategic South West Asia region, this landmass is bounded on the north by the former Soviet Republics of Tajikistan, Uzbekistan and Turkmenistan, on the west by Iran, and on the east as well as to the South by Pakistan. It shares a narrow fifty miles border with the People's Republic of China on the northeast from which runs the so-called Durand Line, the frontier that divides Afghanistan from Pakistan. The mountainous land of Afghanistan comprises of independent-minded, religious and highly tradition-bound people who are called the Afghans.

While Afghanistan is basically a land-locked buffer state, in many respects, it is an artificial, accidental country. Its size is about 252,100 square miles, and approximately two-thirds of it lies above 5000 feet. The maximum east-west distance of the country is about 900 miles, while the north-south distance is about 550 miles. This landmass is full of mountains, deserts, and grassy plains. The climate of the country varies sharply between the highlands and lowlands. For instance, the temperature in the southwest in summer reaches 48.8 degree centigrade, but in the central core of the country containing the Hindu Kush Mountains, it falls sharply down to –26 degree centigrade during the winter. In the rugged terrains of the central core lie the mass of the Hindu Kush, which rises above 25,000 feet and its affiliated mountain ranges from which much of the melted water comes to irrigate the seasonal crops of the country.[4] The two major rivers of the country are Amu-Darya and the Helmand. The Khyber Pass in the southeast is the most important of the passes that link Afghanistan with Pakistan.

The average rainfall of the country varies between two inches in the southern deserts to about ten inches in the central highlands. Plant life, varies widely according to altitude. On the mountain ranges are found large forest trees, (mostly ever green) as well as yew, walnut and peanut trees, while the lowest ridges are mostly barren. Also in the highest ranges grow ferns and mosses and that in the desert regions hardly plants have cropped up.[5]

For centuries, Afghanistan has been a homogeneous country with a lot of cultural, linguistic and geographical diversities. Ethnic diversities and national borders have cut across local ethnic groups in all directions. For instance, out of the total Pushtun population, about half live in Pakistan. This has been so because of the creation of an arbitrary border called Durand Line, agreement signed in 1893 between Sir Mortimer Durand, Foreign Secretary of the Government of India, and the Afghan ruler Amir Abdur Rahman Khan. This border marches into Pakistan for about 1,510 miles, and in the process keeping the Pushtuns divided as a legacy of the British imperialism. Also, similarly, the Afghan-Soviet border had been drawn with that kind of "colonial carelessness." This border agreement signed in 1895 had come to divide the Uzbek, Tajik, and Turkmen peoples who belong to similar ethnic, economic, cultural and historic origins. The agreement between the British and the Russians had identified Amu Darya as the border, which had kept the status of many disputed islands unclarified between them. The Afghan-Soviet frontier agreement signed in 1946 had ultimately sorted out the problem. In fact, the vast stretch of Afghan-Soviet border extends to about 1481 miles. This border also touches China in its extreme northeastern part, which had remained undefined until 1963 when both the countries had demarcated a 47 miles area between them; thus creating a permanent border, which is known as the Wakhan Corridor.

As per the western part of Afghanistan, it is an extension of the Iranian plateau in which sandy deserts dominate the area (especially the Registan, south of the Helmond river). The border between Afghanistan and Iran had been demarcated as far back as in 1857 by the British supervisor after the Shah of Iran had renounced his rights over what had been identified as Herat and Afghanistan. This approximately 550 mile-long Afghan-Iranian border also divides many ethnic groups on both sides embracing the Baluch, Brahui, Turkmen, and Farsiwan population. Further, a fairly large number of Baluch and Brahui people also live in Pakistan. These people of different communities have their own diverse histories and origins. At the same time, due to these boundary complications it is very difficult to know the accurate population of Afghanistan belonging to its different communities. However, according to a latest estimate, the total population of the country is 27, 755, 775, out of which Pashtun constitute 44 per cent, Tajik 25 per cent, Hazara 10 per cent, minor ethnic groups (Aimaks, Turkmen, Baloch, and others) 13 per cent, and Uzbek 8 per cent.[6] About 99 per cent people believe in Islam as their religion, out of which about 84 per cent are Sunni, 15 per cent Shi'a, and others 1 per cent.[7]

The standard of living of the Afghan people is extremely low. It has been estimated that the infant mortality rate has reached a figure of 15%, which is one of the highest in the world. In fact, about a third of all Afghan babies died in childhood, and those who survived, life expectancy has gone up to only forty-six years. Malnutrition, tuberculosis, malarias, measles are the commonly known diseases of Afghanistan.

Despite these handicaps, Afghanistan has some rich natural resources. Natural gas has been discovered around Sheberghan on the north slope of the Hindu Kush, and oil resources have been reported both in the north and southeast parts of the country. Also, rich deposits of iron ore are found near the Hajighat Pass, while copper deposits are discovered near Kabul, as well as high-grade chrome near the Pakistan border. Further, Uranium is found in the southwestern deserts, and that gold, emeralds, and other mineral resources are available in other parts of the country. But lack of scientific technology, as well as lack of access to seaports prevents these resources from being exploited.

The country has come to occupy a geographic position, which has long been recognized as "providing a buffer between the Soviet Union and the Indian Sub-continent, as well as protecting certain routes of access to Iran." The strategic significance of Afghanistan has been recognized as far back as by Alexander the Great who had "coveted it as a stepping stone to his conquest in India."[8] This geographical location and buffer status has influenced

Afghanistan's history and politics in a significant way. In fact, the continued survival of Afghanistan as an independent political entity was due to her location as a buffer, first between the Tsarist Russia and the British Indian Empires and later between the Soviet Union and the American-sponsored military alliance called the Baghdad Pact.[9] Thus, Afghanistan's strategic position has made it an important Asian crossroads.

Finally, the geopolitical location of Afghanistan has contributed to its uniqueness in world politics. This has been due to the following factors. Firstly, Afghanistan is a landlocked country, the nearest point to the sea being the Arabian Sea, which lies some 300 miles to the south. In between the sea and Afghanistan lie the Baluch–inhabited areas of Pakistan and a large portion of Iran. Thus, outlet to the seas constitutes the major impediment to Afghan trade and commerce. In fact, its population has to rely heavily on inland transportations through the inaccessible mountain passes for their economic activities. Secondly, its geographic location is unique because not only it is relatively isolated, but also that its location has made it the only country through which the power game could be played in the Indian Sub-continent. Thirdly, during the overland communication between Europe and the Middle East on the one hand and India and the Far East on the other, Afghanistan had served as the crossroad of trade and cultural exchange. Fourthly, the location of Afghanistan has made it rather insulated from the "winds of change" which had blown across the Asian continent since the beginning of the twentieth century. For instance, with the notable exception of the Afghan King Amanullah's "decade of reform" (1919–1929), the country had witnessed particularly little march towards socio-economic reforms and political modernization. In fact, these special characteristics as well as the relative isolation of the country had prompted some observers to opine that these features have resulted in an "impenetrability" of Afghanistan. But such a view has been discarded by a number of scholars who hold the position that the geo-political character of Afghanistan corroborate the terse fact that "it can be easily influenced by outside forces if they are powerful and determined enough."[10] Thus, the country's strategic location at the crossroads of Asia has contributed to attract worldwide attention towards happenings in that country, at least since the days of the Great Game.[11]

A Record of Conquests

The geo-political environment and the land-locked image of Afghanistan have contributed to the centuries of outside interference in the internal affairs of the country. In fact, Afghanistan has witnessed hundreds of invasions, and has passed through turbulent periods of history. Given this context, the Soviet occupation and withdrawal in the 1980's is but a short interlude to many Afghans although it looks an extended period to the people around the world. Afghanistan is known as the "highway of conquests" for the peoples and empires in Central Asia.[12]

History does not adequately record the number of invasions and conquerors who had swept through the land what was later called as Afghanistan. The earliest mention of Afghanistan had been recorded in the writings of the famous Indian astronomer Varahamihira who had blossomed during the Gupta period. According to him, the Afghan race (Avagana) comprised a group of tribes speaking an Iranian language, "Pusto" who had concentrated themselves in the Sulaiman Mountains in the eastern region of what is now described as Afghanistan.[13] The routes in ancient times between India and China as well as between China and Central Asia had passed through Afghanistan. In fact, cities like Kabul and Kandahar had formed the two main gateways through which various tribes and races had poured into the Indus and Gangetic Valleys.[14] It is now known that sometime around 1500 B.C., great waves of Aryan tribes (of Indo-European origin and speaking) had swept through the Afghan mountain passes into what is now called Pakistan and had destroyed the highly developed Indus Valley civilization. Afghanistan came under the rule of the Greeks during the fourth century B.C. In between 549 and 545 B.C., Cyrus the Great had conquered the country, and Darious I had consolidated his rule. Their rule continued up to 331 B.C. Then came Alexander the Great who entered Afghanistan sometime in 329 B.C., but had to meet with fierce resistance in the country. In fact at the time of his death in 323 B.C., Alexander's empire had stretched from Macedonia to India, which had been divided among his generals. As a result, many small kingdoms had been founded while many had perished. In the process several Greek kingdoms had existed in Afghanistan, which lasted for about 200 years. With the eclipse of the Greek Empire, a part of Afghanistan, especially its eastern provinces had come under the rule of Gupta dynasty.[15]

In the Christian era, the Kusana dynasty under its illustrious ruler Kaniska had come to dominate Afghanistan by uniting the country under his central administration. After the Kusanas, Turks had come to Afghanistan and ruled the country till about 658 A.D. The Turks, however, had been defeated and replaced by the Chinese Mongols in course of time.[16]

With the advent of Islam, Afghanistan had to wrestle with a twin problem, i.e., external attacks and internal revolts. It was in 699 A.D., the Arabs brought Islam to Afghanistan. As stated earlier, the Hindus under the Mauryas had invaded and established themselves in eastern Afghanistan. But within a period of one century, Afghanistan produced one of its most famous kings, Mahamud of Ghazni who had not only chased the Hindu out of his country, but had occupied much of northern India and eastern Persia. But the Ghorids overthrew the Ghaznivids in 1186 A.D. During the thirteenth and fourteenth century A.D. came the Mongol general Chenghis Khan and Tamerlane who had ruled most part of the Middle East. For about two hundred years there after, the Persian Safavid dynasty and the Indian Moghul dynasty had wrestled for the control of Afghanistan. In fact, the Moghuls under Babar had established their sway over India following the battle of Panipat in 1526. The Moghul rulers thereafter had begun to perceive the country as the "outer bastion" of the Moghul Empire and in the process, the defense of the empire had become closely interlinked with the security of Afghanistan. Around this time, Afghanistan had clearly come under the ascendancy of the Moghul rulers of Delhi.[17] This situation had altered with the invasion of Nadir Shah Afshar, who led a great Persian sweep across Afghanistan to India in the 1730's. Finally, as the Moghul rule began to decline sharply (following the advent of the British and especially after the battle of Plassey and Buxar in 1757 and 1764 respectively), Ahmed Shah Abdali had successfully unified the country to establish his dynasty in Afghanistan. Thus, for the first time, a native dynasty had been established in the country. In course of time, Ahmed Shah Abdali had emerged as a powerful contender for power in the northeastern part of India. He had also consolidated Afghanistan into an empire, which had exceeded far beyond the present territory of the country.[18] In the meanwhile dramatic changes were taking place both in India and Afghanistan. Under the impact of industrialization, European powers like Britain, France, and Russia had engrossed imperial ambitions. In fact, the opening years of the nineteenth century witnessed intense political rivalry among the European powers. Central Asia had come under the influence and control of Czarist Russia while both France and Russia had made successful advances in the West Asian region. This situation had created a grave concern in the minds of British policy-makers, who perceived such penetration as a threat directed against their newly acquired dominion in India. Afghanistan and Persia had attracted the attention of both France and Russia for domination and control. The British were quite apprehensive that a combination between France and Russia might jeopardize the British interests in India. But with the downfall of French emperor Nepolion in 1815 such an apprehensions was nullified. Thereafter, the British had concentrated their attention as how to reckon with the expansion of Tsarist Russia into Central Asia, as they conceived such a penetration detrimental to their imperial interests in India.[19] Thus the fear of Russia had become the decisive factor in British frontier policy since the early nineteenth century. In fact, as a sequel to this, the British had followed a policy to preserve the independence of Afghanistan as well as to secure the friendship of the Kabul government. This British – Russian rivalry over Afghanistan has been described as the "Great Game." But as far as Afghanistan was concerned, its survival as an independent entity had largely been ascribed more to the "dynamics of the competing British and Russian imperialism than to the diplomatic or political skills of its rulers."[20]

The Great Game

The "Great Game," a tussle for power and supremacy in Afghanistan between Russia and England had continued unabated until the withdrawal of Great Britain from the Indian Sub-continent in 1947. Afghanistan had continued with its existence with the role as a buffer between the Russian and the British empires, with each rival being out to expand its influence and domination over the land-locked territory. In fact, both the countries strongly believed that any strategic gain by one was the loss of the other. The British had believed that the Russian influence in Afghanistan would tend to distract them and keep them off balance in India. On the other hand, the Russian diplomats had entertained a hope that the weaker Britain would be in India; they would be more accommodating in respect of their role in Europe.[21] This Anglo–Russian maneuvers over Afghanistan had been described as "the Great Game" by a junior British Officer and popularized by Rudyard Kipling, a British author, in his famous book *Kim.*[22]

The British apprehension over the Russian designs in Afghanistan had increased considerably following the Treaty of Guelistan in 1813. Following the sharp increase in Russian influence over Persia, the latter had been forced to sign the humiliating treaty of Guelistan. In fact, this treaty had provided the genesis for the emergence of conflict between England and Russia over Afghanistan. For instance, following the treaty, Persia had threatened the ruler of Afghanistan in 1837 with the active assistance and instigation from Russia. This intension of St.Petersburg prompted the English government to checkmate the Russian designs in Afghanistan. In fact, overtures had been sent by the British government in India to the rulers of Afghanistan not to yield to the Tsarist pressures. But when the ruler Amir Dost Mohammed of Afghanistan had refused to yield, the British had launched the First Afghan War in 1839. In fact, Afghanistan had witnessed two major British invasions during the nineteenth century, one in 1839, and the other in 1879.[23]

The British invasion of Afghanistan in 1839 resulted in the seizure of Peshawar and the Pushtun tribal areas east of the Khyber Pass. In an attempt to recapture the lost territories, Amir Dost Mohammad had appealed to the Russians for help. Although St.Petersburg had declined to intervene, the British had felt alarmed over the readiness on the part of Afghanistan to turn to the Russians for help.[24] As per the British, the then Governor General of India, Lord Auckland and his advisors had decided that a friendly government must be established in Kabul and had succeeded in replacing Dost Mohammad with an ex-Amir, Shah Suja. The British had also put an occupying force to protect the new ruler, but in due course they had left Afghanistan to suffer from great political, military, and humanitarian ordeals. However, they could not pacify the Afghan refractory tribes, who following the British withdrawal had once again installed Dost Mohammad back on the throne of Kabul.

In the meanwhile, the Russians had interpreted the British invasions on Afghanistan as a direct threat to their security interests in the region and had, thereafter started penetrating into the independent Khanates of Central Asia. In the process, the Khan of Bukhara had become a Tsarist vassal by 1869 and that the Russian influence had already reached the Amu Darya (the Oxus of classical antiquity). By this time, the British had consolidated their empire in India and therefore looked nervously towards these developments in

Afghanistan.

It may be mentioned that since the early 1850's, the British had been thinking about schemes as how to annex Afghanistan into their Indian empire.[25] In fact, when the Russians had established diplomatic relations with Kabul and simultaneously deployed troops north of Afghanistan, the British fear of an Afghan collusion with the Russians had aroused. Out of this fear, the British had launched the Second Afghan War in 1879 and the ruler Amir Sher Ali, like his predecessor Dost Mohammad had appealed for Russian help. But the Russian commander in Central Asia, General Kaufmann had tactfully refused to the Afghan request by emphasizing on the impossibility of transporting troops and war materials across the Hindu Kush during winter. But once again the British had succeeded in bringing about a change of regime, this time by putting in power a nephew of Sher Ali, Abdur Rahman, as the Amir of Afghanistan. The British had also succeeded in repudiating their existing diplomatic relationship with Russia, and in the process had ensured some territorial concessions, as well as a complete surrender by Afghanistan of its external relationship with Great Britain.[26]

The Anglo-Russian rivalry had continued to dominate developments in the region. By 1907, a series of agreements were signed between the two great powers. Under the agreements, the British had agreed not to annex any additional portions of Afghanistan, whereas the Russian had reciprocated by agreeing to accept the Amu Darya River as its frontier with Afghanistan. This step had marked the end of Russian imperial expansion into Central Asia. All these had been included in the St.Petersburg Convention of 1907, which, in fact, had moderated the Anglo-Russian rivalry to a great extent. In the process, however, the Afghan experience of the "Great Game" in their own land had contributed to the emergence of a sense of nationalism, which had begun to make them convinced that Great Britain and Russia had been making efforts to settle their own problems at the expense of Afghanistan.[27]

Although to a certain extent an atmosphere of peace had prevailed in the region, Afghanistan had continued to be under the British influence for a long time. One of its rulers, Amir Habibullah had tried his best to neutralize such influence but had failed to regain the lost Pushtun tribal lands from the British. After the assassination of Habibullah in 1919, his third son Amanullah had occupied the throne of Afghanistan. But very soon, to gain national solidarity, the new ruler had launched the Third Anglo-Afghan War in the spring of 1919 by attacking the Pushtun areas beyond the Khyber Pass. As a result, the British had been compelled to agree to renounce their special role and had to recognize the existence of Afghanistan as an independent state. The final agreement signed in November 1921 between the two countries had reiterated the concept of internal and external independence for Afghanistan.

By the time Afghanistan had achieved her independence in 1921, a change of government in Moscow had also taken place with the rule of Lenin having been replaced the Tsarist Russia. Following the British recognition of Afghanistan, Soviet Union had also agreed to sign a treaty of friendship with Kabul. Under the treaty, the Soviet Union agreed to provide some economic aid to Afghanistan basically to offset the cessation of the British subsidy, which were being provided to them since 1880. Afghan ruler Amanullah had also sought security assistance from the Russians in order to continue with his internal reform program. By 1929, however, wide spread revolutions had erupted, and in the process Amanullah had been overthrown by a semi-literate Afghan Tajik known as Bacha-i-Saqao. In fact, the orthodox Islamic society of Afghanistan had not been able to accept the modernization initiatives of Amanullah with favour.

But developments in Afghanistan had moved fast as Bacha-i-Saqao had been overthrown very soon by Mohammad Nadir Khan (a cousin of Amanullah) who had somehow been able to manage the tacit support from the British quarters. But Nadir Khan again could not continue for long as he had been executed soon and replaced on the throne by the teenage son of Amanullah called Zahir Shah. The new king of Afghanistan had generally pursued pro-British (later pro-American) policies during most part of his forty-year rule.[28]

The British-Russian rivalry over Afghanistan had never ceased to exist until Great Britain withdrew from the Indian Sub-continent in 1947. By the beginning of the Second World War, both powers had begun penetrating into its territory to garner their support. In December 1939, the British had sent a military delegation to Afghanistan, which had visited its Prime Minister Hashem in order to discuss about the potential threat to Afghanistan and India by the Soviet Union. In fact, by March 1940, Great Britain had decided to get ready "to meet Soviet aggression on Afghanistan by declaration of war."[29] The British had also decided to provide armaments and commercial credits worth two and half million pounds to Afghanistan.[30] In the meanwhile, however, the course of the Second World War had taken a dramatic turn, and that the two rival powers—the British and the Russian—had become war-allies who had decided to jointly invade Afghanistan's neighbor Iran in order to counter the influence of the Axis powers over Teheran. All parties, however, had been satisfied with the Afghan stance of neutrality during the Second World War. But the cold war between the United States and the Soviet Union, that followed the Second World War, brought Afghanistan back to the "Center" of superpower relationship, and the 18th century's Great Game was continued to be played through this landmass till the end of the cold war in late 20th century. In the new Game, Americans had replaced the British as the Russian adversary.

Early American Contacts with Afghanistan

Despite their independent existence in the world map for over two hundred years, the history of bilateral relationship between the United States and Afghanistan has been of (rather) short duration. Meaningful contacts between the two countries hardly did go beyond the twentieth century. In fact, except a few instances of individual American visitors to Afghanistan in the nineteenth century, there has been no other recorded evidence of interaction at the inter-governmental levels between the two peoples almost up to the early twentieth century.[31]

Described as a "colorful soldier of fortune," the name of Josiah Harlan has been recorded as the first American who had visited Afghanistan sometime in 1828. In fact, the first American visitor had the proud privilege of serving under the military hierarchy of Afghan ruler Amir Dost Mohammad. Harlan is reported to have defeated various Hazara chiefs for his Afghan ruler. He seemed to have been given the title as the "Prince of Ghoree."[32]

The next American visitor to Afghanistan had been an elderly lady named Olney who had undertaken her travel from Kabul to Peshawar sometime in 1906. Around this time there was reports about the visits of some American missionaries to Afghanistan with the possibility of testing the receptivity of potential converts. Their works had been followed up by Reverends Dwight M. Dondaldson and Christy Wilson (the known covert missionaries) who had entered Afghanistan during the 1920's and 1930's respectively. In the meantime, however, an American engineer named A.C. Jewett had been hired by a British company under contract with Amir Habibullah in 1911 to construct an electric generating plant in Afghanistan. Jewett is reported to have lived there for seven years and had earned a good rapport for himself among the Afghans.[33]

In the meanwhile during the 1920's a number of other Americans had managed to enter Afghanistan. In 1922, Cornelius Van H. Engert, who was to become the first American minister to Kabul, had visited the country and earned the friendship of the Afghan people. In fact, Engert, who had been posted as the resident American diplomat of Persia in 1920 and later transferred to China in 1922, had preferred to go to China through Afghanistan. During his stay in Kabul, he traveled extensively and prepared a lengthy report on Afghanistan, which he later sent to the U.S. State Department. Engert had made a strong recommendation in his report suggesting that the United States should grant diplomatic recognition to Afghanistan.[34] The State Department, however, had not attached any importance to his recommendation and merely placed the same as a classified document. During this period few other Americans also visited Kabul, well known among them were journalist Lowell Thomas (along with his photographer David Chase) and a businessman named David Wooster King. These personalities were reportedly well received by the Afghan officials. Following this, further visit was made in 1923 by a distinguished American lady, Jeanne Vancouver (who had traveled extensively in and around Kabul) who recommended to the State Department for placing greater American interest in the country as well as for according recognition to the government of Afghanistan. While her views had been duly noted and recorded, the State Department did not take any effective action on the matter.[35]

In the 1930's, a substantial stream of American travelers, adventurers, journalists, historian and businessmen had started flowing to Afghanistan. Prominent among them were Colonel Theodore Roosevelt and his wife who had been the personal guests of king Nadir in 1933. Some of these American visitors had also left more permanent records of their experience pertaining to Afghanistan.

In the meanwhile, a major American company called Inland Exploration Oil Company had received permission (on concessional terms) from Afghan government in 1936 to explore oil resources in Afghanistan. Following this deal Charles C. Hart, the principal American negotiator had written privately to the State Department urging for the diplomatic recognition of the country. Also, an American geologist, Ernest F. Fox (who had visited Afghanistan in connection with the Oil Company work) had reported favorably on the country in his book, *Travels in Afghanistan:*

. . . I want to emphasized that no where in the world where I have been, among people so different from my own, have I met those whom I esteem more highly than the Afghans, or those with whom I would rather work again. Their honor is their bond, their hospitality is full and generous; and their toleration is more honest than our own . . .[36]

In the 1930's, many American teachers and èducators had visited Afghanistan to arouse a long-lasting friendship between the two countries. Also, around this time, many distinguished Afghans started traveling to the United States. Noted among them were Fatima Begum, a close relative of the Afghan royal family and Faiz Mohammad Zikria, who later became the Foreign Minister of Afghanistan. Many Afghan students also visited the United States for studies who in their later life had occupied good positions in the government. Noted among them were the former Prime Minister Abdul Zahir and his brother Abdul Kayeum, who had also occupied the office of Deputy Prime Minister in the Afghan government.

People to people contacts had been increased to a considerable extent, but no meaningful governmental relationship could be established between Kabul and Washington for a long time. This had been so mostly due to two factors. First, being comparatively a small country with poor economy Afghanistan could not offer many economic and commercial incentives to the Americans. It also could not become an attractive market for American goods due to lack of purchasing power on the part of the Afghans. Secondly, Afghanistan had been buffeted by the "Great Game" politics that had ensued between Russia and Great Britain almost to the 1940's. Also, for several political reasons, Americans could not act independently from the London government as the region was considered as the "sphere of influence" of the British. With the outbreak of the Second World War, however, interests of the United States had increased considerably, leading to the establishment of diplomatic relations between the two countries.

When Amanullah Khan became the Amir of Afghanistan in 1919, one of his first priorities had been to obtain international recognition to his newly independent country. So he sent a mission to the major European capitals and the United States under the leadership of his trusted adviser Mohammad Wali. During its stay in Washington, the Wali mission had held meetings with the Secretary of State Charles Evans Hughes, and President Harding and highlighted Afghanistan's desire to establish diplomatic and commercial relations with the United States. The President and the Secretary of State however, had remained cool towards these Afghan overtures. They had merely hinted that the establishment of diplomatic relations was contingent on Congressional initiative and actions.[37] Despite this frustration, the Afghans had continued to request Washington through different channels for recognition because they strongly believed that the British pressures had influenced the American attitude, to a great extent.

A similar embarrassing development occurred in 1927 when king Amanullah, during the course of a celebrated foreign tour, had decided to visit Washington to get his country's recognition as well as to establish diplomatic relations with the United States. His attempt had been frustrated as he was "diplomatically" asked through a carefully drafted message not to visit Washington. Despite this denial letter, its message had contained at least one good line for the Afghans namely, that the United States had already recognized Afghanistan.[38] But in real action, the State Department time and again had continued to maintain that the United States had not done so.

In the meantime, many American diplomats (who had established strong links with the Afghans) had strongly advocated for the diplomatic recognition of the country. These had included Cornelius Van H. Engert, who had paid a private visit to Afghanistan in 1922, and Charles C. Hart, the American Minister in Iran. The changing environment in American foreign policy had begun under the leadership of President Franklin D. Roosevelt. A meeting in this context had taken place between Jesse Isidor Straus, American Ambassador in France and Shah Wali, the Afghan Ambassador in the Paris Post, which eventually produced a letter from the Afghan King Zahir to the U.S. President Roosevelt requesting recognition. The letter had voiced strong "desire of the Afghan government to strengthen the political and economic relations . . . with the high government of the United States."[39] This letter had eventually reached the office of Wallace Murray (who headed the Near East Division in the State Department). Murray had been reported as being mostly responsible for withholding the United States recognition to Afghanistan, had eventually decided to change his tune and to draft his recommendation for the attention of Under Secretary of State William Philips. In his note, Murray had stated:

> . . . I assume that no notice need be taken of this fact in drafting the President's reply to Zahir Shah since there would appear to be no reason under the circumstances as to why recognition should not be accorded to him at the present time . . .[40]

A memorandum had followed such a note from Williams to the President, which had also accompanied the Murray recommendations. The note had contained draft letter for Roosevelt to be sent to the Afghan ruler for diplomatic recognition of Afghanistan. In this process, the Afghans had received their long-delayed recognition.

Following this, the Afghan ruler Shah Wali had proposed to the American Ambassador in Paris that the two countries should sign a treaty of friendship. The question of granting Most Favored Nation (MNF) status to each other had also been discussed between the two countries and eventually a Provisional Agreement of Friendship and Diplomatic and Consular Representation had been signed in Paris on 26 March 1936 between Shah Wali and the US Ambassador Jesse Isidor Straus. The agreement had highlighted on the evolution of strong friendship between the two countries as well as for conferring special privileges and immunities under international law concerning each other's diplomatic and consular representation.[41]

Soon after these developments, President Roosevelt had appointed William H. Hornibrook, the American Minister in Teheran, as the non-resident Minister to the court of Kabul. Hornibrook had traveled to Afghanistan to present his credentials before King Zahir on 4 May 1935. He was reported to have greatly impressed by the Afghan hospitality, and had very strongly recommended to the State Department for opening a legation in Kabul.[42] Other Afghan diplomats who had also pressed Washington to open its legation in Kabul had supported his voice. However, the Americans had decided to delay this process on the ground that funds were not actually available to open new and additional posts.

But such an American stance had changed very soon with the outbreak of the Second World War. The new American Minister in Teheran Louis G. Dreyfus, who had presented his credentials in Kabul on 19 May 1941, had strongly pressed for the opening of a legation in Kabul. It was also Dreyfus, who for the first time, had emphasized on the strategic importance of Afghanistan for the United States. He had stated that Washington was expected to carefully examine the growing power of the German, Italian, and Japanese influence in Kabul. In his recommendation letter to the State Department, he had observed clearly that Afghanistan "may eventually become a strategic spot in Asia."[43] This message in fact had wielded a great impact on the war planners in the United States as the country had lately entered the war against Germany and Japan. The War Department had realized the strategic importance of Afghanistan and transmitted their concern to the State Department. Also by then, Wallace Murray, the Under Secretary of State had realized the importance of opening a legation in Kabul. This has been clearly reflected in his memorandum to the Secretary of State Summer Welles:

. . . Recent developments in the Near East have increased the geographical importance of Afghanistan . . . it is the recommendation of the Division of Near Eastern Affairs that a legation be established at Kabul. If a successful German attack upon the Caucasus region should cut off the route through Iran for the transportation of supplies to Russia, it appears inevitable that the British and Soviet Governments would undertake to establish a supply line through India and Afghanistan . . . The Afghan Government has already acceded to British and Russian requests to expel Axis nationals from the country.

. . . It appears not altogether improbable that a situation may develop in Afghanistan similar to that obtaining in Iran, where certain areas of the country are under British and Soviet military occupation . . . it is not unlikely that this Government (the United States) would be called upon as it has been in the case of Iran, to cooperate in the transportation of "lend-lease" materials. . . This government has no choice but to plan for such a contingency and to secure useful information enabling these plans to be made. Adequate information of this character, of course, cannot be secured without the presence of American officials in Afghanistan to obtain it . . .[44]

Thus, Washington had finally decided to open a permanent legation in Kabul and had appointed Cornelius Van H. Engert as the first American Minister to Afghanistan. Following this, Engert had immediately traveled to Afghanistan to present his credentials to King Zahir on 25 July 1942.[45]

From the above, it is clearly evident that the strategic importance, and geographical setting of Afghanistan had finally compelled the Americans to open a legation in Afghanistan. And this geo-strategic significance of the country later continued to impress upon the superpowers to play their dirty games over this land-locked country.

Conclusion

It may be mentioned in the concluding observation that the historical setting of Afghanistan has affected its external relationship in a great way. It is a fact that Afghanistan has been a country without ethnic or geographic cohesions and that it has been formed not by internal coalescence but by external pressures from the competing colonial powers and conquerors. It was because of these reasons as well as its land-locked buffer status, Amir Abdur Rahman once said, "Afghanistan is like a goat on which the lion and the bear have both fixed their eyes."[46]

In fact the "lion and the bear" had their fixed eyes over Afghanistan for a long time: from the colonial era to the present day. The strategic importance of the country for the Russians in search of their traditional warm water port in the Arabian Sea in the Indian Ocean, and the British (later American) determination to check the Russian ambition (and expand their own influence) had led to greater stakes and ramifications in the superpower relationships. To illustrate this fact, it may be mentioned that at the height of the "Great Game" in 1903, British Foreign Secretary Lord Lansdowne had proclaimed: "We should regard the establishment of a naval base or a fortified post on the Persian Gulf by any other power as a very grave menace to our interests and we should certainly resist it with all the means at our disposal."[47] Such a perception had once again surfaced and affected the American policy-makers after the Soviet invasion of Afghanistan in December 1979. This time, American President Jimmy Carter in his State of the Union address in January 1980 unambiguously declared: "An attempt by any outside force to gain control of the Persian Gulf region will be regarded as an assault on the vital interests of the United States of America, and such an assault will be repelled by any means necessary, including military force."[48]

From the above two statements it may be inferred that following the British withdrawal from the region, the United States had assumed the responsibility of checking the Soviet power. In fact, after the Soviet invasion in 1979, many American observers had begun to perceive the scenario in Afghanistan vis-à-vis the USSR as one of "Great Game."[49] Even after the end of the cold war and the disintegration of the Soviet Union, the strategic importance of Afghanistan has not disappeared, and the United States is still greatly involved in the Afghan affairs, directly or indirectly. Thus the historical setting of the "Great Game" and the country's geo-strategic importance has remained valid and pertinent as of today.

Notes and References

1. Ernest F. Fox, *Travels in Afghanistan,* McMillan, New York, 1943, as quoted in Leon B. Poullada and Leila D.J. Poullada, *The Kingdom of Afghanistan and the United States: 1828-1973,* University of Nebraska, Omaha, 1975, p. 25.
2. For details see David Fromkin, "The Great Game in Asia," *Foreign Affairs,* Vol. 58, Spring 1980, pp. 936-951.
3. For details see Chapter 2.
4. For details see *Britannica Junior Encyclopedia,* Vol. 2A, Chicago, 1983, pp. 66-67.
5. *Ibid,* p.67.
6. Detailed statistical data reflecting CIA's estimate for 2002 are available at http://www.cia.gov/cia/publications/factbook/geos/af.html
7. *Ibid.*
8. For details see William H. Overholt, "The Geopolitics of the Afghan War," *Asian Affairs,* March/April 1980, p. 205.
9. M.S. Agwani, "The Saur Revolution and After," in K.P. Mishra ed. *Afghanistan in Crisis,* New Delhi, 1981, p. 1.
10. Dev Murarka, "The Russian Intervention: A Moscow Analysis," *Round Table,* April 1981, p. 124.
11. B.P. Sinha, "The Afghan Revolution and After," *Foreign Affairs Reports,* Vol. 28, 1980, p. 111.
12. Arnold Fletcher, *Afghanistan: Highway of Conquest,* Ithaca, Cornell University Press, New York, 1965.
13. As cited in *Encyclopaedia Britannica,* vol.I, Chicago, 1977, p. 173.
14. O.P. Bhatnagar, "Indo-Afghan Relations: A View Point," in D.D. Khanna ed. *South West Asian Crisis,* Calcutta, 1981, p. 39.
15. For details see *Ibid.*
16. For details see *Encyclopaedia Britannica,* p.173.
17. For details see Bhatnagar, "Indo-Afghan Relations: A View Point," p. 40.
18. *Ibid.*
19. For details see G.P. Tripathy, *Indo – Afghan Relations,* New Delhi, 1973, p. 1.
20. Bhawani Sen Gupta, *The Afghan Syndrome: How to live with the Soviet Power,* New Delhi, 1982, p. 11.

21. J. Bruce Amstutz, *Afghanistan: The First Five Year of Soviet Occupation,* National Defence University, Washington DC, 1986, p. 5
22. For details see David Fromkin, "The Great Game in Asia," pp. 936-951.
23. For details on the Indo-Afghan Wars see G.S. Chhabra, *Advance Study in the History of India,* New Delhi, 1978, Vol. 2, pp. 90-108.
24. Henry S. Bradsher, *Afghanistan and the Soviet Union,* Duke Press Policy Studies, Durham, 1983, pp. 9-10.
25. Louis Dupree, "Afghanistan's Big Gamble: Part I," *American Universities Field Staff (AUFS)* Reports, Vol. 4, No. 3, 1960, p. 7.
26. For details see Bradsher, *Afghanistan and the Soviet Union,* p.10; Louis Dupree, *Ibid,* p. 8, and Vartan Gregorian, *The Emergence of Modern Afghanistan: Politics of Reform and Modernization, 1880-1946,* Stanford University Press, Stanford, 1969, pp. 108-110.
27. Gregorian, *Ibid,* p. 211.
28. Bradsher, *Afghanistan and the Soviet Union,* pp. 15-16.
29. Cited in Ashraf Ghani, "The Afghan State and Its Adaptation to the Environment of Central and South-west Asia," in Hafeez Malik ed. *Soviet-American Relations with Pakistan, Iran, and Afghanistan,* New York, 1987, p. 326.
30. *Ibid.*
31. See Vartan Gregorian, *The Emergence of Modern Afghanistan,* pp. 69-75. Also see Leon B. Poullada and Leila D.J. Poullada, *The Kingdom of Afghanistan and the United States: 1828-1973,* pp. 7-31.
32. Leon B. Poullada and Leila D.J. Poullada, *The Kingdom of Afghanistan and the United States: 1828-1973, Ibid,* pp. 9-10.
33. *Ibid,* p. 13.
34. *Ibid,* pp. 15-16.
35. *Ibid,* p. 18.
36. Ernest F. Fox, *Travels in Afghanistan,* McMillan, New York, 1943, as cited in *Ibid,* p. 25.
37. *Ibid,* pp. 38-39.
38. *Ibid,* pp. 47-48.
39. As cited in *Ibid,* p. 52.
40. *Ibid.*
41. As cited in *Ibid,* p. 54.
42. Vartan Gregorian, *The Emergence of Modern Afghanistan,* p. 379.
43. Leon B. Poullada and Leila D.J. Poullada, *The Kingdom of Afghanistan and the United States: 1828-1973,* p. 57.
44. As cited in *Ibid,* pp. 58-59.
45. As cited in *Ibid,* p. 60. Also see, U.S. *Department of State Bulletin,* March 1982, p. 5.
46. As quoted by Mir Sultan Mohammad Khan Munshi, *The Life of Abdur Rahman: Amir of Afghanistan,* cited in Mahanas Z. Ispahani, *Roads and*

Rivals: The Political Uses of Access in the Border Lands of Asia, Ithaca, Cornell University Press, 1989, p. 98.

47. Reader Bullard, *Britain and the Middle East: From Earliest Times to 1963,* London, 1964, p. 54.
48. *US Presidential Documents,* Washington DC, 20 January 1980, p. 197.
49. See Bradsher, *Afghanistan and the Soviet Union,* p. 19. Also see, Rosanne Klass ed., *Afghanistan: The Great Game Revisited,* Freedom House, New York, 1987.

1
United States and Afghanistan: A Historical Perspective

Turkestan, Afghanistan, Transcaucasia, Persia.... are the pieces on a chessboard upon which is being played out a game for the domination of the world.

—*Lord Curzon, Viceroy of India, 1899-1905*

Afghanistan had never been a high priority area in the U.S. global strategy to contain communism until the Soviets invaded that country in late December 1979. But at the same time, Washington had never written it off as a land of no strategic value or a Soviet sphere of influence. What the U.S. policy sought was a "visible presence" in Kabul and, over the years, Washington continued in its efforts to maintain Afghanistan's traditional buffer status between the Soviets and the Pakistanis. The United States had periodically warned Kabul not to rely too much on the Soviets because the latter could be a threat to Afghanistan's sovereignty. By contrast, Washington was also not prepared to provide "too much" economic and military aid to this landlocked country partly because Kabul refused to join in the Western-sponsored military alliance, and also because neither country wanted to bring the cold war into Afghanistan. It seems that Washington was satisfied with its limited leverage in Afghanistan. This chapter surveys and evaluates how the United States viewed Afghanistan between 1945 to 1978, and seeks to demonstrate that Washington, trying to develop a realistic policy had never accepted Kabul as a Soviet satellite. The study finds, moreover, that whenever Afghanistan moved close to the U.S., it led to a negative Soviet response.

Background

The United States showed little interests in Afghan affairs so long as Great Britain was in the helm of affairs in the Indian sub-continent. Washington had turned down the time-to-time Afghan requests for the U.S. financial assistance and diplomatic recognition and support under British pressure. But with the sign of an impending withdrawal of the British power from the region soon after the Second World War, Washington tried to maintain a minimal presence in Kabul. In fact, Washington's interests was mostly the outcome of the wartime allied experience of the strategic importance of the region. During the war, it was the German advance through the Caucasus toward Iran that made the United States realize that land-locked Afghanistan was a "strategic zone" in the rim of Asia. American policy-makers realized that Afghanistan was the gate to India—a land mass where the Japanese and Germans had dreamed of a "link-up point" for the axis powers. So, although the United States had granted diplomatic recognition to Afghanistan in 1934, it was during the wartime that on June 6, 1942, Washington opened its legation in Kabul. Cornelius Van H. Engert was appointed as the first American resident minister in Afghanistan.[1]

The United States objective of opening a legation during the war was aimed more at the wartime allied strategy than an interest in Afghan friendship. Secret orders were issued from Washington to the embassy in Kabul to "prepare the ground for alternative lend-lease transit routes to Russia and China should German and Japanese offensives interrupt those through Iran and Burma."[2] This "strategic compulsion" came to Washington as a result of the growing activities of the Axis powers in Afghanistan. German, Italian, and Japanese secret agents were actively involved in stirring up the frontier tribes against the British troops in India. There were also many people from the Axis countries working in different projects such as dams, roads, radio communications, and light industrial plants, who were seen by the allied powers as a threat to their interests in Afghanistan.

So along with Britain and Russia, the opening of the American legation in Kabul helped putting considerable pressure on Afghanistan to expel Axis intelligence agents and workers. This inflicted a severe damage to the Afghan economy, in the form of a steep inflation. The war also restricted Afghanistan's export of its goods and import of its vital necessities. As a result, the Afghan government asked for the United States aid during the war to deal with its damaged economy. Ambassador Engert managed to provide the most urgent needs of the Afghan people during the war. This, in turn, "earned much gratitude, admiration and goodwill for America."[3] So, under allied pressure, Axis agents were expelled, and in turn, the United States help earned a good image of the Afghan people. It is therefore, not surprising that the allied powers, especially, the United States had recognized Afghanistan as a possible future zone of conflict. Washington was also considering of building a railway line through Afghanistan.

Afghanistan emerged from the war as a neutral country, but with a ruined economy. The war also exposed Afghanistan's vulnerability to outside forces. From the beginning, however, Afghan leaders were cautious about their northern border and the motives of the Soviet Union. So in order to maintain Afghanistan's neutrality, they sought the U.S. aid for their developmental programs. The wartime American assistance also encouraged them to seek greater assistance from Washington. Significantly, the leaders felt that the United States would not pose a threat to their national sovereignty, especially, because of the geographical distance from Afghanistan. Afghan Prime Minister Shah Mahmud Khan Ghazi declared in 1946:

> *I am convinced that America's championship of the small nations guarantees my country's security against aggression. America's attitude is our salvation. For the first time in our history we are free of the threat of great powers' using our mountain passes as pathways to empire. Now we can concentrate our talents and resources on bettering the living conditions of our people.*
>
> *I propose to reduce the army in size to that of a small but well-trained internal security force charged with maintaining order among the nomadic tribesmen. Money once used in maintaining a large army will find better use in the already started national improvement program.*[4]

American Strategic Interest

Soon after the World War II, the U.S. policy of containing communism came to Southwest Asia. Washington's policy to "encircle" the communist countries, especially, the Soviet Union and China was on the mind of the U.S. policy makers even though a consistent policy did not materialize until John Foster Dulles came to power as the Secretary of State in 1953. The United States had already been involved in the Northern Tier security since the day in 1947 when President Harry Truman requested the U.S. Congress for aid to contain communist guerrilla warfare in Turkey. Accordingly, to a certain extent, Washington assumed responsibility for Great Britain in Southwest Asia when the latter withdrew from the Indian sub-continent in 1947. The rivalry between India and Pakistan following partition greatly affected the American involvement in Afghanistan. In the subsequent years, Pakistan remained as a principal factor in the U.S. relations with Afghanistan, a country that Pakistan leaders saw as an enemy from the very beginning. Over the years, Islamabad successfully convinced Washington that both India and Afghanistan were Soviet satellites and that Pakistan was the only pro-Western country in the region. And for that matter, Islamabad deserved American military and economic aid. Over the years, Pakistan did get substantial aid from the United States, but Afghanistan did not remain as a "forgotten land" in the American strategic thinking. So a careful analysis suggests that, Afghanistan had repeatedly sought American assistance on the military, economic, political, and diplomatic fronts. In return, Afghanistan had, to a considerable extent, succeeded in its goal of maintaining neutrality, sometimes tilting towards the West up to 1978 when the communist captured power in Kabul.

For the U.S. containment policy, Afghanistan was strategically important. But at the same time, U.S. policy-makers believed that this land-locked country for geographical reasons was more or less vulnerable to the Soviet pressure. When the United States sponsored Central Treaty Organization (CENTO) in 1954, Washington tried to persuade Kabul to join. Vice President Richard Nixon visited Kabul in December 4-6, 1953 after his triumphant tour of Pakistan, which had already been militarily aligned with the United States. Nixon's purpose of visiting Kabul was in connection with "Afghanistan's neutrality, vitality and suitability as an ally," without which he seemed disinterested and antagonistic toward Kabul's notion of an independent Pushtunistan. During his talks with Afghan rulers, Nixon tried to convince that "an alliance with Pakistan and Iran (and with the U.S.) would answer all Afghanistan's problems." Afghan neutrality, he meant, "was equivalent to political leprosy."[5] However, the Vice-President's visit could not bring about any understanding between the two nations; rather it disappointed the Afghans to a great extent. Afghan Prime Minister Mohammed Daoud Khan refused to join in the U.S. sponsored military alliance mainly because of two reasons. He believed that joining in the alliance would tantamount to bringing cold war into Afghanistan that might one day lead to a hot war as in the Korean Peninsula, and second, he feared that joining would only increase tension in the region and place Kabul in a direct confrontation with Moscow. For that reason, Daoud not only refused to join in the Western sponsored military alliance, he also criticized Pakistan for doing so. He argued that the Pakistanis had betrayed the people of Afghanistan as well as the region by replacing the British with the Americans. Despite this, Daoud continued to seek military aid from Washington in order to strengthen his armed forces, which the United States declined to provide. The American version of Afghan "reluctance" to join the pact differs somewhat. Apparently, some in the Afghan military were interested to join the pact, but under certain conditions. They demanded that Washington agree to come to their rescue if they were threatened by the Soviets. The United States refused to give such an assurance. According to the U.S. diplomats, a guarantee of this sort was not feasible due to Afghanistan's geographical and land-locked position, and its vulnerability to the Soviet Union.[6]

American policy-makers also believed that Afghanistan was a truly non-aligned country in the cold war competition between the Soviet Union and the United States. In fact, Kabul was more inclined towards the West, especially towards the United States, rather than the Afghan's northern neighbor, the Soviet Union. Afghan leaders had a traditional fear of the Soviet expansion in their region. On numerous occasions, Afghan leaders explained their case before the Americans by demonstrating their anti-Sovietism. Commenting on this Afghan rhetoric, Secretary of State Dulles once remarked: "If Afghans are already so anti-Russian we don't have to worry about them."[7] Even when the U.S. sponsored "Northern Tier" excluded Afghanistan for the above mentioned reasons, and Kabul turned to Moscow for economic and military aid which had followed Khrushev-Bulganian visit to that country, there were reasons for the Americans to believe that the moves were tactical rather than ideological. So paradoxically, Afghanistan was not a Soviet satellite by 1954; United States' "presence" was very much there (see the sub-section, American aid below), and Afghanistan's non-aligned status remained.

It seems that the United States was content with this status of Afghanistan in the mid-1950's. During the visit of a special ambassador of President Eisenhower, James P. Richards (who visited the Middle East to explain the Eisenhower doctrine) to Kabul in 1957, both sides maintained "restraint" about Afghanistan's involvement in the cold war and in the new doctrine of the American President. The Eisenhower doctrine was committed to loosely protecting the Northern Tier—all along the Soviet border from Islamabad to Ankara. "Neither the U.S. nor the Afghans, however, wanted Afghanistan to openly and publicly place itself under the American protective wing, and the resulting communiqué was a masterpiece in diplomatic doubletalk." So Afghanistan remained uncommitted to the American security system.[8]

Similarly, President Eisenhower's visit to Kabul on December 9, 1959, helped establish a cordial relationship between the two countries. People within and outside Afghanistan wondered why an American President should be so interested in a neutral country. But according to the then US ambassador to Kabul Henry Byroade—who had strongly endorsed the King's invitation to the US President—Eisenhower visit would atleast bolster sagging American prestige caused by dissatisfaction with several ICA programs in Afghanistan, continued military aid to Pakistan, and seeming American indifference to the Pushtunistan problem.[9] The President's visit also provided an opportunity to both head of states to clarify their respective positions on regional issues, and strengthened their personal relationship. The Presidential entourage which includes a group of newsmen was convinced about Afghanistan's genuine desire to remain neutral in the ongoing superpower competition.[10]

However, the United States strategic interest in Afghanistan is reflected from its "outlook" in the early years of the cold war which had originated during the war itself. American war strategists believed that the U.S. sponsored Qandahar international airport was meant for the possible wartime use. When U.S. diplomats negotiated about the funding of this airport with their Afghan counterparts, they had several strategic factors in their mind. They believed among other things, that "rejecting the project would mean. . .running the risk of having the Soviets organize it and use it to penetrate nearby Asian countries."[11] They also perceived that Qandahar could be a potential U.S. Air Force base in future wartime use. It would be a "recovery base" for refueling the American bombers after attacking the Soviet targets, since their takeoff points in the Western Europe or North Africa were too distant from the Soviet border.[12] So, it is evident that the United States financial support for Qandahar international airport was not meant for "only" civilian purposes or for organizing the Afghan airline, Ariana; it had its strategic reasons and implications. No documentary evidence however available, whether by then, the U.S. diplomats had been guided by the vision of a traditional Russian ambition of reaching the warm water ports, or threatening the Persian Gulf oil supply to the West; an idea of strategic threat, that had been exaggerated to a great extent, and had created a sharp American reaction to the Soviet invasion of Afghanistan in December 1979.

Nevertheless, if we analyze the American strategic stakes in Afghanistan in view of the Soviet penetration and the communist expansion in the region, the former's stand sounds more superficial and exaggerated than that of the latter. American power remained more influential, especially in Iran and Pakistan, than the Soviet power. Both Islamabad and Teheran joined the U.S. sponsored security alliances and were known as the "two pillars" in the region to further American objectives and protect its interests. On the other hand, despite Soviet strategic interests in and substantial aid to Afghanistan, the latter pursued a policy of non-alignment, a policy that was more tilted towards the West than the East. So all the Northern Tier states, such as Afghanistan, Iran and Turkey, which had combined, a common borders on Soviet territory of over 2,666 miles, were under the American influence. All that Washington remained uncommitted with regard to Afghanistan was a direct security guarantee, that it already had with the other two countries. Afghanistan's non-alignment policy had more to doing with its leaders rather than the cold war warriors; the United States and the Soviet Union. During a visit of the U.S. Senate delegation to Afghanistan in December, 1965, the American Embassy in Kabul noted:

> *Afghanistan maintains a staunch policy of "positive neutralism," conditioned by its history and geographic position, especially its past experience as a buffer state and interference in its affairs by neighboring powers. Its policy is to avoid foreign entanglements while welcoming and utilizing the assistance of foreign countries in its economic development."*[13]

The United States believed that this position of Afghan neutralism would best serve its interest in the region. Because, by then, Pakistan had become an American satellite state, and had already joined in several military alliances sponsored by the West. So, Washington viewed its political-military relationship with Islamabad as far more conducive than that of with Kabul. For the United States, limited leverage in Afghanistan was taken for granted as maintaining its traditional buffer status between Pakistan and the Soviet Union. As early as late 1940, Iran had come under the American strategic sphere, a country that continued to be a close ally of Washington up to 1979. With this, the American policy-makers contented themselves on the ground that their interests in the Persian Gulf region would be fully protected.

Pakistan's joining of the American security umbrella undermined the Afghan request of military aid from Washington. This was so because of the continuous strained relationship between Islamabad and Kabul over their border disputes. To repeated Afghan requests for military aid, U.S. officials cited a rapprochement with Islamabad as a crucial precondition.[14] Even long before that, the United States had accepted Afghanistan as a land of strategic importance, but was skeptical about its proximity with the Soviet Union. But at the same time, American officials explained that Afghanistan would be of no use to further even the Soviet interests in the region. So the Kremlin would not invest too much of its assets in that landlocked country. Washington also apprehended that in case of any aggression against Afghanistan, some sort of resistance would continue to be there for the preservation of the Afghan independence. So it was not strategically threatening to the American interests in the region even if Washington did not give any military aid to Kabul. As a study prepared for the Senate Committee on Foreign Relations reveals:

In the vacuum left by Britain's withdrawal from the Indian sub-continent in 1947, the Afghan ruling family envisaged creating an American military connection as crucial defense against Soviet power. Despite its prodigious security assistance efforts elsewhere, the Truman administration remained unimpressed either with Afghanistan's strategic importance or with the efficacy of American military aid containing Soviet expansion in that theater. A Pentagon study in 1949 concluded that Afghanistan's "geographical location coupled with the realization by Afghan leaders of Soviet capabilities presages Soviet control of the country whenever the international situation so dictates." Two years later, an NSC assessment of Afghanistan's situation was equally resigned: "The Kremlin apparently does not consider Afghanistan's meager assets to be worthy of serious attention...(but) there is little doubt that Afghanistan could be conquered..." The analysis did note, "in the event of an invasion, it is possible that certain elements...would continue to resist.[15]

However, in an apparent strategic and diplomatic development in 1950, the United States was on the verge of giving military aid to Afghanistan. The American Embassy in Kabul recommended approval of military aid "to exclude Soviet influence, cement Afghan-American friendship, maintain internal security, and promote settlement of differences with Pakistan."[16] This recommendation followed at least a visit to Kabul by an Assistant Secretary of State, George McGhee on March 12, 1951. However, though his talks with the Afghan officials did not produce any concrete results, mostly because of Afghanistan's stand on the border dispute with Pakistan, the Afghans became more hopeful of arms aid in future. So they continued their requests until 1954 when Pakistan joined the Western sponsored military alliance and the United States finally turned down all their appeals. In order to modernize armed forces to meet the increasing threat from Pakistan, Kabul turned to Moscow for military aid.

But that did not mean that the United States had written off Afghanistan from its strategic sphere of influence. Over the years, Washington had kept an alerted eye on the Soviet influence in Afghanistan, and even considered the prevailing "Russophilia" as more tactical then ideological. Washington also continued its economic support and maintained a "visible presence" in Afghanistan. The United States denied military aid mostly because of the location and poor communications of Afghanistan, which would require Washington to undertake "an enormous logistics efforts." The cold war strategists in Washington also feared that providing military aid to Afghanistan would be nothing but risking an escalation of the cold war with the USSR.[17]

Robert G. Neumann, who was United States ambassador to Afghanistan from 1966 to 1973, prepared a policy review for the State Department in June 1971. In this review he emphasized:

For the United States, Afghanistan has at present limited direct

> *interest; it is not an important trading partner; it is not an access route for US trade with others; It is not presently...a source of oil or scarce strategic metals... there are no treaty ties or defense commitments; and Afghanistan does not provide us with significant defense, intelligence, or scientific facilities...However, Afghanistan has important interests for us which have in large part derived from its strategic location between Central Asia and the Indian subcontinent.*[18]

So it is evident that inspite of all these "pulls and pressures," Afghanistan remained as a strategically important country in the American scheme of things. Afghan neutralism was considered as the best way to preserve the Afghan sovereignty. It seems that Washington remained satisfied with the prevailing leverage of superpowers in Afghanistan and had nothing to worry about the Afghan neutralism and the so-called Soviet push towards the warm-water ports of Karachi or Gwadar, as most American observers predicted through the 1970s and 1980s. But it is true that the American perception of the Soviet strategic threat to its interests was closely related to the US-Soviet balance of power and influence in Afghanistan. So, inspite of Washington's unchallenged influence and power, there remained a popular perception that the Soviet Union was out to dominate the region. Also according to this perception, the Soviets intended to control the Persian Gulf, and in that case, the Western alliance would not be able to survive longer in opposition to a power that controls its oil supplies. So, in 1979, when the Soviets invaded Afghanistan, Western fear doubled, and Carter Doctrine drew a clear line in Southwest Asia and committed to using American military force in the eventual further Soviet expansion in the region. With the withdrawal of Soviet soldiers from Afghanistan in 1989, the American fear of the communist penetration in the region disappeared.

The American Aid

No country invests millions of dollar in a foreign land without seeking some conformity with its own interests. As stated earlier, Afghanistan fell under the American "strategic compulsions" to contain the Soviet communism first, and then, the Chinese communism. Afghanistan, as traditionally believed, was a "crossroad of Asia," and obviously a land of potential strategic importance. This idea had been developed in the American strategic eye during the World War II. And first time it was reinforced and made public in the U.S. Congressional Hearing in 1951 when George McGee testified that, "Afghanistan is an important country of South Asia and its strategic location further augments its significance."[19] In view with its intention to keep Afghanistan under its influence, the United States provided moderate aid for various developmental projects. In the initial years after the war, Washingtoh moved slowly, but adequate economic aid started flowing from the early fifties. The purpose of this aid was to maintain Afghan neutrality, and possibly, to keep Afghanistan under the U.S. sphere of influence, so that in case of any future war, it could be a "military base" of the Western powers against the Soviet Union and China. American aid was meant for the furtherance of these objectives. But when the Soviet Union started supplying both military and economic aid about two times more than that of the U.S. aid, the latter maintained restraint from the competition with the former. But American aid continued up to 1979, when the Soviets invaded that country. It is evident that over the years, it was American influence in Kabul that had alarmed the Soviets; it was the Americans who started the "game" first in the form of economic aid, not the Russians; it was Washington's struggle for supremacy in the region that had pulled Moscow into Afghanistan. Invasion of a country is obviously an extreme case; otherwise, Afghanistan would have been a "cold war beneficiary."[20]

Long before World War II, the United States had granted diplomatic recognition to Afghanistan in 1934. Soon after that, a couple of American private entrepreneurs visited Afghanistan to study the market and sources of investment in that country. They conducted research to examine the possibility of oil deposits and its extraction. The U.S. oil company known as Inland Exploration Company had discovered the formations of oil in Afghanistan. However, due to the land-locked situation of this mountainous country, the company abandoned its exploration on the ground that it was not economically feasible to extract oil for the U.S. market.

Soon after the war in 1945, the United States signed a contract with Afghanistan to provide $20 million loan for construction of the Kandahar-Herat highway, the Arghandab and Kajaki water reservoirs, and for completing the Helmand Valley Project (HVP).[21] Using the paltry foreign exchange reserves built up during the war and money earned from the export of its Karakul skins along with the modest American assistance, the Afghan government initiated the economic development programs for the construction of dams, irrigation canals, main drains, electric power facilities, roads and high ways. In 1946, the Afghan government hired an American company known as Morrison-Knudsen Construction Co. (MKC) to help in their land developments scheme in the Helmand Valley. But their limited resources proved inadequate to initiate more ambitious programs. So the Afghans again turned to the United States for economic aid. A high level delegation led by the Minister of National Economy Abdul Majid Zabuli visited Washington in 1949. Zabuli was referred to the Export-Import Bank by the State Department to negotiate the economic package. He asked for $55 million, from which the Bank approved a $21 million loan in 1949. The Export-Import Bank also insisted that a Helmand Valley Authority be formulated, modeled on the Tennessee Valley Authority, to integrate the project. MKC, however, was able to complete two dams and Boghra canal system ahead of time in 1951.[22]

During the period from 1945 to 1954, the United States supplied moderate aid for the Afghan economic development programmes. This period also include first Five Year plans, which the Afghan government started in 1950. With the initial loan of $21 million from the Export-Import Bank at an interest rate of 4.5 percent, the government renewed its contract with the MKC. Within two years the Company's activities expanded to other development projects. Prior to the five first year plans, the United States loan totaled $91.5 million, and during the first five-year plan, it provided a loan package of $93.3 million.[23] In addition, a sizeable program of food assistance was started in 1953, under the provisions of the U.S. Public Law (PL) 480, the Food for Peace program.

The year 1954 is considered by many observers on the history of the Afghan foreign policy as a year of turning point. In this year, Pakistan joined in the Western sponsored military alliance, and Afghanistan decided to seek military assistance from the Soviet Union. But a careful study of the situation suggest that it was not so. Rather Afghanistan returns to its traditional policy of nonalignment from its more Western tilted policy. In 1953, when Mohammed Daoud Khan became the Prime Minister of Afghanistan, he tried to maintain the Afghan neutrality. Louis Dupree writes, "among the reasons for his (Daoud's) seizure of power in 1953 was the fear that the Afghan government, to its detriment, had become too pro-American."[24] In fact, the new government wanted to modernize Afghanistan's armed forces to confront the possible internal rebellion and also to confront Pakistan for its disputes over the Pashtunistan issue (see the discussion below) and the controversial Durand Line. It is also true that Daoud never turned back to the Western nations while accepting military aid from the Soviets. He wanted to maintain neutrality and at the same time modernize Afghanistan's economy and military. As such, it was during Daoud's rule that aid flowed to Kabul both from Moscow and Washington.

Daoud's policy of seeking military aid from Moscow created a debate in Washington. Some officials believed that "Afghan leaders had abandoned the West and joined the communist bloc." They urged that Washington stops all investment in a country that had moved too close to the Soviet Union. Another group of officials viewed that there was "no ideological leanings" in Afghanistan's relations with the Soviets, and that the Afghans, including Daoud, are fiercely independent people. So, according to this view, the United States should increase its aid program and maintain an East-West balance in Afghanistan. Former ambassador Leon B. Poullada writes:

Such a foreign policy debates are seldom settled by clear-cut decision, but in a pragmatic way American economic aid did greatly increase and project-by-project, and case-by-case, the United States fashioned a program aimed at restoring the cold war balance.[25]

From 1954 onwards, the United States aid flowed to Afghanistan, and increased year by year. From 1950 to 1971, U.S. aid reached $81.2 million in loans and $204.8 million in grants (see table below). Most grants were for the construction of highways and educational exchanges and programs. However, the United States also provided a substantial amount under its PL 480, which is known as the Food for Peace Program.

TABLE 1
United States Assistance to Afghanistan: 1950-1971
(US Fiscal Years)

	Total Loans ($ millions)	*Total Grants ($ millions)*
Transportation and Infrastructure	20.8	106.6
Helmand Valley Project	59.3	79.2
Education	—	39.1*
Government Management and Economic Planning	0.4	13.2
Agriculture	—	10.6
Population/Family Planning**	—	0.2
Mining and Industry	0.7	3.8
Fruit Airlift (1961-1962)	—	0.8
Commodity Assistance (wheat, flour)	1.4	1.2
Wheat (PL 480)	1.6	—
Wheat and Edible oil (PL 480)	12.6	—
Agricultural Commodities and Fertilizer	2.5	—

* About $10.3 million of the technical assistance program (1958-1969) was used to send 2,142 Afghan students to the United States and other countries for advanced training.

** In 1972, population/family-planning grant grew to $2.1 million.

Sources: Briefing Book, Afghanistan, United States Agency for International Development/Afghanistan, January 1970. Louis Dupree, *A Note on Afghanistan: 1971*, American Universities Field Staff Reports, Vol. 15, No. 2, July 1971, p. 23. Also see Louis Dupree, *Afghanistan*, Princeton University Press, Princeton, 1973, pp. 630-631.

Besides this, the United States also extended $5.9 million in military aid to Afghanistan during the period from 1957 to 1972.[26] In fact this period is known as a period of cold war competition in Afghanistan between the United States and the Soviet Union. Though Moscow provided more military and economic assistance to Kabul[27] than did Washington, the American presence was not invisible. United States not only supplied substantial economic assistance, it also repeatedly warned Afghanistan against Kabul's excessive dependence on Moscow. As early as 1956, the National Security Council (NSC) recommended that the United States should "encourage Afghanistan to minimize its reliance upon the communist bloc for military training and equipment, and to look to the United States and other Free World sources for military training and assistance."[28]

In fact, by the end of 1960s, the United States did succeed in encouraging Afghanistan to maintain its nonaligned posture to a considerable extent. Truly,

Afghan government was not aligned to either the United States or the Soviet Union. The government was only concerned about the economic and industrial development of the nation. Huge project works by both the Americans and the Soviets continued. It is interesting that both the superpowers worked hard to improve Afghanistan's communication network. They put more emphasis on roads and highways construction. The United States build Kabul-Jalalabad and Kabul-Qandahar highways that connected Kabul to Pakistan borders of Peshawar and Quetta. Similarly, the Soviets built highways north of Kabul connecting Mazar-I-Sharif and up to the Soviet Union's southern border. The Afghan government even located projects for the Soviets near Pakistan border, and projects for the Americans near the Soviet border: The United States built a number of airfields in the north, near several Soviet projects, whereas, the Soviets constructed large-scale irrigation projects in the Jalalabad area near many American projects and Pakistan border. The runways and buildings of the new International Airport at Kabul were built by the Soviets, whereas, the electrical and communication equipments were installed by the Americans. Officials of both countries had to come to the same conference hall in the Afghan Planning Ministry to decide their plans and programs. For the time being, they had to forget their cold war rivalry, and they became friends. An American newsman wrote:

> *On the third floor of the Royal Afghan Planning Ministry, Russian and American advisers use the same teacups and telephones (both are in short supply in Afghan government offices) and lecture the Afghans with equal vigor on the blessings of economic progress. At noontime Russians, Americans, and Afghans all queue up for GI style hamburgers and chocolate pie at the chrome-lined Khyber Cafeteria, one of the showplaces of the Afghan capital.*[29]

Whatever might have been the cooperation or cold war confrontation between the two superpowers in Afghanistan, the American aid during this period had a great impact in at least two economic fields: aviation and public finance. Undoubtedly, the land reclamation program of the Helmand Valley Authority, a joint Afghan-American project, had the greatest impact of all, especially, in the development of agricultural sector. PanAmerican Airways (PAA) developed the Afghan national airlines, Ariana, which was under contract from the International Cooperation Administration (ICA). Not only did the Afghans got an airline of their own, connecting Kabul with Karachi, Delhi, Ankara, Prague, Frankfort, and many other state capitals, but substantial revenue also came home. The most spectacular achievements of the American aid however, was in the field of budgetary and financial reforms along with the system of taxation. The Public Administration Services of Chicago under contract to the ICA instituted these reforms, and interestingly, it was completely patterned after American methods.

But the Soviets were uncomfortable about America's increasing success in the field of Afghan economy, and the American activities in every sphere of Afghanistan's internal and external policies. What alarmed the Soviets most was that the Afghan government and the entire state apparatus had been divided into the American and the Soviet camps. The struggle for power and influence was no longer confined with the economic activities such as building of roads, highways, irrigation projects, or airports, supporters of both camps were clearly visible in the Afghan government. So, when in 1965, Mohammad Hashim Maiwandwal took over as Prime Minister, replacing Dr. Yousuf, "Russian diplomats chided Americans at the nightly diplomatic cocktail parties: Well, you Americans should be happy, at last your man got in."[30]

United States was really not happy with that. The main purpose of Washington was to minimize the Soviet influence, and to convince the Afghan leadership that the country would remain neutral only if it checked the growing Soviet activities. U.S. aid was not confined to the developmental programs. It also expanded in many other aspects. While the Soviets trained Afghan military officers, the Americans trained the civilian officers. Under Washington's technical assistance, 2, 142 Afghan students were sent to the United States and other countries for advanced training during the period from 1958 to 1969.[31] Up to 1978, some 487 courses were offered to the Afghan army personnel in the United States Command and General Staff School, tank maintenance school, and other specialties. This was provided free to the Afghans.[32]

There was also growing resentment of both the Americans and the Soviets against each other, and that animosity brought more and more aid to Afghanistan. Both actors were determined not to leave Afghanistan for the other. For Washington, Afghanistan was an "emergency action area," and it started competing with the Soviets starting from the early 1960s. A secret document of the National Security Council recommends that the United States should "not undertake an economic aid program aimed at matching in size and scope the credit and aid activities of the Soviet Union." It however, reveals that the Soviet military aid posed "problems for the United States government which are primarily of a political-economic nature and should be included among the factors affecting our political relations with Afghanistan and the size and nature of our economic assistance."[33] On the other hand, the Soviet resentment against the Americans is clearly reflected from the memoirs of the Soviet leader N.S. Khrushchev, which he articulates from his 1955 visit to Afghanistan:

> *I went there (to Afghanistan) with Bulganin on our way back from India. It was clear that America was courting Afghanistan...The Americans were undertaking all kinds of projects at their own expenses...The Americans hardly bother to put a fig leaf over their self-centered, militaristic motives...It is my strong feeling that the capital which we have invested in Afghanistan hadn't been wasted. We have earned the Afghan's trust and friendship, and it hasn't fallen into American trap; it hasn't been caught on the hook baited with American money.*[34]

The large-scale American investment along with economic and military aid not only alarmed Moscow; it also created a stalemated situation in Soviet activities in Afghanistan. The Soviets viewed the American presence as their security problem. In 1959, Louis Dupree was told by a Soviet oil exploration team, "we are here for a long time. The Afghans need our help...why don't you Americans go home? Afghanistan is our neighbor not yours."[35]

Under no circumstances, the United States was ready to leave Afghanistan in the Soviet hand. The aid program initiated in the mid-1940s, continued through the end of 1970s. The most important factor of the American aid was that, it was given more on political basis than for the economic development of the country. The International Cooperation Administration (ICA) later became known as the Agency for International Development (AID), which channeled aid to Afghanistan, had been instructed by the U.S. government to help the Afghans on political basis. Before the Soviet invasion of Afghanistan, American aid reached a figure of about $1 billion, whereas the Soviet aid was totaled $1.5 billion.[36] However, the American magnitude of economic and military aid could not buy "pro-Americanism" mostly because of Washington's stand on the Pashtunistan issue and its support to Pakistan. It seems that the Soviets support to Afghan nationalism over the latter's claim of Pashtunistan paid off well in the Afghan society, at least upto their invasion of that country. Pashtunistan issue remained as a major irritant in the US-Afghan relations.

The Pashtunistan Issue

United States never tried to understand the depth of Afghan nationalism over the Pashtunistan issue. Washington believed that in course of time this issue would fade out from the Afghan minds and that the improvement of Pakistan-Afghanistan relations would serve the best American interests. So the United States decided to take a neutral stand over the Pak-Afghan border skirmishes that occurred from time to time. Though the American neutrality was understood as its opposition to the Afghan case, Kabul never denied, as stated above, Washington's offer of several aid packages over the years. At the same time, the United States correctly articulated that in spite of its stand on the Pashtunistan issue, Afghanistan would not go too far in her relations with the Soviets. This policy paid well in furthering the American interests in the subsequent years.

The Pashtunistan issue was already old when Pakistan was created after the partition of India in 1947. Like many other issues that generated border conflicts in the fifties and sixties, Pashtunistan issue was a legacy of the British imperialism in South Asia, especially between Pakistan and Afghanistan. The origin of this problem goes back to 1893, when British-Indian foreign secretary Sir Mortimer Durand erected the so called zone of British and the Afghan sphere of influence; thus dividing the Pashtun tribe in both sides of the line, what later came to be known as Durand Line.[37] The fact, Durand failed to recognize that this Pashtun tribe had ruled Afghanistan for about 200 years. Over the years however, this "zone of influence" had assumed the character of an international border, though it had been imposed on the Afghan ruler under duress, and no successive Afghan governments had accepted this line as an actual border between the two countries.[38] When the British withdrew from the Indian sub-continent, orchestrating the creation of Pakistan, they did not give a choice to the present Pakistani occupied Pashtun areas whether they would join in Afghanistan. Thus the "imperial hangover" continued and, in later years, it badly affected the relations between Pakistan and Afghanistan. Afghanistan was the only country to vote against the admission of Pakistan into the United Nations in 1948. To pressure Afghanistan, Pakistan closed the border in 1950, 1955, and 1961, interrupting the transit of goods to the landlocked Afghanistan, which badly affected the country's economy. Afghan irredentism increased, and Kabul retaliated by advocating an independent Pashtunistan, which would be carved out from Pakistan's North-West Frontier Province.

In the initial years, the United States reaction to the Pak-Afghan border skirmishes was cool, and Washington tried to maintain a sort of neutral stand over the issue. In fact, very few Americans tried to understand the real problem about what was going on between Islamabad and Kabul. For U.S. policy-makers, the strategic stakes was the security of Northern Tier, and containment of the Soviet communism. The United States only expressed its disappointment against the Afghan stand when the latter refused to join in the American sponsored military alliance in the mid-1950s. Washington's policy was to bring Afghanistan under its military umbrella, and for that reason, American officials always encouraged Kabul to improve its relations with Islamabad. The United States believed that, if not western-oriented, a neutral Afghanistan was necessary to promote American interests in the region.

But how far did the United States succeed in maintaining Afghan neutrality and its own "neutral" stand on Pak-Afghan conflicts? From the very beginning, Mohammed Daoud Khan was known as a Pashtun nationalist in the Afghan Royal family. When he assumed power as the Prime Minister of Afghanistan in 1953, it was obvious that the Pashtunistan issue would be raised and become more acute. It took a serious turn in 1955, when Pakistan announced the "One Unit Plan," to consolidate all the four provinces of West Pakistan, including the Pashtun-dominated North-West Frontier Province, into its so-called one unit system. The Afghan indignation was inflamed, leading to the burning of the Pakistani flag and attacking of its embassy in Kabul by a violent mob. Similarly, in Islamabad, government supported mob attacked the Afghan embassy, and Pakistan government blocked the Afghan transit route, bringing grievous harm to the Afghan economy. The two countries came to the edge of war.

The Americans faced a dilemma. On the one hand its closest ally Pakistan, and on the other, Afghanistan had to be supported, at least to prevent the Soviets from entering into the scene and thus exacerbating the chances of Soviet influence in Kabul. With the American initiative, Iran, Saudi Arabia, and Egypt came to the rescue of the two countries, and the problem was partially solved, even though it could not fully meet the Afghan expectations. Though the American diplomacy was of "uneven quality," its economic aid packages and active participation in ambitious development programs of Afghanistan helped subside the Afghan irredentism to a considerable extent.

In spite of sporadic border clashes between Pakistan and Afghanistan over the Pashtunistan issue, very few people in the West tried to understand what it meant. The 1960-61 border closing and break-off of diplomatic relations internationalized this issue to a great extent. Land-locked Afghanistan had to pay a heavy price in terms of the transit of goods that Pakistan blocked, and for about 18 months Afghan suffering continued. The Soviet Union extended the essential commodities, and the United Nations, the West Germans, and others send their goods through the Russian transit route. Also, by this time, several Western journals and newspapers discussed the Afghan point of view sympathetically.[39] But the American policy did not change. The Afghans suggested that the Americans supply their goods through the Soviet border. A close ally, Pakistan, was more important to Washington than a neutral Afghanistan. Above all, it was unacceptable for American officials to ship aid through the Soviet Union which would undoubtedly create a sharp reaction from the American Congress and the public. However, the American policy of neutrality over the Pak-Afghan disputes could not convince the Afghans and even some of them believed that in case of any direct confrontation, the United States might send troops to support the Pakistanis.[40]

The Pashtunistan issue, which resulted in the Pak-Afghan border closing also adversely affected the American aid program which had "boosted" the United States prestige after President Eisenhower's visit to Kabul in December 1960. Several projects, which had been seriously affected on the ground of logistics and administrative incompetence in the past, had gotten a new impetus. But now the border closing forced the American workers and officials to slow down their construction work. It also seriously undermined several heavy engineering construction projects, including the Kabul-Qandahar road, the Spin Baldak-Qandahar road, the installation of electric power facilities at the Arghandab Dam site, and improvement in the Helmand Valley land reclamation project. As one American official bitterly remarked, "The damned border closure wastes two years of solid preparation."[41] The border closure was also costly for the United States for it had to spend some $10,000 per day in salaries and allowances of their workers.

Significantly, the United States had to invite Pakistani displeasure by showing a sympathetic attitude towards the Afghans. When President Kennedy decided to send Mr. Livingston Merchant, a special emissary and ambassador to Canada, to mediate the Pak-Afghan conflicts, President Ayub Khan of Pakistan accused the United States of indecisiveness, and in an interview to an American reporter said, "Are all countries prepared to be friendly to you? Whose friendship is of any worth to you? The time for a choice has come—in fact it came a long ago. A great deal of hard, pragmatic thinking is required. The Russians have friends whom they back up to the hilt, right or wrong."[42]

Ultimately, the United States and the Iranian efforts prevailed, and Livingston arrived in Islamabad and Kabul. Though the Pakistanis did not consider any compromise, Mr. Merchant's proposal was greeted in Kabul in "glowing terms." The Afghans repeatedly stated that it was the Pakistanis who had closed the border and expected Washington to put pressure on them for it's reopening. It seems that the United States policy during this period was just to help the Afghans, and at the same time not to displease the Pakistanis, so that the policy of maintaining Afghan neutrality would remain intact. Afghanistan and Pakistan reestablished their diplomatic relationship, and the transit route for the Afghan goods were open, but the Prime Minister, Daoud, had to quit his office because of the emerging differences in the Royal family over the Pashtuinistan issue.

Once Daoud quits his office, the relations between Pakistan and Afghanistan improved to a considerable extent. So did Kabul's relations with both the superpowers. Substantial aid flowed from both sides. King Zahir Shah's efforts to maintain good relationship with both Pakistan and the United States were appreciated by Washington. But, in the meantime, in 1971, Pakistan had to fight a war with India over Bangladesh, and during the war, there was rumor that the Afghan army prompted by Mohammed Daoud (although he was out of power) was about to invade Pakistan in an apparent effort to "liberate" Pashtunistan from the Pakistani occupation. It was also widely believed in Afghanistan that Daoud's attempt had been restrained by the Soviet Union.[43] Afghanistan's westward leaning was clearly evident from the King's visit to London in December 1971 and the two government, among other things, agreed to terminate their long period of enmity. Citing the Western skepticism about the Afghan government, the King categorically stated in London that his armed forces were fully under his control and that Afghanistan was politically stable. The reopening of the British-Afghan friendship along with the American support to the famine affected people and increasing aid packages must have alarmed the leadership in Moscow. No doubt, there were some misgivings about the governmental stability in Kabul. It was only because of the emergence of a new class of people who supported the communist philosophy. It might be, however, possible that Daoud was trying to capture power with the help of the Soviet supported communist parties known as *Parcham* and *Khalq*. Whatever might have been the internal political dynamics in Kabul, it was true that during this period when Daoud was out of power, Afghanistan earned a good reputation in the Western world, especially its relations with the United States, and for that matter, Kabul had been accused of "even-handed policy" by the Soviets.

Another remarkable American effort paid off well in 1972 when Afghanistan severely suffered from a devastating famine in the northern and central region of the country. Officials in Kabul estimated that death toll was approximately 80,000. There was an acute food shortage, and Afghanistan needed an emergency relief operation to sustain the people in the affected areas. At this juncture of time, the United States ambassador, Robert G. Neumann came forward with a package of American assistance programs to help the Afghans in their fateful period. "Operation

Help" was carried to the worst affected areas. Assisted by several Afghan bureaucrats and army, the United States earned a good image. Though this emergency relief works revived Afghan faith and confidence in the Americans, the issue was exploited by the leftist elements in the regime. For the time being, Afghans forgot the Pashtunistan issue, and appreciated the American help in their crucial period of history.

Daoud's Westward Look

When Daoud came to power after a *coup 'd etat* in 1973, many observers, especially in the Western world believed that there might be a "Soviet hand" in engineering the coup. These accusations were further substantiated by the immediate support of the leftist political parties known as *Parcham* (banner) and *Khalq* (masses), which were formed as a communist party in 1965 and splited in 1967 into two factions. The Western observers also cited Daoud's achievements in successfully bringing massive Soviet aid to Afghanistan. But an American anthropologist who spent most of his lifetime in studying Afghanistan refused to accept this popular perception. Instead, paradoxically, in his book *Afghanistan*, he stated:

> *Daoud Khan is neither pro-Russian, pro-Chinese, nor pro-American: he is vigorously pro-Afghan.*
> *Among the reasons for his seizure of power in 1953 was the fear that the Afghan government, to its detriment, had become too pro-American. This may also be ultimately listed as a reason for the July coup.*[44]

Daoud also publicly declared that the overthrow of the monarchical rule of King Zahir Shah was purely a domestic affair. He categorically stated that his intension was to establish a republican form of government and that would be in strict conformity with the tenets of Islam.[45] In contrast, a popular perception emerged in Washington that the Soviets had a complicity in the coup, and that Daoud's regime would be not less than a satellite of Moscow. Daoud did receive millions of dollar worth of arms and economic aid, but that was only to strengthen and modernize his armed forces and to continue Afghanistan's five-year plans of economic reforms. He once again raised the Pashtunistan issue and started a confrontationist approach towards Pakistan. But, within a short period of time, Daoud had to turn to Pakistan, Iran, Saudi Arabia, Egypt, and the United States, a "turn" that cost Afghan sovereignty. Why did Daoud turn to the West and the United States, especially, at a time when he was receiving millions of dollar worth military and economic aid from the Soviet Union?

There were many reasons for Daoud's change in foreign policy. Internally, the two factions of the communist party were getting more and more popular support among the civil servants, military, and student populations. Most people saw his populist slogan of the Pastunistan issue as a sort of plea for him to continue in power. Moreover, in spite of substantial Soviet aid, economic condition deteriorated, and the communists started exploiting the situation. Externally, Zulfikar Ali Bhutto, the Prime Minister of Pakistan had already succeeded in suppressing the Afghan army trained rebellion in the North-West Frontier Province in which Daoud was reportedly involved. Significantly, Bhutto had also initiated several counter insurgency measures against the Daoud regime to put pressure on him to drop the Pashtunistan issue. The Panjsher Valley rebellion of 1975 signaled to Daoud that he had to be very careful about the Pashtunistan issue. Bhutto was determined to bring Daoud to the negotiating table, and to change the course of Afghanistan's foreign policy. Another most remarkable development within Kabul was that the U.S. ambassador Theodore Eliot, Jr. had been pursuing Daoud not to go too far in his Pashtunistan policy and to improve relations with Pakistan, Iran, and the other countries of the Middle East. Interestingly, during this period, the United States asked Iran, Saudi Arabia, Kuwait, and Japan to extent more economic assistance to Afghanistan. Ambassador Eliot had told Daoud that the Pashtunistan issue was making him more dependent on Moscow, and that for that reason he must open his door to Pakistan. In this effort Eliot was not entirely unsuccessful.[46] At this point of time, Shah Reza Palhalvi of Iran offered his good offices to mediate the Pak-Afghan dispute. Daoud had no other alternatives left but to cave in the Shah's efforts.

Within two years, Daoud expelled all his communist supporters, both from the *Parcham* and the *Khalq*, by virtue of whom he had come to power, and attempted to pursue an independent and non-aligned foreign policy. In February 1977, he appointed Abdul Qadir Nuristani, a hard-liner, as his minister of the interior, and intensified repression of the communists and other opposition elements. He also halted Afghan mass media attacks on Pakistan and, in 1977, he was about to reach a tentative agreement with the Bhutto government over the Durand Line and the Pashtunistan issue. But the domestic development in Pakistan and the overthrow of Zulfikar Ali Bhutto by General Zia-ul-Haq blocked the negotiating process to a considerable extent even though soon after coming to power, Zia had expressed his willingness to continue the negotiation initiated by the Bhutto government. In fact, these changes in Daoud were mostly affected by his policy of economic modernization and Afghanistan's regional considerations, such as improving relations with Iran and Pakistan. The Shah of Iran played a dominant role in this regard. The Shah had his own reasons to sort out the Pak-Afghan disputes, and bringing Afghanistan to its own sphere of influence. Because of its fairly large Baluch minority, Iran had a traditional fear of the Afghan demand of a separate Baluch state, which the former perceived, could be a threat to Iran's territorial integrity. So, under a $2 billion 10-year economic agreement with Kabul, the ambitious Shah Reza Palhlvi attempted to replace Moscow as the principal aid donor. He also persuaded Daoud to build a railroad linking Kabul to the nearest railhead in Iran. Had this project been completed, it would have significantly reduced Afghanistan's trade dependencies on the Soviet Union.[47] The Shah wanted to draw Kabul into a "Western-tilted, Teheran-centered regional economic and security sphere embracing

India, Pakistan, and the Persian Gulf states," a policy encouraged by the United States.[48]

So, internally through the U.S. ambassador, and externally through the Shah of Iran, the United States persuaded Daoud to turn towards the West. Daoud sent large number of his soldiers to Egypt, India, and the United States for training. Before that he had also reached an agreement with Pakistan for the military training of the Afghan soldiers, and in exchange, he pledged to oust Pakistani Baluch and Pathan guerrillas who were using Afghanistan as their sanctuary. During the Non-alignment Movement summit in Havana, Daoud succeeded in projecting himself as the leader of a "purely independent nation" by closely working with the "centrist group" rather than the "Soviet cluster" led by Cuba and Vietnam. In March 1978, Daoud visited many countries including India, Pakistan, Egypt, Libya, Saudi Arabia, Turkey and Yugoslavia. He was also preparing for a trip to Washington in September that year, in which the Carter administration was likely to increase the level of American aid and support the new initiatives of the Afghan President. Adolph Dubs, then Deputy Assistant Secretary of State for Near Eastern and South Asian Affairs, on March 16, 1978, in a statement before a Congressional Committee, just six weeks before the coup in Kabul, had remarked that "internally the political situation is stable (in Afghanistan)" and "President Daoud remains very much in control and faces no significant opposition."[49]

Commenting on Iran's determined efforts to snatch away Afghanistan from the Soviet orbit—into the Western sphere of influence, British ambassador to Afghanistan Roy Crook, a well known Afghan specialist, had predicted that, "if it goes too far and too fast, it (Teheran's diplomacy) will surely upset the Russians and produce reaction. The Soviets had just begun helping the Afghan communist in order to keep Daoud in line and to prepare for an increasingly uncertain future. But they are still generally satisfied with the degree of influence they have, provided that the drift to the right does not go too much further."[50]

Daoud had already gone too far right. But ironically, the April coup of 1978, which was later known as the *Saur* revolution, had not been directly instigated by Moscow, even though the revolutionaries had personal and ideological links with it and that the Soviet-trained military officers were directly involved.[51] Both Daoud and the Americans had misjudged the strength of the Afghan leftists, which was deeply entrenched in the government and military. When Daoud realized the strength of his opponents, it was too late to save him or his regime.

Conclusion

It can be stated that in 1953 and in 1973, Mohammed Daoud Khan had come to power to neutralize Afghanistan from "going too far" towards the west. And contrary to the popular perception, Daoud was not a pro-Soviet leader; rather, he was a "pro-Afghan" nationalist as he had been through out his political career. He was committed to keeping Afghanistan's non-aligned status, no matter how much economic or military aid his government received from the Soviet Union or the United States. He was truly a nationalist. His assertive nationalist rhetoric is reflected from his statement:

> *Our whole life, our whole existence, revolved round one single focal point—freedom. Should we ever get the feeling that our freedom is in the slightest danger, from whatever quarter, then we should prefer to live on dry bread, or even starve, sooner than accept help that would restrict our freedom.*[52]

When Daoud recaptured power in 1973, he mainly drew support from a large numbers of young reform-oriented army officers. No doubt the officers who supported Daoud had had training in the Soviet Union, they were more nationalistic in their political fervour, than any ideological leanings towards the Soviet communism. Daoud's purpose was not to follow dictates from Moscow, but to remain non-aligned. It may be stated that the most immediate reason of his coming to power in 1973 was to stop King Zahir Shah's apparent moves to improve relations with the United Kingdom and the United States, and the King's lack of interest in the Afghan claim of an independent Pashtunistan state. But after five years of authoritarian rule, he ended up with the same line of foreign policy: a desire to improve relations with the United States. Interestingly, in 1978, Daoud's own moves towards the West, in order to maintain a balance of his foreign policy, created a sharp reaction among the opposition leftist elements that ultimately resulted in his assassination and coming to power of the communists with immediate support from the Soviet Union.

What emerges from above is that, in spite of Afghanistan's land-locked geographical status and "proximity to the Soviet Union," over the years after World War II, up to 1978 (as this chapter deals with), the Americans had maintained a clearly visible presence. And paradoxically, the United States had never wholly accepted Afghanistan as within the Soviet sphere of influence. Rather whenever Kabul was seen moving closer to the United States, it had led to a negative Soviet response, directly or indirectly. The Americans continued their presence—sometimes in a small way, sometimes in a big way.

Notes and References

1. Cornelius Van H. Engert was the first American official to visit Afghanistan in 1922. After 20 years, he became the first American resident diplomat in Kabul.
2. Leon B. Poullada, "Afghanistan and the United States: The Crucial Years," *The Middle East Journal,* Vol. 35, Spring 1981, p. 181.
3. *Ibid.*
4. *The New York Times,* August 9, 1946. Cited in J.C. Hurewitz, *Middle East Politics: The Military Dimension,* Frederick A. Praeger, New York, 1969, p. 300. Also see *Hidden War: The Struggle for Afghanistan,* a staff report prepared for the Committee on Foreign Relations, United States Senate, April 1984, Washington DC, US Government Printing office, p. 6.

5. Louis Dupree, "The Mountains go to Mohammed Zahir," *American Universities Field Staff Reports* (here after AUFS,) Vol. IV, No. 6, 1960, pp. 23.
6. Louis Dupree, *Afghanistan,* Princeton University Press, New Jersey, 1973, p. 511.
7. Poullada, "Afghanistan and the United States," p. 184.
8. Dupree, *Afghanistan,* p. 511.
9. Louis Dupree, "The Mountains go to Mohammed Zahir," p. 6.
10. *Ibid*, p. 17.
11. Henry S. Bradsher, *Afghanistan and the Soviet Union,* Duke Press Policy Studies, Durham, 1983, p. 30.
12. *Ibid.*
13. Report of Senate Delegation, Named by the Vice President to Respond to Certain Official Invitations From Foreign Parliamentary Bodies and Governments, by Senator Wayne Morse, February 10, 1966, U.S. Government Printing Office, Washington: 1966, p. 15.
14. *Hidden War*...p. 5.
15. *Ibid.*
16. Airgram No. A-2, January 4, 1950, from the American Embassy in Kabul to the Department of State. This is one of many classified State Department documents obtained by the author under the Freedom of Information Act.
17. This was the perception of the Secretary of State John Foster Dulles who turned down the Afghan request for military aid in 1954. For details, see Robert G. Neumann, "Afghanistan Under the Red Flag," in *The Impact of the Iranian Events Upon Persian Gulf and U.S. Security.* Ed. By Z. Michael Szaz (Washington D.C., American Foreign Policy Institute, 1979), p. 130.
18. Airgram no. A-71 from the American Embassy in Kabul to the State Department, June 26, 1971, p. 1. This airgram contained the policy review. Cited in Thomas T. Hammond, *Red Flag Over Afghanistan: The Communist Coup, the Soviet Invasion, and the Consequences,* Boulder, Colorado, Westview Press, 1984, p. 26.
19. U.S. Congress, House Committee on Foreign Affairs Hearing, *Mutual Security Programme,* 82nd Congress, 1st session (U.S. Government Printing Office, Washington D.C., 1951), p. 996.
20. A very analytical discussion is available in J.C. Hurewitz, *Middle East Politics: The Military Dimension,* Published for the Council on Foreign Relations by Frederick A. Praeger, New York, 1969, pp. 296-307.
21. Out of these three projects, the Hilmand Valley Project was the oldest one. The Afghans had initiated the HVP in the early years of the 20th century. They constructed first new functional canal between 1910 and 1914. The Germans and Japanese technical assistance in the 1930s and early 1940s helped dig nine miles of canals at Boghra. From 1941 to 1946, Dr. S.W. Shah, a Cornell-educated Afghan engineer led digging the canals for another 16 miles.

22. Dupree, *Afghanistan*, p. 484.
23. Afghanistan, Ministry of Planning, *Majmuaei Aisayawi-e-Sali 1350* (Statistical Dictionary of 1971), Kabul, 1971, p. 161.
24. Dupree, *Afghanistan*, p. 759.
25. Poullada, "Afghanistan and the United States: The Crucial Years," p. 184
26. United States Embassy in Kabul, *Helping People: Agency for International Development Mission to Afghanistan*, April 1979, p. 35. Also see Afghanistan Ministry of Planning, p. 161.
27. During this period, the Soviet Union provided $516.9 million in economic aid and $100 million in military aid. See *Ibid.*
28. Note by the Executive Secretary to the National Security Council (James S. Lay, Jr.) on "U.S. Policy Toward South Asia," December 7, 1956, in a *Declassified Documents Quarterly Catalog 5* (January-March 1979), No. 44B.
29. Quoted in J.C. Hurewitz, *Middle East Politics: The Military Dimension*, p. 305.
30. Dupree, *Afghanistan*, p. 593. Also see Dupree, *AUFS Reports*, Vol. 10, No. 4, July 1966, p. 6. Maiwandwal was a long time ambassador to Washington.
31. Louis Dupree, "A Note on Afghanistan: 1971," *AUFS*, Vol. 15, No. 2, p. 23.
32. Security Assistance Agency, Department of Defence, "Fiscal Year Series, 1979," Washington, 1979, p. 71.
33. Bradsher, *Afghanistan and the Soviet Union*, p. 29. Bradsher quoted from "Expansion of Soviet Influence in Afghanistan and U.S. Countermeasures," 11 May 1956, in *Declassified Documents* 1980, No. 280B; report by the Operations Coordination Board, National Security Council, dated 28 November 1956, in *Declassified Documents* 1981, No. 76B.
34. Nikita Khrushchev, *Khrushchev Remembers*, Little Brown, Boston, 1970, pp. 507-8.
35. Louis Dupree, "American Private Enterprise in Afghanistan: The Investment Climate, Particularly as It Relates to One Company," *AUFS Reports 4*, December 1960, p. 15.
36. Louis Dupree, *AUFS Reports*, No. 27, 1980, pp. 5-6.
37. Pashtun population of about 14 millions presently divided almost equally between Pakistan and Afghanistan across the Durand Line. The historical fact is that the Pashtun dynasties in Kabul ruled a united Pashtun kingdom, encompassing most of what is now northern Pakistan, until 1880, when the British-India pushed the Afghan boundary to the Khyber Pass.
38. The then king of Afghanistan, Amir Abdur Rahman Khan claimed that the Durand Line was imposed on him under threat and duress. See Louis Dupree, *Afghanistan*, pp. 417-429.
39. For example, see *Eastern World*, October 1961, and *The New Republic*, October 30, 1961.

40. Louis Dupree, *The AUFS Reports,* Vol. 5, No. 3, November 1961, p. 9.
41. *Ibid,* p. 10.
42. *The New York Times,* October 3, 1961. Also see *Ibid,* p. 11.
43. Larence Ziring, *Pakistan: The Enigma of Political Development,* Kent, England, Dawson Publishing, 1980, p. 237.
44. Louis Dupree, *Afghanistan,* p. 759.
45. Zubeida Mustafa, "Afghanistan and the Asian Power Balance," *Pacific Community,* January 1975, p. 238.
46. Thomas T. Hammond, *Red Flag Over Afghanistan: The Communist Coup, the Soviet Invasion, and the Consequences,* Westview Press, Boulder, Colorado, 1984, pp. 38-39.
47. Louis Dupree, *Afghanistan 1977: Does Trade Plus Aid Guarantee Development?* AUFS Reports, Vol. 21, No. 3, p. 4.
48. Selig S. Harrison, "Dateline Afghanistan: Exit Through Finland," *Foreign Policy,* No. 41, Winter 1980/81, p. 165.
49. Hearings before the Sub-committee on Asia and Pacific Affairs, House Committee on Foreign Affairs, in the *Department of State Bulletin* 78, 2014 (May 1978): 50.
50. Selig S. Harrison, "Dateline Afghanistan: Exit Through Finland?" pp. 167-168.
51. As a matter of fact, Najibullah who had been an active participant of the April 1978 events, in his 1987 conversation with Shevardnadze bluntly said, "In April 1978 neither a revolution, nor a rebellion, but a coup happened in Afghanistan." Cited in G.M. Kornienko, "The Afghan Endeavor: Perplexities of the Military incursion and Withdrawal," *Journal of South Asian and Middle Eastern Studies,* Vol. 17, No. 2, Winter 1994, p. 2. By the time of the coup, Kornienko was an alternate member of the Politburo, as were Gorbachev and Shevardnadze.
52. Cited in Gunther Nollan and Hans Jurgen Wiche, *Russia's Southern Flank,* New York, Praeger, 1962, p. 136.

2
Carter and the Road to Afghanistan

The victory of the opposition and the collapse of a pro-Soviet leftist radical regime would certainly serve the U.S. interest and it would show the Third World that the perspective of our rival Marxist-Leninist on the "inevitability" of world history is not necessarily true.

—U.S. Intelligence Assessment, 1979.

This chapter examines the evolution of U.S. policy towards Afghanistan in the first years of Carter Presidency in order to understand the dimensions of the Soviet threat and the subsequent American reaction. Most writers on the Afghanistan crisis believed that President Carter had no viable policy to contain the increasing threat of communist expansion in South Asia after the April 1978 coup in Kabul. Instead they described the administration's response as one of ambivalence and benign neglect. They saw increasing Soviet assertiveness and erosion of American power in the region. This is, however, an oversimplification of Carter's policy. Washington's policy was influenced by several external factors such as the cold war rhetoric in the international environment and, simultaneously, internal factors such as differences between the State Department and the National Security Council (NSC) on the one hand, and the domestic developments in Afghanistan and neighboring Iran and Pakistan on the other. Delving into the background of the crisis, the evidence suggests that the Carter policy did not suffer from any dovish ideas, rather up to the day of the Soviet takeover, the United States had tried its best to preserve Afghan sovereignty by giving substantial aid and supporting the successive regimes in Kabul. Up to the Soviet invasion of that country, Washington worked hard to preserve the Afghan non-aligned status by maintaining its own presence in Kabul. But when it became certain that the Soviets were invading Afghanistan, Washington did not warn the Soviets in the "top level" for any possible restraint from Moscow or commit any military force to protect Afghan sovereignty. Instead, it allowed the Soviets to get involve in a protracted war.

How did the United States evolve a policy from the communist coup in Kabul and beyond? What motivated the administration to maintain a visible presence in Kabul even though it was clearly known as a communist regime?

How far Carter's policy influenced the subsequent Reagan administration in making the Afghan war costly for the Soviets? In order to answer these questions, it is necessary to examine the badly signposted road to Afghanistan, keeping in mind both internal developments in Afghanistan and the regional political development.

The Coup

As discussed in the last chapter, the United States was not expecting any major political upheaval in Kabul and everyone in the Carter administration had believed that there was no internal or external threat to the Daoud regime. But within a short period of time rapid political developments took place, and even Prime Minister Daoud himself could not properly comprehend the strength of his leftist opponents in Afghanistan. Things began to change when the Parcham (one of the break away factions of the People's Democratic Party of Afghanistan, PDPA) leader Mir Akbar Khaiber was murdered on April 17, 1978. It is still clearly not known who killed Khaiber but many expe ts at the time believed that the murder was conspirated by Daoud's hard-liner interior minister Abdul Qadir Nuristani, who had told many of his friends that it was time for the government to "finish off' the communists before they became too strong.[1] This speculation had been intensified by two previous killings allegedly, related to a greater conspiracy.[2] Whatever might have been the "behind the scene" plot, the murder of Khaiber led to a sharp reaction from the people, and about 15,000 slogan-shouting sympathizers turned up for his funeral. Public resentment against the Daoud regime continued and the President ordered mass arrests of the communist leaders in an apparent effort to suppress them. But his inefficient police force failed to arrest Hafizullah Amin, a leading Khalq leader, until 10.30 AM on April 26. Although Amin was under house arrest before that, he managed to orchestrate a coup by sending messages by his teen-aged son to his party leaders and key supporters in the military. The coup succeeded. And accordingly, April 27 proved a fateful day for Daoud. Along with him, all his family members were killed in the Royal Palace itself, marking the end of about 150 years of political domination by the Mohammadzai lineage in Kabul. The communist had come to power under the leadership of Nur Mohammed Taraki and Hafizullah Amin.

Many people, especially in the West, believed that the coup had been orchestrated by the Soviets. But the evidence suggests that there was no linkage between the Afghan communist leaders and the Soviets to plot a coup at that period of time. The Soviet trained military officers, who played a critical role on April 27, were also more nationalist than communist in their political fervor. Not surprisingly, popular opinion in Kabul pointed the finger at the US embassy or even CIA as the culprits of Khaiber murder and alarmed the Daoud regime through an unprecedented anti-American demonstration in the street of the capital.[3] Another interesting fact is that of the 21 men who constituted the first PDPA cabinet immediately after the coup, no fewer than 10 had been educated in the United States and a mere three in the Soviet Union. So the 1978 *Saur* (April) revolution, as it was called later, was basically an internal development in Kabul. However, the Soviets accepted the developments as a fait accompli and "envisioned Afghanistan as a second Mongolia which would leap from feudalism to socialism."[4]

For the United States, it came as a surprise and Washington pursued a policy of "watchful waiting." In fact, most people in the Carter administration were confused about the nature of the coup and for that reason; there were conflicting stands among the officials in the White House and the State Department. Washington was also not anticipating any threat to its interests in the region, since its closest friend Shah Reza Pahlvi was very much in power in Iran, and Persian Gulf oil for the U.S. allies seemed fully protected.

However, the Russian-speaking CIA station chief and the American ambassador in Kabul had been instructed from Washington "to regard watching Soviet activities as a higher priority than monitoring Afghan domestic affairs."[5] But in fact, the attitudes and affiliations of the new rulers could not be properly assessed by either the U.S. embassy in Kabul or the State Department. In fact, mainly because of two principal factors, there was some difficulty in knowing exactly what happened in Kabul. Firstly, for a few days, the new Afghan regime resented being called communist, Marxist-Leninist or Scientific Socialist. Nur Mohammed Taraki, who emerged as the leader of the coup and President of Afghanistan, declared at a press conference on May 6, "We are non-aligned and independent." He denied that his party was communist or Marxist, and he appealed to all the countries of the world, including the United States, for economic aid. He said nothing of his government's connections with the Soviet Union.[6] Taraki also declared that his government was trying to maintain friendly relations with the United States and added that this would depend on "the amount of economic and political support the revolutionary government received."[7] If this was a tactical move by the President, it worked well for a few months especially in terms of American responses to the new regime. Secondly, some observers in Washington ruled out any Soviet hand in the coup. Selig Harrison, a frequent commentator on Afghanistan, wrote, "The coup was a hastily improvised, 11th-hour affair and thus did not represent a deliberate Soviet gambit in the global strategic chess game."[8]

The U.S. Embassy in Kabul expressed similar uncertainty about those involved in overthrowing President Mohammed Daoud and cautioned the State Department "against any premature conclusion that the new leaders are communist."[9] The following day the State Department sent messages to various American embassies arguing, "fragmentary evidence suggests that they (the coup leaders) may be leftist and /or strongly Islamic nationalists."[10] But after a few days, this misconception was cleared up when the regime declared its ideology as "scientific socialism" and that the Afghan coup as the "true continuation of the Great Soviet October Revolution." Even at this stage, the policy makers in Washington did not regard the coup as an adverse development or the upheaval for altering the strategic balance in the region and, therefore, the U.S. had a low-keyed response. Washington wanted to continue its aid and diplomatic relations with the new regime for several reasons.

As the leaders of the coup sounded more nationalistic than communist, and given that Hafizullah Amin instead of Nur Mohammed Taraki orchestrated the coup, U.S. officials believed that the new regime would develop its relations with the West and the United States, and would not succumb to the wrath of Soviet power. Some people in the U.S. government remarked, "despite his (Taraki's) longstanding Marxist views he had never appeared to be hostile to the Americans."[11] As to the new government's relations with Moscow, even the *London Times* of May 29, 1978 commented that it might be even more nationalist and independent than the government of Daoud.

The United States feared that once it recognized the new regime as communist, it would have to withhold all aid to Afghanistan. Since 1962, the U.S. Congress had prohibited aid to communist countries unless the President made a formal determination that the particular case served the American national interest. So the U.S. Embassy in Kabul was ordered not to apply the communist label in its political analysis of the regime because of the fear of triggering the 1962 law.[12]

Some officials in the State Department argued that if they closed their aid mission, they would lose what little leverage they had retained in the country. So according to them, even if the Prime Minister Nur Mohammed Taraki and his Khalq party were openly communist, the Afghan society and most people in the government were not. So stay in touch and hope for a change in the direction. "And anyway when Congress tries to dictate the tactics of foreign policy, it generally makes stupid laws."[13]

By pursuing this policy, Washington not only legitimized the communist regime in Kabul, but also demoralized the Islamic resistance forces to the regime (who were fighting against Daoud and later against Taraki and Amin), to a great extent. Nevertheless, at the regional level, the United States discouraged both Pakistan and Iran from following a hostile attitude or to "take any hasty moves" against Kabul's new rulers. Both Islamabad and Teheran were however, seriously worried about the developments in Kabul. They had warned Washington about the possible communist takeover in Kabul and wanted the United States to respond by strengthening Pakistan. Iran and Pakistan were uneasy about the American policy of continuing aid to a communist regime. There was fear that the Soviets would encourage the Afghan revolutionaries to stir up old ethnic separatist movements among Pakistan's Baluch and Pashtuns. For Pakistan, the coup in Kabul eliminated Afghanistan as a buffer state, now in effect, leaving the country with a common border with the Soviet Union. A high-ranking official said, "the U.S. must realize that there has been a historic readjustment in this part of the world and act accordingly."[14] The Shah had also told the U.S. Ambassador in Teheran, William Sullivan that "coddling" the new Afghan rulers would not change their policies or buy any influence in Afghanistan. However, he felt obliged to go along with Washington's policies.

During this period of time, as a part of its "wait and see" attitude, the State Department was trying to test the Afghan leaders' declared goal of non-alignment policy. In fact, Washington maintained a two-track approach. Privately, U.S. officials encouraged the Foreign Minister, Hafizullah Amin, to adopt a less hostile public posture towards the United States in order to avoid Congressional pressure for aid cut off. Publicly, the administration maintained that the new regime was not communist and that if they cut off aid, there was possibility of Kabul being totally dependent and aligned with Moscow.

Two School of Thought

After the 1978 coup in Kabul, the entire U.S. government and academia had been divided about what had happened in Kabul and what should be the United States response. Louis Dupree, a longtime educator in Kabul and a leading scholar on Afghanistan wrote, "Governments, like persons, should be considered innocent until proven guilty."[15] Even he went to the State Department and argued "the coup was more nationalist than communist and that the United States should follow a wait-and-see policy."[16] Theodore Eliot, former U.S. Ambassador to Afghanistan agreed with this approach. He emphasized "this policy made sense because cutting off these programs unilaterally would only reduce Afghan options and drive the Afghan government deeper into the Soviet embrace."[17] Zbigniew Brzezinski, President Carter's National Security Advisor, who was later known as a hardliner in his approach towards the Afghan crisis, also approved of this restrained response to the communist coup. He believed it an internal development in Afghanistan and since, "there was no evidence of Soviet involvement, there was no ground for an American protests. As long as we could have some influence in Kabul why cut off aid?"[18] The then Under Secretary of State David Newsom visited Kabul in July 1978 to discuss economic assistance. Along with ambassador Adolph Dubs, Newsom met with Taraki and Amin. In their meeting, the Afghan leaders asked for more aid than the $20.6 million already programmed for 1978. Cyrus Vance, Carter's Secretary of State later wrote, "Newsom returned with a pessimistic assessment of the new regime's capabilities and intentions. He believed however, that the political situation was still fluid and that it would be a mistake for us to halt economic assistance and lose the prospect of any influence in Kabul."[19]

Another school of thought was supported by at least two former U.S. ambassadors to Afghanistan. Robert Neumann argued in the State Department that he had known the Afghan leaders for a long time and that "they were definitely communists and would follow orders from Moscow." He believed that the "failure of the United States to respond more forcefully to the coup of 1978 led the Soviets to think that Washington would not do much when they invaded Afghanistan in 1979."[20] Another supporter of a tougher approach was ambassador Adolph Dubs, who had been posted to Kabul shortly before the coup. Dubs repeatedly recommended, "The Carter administration do some contingency planning for a Soviet military takeover of Afghanistan." But some South Asian specialists in the State Department dismissed this as madness.[21]

Cyrus Vance later writes that the United States' response to the April 1978 coup was not appropriate. In his *memoir*, he has stated:

> *In looking back, I think we should have expressed our concerns more sharply at the time of the April coup that brought Taraki to power. There were reasons why we did not protest more vigorously. Although there was little question that the Taraki government would make itself responsive to Moscow, there was room for doubt whether the Soviets had planned the coup or were involved in its execution. And there was reason to think the strong Afghan nationalism of Taraki, and even more of Hafizullah Amin, might keep Afghanistan from becoming a Soviet satellite . . .. Although we were contacted from time to time about coup plots, my advice was that we not get involved.*[22]

Dubs' Death and Shift in American Policy

This policy of "wait-and-see" took a serious turn and compelled Washington toward a fundamental reassessment of its policy when ambassador Adolph Dubs was kidnapped and killed at a Kabul hotel by a militant group known as Setem-i-Melli on February 14, 1979. After Dubs was taken hostage, the United States urged the Afghan authorities not to do anything that might endanger the ambassador's life. But overriding these pleas, the police opened fire and Dubs was killed on the spot.[23] Now that Dubs death acted as a catalyst in US-Afghan relations although even before this incident, Washington's policy had already suffered a setback due to the increasing guerrilla resistance to the government.

When Dubs had come to Afghanistan some eight months before, for the first few months, he had found it virtually impossible to have any meaningful dialogue with the Afghan authorities, especially because of the growing Soviet influence both in the Government and armed forces of the communist regime. However, he had been able to develop a personal rapport with the Foreign Minister Hafizullah Amin and as a Russian-speaking Soviet and South Asian specialist, (who had also served in Moscow), and was unusually well equipped by training and temperament, Dubs had no difficulty in monitoring the Afghan situation.

With the loss of its envoy, Washington cautiously became more sympathetic to the opponents of the regime and slowly disengaged itself from the Kabul government. Afghan leaders also wanted a reduced American presence in the country restricting the number of peace corp volunteers, and cultural exchange program between the two countries. To the dismay of the Carter administration, Taraki's government also refused American requests for an investigation into the circumstances that led to the death of Dubs.

The outraged Carter administration slashed all aid programs except the humanitarian ones, and on July 23, Washington announced the withdrawal of most United States officials from Kabul embassy because of security reasons. By then the resistance had already spread to almost all parts of Afghanistan. Only a charge d'affairs rather than an ambassador replaced dubs. However, Washington continued its minimum economic support to Afghanistan until the Soviet occupation of that country in December 1979. By now, the United States had only about 20 officials remained in Kabul and Washington's leverage was by any measure extremely limited. "This may not be what the U.S. wanted, and it is unlikely to help the Afghans, whichever side of the current battle they are on. But what else could the U.S. do?"[24]

The Amin Factor

One of the most important reasons why the Carter administration did not take a hard line approach towards the communist regime after the 1978 coup was obviously the Amin factor. Hafizullah Amin, who led the coup and became the Foreign Minister of the new government, was more a nationalist than communist in his spirit and temperament. Though he was one of the founding members of the People's Democratic Party of Afghanistan (PDPA), which was formed in 1965 and preached Marxism-Leninism along Soviet lines, Amin was "less sycophantic" in his relations with Moscow than other communist leaders. In fact, the Soviets were not prepared for a communist revolution in Afghanistan as early as April 1978,[25] and were suspicious about the strength of the Amin faction in the PDPA because of its nationalist rhetoric. As a foreign minister, Amin had been committed to pursuing a balánced policy in Afghanistan's relations with both Washington and Moscow. In spite of his government's total dependence on Moscow, he continued to behave in his "free-wheeling fashion" because of the strong personal loyalty to him among key officials in the military and intelligence and "jealously guarded his grip over the security forces, refusing to let the KGB assume the degree of control it customarily expects in a satellite state."[26]

Hafizullah Amin never enjoyed Soviet blessings and was always looked upon suspiciously by the Soviet officials and especially those of the KGB. This was because of the fact that he had studied at Columbia University, New York, for three years, and subsequently had worked for the U.S.-aided Afghan teacher training programs. As a foreign minister, Amin had developed a good rapport with U.S. Ambassador Adolph Dubs and met him frequently, which must have worried the Soviet leadership in Moscow. In fact his meetings with the American diplomats were not unintentional. He "wanted to preserve a discreet link with the United States" as a guarantee against the increasing Soviet pressure to make Kabul accept satellite status.[27] He had also refused to go along with the Soviets in his policy towards Iran and over ambitious reform programs in Afghanistan that brought widespread guerrilla movements in the countryside.

These "discreet links" with the United States and distrust of the Soviets came into the open following the internal power struggle between Taraki and Amin that ended in a "Palace shoot-out" and the death of Taraki. In the aftermath of this event, the disaffeotion between Moscow and Amin was intensified and Amin's foreign minister, Shah Wali, openly accused the Soviet embassy in Kabul of complicity in an abortive attempt to remove his prime minister.[28] He demanded the removal of its longtime ambassador, Aleksandr Puzanov, who was ultimately recalled to Moscow in November 1979. Moscow no longer trusted Amin but the latter's control over the armed forces and intelligence made it difficult for Moscow to engineer an internal coup. Soviet officials also feared that a desperate Amin might seek help from the United States and Pakistan.

As a matter of fact, Amin did make some late efforts to improve his relations with the United States and Pakistan. When he assumed power after the death of Taraki, he probably knew that the Soviets were quite displeased with him and his policies, and that he needed to strike a deal with Islamabad and Washington. So apparently, he made a last attempt to either make a diplomatic breakthrough with the help of the United States or Pakistan, or seek asylum. Accumulating evidence suggests that Amin was not ready to compromise with Afghan sovereignty. He told an American diplomat in Kabul that if asked by the Soviet leadership to make a move against Afghan independence, he would not hesitate to sacrifice his life in opposing such a request.[29] A few days earlier, Amin had also clearly signaled his willingness to develop good relationship with the United States. He had an "amicable" and "relaxed" meeting with American Charge d' Affairs, J. Bruce Amstutz, in Kabul. Afghan officials told the American diplomats that Amin was intending to improve Afghanistan's bilateral relations with the United States and that he was even considering "an official letter of apology over the February 14 death of Ambassador Dubs."[30]

The United States decided to respond and made several minor gestures of friendship. The State Department "explored the possibilities for a less contentious relationship" and, at Pakistan's request, the United States waived PL480 regulations to enable the export of 200 tons of wheat to Afghanistan to meet the emergency needs. An American passenger plane for Ariyana (Afghan National Airlines) was delivered, and aid for the rural schools and health centers was extended. Because of this symbolic improvement in relations between United States and Afghanistan, Amin was branded an opportunistic leader. As a senior American diplomat observed: "Amin had Brezhnev's build, but Tito's mind and ambitions."[31]

However, relations remained stagnant. President Carter's concern over Amin's human right records, the Dubs issue, and the size of the American embassy staff continued to be the obstacles to improve relations. The Amin government's various foreign policy issues also troubled the Carter administration. Moreover, Amin did not make any concrete move to improve his relations with the U.S. An American diplomat in Kabul concluded that Amin was "content for the time being with a polite but limited relationship, which both countries would refrain from exacerbating by word or action."[32]

The U.S. Protest

As stated earlier, the Carter administration had been divided over U.S. policy towards Afghanistan before the Soviet invasion. While the National Security Council was pushing for a hard line approach, the State Department was pursuing a moderate policy. Brzezinski believed that because of the inconsistency of the administration's reactions to other "Soviet gains," Moscow invaded Afghanistan. In his memoir he notes: "Had we been tougher sooner, had we drawn the line more clearly, had we engaged in the kind of consultations that I had so many times advocated, maybe the Soviets would not have engaged in this act of miscalculation."[33] He claims that American protests to the Soviets about Afghanistan had been only initiated by him, and that the State Department was always reluctant to do so because it had lacked credibility in various foreign policy issues before that. But Secretary of State, Cyrus Vance denies these allegations.[34] In any case, the United States continued to warn the Soviets against the increasing military build up near the Afghan border.

As early as March 23, 1979, Washington sent a note to Moscow in which it stated that the United States and its allies "regard external involvement in Afghanistan's internal problems as a serious matter with the potential for heightening tensions and destabilizing the situation in the entire region."[35] In May, a report prepared for the Defence Intelligence Agency (DIA) accurately assessed that there was a high probability that the Soviets would invade Afghanistan. With more and more intelligence reports coming in, Washington cautiously tried to change its policy towards the region and warned Moscow against its possible invasion. In August, Brzezinski, with President Carter's consent, warned the Soviets against possible invasion of Afghanistan. The National Security Adviser cited "prudent" American restraint during the hostage crisis in Iran and said: "We expect others similarly to abstain from intervention and from efforts to impose alien doctrines on deeply and nationally conscious people."[36]

Beginning in September, when the intelligence reports came about the Soviet troops concentration in Central Asia, American officials had repeatedly asked for explanation and cautioned Moscow against moving troops into Afghanistan. But they received no response. After the killing of ambassador Dubs, the administration's attitude hardened. Harold Saunders, the Assistant Secretary for Near Eastern and South Asian Affairs, stated before the House Committee on Foreign Affairs that the administration had warned the Soviets of the dangers of a more direct involvement in Afghanistan.[37] However, Vance and his Soviet Affairs Adviser Marshal Shulman argued that warnings to the Soviets had no impact on its leadership because the relationship between Moscow and Washington had reached such a point that the Soviets had little to lose by further antagonizing the Americans. "Prior to Afghanistan," Shulman said, "Carter had dismantled all of the apparatus of cooperation between the United States and the USSR. We had little leverage left."[38]

In fact, the United States had both privately and publicly warned the Soviets against their increasing presence in Afghanistan. But, ironically, no major efforts were made in the "top level." It seems that Washington was pre-occupied with the hostage crisis in Iran, which was an emotional issue among the American public and so, paid little attention to the Soviet influence in Afghanistan. President Carter never warned Brezhnev privately or publicly saying that if the Soviets invaded Afghanistan, he would take the kind of steps that he took after the invasion. In that case, the Soviets probably would have thought twice before they ordered their troops to cross their southern border. It could also be possible that the Carter administration had already been "overpowered" by "hawkish" influences by the mid-1979 and, intentionally, the United States maintained a low-keyed policy towards Afghanistan, exacerbating the chances of more and more Soviet involvement in that country—intending to make Afghanistan, the Soviet's Vietnam. This idea is speculated from Brzezinski's statement before the first SCC meeting after the Soviet invasion when he said "the Soviets have overextended themselves. Afghanistan is there Vietnam, bleed them."[39] In that case, might be Washington was applying the dictum that Louis Dupree said some thirty years ago: "If you want to destroy the Soviet Union, give it Afghanistan."[40]

United States and the Afghan Rebels

By nature, Afghans are fierce and independent people. They have always killed each other in a small way and started to do it in a big way only when foreign armies, money, and weapons became involved. After the 1978 coup and capture of power by the PDPA, no one had to create a resistance to the communist regime. It was already there. In fact the origin of this resistance goes back to 1973, when Mohammed Daoud ousted Zahir Shah's monarchical rule and declared Afghanistan as a republic. Some supporter of the king and a group of militant Muslim fundamentalists fled to neighboring Pakistan and started guerrilla warfare against the Daoud regime. The Bhutto government took full advantage of these developments because of Pakistan's longstanding dispute with Afghanistan over the Durand Line as border between the two countries. Islamabad clandestinely trained a 5,000 strong military force at secret camps in Pakistan to pressurize the Daoud government and "neutralize" any pro-Pashtunistan movements. In 1974-75, the Pashtunistan issue re-emerged and there were frequent bomb blasts in Peshawar and other parts of the North-West Frontier Province. In July 1975, a major uprising against the Daoud government was initiated under the leadership of Gulbuddin Hekmatyar, who later became a dominant exile Afghan politician in Peshawar and *amir* (chief) of the Hezb-i-Islam insurgent group. The immediate aim of the Bhutto government was partly solved. With the help of the Shah of Iran, Bhutto succeeded to bringing Daoud to the negotiating table and change the direction of Afghan foreign policy, but he never stopped his masqueraded guerrilla war against Afghanistan. Thus the insurgency against the Daoud regime was primarily a product of Pakistan. So, by the mid-1979, when the United States slowly started supporting the resistance by giving them light weapons and some communication equipments to fight against the communist, Washington did not have to create a force, it was already there.

With the overthrow of Daoud and assumption of power by the PDPA, and subsequent 'reform, repression, and revolution' in Afghanistan, thousands of people fled to Pakistan and Iran and joined in the resistance movements. Many Muslim countries as well as some Western nations started supporting the rebels with money and arms. Although the American officials involved contend that they were not seeking the removal of the DRA government, later evidence indicated that Washington had cautiously encouraged the resistance against the Kabul regime. According to an August 1979 assessment by the U.S. Embassy in Kabul:

> *On balance, however, our larger interests especially given the DRA's (Democratic Republic of Afghanistan) extremely close ties to Moscow, this regime's almost open hostility to the U.S., and the atmosphere of fear it had created throughout the country, would probably be served by the demise of the Taraki-Amin regime.*[41]

In a separate dispatch, the U.S. Embassy in Kabul wrote to the State Department:

> *The victory of the opposition and the collapse of a pro-Soviet leftist radical regime would certainly serve the U.S. interest and it would show the Third World that the perspective of our rival Marxist-Leninist on the "inevitability" of world history is not necessarily true. A truly international non-aligned movement would be welcomed by us. The U.S. participation in economic construction would be possible in the case of the collapse of the DRA.*[42]

As early as April 1979, Carter's National Security Adviser, Zbigniew Brzezinski, "pushed a decision through the SCC (Special Coordinating Committee) to be more sympathetic to those Afghans who were determined to preserve their country's independence."[43] Brzezinski's memoir does not provide any details of what concrete form this sympathy took. However, based on available evidence, the United States was reported to have provided the resistance with covert aid limited to small amounts of medical supplies and communication equipment along with technical advice about from where they could acquire arms on their own.

With the mass uprising against the DRA government, the United States saw benefits in supporting the opposition forces, and greater publicity was given to the difficulties of the government in Kabul and increasing Soviet involvements in Afghanistan. Washington appointed Adolph Dubs as a new ambassador to Afghanistan with the hope that the new diplomat would be able to support the resistance forces.[44] By this time, the CIA had already started its operation. It's Afghan agents smuggled some tapes of speeches by partisan leaders such as those by the Iran based Islamic Movements of Afghanistan Mohammed Assef

Mohseni Qandahari, and distributed in Afghanistan. The agency financed demonstrations among the Afghan exiles in Pakistan and Iran, and cultivated alliances with the guerrilla leaders by donating medicine and communication gear. In fact, the CIA officials had been in touch with the rebel leaders based in different training camps in the North-West Frontier Province and Baluchistan starting from the April 1978 coup in Kabul.

The United States supported the resistance. But at the same time American officials were cautious about their support to the fundamentalists resistance groups based in Pakistan who carried out a repressive policy against the "nationalist, revolutionary, and patriotic" forces throughout the country under the pretext of fighting "communism."[45] Washington believed that American interests would not be served if the fundamentalists' parties overthrow the Kabul regime. In a secret memo to the State Department, the U.S. Embassy in Kabul writes:

> *(T) he available manifesto issued by some opposition group's call for a social and economic reforms (so necessary for this backward country high on its priority list). Thousands of personal vendettas would probably be carried out against surviving Khalqi officials, thereby probably tarnishing a post-DRA regime's human rights record. No matter how justified retribution against some officials might appear to be.*[46]

In fact, the United States wanted to support the traditionalist groups and supporters of the former king Zahir Shah and former Prime Minister Mohammed Yusuf. But most pro-Western groups lacked fighting strength and did not succeed in asserting themselves in the resistance movement. So the United States had no other option but to support with money and arms to the fundamentalist parties like the Hezb-I-Islami and Jamiat-I-Islami, headed by Gulbuddin Hekmatyar and Burhanuddin Rabbani respectively.

The Regional Scenario

By the end of its term, the Carter administration had been charged with indecisiveness, vacillation, and failure, in its policy towards Afghanistan, Iran, and Pakistan. The burning of the U.S. Embassy in Islamabad; the fundamentalist revolution and the overthrow of the Shah, and the hostage crisis in Iran; and the communist revolution and the Soviet invasion of Afghanistan, infuriated the Americans more than anything else since the Vietnam war. Most people felt that there was growing erosion of American influence and power, while the Soviets were more assertive and expanding their influence in the region. But a closer look at the developments in the region reveals a different picture. It suggests that the setbacks of American policy were not a consequence of the U.S. military weakness or the incapability of making a viable policy towards the region; they were a natural result of political conflicts that were local and indigenous in origin. So, before examining the Soviet invasion in Afghanistan and the intensity of American response, a look at the developments in the neighboring Iran and Pakistan will be worthwhile to understanding the implications of the crisis and the role of the regional actors.

Iran: To begin with, when the rising tide of fundamentalist putsch engulfed Iran soon after the arrival of Ayatollah Rahollah Khoemeini in February 1979; no one could judge the intensity of the revolution. Many people in and out of the Carter administration had believed that there was no threat to the Shah's government from the opposition. Even the CIA's assessment was wrong. The intelligence had stated that there was no cause for concern and that Iran was not in a revolutionary or even a pre-revolutionary situation. "Those who are in the opposition, both violent and non-violent," the report said, "do not have the capacity to be more than troublesome. There is dissatisfaction with the Shah's tight control of the political process, but this does not threaten the government."[47] However, within a short period of time, the Shah's hold of power took such a turn that it was beyond the control of Iranian authorities and the Carter administration. Khomeini not only called upon his followers to sacrifice their life "to protect Islam" and oppose the authoritarian rule of the Shah, he also urged the armed forces personnel to desert the government and join with him in the Holy War. Within weeks, desertion in the military started and came to a point of virtual collapse. Iranian armed forces was onetime the center of influence for Washington. Now with the virtual disintegration of the military, the Carter administration feared that the leftist revolutionaries, supported by the Marxist-Leninist Tudeh party would create more chaos, if come to power overthrowing the Shah. The fear was exacerbated due to the developments and coming to power of the communists in the neighboring Afghanistan eight months before. Therefore, President Carter sent General Robert Huyser to Iran to assess the state of morale in the armed forces. However, there were conflicting views in Washington about Huyser's mission. Some people speculated that he was assigned to organize a pro-Shah military coup in Teheran. This idea was led by the National Security Adviser, Zbigniew Brzezinski.[48] Others believed that his intention was to oppose such a possibility. However, the General could not succeed to achieve anything and his trip was a failure one.

When Ayatollah Khomeini arrived in Teheran in February 1979 after a long political exile and denounced the newly appointed Bakhtiar government, the U.S. had by all means, very limited leverage left in Iran. Because, after the Shah, Carter had supported the Bakhtiar government. The Ayatollah denounced the Bakhtiar government and appointed Mahdi Bazargan as his own Prime Minister. Although the new government had assured the United States to keep normal relationship with Washington and to protect American life and properties in Iran, the growing anti-U.S. rhetoric in the majority did not allow him to do so. In fact, Carter administration's responses to the domestic political developments in Iran were very much systematic and correct. The hue and cry about the President's inability to tackle the situation was spread in Washington mostly because of the distorted media coverage and by the people who themselves were not familiar with the ideological and religious dimension of the revolution which was deep rooted in the minds of the Iranian people. As an American expert on the field, who investigated the historical aspect of the revolution in Iran notes:

> *No conceivable change in U.S. policy would have induced the revolutionary government to be pro-American. After nearly two centuries of domination by powerful outsiders (the British and the Russians before us), Iranians intensely hated foreign powers and foreign influence. A study of Iran's past suggests that current anti-American feeling is as much a product of this history as of three decades of U.S. support for the Shah.*[49]

As a matter of fact, the religious fever did not originate against the United States; rather its origin was against the Shah's authoritarian rule, corruption, and his program of modernization, which inflicted a heavy burden on a large segment of the rural and urban population. The reform programs created sharp resentment among the clergy who lost their lands under the new law of the government. This maximized the power of the mullahs and solidified extremist organizations into an army of revolutionary action. Khomeini, though in exile, sent periodical "sermons" to his followers condemning the Shah and his foreign friends as anti-Islamic and traitors of the Iranian people. These sermons were being clandestinely propagated in the mosques throughout the country. SAVAK, the secret police of the Shah, was reportedly involved in a number of dastardly killings of his political opponents. When some 430 people were killed in a movie theater fire in Abadan, most people followed their religious leaders insistence that the fire was set by the SAVAK.

As such, when petroleum workers went on strike starting from October 1978, responding to the call of the Ayatollah, the law and order situation deteriorated rapidly. In December, about seventy percent workers stayed off the job. The military government failed to restore normalcy. General strike continued for months, paralyzing all trade and commerce. Not only it created chaos and confusion among the people, it had also a lasting impact on the nation's economy; drastically reducing Iran's oil production. With the increasing religious fever, anti-American feelings also reached to its peak. Even with Washington's support, the Shah's maneouvre had not been sufficient to preserve the monarchy. So he left Iran on January 16, never to return.

President Carter had to take a hard decision to admit the Shah in the U.S. for medical treatment. People from both the left and right in the administration supported such a decision—though most people criticized the President after the hostage crisis. The revolutionaries under the Ayatollah perceived it as an act of arrogant defiance on the part of Washington and insult against them. On November 4, 1979, radical Iranian students broke into the American Embassy compound and took some sixty U.S. officials as hostages; thus creating the hostage crisis, from which the Carter administration never recovered. Initially, Washington hoped to release the hostages soon. But with the dismissal of the Bazargan government and the sanctioning of the takeover by the Ayatollah, the situation became very complicated and the U.S. perception and policy towards Iran changed overnight. President

Carter reacted sharply. He declared, among other things, unilateral economic sanctions against Teheran, froze Iran's foreign assets, and sent two aircraft carrier task forces to patrol the Arabian Sea and the Persian Gulf region. Other forces at Diago Garcia and elsewhere were put under alert and even he was considering a direct military action against Iran. But since such action would jeopardize the lives of the hostages, Carter left the option open, without taking such move. However, he warned that in case of any punishment or execution of the hostages, he was prepared to take direct and immediate military attack against Iran. In his memoir, Carter notes: "We pored over aerial photographs of oil refineries and many other targets of strategic importance there and planned how best to carry out our threat to the Iranian leaders of quick punitive action. We were not bluffing and they new it."[50] The ill-fated rescue mission of April 1980 had been the consequences of this policy.

Pakistan: Since the early 1970s, it had been a debatable question in Washington, whether Pakistan was a part of South Asia or Southwest Asia. If Pakistan is regarded as a part of South Asia, it is obvious that, it would be thought of largely in connection with India and the outside powers may be heavily influenced by India's greater size, military strength and potential, and democratic political system. If Pakistan is regarded as a Southwest Asian country, because of its geographical location and its growing links with the Arab World and the Gulf, the policies of the outside powers toward Islamabad are likely to be less influenced by a concern for Indian views. Washington accepted the former view and recognized India as a regional power,[51] when after its defeat in the 1971 war with India and loss of East Pakistan, Islamabad started turning into the oil-rich Muslim countries in the Middle East and West Asia and put less importance to South Asia in its foreign policy. This 'westward' look of Pakistan puzzled the Americans most throughout the 1970s. Viewed from Washington, it looked as if Pakistan was committed to carving out a role in an increasingly anti-US Islamic world and part of the revival of the Pan-Islamic fundamentalist putsch in the region. This perception was later intensified in Washington when Pakistan followed Iran's lead and withdrew from CENTO (Central Treaty Organization, a military alliance carefully constructed by Dulles in the 1950's), and General Zia-ul-Haq's emphasis on Arab states, rather than the United States and the West.

Carter acknowledged that previous Presidents, such as Nixon and Ford, recognized India as a regional power, but neglected to explore its potential as a partner in promoting the United States interests in the region. So, he attempted to correct the past U.S. mistakes and tried to improve relations with New Delhi. His National Security Adviser, Zbigniew Brzezinski sketched out a foreign policy agenda and listed India, among other nations, as a "regional influentials."[52] Carter's Deputy Secretary of State Warren Christopher meeting the press in New Delhi praised India "as the leader in South Asia."[53] Carter also visited India in December 1978 and helped strengthen Indo-US relations. While Iran was strategically important to Washington, both as a "policeman" of the Gulf to protect American and Western interests, and the largest source of oil, Pakistan was neither of the two. So the Carter administration saw no American political or military interest at stake in Pakistan. The domestic political developments in India and Pakistan also contributed to a great extent for the American tilt towards India. The civilian government of Zulfikar Ali Bhutto had been overthrown and replaced by a military junta; Zia-ul-Haq[54] in Pakistan and across the border in India, the pro-Soviet Congress Party government of Indira Gandhi had been defeated in the national elections by a pro-American Janata Party. Even during their election campaign, the Janata Party leaders had expressed their willingness to improve India's relations with the United States.

U.S.-Pakistan ties was also inevitably complicated by disagreements over issues such as nuclear nonproliferation, Islamabad's non-recognition of Carter's Camp David Accords and overall American policy towards the Arab-Israeli conflicts, and General Zia's canceling of the general elections. To the dismay of the administration, Pakistan insisted on developing its nuclear capability and continued to seek its technology and parts abroad. Since Washington was very critical on this issue, on Carter's own consent, Congress applied the Symington-Glen Amendment to the International Security Assistance Act of 1977 and terminated all aid to Pakistan in April 1979.

The two countries relations were also greatly influenced by the burning of the U.S. Embassy in Islamabad and killing of two Americans in the action. A rumor that the United States was involved in the takeover of the Grand Mosque in Mecca incited this incident. Pakistani authorities apparently made only delayed efforts to control the violent mob.

Conclusion: The developments in Afghanistan, Iran, and Pakistan during the Carter Presidency were not because of faulty policies of Carter administration. Nor was it a result of an erosion of American influence. Rather they were indigenous in origin, and expressions of nationalism in the region. As described earlier, the United States was pursuing its policy of "wait-and-see" and its visible presence in Kabul, at least up to the death of ambassador Dubs when Washington curtailed most aid except the humanitarian ones. Only after the Soviet invasion of that country that Washington seriously marked the geopolitical implications of the developments and the possible Soviet control of the oil fields in the Persian Gulf. But, as stated before, the Soviet move to Afghanistan was not an offensive one and that it was based on traditional Soviet fear of spillover of the Muslim fundamentalism from the South to the former Soviet Central Asian Republic.

Iran was made the protector of American interest in the Persian Gulf under the Nixon doctrine. Throughout the years, Washington had shipped huge quantity of arms and sophisticated aircrafts, and extended military, political, and economic support to Teheran. But it is true that there was no treaty or any military alliance between the United States and Iran committing Washington to come to the rescue of the Shah against either external or internal threats. The growth of religious fundamentalism combined with the rhetoric of nationalism percolated in such a way that no U.S. policy could have forestalled. Similarly, the developments in Pakistan such as from Bhutto's democracy to Zia's military dictatorship, and Pakistan's insistence on its nuclear option, its policy towards Carter's camp David Accords, burning of the American Embassy in Islamabad and violations of human rights in Sind and Beluchistan forced Carter to leave Pakistan "to the wolves." By contrast, India, as the largest democracy in the world, after a change of government from pro-Moscow Congress Party to pro-Washington Janata Party, tilted Carter to New Delhi. He saw Indian power and potential as conducive to the American interests.

So, in spite of the political upheaval in the region, Carter administration's policy towards Afghanistan was quite balanced and up to the last moment Washington tried best to maintain its presence in Kabul. The United States traditional policy of maintaining Afghan neutrality however, had already in favor of the Soviet communism, and, more and more political, economic, and military investments flowed from Moscow. It is interesting to note that, whenever, Kabul was looking towards Moscow before the 1978 communist coup, it was Pakistan or Iran or the United States, used to emerge in the scene to pull Afghanistan from the Soviet orbit (or vice versa). But now that Washington tried to apply a two-track policy. Firstly, American officials wanted to bring the Prime Minister Hafizullah Amin to their own umbrella, and Amin's willingness to play the American game ultimately proved catastrophe and led to the Soviet military invasion. Secondly, the United States very cautiously initiated a program of secret arms to the resistance forces which subsequently to be a major CIA operation against the Kabul regime. But these policies were designed to serve American interest in some way or the other.

Notes and References

1. For example, Selig S. Harrison, "Dateline Afghanistan: Exit Through Finland?" *Foreign Policy,* No. 41, Winter, 1980/81, p. 168.
2. See Louis Dupree, *American University Field Staff Reports,* (here after *AUFS*), No. 45, 1979, p. 4.
3. Martin Ewans, *Afghanistan: A New History,* Curzon Press, Richmond, 2001, p. 135.
4. G.M. Kornienko, "The Afghan Endeavor: Perplexities of the Military Incursion and Withdrawal," *Journal of South Asian and Middle Eastern Studies,* Vol. 17, No. 2, Winter 1994, p. 3.
5. Henry S. Bradsher, *Afghanistan and the Soviet Union,* Duke Press Policy Studies, Durham, N.C. 1983, p. 83.
6. Report of Taraki's press conference of 6 May 1978 in *FBIS* 9 May, 1978, pp. 1-2.
7. *The Times* (London), May 8, 1978.
8. Selig S. Harrison, "Dateline Afghanistan: Exit Through Finland?" p. 169.
9. From the American Embassy Kabul to the Secretary of State (confidential) 3242, April 27, 1978. Document obtained from the State Department under the Freedom of Information Act.

10. From the Secretary of State to various American embassies (confidential), 108913.
11. *The New York Times,* May 2, 1978, p. 4.
12. "The Chill in Kabul" ed. *The Wall Street Journal,* March 2, 1979, p. 12. Section 620 (F) of the Foreign Assistance Act forbids aid to Communist government.
13. *Ibid.*
14. *The New York Times,* May 20, 1978, p. 4.
15. *Ibid,* p. 18.
16. Cited in Thomas T. Hammond, *Red Flag Over Afghanistan: The Communist Coup, the Soviet Invasion, and the Consequences,* Boulder, Colorado, Westview Press, 1984, p. 62.
17. Theodore L. Eliot, Jr. "Afghanistan after the 1978 Revolution" *Strategic Review,* Vol. 7, No. 2, Spring 1979, p. 61.
18. Hammond, *Red Flag Over Afghanistan,* p. 63.
19. Cyrus R. Vance, *Hard Choices: Critical Years in American Foreign Policy,* Simon and Schuster, New York, 1983, p. 385. Also see Bradsher, *Afghanistan and the Soviet Union,* p. 86.
20. Hammond, *Red Flag Over Afghanistan,* p. 63
21. Bradsher, *Afghanistan and the Soviet Union,* p. 86.
22. Vance, *Hard Choices,* p. 386.
23. Bradsher argues that Soviet advisers were directly involved and present on the spot, and according to their directions Dubs was killed. See Bradsher, *Afghanistan and the Soviet Union,* p.99. But Soviet denies that any advisers had role in U.S. Envoy's death. See *The New York Times,* February 18, 1979, p. 12.
24. Louis Dupree, "Afghanistan Under the Khalq," *Problems of Communism,* Washington DC, July-August, 1979, p. 50.
25. Selig Harrison, "Dateline Afghanistan," p. 170. Also see Kornienko, "The Afghan Endeavor", p. 3.
26. Selig Harrison, *Ibid.*
27. *Ibid,* p. 172.
28. Bradsher, *Afghanistan and the Soviet Union,* p. 117.
29. Cable No. 07726 from the U.S. Embassy Kabul to the State Department, October 28, 1979, p. 4.
30. From the U.S. Embassy in Kabul to the Secretary of State (confidential) 5727, October, 1979.
31. *The Guardian,* April 19, 1981, p. 17.
32. Cable No. 07726 from the embassy in Kabul to the State Department, October 28, 1979. p. 1.
33. Zbigniew Brzezinski, *Power and Principle: Memoirs of the National Security Adviser,* Farrar, Straus, Girous, New York, 1985, p. 432.
34. *Ibid,* Also see Hammond, *Red Flag Over Afghanistan,* p. 114.

35. Louis Dupree, "Afghanistan Under the Khalq," Problems of Communism, Washington D.C.: U.S. International Communications Agency, July-August, 1979, pp. 48-49.
36. *The New York Times,* August 3, 1979. Also see Brzezinski, *Power and Principle,* p. 427.
37. Testimony of H. Saunders, 26 September 1979, Subcommittee on Asia and Pacific Affairs, House Committee on Foreign Affairs, p. 53.
38. Hammond, *Red Flag Over Afghanistan,* p. 115.
39. Bob Woodward, *Vail: The Secret Wars of the CIA 1981-1987,* Simon and Schuster, New York, 1987, p. 79.
40. Dupree said this in course of an American University Field Staff (AUSF) lecture in 1960. Also see Louis Dupree, AUSF, Asia No. 37, 1980, p. 9.
41. From U.S. Embassy in Kabul to the Secretary of State (confidential) 5269, August 1979.
42. Cited in Hafizulla Emadi, *State, Revolution and Superpower in Afghanistan,* p. 112. Emadi has quoted from *The Documents from the U.S. Espionage Den,* (Translated from Persian version of the document).
43. Brzezinski, *Power and Principle,* p. 427.
44. Hafizullah Emadi, *State, Revolution, and Superpower in Afghanistan,* Praeger, New York, 1990, p. 110.
45. *Ibid,* p. 111.
46. Cited in *Ibid,* p. 112.
47. Jimmy Carter, *Keeping Faith: Memoirs of a President,* New York, Bentam Books, 1982. Also see Abdul Kassim Mansur, "The Crisis in Iran: Why the U.S. Ignored a Quarter Century of Warning," *Armed Forces Journal International,* January 1979, p. 28.
48. Brzezinski, *Power and Principle,* pp. 354-400. Also see Ambassador William Sullivan's account in his *Mission to Iran,* W.W. Norton, New York, 1981, pp. 36-37.
49. Stephen P Cohen, "Who Lost Iran: Revising Revisionist History," *The Washington Post,* September 5, 1980, p. 26.
50. Jimmy Carter, *Keeping Faith,* p. 466.
51. The Nixon administration recognized India as a potential power in South Asia region in 1973. A year later, Secretary of State Henry Kissinger during his October 1974 visit to New Delhi stated that the "size and position of India give it a special role of leadership in South Asian and world affairs." See Secretary of State Henry A. Kissinger, "Toward a Global Community: The Common Cause of India and America," *Department of State Bulletin,* November 25, 1974.
52. Brzezinski, *Power and Principle,* pp. 53-56. Also see *The New York Times,* February 11, 1977.
53. *The New York Times,* October 2, 1977. A specialist on the field points out: "Christopher's statement was seen as conclusive proof that Washington had

abandoned Pakistan to the wolves, leading to a sense of isolation that was punctuated by reliance on Chinese friendship and recognition that the future of Pakistan lay with the conservative Arab states who alone could underwrite the costs of Pakistan's independence and security needs." See Shirin Tahir-Kheli, *The United States and Pakistan,* New York, Praeger, 1982, p. 73.

54. Though some people at the time alleged that the Carter administration "had a hand" in Zia's coming to power, subsequent evidences and bitter relationship between Carter and Zia proves otherwise.

3
Soviet Invasion and the American Reaction

An attempt by any outside force to gain control of the Persian Gulf region will be regarded as an assault on the vital interests of the United States of America and such an assault will be repelled by any means necessary, including military force.

—*President Jimmy Carter, State of the Union Address, 23 January 1980*

The Soviet invasion of Afghanistan in December 1979 led to a sharp and unambiguous reaction from the United States as Washington clearly drew a line in Southwest Asia and the Persian Gulf to contain the Soviet threat. Superpower antagonism ushered in the New Cold War era, and the American policy of seeking détente with the Soviet Union was severely jolted. For the United States, it was a challenge of great magnitude and Washington sought to demonstrate its political will and military superiority over Moscow by invoking several punitive measures against the Soviet Union. Notable among them were: recalling ambassador from Moscow, postponing the SALT process, boycotting the Moscow Olympics, establishing the Rapid Deployment Force (RDF), enhancing the defense budget, playing the China card, invoking several economic sanctions, and most importantly, demarcating a clear security zone in Southwest Asia stipulating that in case of any eventual Soviet push towards the region, the United States would use military force to protect its vital interests. Also, as a part of Washington's policy which was aimed at increasing the political, economic, and military cost to Moscow of its invasion, the United States made a deliberate effort to supply arms and financial assistance to the rebels who were fighting the Soviet supported communist regime in Afghanistan. In short, cold war rhetoric had gone deep into the minds of policy-makers in Washington.

What made the Carter administration take a hard-line on the Afghanistan crisis? What were the factors that motivated Washington to declare a "doctrine," in the format of the Truman Doctrine, which was enunciated in 1947 to aid Greece and Turkey? To answer these questions, most evidences suggest that Carter's punitive measures against Moscow and the U.S.' return to the cold war had very little to do with the Afghanistan crisis. The Soviet action "only triggered the release of tensions that had been growing in superpower relations and within the Carter administration over how to handle them."[1] The "hawks" within and without the Carter administration had already overpowered, and assumed the responsibility of steering American foreign policy. So, in order to understand the U.S. reaction to the Soviet invasion of Afghanistan, it is necessary to have a look at the evolution and depth of the "moderates" vis-à-vis the "neo-conservatives" thinking and influence in Washington in the context of the Southwest Asian region in general and Afghanistan crisis in particular. This chapter demonstrates that the United States response to the Soviet invasion of Afghanistan was mostly based on the hardliners stand of maintaining American military, political, and economic superiority over the Soviet Union and to make Moscow pay a heavy price for its misadventure to a non-aligned country. The chapter will show that even at the cost of American domestic self-interests, Washington went to the maximum possible extent to put pressure on Moscow and to maintain its unchallengeable presence in the Indian Ocean, Persian Gulf and the Middle Eastern region. The Carter administration also initiated a moderate aid and arms program for the rebels who were fighting the Soviets in Afghanistan, a factor often credited with the disintegration of the Soviet Union itself and dubbed as the Soviet's Vietnam in the long run.

Throughout the cold war years, a sort of "conflict of perceptions" about the Soviet threat continued between the liberals and conservatives in Washington. The liberals believed that there was competition between the two superpowers. But they argued that the Soviets should be viewed as a traditional great power attempting to expand its reach within the existing international system, mainly through defensive strategy. The conservatives, in contrast, believed that the Soviet Union was basically an international revolutionary state committed to unrelenting ideological warfare. They also accepted the view that Moscow was out for world domination. Accordingly, they thought that all that the United States needed to do was anti-communist liturgy and that that would solve all problems. Within the Carter administration, it was after the Soviet invasion of Afghanistan that the conservatives led by the National Security Adviser Zbigniew Brzezinski prevailed over the liberals, headed by the Secretary of State Cyrus Vance. What then was the American perception of Soviet threat? In order to answer this question, it is necessary to look at the problem from two perspectives—both liberal and conservative—about why Moscow decided to invade in the first place? Like all other international issues, the hard-liner conservatives interpreted the Soviet move as an offensive one, whereas the liberals viewed it as defensive.

Liberal View

What was called the liberal view in Washington in early 1980 has become widely accepted as the more realistic assessment of the Soviets motive behind their decision to invade Afghanistan: that it was a defensive move by Moscow to protect its political interests in Afghanistan and to defend its own territory from the spillover of a Muslim fundamentalist effects into Central Asian Republics. The following is based on this argument.

At a time when the United States was acting very quickly to make the Soviet Union pay a political and economic price for its invasion of Afghanistan, two known figures in American politics—Howard Baker and John Connally—advised President Carter "to whine loudly and go on with business as usual."[2] George F. Kennan, the veteran specialist on Soviet affairs, commenting on Washington's stand on the Soviet action, argued that "the American official reaction has revealed a disquieting lack of balance, both in the analysis of the problem and then, not surprisingly, in the response to it." He further stated, "In the official American interpretation of what occurred in Afghanistan, no serious account appears to have been taken of such specific factors as geographic proximity, ethnic affinity of peoples of both sides of the border, and political instability in what is, after all, a border country of the Soviet Union. Now, specific factors of this nature, all suggesting defensive rather than offensive impulses."[3] As a career diplomat, Kennan was convinced that no American pressure of "this nature" against the Soviets would help bring troop withdrawal from Afghanistan.

Many American scholars and policy-makers who were realistic about the assessment of the American-Soviet rivalry in the cold war years had given their account on Soviet perception of threat about the "spillover" effect.[4] They argued that a measure concern in the Soviet foreign policy used to be the security of their volatile borders into the South. The geographical area from Turkey to Afghanistan was known to the Kremlin as the "softest under belly." Like the Russian activities in Cuba, which disturbed the Americans, U.S. activities in these sensitive borders have always upset Moscow. Turkey was a NATO country. Iran under the Shah was known as a strong ally of the United States. With the fundamentalist revolution in Iran and the revival of the Islamic militancy in the region in the early 1980s, the US lost an ally, but the Soviets had reasons to fear the spillover of militancy into its own territory. Under these circumstances, a pro-western or an instable Afghanistan would undoubtedly be a direct threat to the Soviet territory. It was obvious that a militant fundamentalist regime in Kabul would be a threat to the 54 million Central Asian Muslim population of the Soviet Union, and so bound to create a reaction from Moscow.

Accordingly, experts viewed that the Soviets fear had been exacerbated when the Afghan Prime Minister Hafizullah Amin showed his willingness to improve his relations with the United States. In fact, by the end of his rule, Amin was clear about his desire to improve Afghanistan's relations with the United States. Selig Harrison has written that the Soviets were very much concerned about a desperate Amin who might strike a deal with Washington or Beijing. What worried the Soviets most was that Amin was firmly in control of the military and intelligence internally, and trying to come closer to the U.S. externally. So the only option left for Moscow was to move in with its own army to dislodge the "opportunistic Amin."[5]

The Soviets were also worried about the possible American invasion of Iran after the fundamentalist revolution and the subsequent hostage crisis. There was a strong public opinion about "doing something," and a military attack against Iran would have been applauded in the United States. Cyrus Vance wrote in his *memoirs:* "There were background news stories coming out of Washington to the effect that there was a possibility of some form of U.S. military action against Iran." However, at the same time, Vance had realized that "U.S. military presence in the area would make a collapse of the Kabul regime more dangerous for the Soviets and thus enhance the possibility of Soviet intervention."[6] Marshall Shulman, a longtime expert on Soviet affairs and special adviser to Secretary Vance, believed that the Soviet invaded Afghanistan because of a "broad fear" of "the creation of a crescent of militant Islamic anti-Soviet states on its southern borders, with the added possibility of Chinese or U.S. influence, and not because it seeks to gain access to the Indian Ocean and control over the Middle East." He did not believe in the hard-liner's view in Washington that the Soviet motive was to attack Iran or Pakistan.[7] Another influential specialist on this area, Raymond Garthoff, whose views were very often debated in the Carter administration, had also supported this argument. Garthoff strongly argued that the Soviet action was defensive and not offensive. Contrary to the popular opinion, he emphasized that the Soviet decision to intervene was not affected by "any perception of American weakness, but by heightened concern over the American buildup of its strength, particularly the Indian Ocean fleet, the quest for new bases in the area, and the development of security ties with China." He also focused on the Soviet concern over possible U.S. intervention in Iran and further massive buildup of American naval presence in the Indian Ocean-Persian Gulf region.[8] By the Christmas Eve 1979, Russian intelligence had reported to Moscow that within days the American would do "something drastic" in Iran. When the U.S. action failed to materialize, one Soviet diplomat in Washington exclaimed, "Carter double-crossed us."[9]

In the Carter administration there were many conflicting stands about the Soviet motive behind the invasion. Because of the very nature of secret decision-making system in the Kremlin, it was undoubtedly very difficult to reach a conclusion about the real Soviet motive.[10] Carter's Secretary of State Cyrus Vance acknowledged that: "Not even the most penetrating analysis can determine with certainty Soviet intentions in the region-whether their motives in Afghanistan are limited or part of a larger strategy."[11] But in his memoirs, Vance writes that in his own opinion, "Moscow had acted as it did for a number of reasons." First and immediate aim of the Soviets was to protect their political interests in Afghanistan. Vance argues that the Soviets had lost their faith in Hafizullah Amin who was considered a nationalist communist and was not listening to Moscow. Secondly, he pointed out that after the Iranian revolution, Moscow "feared that the regime (communist) would be replaced by a fundamentalist Islamic government and that would, in turn, be followed by a spread of "Khomeini fever" to other nations along Russia's southern border." He opined that the Soviets believed that they should "seize this opportunity to position themselves more favorably with respect to China and Pakistan." Finally Vance emphasized:

> *The downward spiral in U.S.-Soviet relations had released the brakes on Soviet international behavior. If, as is likely, Moscow had decided by late December that the Salt Treaty was in deep trouble, that access to American trade and technology was drying up, and that the dangers of American-Chinese-Western European encirclement were growing, it probably had concluded that there was little reason to show restraint in dealing with a dangerous problem on its borders.*[12]

Vance further highlights "two theories" that were discussed in the Carter administration. His first argument is based on the Soviet fear of the spillover of Muslim fundamentalism into their Central Asian Republics. Accordingly, Moscow had decided to replace Amin with more "compliant one" (Babrak Karmal), and sent its troops to "guarantee the new regime's survival and push the insurgents back into remote areas. If this was the case, Moscow's objectives were primarily local and directly to perceived threats to its national security."[13] Secondly, Vance writes, the Carter administration perceived that because of the deteriorating U.S.-Soviet relations, Moscow had calculated that they had nothing to lose in furthering its strategic position in Southwest Asia. It was argued that "Soviet pessimism was augmented by their paranoia about a U.S. "tilt" towards China and their fears of a NATO military buildup. By consolidating their position in Afghanistan . . . the Soviets would be in a position to exploit Pakistan and India as a counter to American moves into the Indian Ocean and Persian Gulf."[14]

Even Henry Kissinger did not believe that the Soviets, like Hitler, had a master plan, a blueprint for step-by-step world conquest. He did not see Afghanistan as an integrated issue in the U.S.-Soviet relations. What he perceived was the overall superpowers' balance of power in the world. In an interview, Kissinger said: "The main issue is not Afghanistan. The issue is what the countries that rely on us can expect of us and what we can expect from them. And what countries have a right or reasonable exploitation to rely on us. Those are the issues."[15]

People, who subscribed to the developments in Afghanistan as a local problem, strongly opposed the arguments of the "neo-conservative" who saw the U.S. "weak" in Africa and Southwest Asia in the 1978-79. They believed that the United States failed to identify events and judge the force of emerging nationalism in the region. About half million American troops, with all strategic superiority and firepower could not prevent the humiliation in Vietnam, nor could Washington use all its military superiority to force Iran to release the hostages. So, what they argue is that, when the Soviet moved into Afghanistan, the United States ignored the regional situation in favor of global advantages.[16] Washington failed to realize the ethnic and religious linkage in the Soviet decision to invade, and only perceived in terms of global "losses" and "gains."

It was also argued that even from the military point of view, it was not feasible to show the Soviet power to threaten the Persian Gulf oil which was regarded as the lifeline of the West and which created a sharp reaction from the United States. A military expert pointed out that the "current Soviet force projection capabilities represent, at best, only a rudimentary potential to project into and to sustain power in distant crisis areas, particularly when opposed by an adversary."[17] In a worst possible scenario, if the Soviets wanted to threaten the Western oil supply, they would have to invade Iran through the north, and here too, the route was not clear. Any invading troops were likely to face the difficult terrain and the Zagros Mountains, which are surely a formidable barrier. And in that case, a huge Soviet military commitment was necessary which the Kremlin was not prepared to make at that time. Further, the Kremlin knew that an attempt against Iran or Pakistan would mean war with the West. Because that would be considered as an outright attack on an ally of the United States, or on one of the chief oil suppliers of the West and Japan, it would represent an escalation of Soviet risk-taking infinitely greater than stepping into the relative military vacuum of Afghanistan. Very probably then, the Soviets did not have any grand strategy and their move into Afghanistan was essentially defensive.

Most importantly, the United States ignored the Soviet concern of the foreign involvement in assisting the Afghan resistance forces who were fighting against the Taraki and later, Amin regime. As mentioned in the previous chapter, the United States, China, Pakistan, and many other Muslim countries were involved in this covert operation long before the Soviet action. Several warnings from Moscow were ignored. Even after the invasion, Soviet leader Brezhnev categorically and vigorously stated that Moscow did not have any military ambition in the region and that once the need for that (i.e. outside support to the resistance stops) was through, they would get out. United States never tries to understand the Soviets security concern in their southern border.

Neo-Conservative View

It is worthwhile to mention that before the Soviet invasion, there were differences in the Carter administration with regards to Moscow's aims and objectives in Afghanistan. Some people in the administration had believed that the Soviet motive was by nature local, while other forecasted in view of a long-term plans and a grand strategy. In the over all American-Soviet relationship, there was talk of "Acquiescence vs. Assertiveness" within the Carter administration by the people who believed that in spite of military, political, and economic superiority of Washington over Moscow, the former was operating from a position of weakness against the latter. At this juncture of time, the Soviet action came as a catalyst in Washington. Already in the United States, the invasion had played into the hand of those who clamed that Washington was so weak that Moscow had no fear of an American response to any move they made. It tended to confirm their views that the Soviets were following a master plan towards world conquest. Then more and more interpretation followed, and more and more people came to accept that idea.

As stated earlier, Soviet move into Afghanistan was only a "clue" for the ascendancy of the conservative ideas in Washington. There was "smoke" in various bureaucratic circles within and without the Carter administration, the Soviet invasion only ended up in "fire." The idea that even though the United States was strategically and militarily stronger then the Soviet Union, Washington was operating from a position of weakness, gained momentum. Strategists who believed this idea looked at the Soviet move as an offensive one and interpreted in terms of Russian thrust for the control of the Persian Gulf oil and even world domination. After the Soviet invasion of Afghanistan, these ideas prevailed in Washington. But it should be remembered that this was not a new "discovery," rather, for a long time, it was in the minds of a certain circle of intelligentsia and academia. Soviet action only "triggered" their ideas. So it would be worthwhile to have a look at the evolution and growth of conservative thinking in order to understand the intensity of subsequent American reaction to the Soviet action.

The growth of this idea in the Carter administration was not new. Its root originated in the era of Nixon-Kissinger policy of détente. By the mid-1970s, the conservatives, who were also known as the "New Right" had achieved considerable support throughout the nation and had occupied a center stage in the national debate about America's foreign policy. They discarded the American policy of détente as a "philosophy of weakness."[18]

Though the "Vietnam syndrome" was very much alive in the minds of the Americans, the New Right tried to exploit the 1973 oil crisis, and linked the embargo with the possible threat from Moscow. They argued in favor of American military intervention to protect the U.S. vital interests in the Gulf and to teach a lesson to OPEC politically and economically. Even though there was doubt about the feasibility of a military operation and fear of the Arabs' blowing off of their own facilities in case of an attack, it was predicted that the seizure of Gulf oil would "markedly improve Israel's position" in the region and the Soviets would not dare to counter the American move.[19] By then, an image was created by the conservatives that in spite of the huge price rise of the Gulf oil, the United States seemed helpless. Interestingly, many people in Washington started talking about the oil crisis at a time when oil prices had already stabilized and, even started declining in real terms. After much "hue and cry," Washington declared that attacking oil installations was not the U.S. goal. But in the popular mind, the oil threat was linked to the U.S. economy and its image abroad, and without any substantial reasons, the conservative portrayed that America was getting weaker militarily. The New Right gained at least one advantage in their favor: pro-Israeli and anti-Arab mood predominated the Congress.

Secondly, the concept of détente with the Soviet Union was the greatest enemy of the neo-conservative. From the very beginning, they were not in favor of the SALT talks and opposed to any American move to "appease" the Soviets. Many prominent figures like Paul Nitze, Richard E. Pipes, James Schlesinger, amongst many others, led the movement. In a book entitled *Defending America* (1977), Paul Nitze warned the nation that the Soviet Union was fast acquiring a "theoretical war-winning capability," and expressed his concern about the consequences of declining defense spending. James Schlesinger directly attacked the "détente minded people" and discussed the weakening American national will. In 1976, he wrote:

> *Worldwide stability is being eroded through the retrenchment of American policy and power. This growing instability reflects visible factors such as the deterioration in the military balance, but also, perhaps more immediately, such invisible factors as the altered psychological stance of the United States, a nation apparently withdrawing from the burdens of leadership and power.*[20]

Many people from the U.S. academic establishment joined this new right group to accept the view of the loss of confidence of the American power, "faltering American purpose," and the U.S. "impotence." The threat from Moscow was no longer confined to the European security, they argued, it had been multiplied to the Far East, Southwest Asia, and the Persian Gulf, thus linking the oil lifeline of the West. It was interpreted as having a direct link between the American domestic unrest, such as unemployment, dollar value, and growing inflation. So the stake was as high as it could be: Washington had to protect its interests abroad in order to maintain its own economy. A turning point in the evolution of the conservative thought came when in 1976 the Committee on Present Danger (CPD) was formed.[21] In its first press announcement, the CPD expressed grave concern over the growing "Soviet drive for dominance" based on a huge military buildup, and recommended that the United States needed to counter the Soviet threat with a tough stance. The Committee also demanded that Washington increase its own defense spending to meet the Soviet threat.

So, by the time Carter came to power, the New Right had already assumed the national platform in the nation's foreign policy, and, from the very outset, the administration came under intense pressure with regard to its policy of arms control with the Soviets and the human rights issue. To the good fortune of the conservatives, by 1978-79, political situation began changing in the Southwest Asian region. The Iranian revolution and the hostage crisis provided a great opportunity to them to criticize Carter's liberal foreign policy, which was, what they said, mostly based on State Department's viewpoints. The turn for the "hawks" had come. Zbigniew Brzezinski, Carter's National Security Advisor, saw an "arc of crisis—along the shores of the Indian Ocean," and warned that any political upheaval in the region was bound to benefit the Soviet Union. Two strong supporters of Brzezinski's view in the Carter administration were Energy Secretary James Schlesinger and the Defense Secretary Harold Brown. Schlesinger alarmed over the balance of power in the region and stated that the U.S. "will have to take steps to shore up the nations around the Gulf."[22] Long before the proclamation of Carter Doctrine, which drew a security line in the Southwest Asia beyond which the possible Soviet military adventure would meet with the American military force, Harold Brown had gone on record, saying: "We will take any action that is appropriate, including military force, if the oil supplies were threatened and the Soviet Union tried to fish in troubled waters."[23]

In the meanwhile, some influential Congressmen had joined in the school of the neo-conservative doctrine. Senators Frank Church and Jacob Javits, who had opposed American intervention in Vietnam, were known as the liberals, became the strong advocates and supporters of this new emerging idea. Carter administration came under intense pressure from the Congress when an influential group of Senators like Sam Nunn, Alan Cranston, and Birch Bayh refused to vote for the SALT II treaty unless the administration substantially increased defense spending. It was also during this time that the conservatives suddenly "discovered" about 2,000 to 3,000 Soviet combat troops stationed in Cuba. They got another opportunity to criticize the government for not taking this issue seriously. They argued that the Soviets had no fear of a U.S. reaction and that they were out to use military force when they feel necessary. Interestingly, it was not an issue in Washington even though the US knew the presence of these forces in Cuba since the mid-1970s. It was only made an issue in an appropriate time to pressure the government on foreign policy.

Since the Vietnam War, the one issue that had most irritated Americans was the Iranian Revolution and the subsequent hostage crisis. It created a great shock and frustration—directed against the Carter administration—and most people regarded the developments as a national humiliation for the United States. During the hostage crisis, an opinion poll showed that a decisive 65 percent people in the U.S. agreed that the Carter administration's handling of the situation had "decreased United States prestige abroad."[24]

It was obvious that at a time of this sort of frustration and anguish in the U.S. public mind, Washington would react very severely to any major international development related to the projection of the Soviet power. The Soviet invasion of Afghanistan in December 1979 simply played into the hands of these people and the New Right's strength increased to a great extent both inside and outside the Carter administration. Already, the prevailing smoke had ended up in fire in U.S.-Soviet relations. Carter administration had completely surrendered its policy in favor of the neo-conservatives and acted vigorously to punish the Soviets for what it called, their misadventure against a neighboring Muslim orthodox and tribally populated country. Paul Nitze,[25] a staunch advocate of this idea stated that "the thrust into Afghanistan advances the Soviet base structure by 50 miles so as to outflank Iran and bear directly on the Arabian Sea." He claimed that the Soviet aim was to control the Persian Gulf oil and ultimately to politically separate NATO and the Western Europe from the United States. He argued that the leverage Moscow gained by invading Afghanistan would provide them a golden opportunity to do so.[26]

Within the Carter administration, Zbigniew Brzezinski, the National Security Advisor, was the outspoken advocate of these reasoning. It was Brzezinski, who had been "the mirror-image of Lyndon Johnson's George Ball—given a hearing but rarely heeded. He lost the B-1 bomber, was rejected on the neutron bomb, helplessly watched the scuttling of the U.S. Navy, was overruled on helping the Shah and on applying greater pressure against the Cubans. Too late, he is being asked for too little."[27] Now that the time had come to show America's strength and military capability abroad and to demonstrate that the United States was not weak but strong enough to deal with the perceived Soviet threat.

Brzezinski had drawn a worst possible scenario of the Soviet invasion. As early as May 1979, that is, eight months before Moscow's move, he had briefed the President that if the Soviets dominate Afghanistan they would be in a position to promote a separate Baluchistan "which would give them access to the Indian Ocean while dismembering Pakistan and Iran." He interpreted the Soviet motives in terms of a grand strategy in which Moscow would occupy a major portion of the region to fulfill its historical ambition. He reminded the President "on Molotov's proposal to Hitler in late 1940 that the Nazis recognize the Soviet claim to preeminence in the region south of Batun and Baku."[28] After the Soviet invasion, this perception was largely taken as granted and was greatly exaggerated by the hardliners led by Brzezinski himself.

In his *memoirs,* President Carter is more or less silent about the possibility of any Soviet threat before the invasion. After the Soviet move, he accepted it as a threat to the region. "A successful take-over of Afghanistan," Carter writes, "would give the Soviets a deep penetration between Iran and Pakistan, and pose a threat to the rich oil fields of the Persian Gulf area and to the crucial waterways through which so much of the world's energy supplies had to pass."[29] It seems that only after the Soviet invasion of Afghanistan, Carter had accepted the view that Moscow's motive was not "local" in nature, and therefore, not a defensive action, rather, it was regional, and more or less global, and so, an offensive move.

The American perception was based on their exaggerated fear that the Red Army was headed towards the Persian Gulf and its oilfields, and /or to the "warm-waters" of the Arabian Sea. The United States emphasized and concluded that the Soviet motive was primarily offensive and, therefore, they decided to remain prepared for further Soviet incursions in the region. Washington saw that the Afghan resistance against the Kabul regime falls under its "strategic compulsions" to resist the communist expansion. So from the very beginning, even before the Soviet invasion, the United States was providing limited economic and military assistance to the resistance, which later grew as a formidable force against a superpower. Washington simply drew a worst possible scenario of the Soviet action.

What emerges from the foregoing is that there was a clear line of demarcation between the liberal and conservatives about the threat from the Soviet move into Afghanistan, and both drew opposite conclusions with regard to the American response.

Interpreting the Soviet move

Analyzing the cold warrior's mood and the interpretation of the Soviet move, a renowned American political analyst and commentator remarked:

> *Each time the Soviet Union has moved one pawn in the game of chess, we have tended to see in the move a prelude to a desperate attempt to win the entire hand at poker. We interpreted Stalin's tactical thrusts in Europe between 1945 and 1948 as steps in an attempt to seize all of Western Europe, and the Korean War as a first stage in a world-wide drive, just as we now talk of a Soviet plan to control our oil supplies.*[30]

Such was the case after Afghanistan. United States interpreted the Soviet intervention in terms of a Soviet grand-strategy that had a domino effect step by step. The Carter administration viewed that if the Soviets were successful in consolidating their communist regime in Afghanistan, they might penetrate into Pakistan and Iran. As such, the administration conceived, the Soviets were in a striking distance from southwestern Afghanistan to the Straits of Hormus and the Persian Gulf, which is known as the oil lifeline of the West. Administration officials perceived that the Soviet invasion altered the strategic situation in the region in a very ominous fashion. It was argued that control over this area would enable Moscow to intimidate the entire region and choke off the oil supply to Europe and Japan. And, in that case, the Western alliance (viz-NATO) would not be able to survive in opposition to a power that controls its essential oil supplies. So, "the loss of the Persian Gulf might lead to the loss of Europe" and in that case, "isn't it vital that we (the U.S.) deter the Soviets from moving into Iran?"[31] In President Carter's view, the Soviet invasion eliminated a buffer state between South Asia and the U.S.S.R., making Pakistan and Iran "far more vulnerable to Soviet political intimidation. If that intimidation were to prove effective, the Soviet Union might well control an area of vital strategic and economic significance to the survival of Western Europe, Far East and ultimately the United States."[32]

Apart from the threat to the Persian Gulf oil and the traditional Russian thirst for the warm-water ports of the Indian Ocean, Washington believed that the continuing Soviet presence in Afghanistan presented chilling prospects of further incursions into the South and the East. Even if Moscow did not exercise further military options, it was argued, the strategic map of the region would remain very unfavorable, with an atmosphere of fear among the neighbors of Afghanistan. American analysts maintained that the Soviet presence in Afghanistan altered the "political and geo-strategic balance of forces" in the entire region, including the Indian Ocean, South Asia and the Middle East.[33]

Soviet action in Afghanistan was also seen by Washington as a test of both "alliance (NATO) solidarity and of the future course of East-West relations."[34] This was more so because of the Western dependence on the Persian Gulf oil and the Europeans increasing skepticism on the subsequent American response to the Soviet intervention. Most European countries felt that there was no alternative to détente and that the U.S. response was more rhetorical than actual. So Washington's fear was heightened with the presumption of the question of Western solidarity against the Soviets.

Besides enumerating the geo-political imperatives of the Soviet action, President Carter termed it as a serious threat to world peace and violation of the norms of international behavior. The President observed that "the explosiveness of the region, its great natural wealth and the Soviet willingness to use the armed forces which have been developed during the Kremlin's enormous military buildup during the last 15 years are what combine to make the invasion of Afghanistan so unsettling to the future of international peace." He argued that the Soviet invasion had disturbed the economic, historic, ethnic, and religious forces, which were not under Moscow's control, and could pose a serious threat to other nations' interests in the region.[35] It was obvious that the Soviet intervention brought about a drastic change in the traditional ethno-religious moral forces in the region, and gave the Soviets a geo-political advantage in the contiguous areas.

U.S. officials also viewed the Soviet move as a challenge to the American influence and power not only in the regional level, but also in the strategic and global level. They argued that Afghanistan was an extension of the Soviet assertiveness beyond its traditional "sphere of influence" (i.e. Eastern Europe), where the West had accepted Moscow's vital security interests. Therefore, it was considered as one of the most serious incidents after the World War II. Deputy Assistant Secretary of State, Robert Peck noted that the Soviet action in Afghanistan "was a challenge to the kind of international system that we have tried to support over years and inconsistent with the kind of East-West relationship . . . that we have tried to develop with the Soviet Union."[36]

Reaction: A Strategic Challenge

The Soviet invasion of Afghanistan was viewed in the Carter administration as a strategic challenge to the United States, and Washington made every effort to make Moscow's expedition as costly as possible. This was a great opportunity for the hawks in Washington who found in the Afghanistan crisis an occasion to erase some of the lessons of Vietnam and to demonstrate their military superiority over Moscow in a relatively risk-free environment. The available evidence suggests that the U.S. policy towards Afghanistan (and the region) was mostly designed by the National Security Council headed by Zbigniew Brzezinski. Brzezinski, who was well known as a hard-liner conservative in the Carter administration and had been advocating a tougher approach towards the Soviet Union, had finally prevailed. A Soviet media accused him of "anti-Communism and morbid anti-Sovietism," and whose "line, which until recently scared many people in the United States with its extremism and fanaticism, has become . . . Washington's official policy."[37]

As the President of the United States, President Jimmy Carter led the worldwide condemnation of the Soviet invasion. "We are the other superpower on earth," Carter proclaimed, "and it became my responsibility . . . to take action that would prevent the Soviets from this invasion with impunity."[38] Within a few days, Carter said that the Soviet action was "an extremely serious threat to peace, because of the threat of further Soviet expansion into neighboring countries in Southwest Asia and also because such an aggressive military policy is unsettling to other peoples throughout the world."[39] In his address to the Congress on 23rd January, Carter emphasized that "the implications of the Soviet invasion of Afghanistan could pose the most serious threat to peace since the Second World War." Carter categorically stated, "Verbal condemnation is not enough. The Soviet Union must pay a concrete price for their aggression."[40] The President declared that the United States was determined to make Moscow's Afghan war as costly as possible.

The United States did make Moscow's Afghan war costly. From the very beginning, the Soviets were kept on the defensive. The cold war rhetoric was at its peak in Washington. Soon after the Soviet action, in the PRC meeting of December 27, and the NSC meeting of December 28, several decisions were taken and it was emphasized that the "ultimate goal is the withdrawal of Soviet troops from Afghanistan." It was also decided that the United States "should use the events in Afghanistan as a rallying point for our policies in the area."[41] So it is clear that the events in Afghanistan shaped the U.S. policy towards the region and brought about a fundamental reassessment of Washington's approach in the 1980s. Not surprisingly, the hardliners had dominated the Carter administration and more or less, it looked like a one-man-show: Zbigniew Brzezinski.

Brzezinski always argued Afghanistan crisis in a broad strategic context. It was he who forcefully committed the United States to deter the Soviets in Afghanistan lest, once Afghanistan was consolidated; Moscow would be in a position to intimidate the entire region and could pose a threat to the neighboring countries. He compared Afghanistan with the situation of Greece and Turkey in 1947, which President Truman had confronted with all American will and power.[42] Opening an SCC meeting on January 14, the National Security Advisor acknowledged that,

> *We must deal with the continued deterioration of the U.S. position in the region. Whatever the Soviet motives for their actions in Afghanistan, they have created an objective threat and a dynamic development in the area as serious for our security and vital interests as Soviet actions in Greece in 1947. We must provide the President with a basis for responding adequately to this change, especially what we should do about Pakistan and about the larger Persian Gulf region. The President believes that there will be lasting strategic consequences.*[43]

Accordingly, Brzezinski wanted the President to specify and declare the American policy in concrete terms. Even long before the President's State of the Union address on 23rd January, which was later baptized as the Carter Doctrine, Brzezinski himself declared that the U.S. would use armed force to preserve Pakistan's independence in case of any Soviet attack to that country.[44] So it seems that Carter's explicit commitment of American troops to protect U.S. vital interests in the

Persian Gulf region was not a "cool-headed" policy statement, rather an exposure of the neo-conservative stand in the administration, a militant foreign policy initiative. In his State of the Union address, Carter formally declared:

> *An attempt by any outside force to gain control of the Persian Gulf region will be regarded as an assault on the vital interests of the United States of America and such an assault will be repelled by any means necessary, including military force.*[45]

Like the Truman Doctrine spawned in the Eastern Mediterranean and the Nixon Doctrine rooted in Southeast Asia, the Carter Doctrine was triggered to contain communist expansion in a specific area: the Persian Gulf and the Southwest Asia. By declaring this as American vital interests, Washington elevated the Persian Gulf region to the level of Western Europe and the Far East, and considered the former as more volatile to the Soviet intimidation than the later. It was argued that in Western Europe and Far East the U.S. had a permanent military presence and obligatory commitments, which would be automatically triggered. In the Persian Gulf region, Washington had to begin an effort to shore up its military capabilities to provide some credibility to its declaratory policies. In order to do so the United States sought military presence in the area, and as a part of its long-term plan, established the Rapid Deployment Joint Task Force (RDF) to meet the immediate military requirement in the region. For a longtime, the hard-liners in the administration had been seeking the establishment of the RDF. The Persian Gulf region had been already counted as an area of U.S. vital interests. Carter's National Security Advisor believed that "the situation in that region is much more nuance and complex than even the Western European area or even the Middle East." He revealed "the trend is towards increased American military presence in the region, towards greater utilization of available facilities, towards a regional security framework including also the U.S."[46]

In conformity with its declared policy, Washington remains prepared to meet any threat from Moscow. The Department of Defense planned to spend approximately $25 billion over the next five years (1980 to 1985) to build the RDF and to equip it with all sorts of sophisticated weaponry to ensure its mobility in the region.[47] The purpose behind this deployment of the RDF was to deter the Soviets from a possible intervention in the Gulf by getting there first. In case deterrence failed, it was supposed to defend the territory.[48] Policy-makers in Washington conceded that if the U.S. used conventional weapons in response to a Soviet incursion, the U.S. forces would quickly be overwhelmed because the Soviet had too many troops conveniently close to the Middle East. So the U.S. had to make it clear that a Soviet attack in the Persian Gulf with conventional weapons would be met with a limited or regional nuclear strike.[49] Officials in Washington believed that by issuing this warning to Moscow, it might prevent the later from putting pressure on Western oil supplies throughout the decade. This announcement was intended to deter possible Soviet action by showing Moscow that force might be used if deterrence failed.

There was even talk of bringing NATO to the Persian Gulf/Indian Ocean area to contain the Soviet threat. However, it was decided that the United States, "cannot duplicate NATO in this region; a more eclectic mix of bilateral, multilateral, and informal arrangements must suffice."[50] Equally strong support came from some circle of the Congress. Many people in the Congress believed the U.S. response should be very explicit and that Washington should make it clear to Moscow that its action in Afghanistan was not acceptable and that had to face serious consequences. In a Congressional hearing in January 1980, a Congressman argued strongly "in 1948, the Soviets first moved into Czechoslovakia. The answer of the West was NATO. It seems to me the proper answer to the Soviet invasion of Afghanistan is a NATO-type security alliance in that region."[51]

In fact, the hard-liners in the Carter administration were virtually preparing a war with the Soviets in the Southwest Asia region. Not long after the Soviet invasion of Afghanistan, the Carter administration decided to resume military sales to Pakistan overriding the Symington Amendment under which the U.S. law had prohibited aid to the nuclear "threshold" country. The President spoke to the Pakistani Foreign Minister Aga Shahi and reaffirmed the U.S. commitment to the 1959 Mutual Defense Agreement between the two countries. It was decided that in case of any Soviet attack to Pakistan, "the US will respond within the limits of our constitutional authority," which means direct deployment of the U.S. troops to protect Pakistan. It was also decided that the U.S. would not get involved in the border skirmishes between the Pakistani and Soviet soldiers in the Pak-Afghan border. The text reveals not less than the blueprint of a hypothetical war:

> *We want our support to help Pakistan to take a firm stand against Soviet forces in the region even if they are faced by a Moscow/Kabul/ New Delhi axis. In that case, the U.S. will develop a U.S./Saudi Arabian/PRC/Pakistan/and eventually Iran axis as a counter.*[52]

Pakistan: the "Melting Pot" of the Intelligence Agencies

The Soviet invasion of Afghanistan was a great opportunity for General Zia-ul-Haq to consolidate his military regime and draw sympathy from the West. From the very beginning Zia and his intelligence, known as Inter Services Intelligence Directorate (ISI) believed that "Afghanistan could be made into another Vietnam with the Soviets in the shoes of the Americans." Accordingly, Islamabad decided to covertly support the Afghan guerrillas with arms, ammunition, money, intelligence, training and operational advice.[53] Given the Soviets "limited contingent" of troops in Afghanistan, Pakistan never believed that Moscow had a grand strategy to occupy the Persian Gulf oil fields or to reach the warm-water of the Indian Ocean. Rather it was an opportunity for Islamabad to wheedle out money from the West and the United States, and build its own military and economy. As one magazine commented:

The Pakistani dictatorship has reason to welcome an event that has reopened the apparently boundless coffers of the U.S. Treasury and led the American government to discover a vital interest in the territorial outlines of one of the worlds more artificial and unstable national entities.[54]

United States-Pakistan relations were at its lowest ebb when the Afghanistan crisis occurred. Washington simply ignored Pakistan's nuclear ambition under which Islamabad had been debarred from the U.S. aid, overlooked Pakistan's stand on U.S.-sponsored peace process in the Middle East, and remain silent on massive human rights violation in the military dictatorship of General Zia. From an international pariah, Pakistan became the third largest recipient of American foreign aid, only after Israel and Egypt. Pakistan became an over-night staunchest ally in the U.S. policy towards the region. The fear of the "Islamic Bomb" for the United States was minimized. Pakistan was no longer a hostile Islamic dictatorship; it was a stalwart ally on the front line of the war against the Soviets. *The New York Times* quoted Zia-ul-Haq as saying; "Pakistan has become the best friend that the United States has in the enormous belt that runs from Turkey to Indochina."[55] Interestingly, it was only eight weeks after the burning of the U.S. embassy in Islamabad, where the Pakistani security forces had arrived too late to prevent the gutting of the embassy and the death of two Americans, and the burning of the American cultural centers in Rawalpindi and Lahore that the Soviet invasion took place.

Now that the stakes were as high as that could be. President Carter invited Pakistan's Foreign Minister Agha Shahi and offered $400 million, half economic, half military. Carter also openly declared that the United States wanted to give Pakistan the ability "to repel invasion if it should occur, and particularly to let Pakistan be known as a strong nation able to protect themselves so that a possible invasion will be prevented."[56] But Pakistan was very cautious. Zia knew that it was time for the Americans to support Pakistan, and it was for Islamabad to bargain from a position of strength. Zia not only dismissed Carter's offer of $400 million as inadequate but also made known to everybody that this meager amount of American aid would not buy Pakistan's security. Instead, Zia publicly stated, "it will buy greater animosity from the Soviet Union, which is now much more influential in this region than the United States is."[57] Later, Pakistan accepted a hefty amount when President Reagan offered $3.2 billion in aid over six years beginning 1 October 1982. Washington also provided forty F-16 jet fighters for $1.1 billion to Islamabad to meet the so-called Soviet threat.

In addition, in February 1980, Brzezinski and then Deputy Secretary of State Warren Christopher visited Pakistan and made arrangements for a CIA operation carrying arm supplies to the Afghan resistance. As stated in the previous chapter, the United States was involved in supplying light weapons, ammunition, and money to the Afghan resistance forces even before the Soviet invasion. Now that Washington made a concerted effort to make the Soviets pay a price for their invasion. In his *memoir* Brzezinski writes that in his talks with the Pakistani leadership and, on the way back home, with the Saudi Arabian leaders, he "held separate negotiations regarding cooperative responses to the Soviet action in Afghanistan, and these yielded tangible results."[58] In Pakistan, Brzezinski even visited the Afghan refugee camps in the North-West Frontier Province and the Khybar Pass areas, and had a view of the Afghan resistance against the Soviets. Within a few days, the CIA pipeline of weapons resumed to the resistance in a greater volume. It is estimated that the amount of U.S. military assistance to the Afghan resistance was about $30 million during the Carter administration.[59]

United States also played the China card again. The timing of playing this "card" in fact had a greater significance not only in view of the U.S.-China military cooperation—which was a nightmare that Moscow had feared ever since Henry Kissinger made his secret trip to Peking in 1971—but also from the Sino-Pakistani strategic perspectives Russians had every reason to worry about. On the other hand, Chinese leaders knew that nothing was more likely to agitate Moscow than the prospect of an emerging Chinese-United States alliance. Washington was ready to go ahead with its game. Defense Secretary Harold Brown visited China in January 1980 and held discussions with Chinese leadership about the significance of the Soviet invasion of Afghanistan. At the end of his visit Brown said in a press conference that American and Chinese views "are very closely parallel about the need to strengthen other nations in the region and each side will take appropriate action on its own towards that end."[60] Few days later, it was reported that during Brown's visit to China, leaders in Peking had suggested that they were ready to increase a covert flow of Chinese small arms to rebels in Afghanistan.[61] In addition, Chinese Foreign Minister Huang Hua visited Islamabad and made a "third party arrangement" to supply weapons to Pakistan and the Afghan rebels through China.[62] Therefore, the visit of the U.S. Defense Secretary was not only significant from the point of view of arms supply to the Afghan resistance, it had a far-reaching impact on the U.S.-Soviet relations and was viewed as a major step of the demonstration of Washington's outrage against the Soviet action.

The militant Muslim fundamentalists were transformed into Mujahiddin, freedom fighters. Actually, most of them had been fighting for political power since 1974, first against the Daoud regime, and later against the communist regimes of Taraki and Amin. But now that they came under American "strategic compulsions" to contain communism, to fight against the Soviet soldiers in Afghanistan, they had to be provided with American money to buy arms to fight a jehad, a holy war. President Carter later wrote in his *memoirs* that he ordered the CIA to begin "arranging for Soviet-made weapons to be delivered to freedom fighters in Afghanistan."[63] It had to be a secret operation and that to only Soviet-made weapons because the guerrillas could claim that their arms were captured from the enemy, and not supplied by the CIA. There was also the fear of the Soviet retaliation against the Pakistanis in case of open support to the rebels.

Within days of the Soviet invasion, CIA Director Stansfield Turner turned to the Agency's largest overseas posts in Cairo and contacted the Egyptian President Anwar el-Sadat to open his huge stockpiles of Soviet-model automatic rifles, land mines, grenade launchers, anti-tank and anti-aircraft missiles for the Afghan rebels. They were the left over weapons of 1960s and early 1970s supplied by the Soviet Union to Egypt when the latter was in friendly terms with the former. In a September 1981 interview with *NBC News*, Sadat recalled: "The first moment that Afghan incident took place, the U.S. contacted me" and "told me, 'Please open your stores for us so that we can give the Afghans the armaments they need to fight,' and I gave the armaments. The transport of armaments to the Afghans started from Cairo on U.S. planes."

United States did start a secret operation of arms to the Afghan rebels, but no one, not even the hard-liners in the Carter administration believed that the Soviets could be pushed back from Afghanistan by military means. All that they wanted was to strengthen the resistance forces so that they could bargain with the Soviets from a position of strength in future. A secret document of January 2, 1980 reveals that the U.S. goal was the withdrawal of Soviet troops from Afghanistan, but "even if it is not attainable, we should make Soviet involvement as costly as possible."[64] So the U.S. was not sure about the military success of the Afghan rebels in the beginning. But in spite of the possibility of large-scale massacred of the rebels, the United States went ahead with its plans of fighting a guerrilla war in a distant land. Carter's CIA Director, Stansfield Turner acknowledged,

> *We had some moral dilemmas in the beginning. The question in the beginning was is it right for the United States to give weapons to people who wind up being killed in order to keep the Russians off balance? I thought that was a tough question, morally, to answer. The whole program of feeding freedom fighters is one of feeding people who cannot win militarily.*
>
> *But at the time, back in 1979, there was surely a benefit to the United States in this. So I said: 'Okay, I think I can morally accept this.'*[65]

For the first time the CIA-supplied weapons would be killing regular Soviet Army troops in Afghanistan. Turner was worried that the U.S. policy was to fight to the last dead Afghan. But as in many other situations when moral questions are hardly a matter of discussions in furthering national interests, Turner had no other option. Just before five days of the Ronald Reagan inauguration, in a meeting with President Reagan, Vice-President George Bush, and Reagan's CIA Director, William Casey, Turner unveiled, "the most important covert action was the secret support to the resistance in Afghanistan."[66] In addition to this demonstration of American challenge and strategic superiority over the Soviet Union, and the CIA operation of arms supply to the resistance forces; Washington also imposed several punitive measures and sanctions against Moscow. The hardliners analysis of implications of the Soviet move presented to the United States a frightening scenario. So it was obvious that Washington would pursue an assertive role because, the administration believed, the future Soviet behavior in the region and elsewhere would depend on the nature of American reaction. President Carter said "the response of the international community to the Soviet attempt to crush Afghanistan must match the gravity of the Soviet action."[67] To make the matter worse for the Soviets, three options were available to the United States: military, political, and economic. Carter ruled out the military option as he deemed it inappropriate and infeasible.[68] The United States resorted to the remaining two options, along with material aid to the Afghan resistance forces.

Carter's economic and political sanctions touched several aspects of U.S.-Soviet relations including, (1) suspension of the opening of new consular offices in Kiev and New York; (2) deferment of a number of economic and cultural exchanges programs under consideration; (3) an embargo on the sale of 17 million metric tons of food grain to the Soviets; (4) curtailment of the Soviets fishing privileges in the American waters; (5) United States withdrawal of the Summer 1980 Moscow Olympics; (6) suspension of the Senate consideration of the SALT II treaty and the arms control talks.[69]

In addition to this, the U.S. also encouraged its friends, allies, and many other Islamic and Third World non-aligned countries to follow its economic and political move against the Soviet Union. Washington's main goal was to alienate Moscow from its own allies and friends, especially from the Islamic nations in the Southwest Asian and Middle Eastern region. It looked for military bases in the region in Somalia, Kenya, Oman, and increased its military capability in the Indian Ocean base of Diego Garcia by expanding the runways and the storage facilities. The United States was virtually prepared for a war with the Soviet Union, and therefore, the latter was kept on defensive position from the very beginning.

Carter Administration in Retrospect

From the above discussion, it can be inferred that before the Soviet invasion, Brzezinski had advocated a tough countermoves to deter Moscow's fateful decision. He claimed that it was because of the "timid opposition" of the State Department under Cyrus Vance, that the U.S. could not initiate large-scale aid program to the Afghan resistance, which he advocated, might have stopped the Soviets from crossing their southern border. But this public posture of the National Security Adviser is clearly contradicted by the evidence of several cables from the U.S. Embassy and CIA station in Kabul, along with other U.S. documents published in Teheran in 1983-84, after their seizure from the U.S. Embassy in 1979. Commenting on these documents, a magazine disclosed that

> *The Soviets had kept the Carter administration well informed of their political and military moves in Afghanistan and had sought a tacit agreement with Washington to stabilize internal Afghan politics and limit Soviet military intervention in exchange for reductions in U.S. support for the Mujahiddin. But Brzezinski wanted to draw the Soviets*

> *deeper into Afghanistan, where they could become easy military targets and their presence used in US relations with the Arab Gulf States, Iran, China and Pakistan.*[70]

So, it might be possible that some elements in the Carter administration presumed the Soviet invasion as a defensive move on the part of Moscow; a fear of the spillover of the Muslim fundamentalism into the former Central Asian Republic. But since Afghanistan could be made an issue in the global superpower relationship and viewed as "an elephant's step" in the broad "chess game" of the globe, it made hardly any sense to Washington whether Moscow's move was offensive or defensive. The resistance to the communist regime in Afghanistan fell under the United States policy of opposing the Soviets, and Washington increasingly engaged itself in supplying money and weapons to the rebels. Zbigniew Brzezinski, who was also quite instrumental, later in Reagan administration's decision-making with regard to Afghanistan, wrote

> *The American engagement was predicted on the strategic premise that, whatever might have been the subjective motives of the Soviet military move into Afghanistan; its objective consequences were profoundly threatening to the region, and could lead to regional Soviet domination.*[71]

The U.S. did not bother much about the offensive/defensive debate and wanted to demonstrate its military superiority over the Soviet Union. But what is ironical is that shortly after the Soviet action, the United States had realized that the Soviet soldiers had been bogged down and there was no further threat to Pakistan or Iran or Persian Gulf oil. As early as February 1980, some officials in Washington analyzing the "intelligence reports" said that nothing had gone right for the Russians since their move into Afghanistan. It is also remarkable that at the same time the State Department noted that with Russian troops so bogged down in Afghanistan, the risk of an invasicn of Pakistan or Iran, as some officials had earlier feared, was receding rapidly.[72] The United States estimated that just to maintain law and order in Afghanistan, Moscow needed 25,000 to 50,000 more troops beyond the 70,000 deployed by then. It was concluded that if the Soviets really intended to crush the rebels and move towards the Indian Ocean or the Persian Gulf, they would need as many as 300,000 to 400,000 more troops, bringing total number to half a million, about the size of troops the Americans had deployed in Vietnam. But in spite of this known fact, the United States continued its military buildup in the region; it continued to argue that the Soviets would battle on until effective and permanent control was established, and the cold war rhetoric continued without any hitch.

Another symbol of a "policy conspiracy" was that the CIA had predicted in 1977 that the Soviet Union would be an oil-importing nation by the mid-1980s. This was highlighted in the United States as a major cause for Moscow's move to make Afghanistan a "steppingstone" for its further march towards the oil fields of the

Persian Gulf region. It was natural that such an estimate would create a fear and that public opinion would support the U.S. military to protect the oil fields. Egyptian President Sadat had echoed the CIA estimate and declared in 1979 that the Soviet Union was the new world power and had joined the United States in the international "battle for energy." However, later the CIA revised its estimates and it was made clear that the 1977 prediction was wrong and exaggerated. But the CIA's prediction of Soviet's oil shortage had a great impact on Carter's reaction to Moscow's move, and the outrage in the U.S. public's mind.

It is ironic about American foreign policy that even at the cost of strong domestic criticism and possible internal economic fallout, Washington was willing to punish other countries. The derailment of SALT II and the grain embargo, and many other Carter's sanctions had definitely negative impact on U.S. policy abroad and brought dissatisfaction to certain people at home. For example, in accordance with the provisions of the SALT, the Soviets had already destroyed their four *Yankee* class submarines by the time the talk about the ratification of the controversial treaty started in Washington. The balance of power in the Western Europe was also in favor of the U.S. In fact, SALT II had allowed the U.S. to pursue the strategic programs it needed; such as the MX, long-range air-launched cruise missile or such weapons not covered by the treaty as the neutron bomb or the Pershing II. But the treaty limited the number of warheads the Soviets could put on the missiles whose throw weight and accuracy were beginning to threaten American land-based missiles. It had also limited the number and the type of new Soviet ICBM systems, or the conversion of the existing launchers. In short, SALT II had made it more difficult for Moscow to pursue a war-winning strategy, whereas there was more scope of "strategy flexibility" for Washington. That is the reason why most people in the Carter administration believed that the U.S. was punishing itself by shelving this treaty. Even President Carter himself believed that the Treaty was in the U.S. national interests. Announcing the derailment of the treaty, Carter's spokesman said "while the President continues to believe that ratification of SALT II is in the national security interest of the United States, he has concluded that the Soviet invasion of Afghanistan, in defiance of the United Nations Charter has made consideration of the SALT II treaty inappropriate at this time."[73]

Similarly, Carter's grain embargo against the Soviets had a more adverse impact on U.S. farmers than on Moscow. The Soviets were able to replace most of the embargoed grain from other sources, most notably Argentina. In the United States, it became a domestic political issue, and on April 24, 1981, President Ronald Reagan lifted the embargo enabling the Soviets to resume large-scale purchasing of American grain.[74]

Conclusion

What emerges from the preceding discussion is that the American reaction to the Soviet invasion of Afghanistan was basically a triumph of the neo-conservatives both within and without the Carter administration. Afghanistan was certainly not a drawback for the U.S. policy, rather paradoxically; it offered an opportunity to demonstrate American power and capability in the region.

In fact, a false perception of the American weakness in the region had developed after the Iranian revolution. American reaction to the Soviet action might well have been low-keyed if the Shah had still been in power in Iran. And in that case, the American ability to punish the Soviets in Afghanistan would have been much higher. Without a setback in Iran, the United States would have responded to Afghanistan rather as it did to the Soviet invasion of Czechoslovakia in 1968: a sort of indignation, contempt, and a realization that it did not affect the balance of power in any way. In fact, if we compare the so-called "strategic stakes" between Czechoslovakia and Afghanistan, the formers geographical position was far more central to the American interests than the later. Yet no military strategist in the Johnson administration suggested that the Soviets were preparing to attack Western Europe and nobody stimulated a climate of national hysteria in a presidential election year.

The evidence have points to the proposition that Carter's reaction to the Afghanistan crisis was based on several other factors not related to any "grand design" of Moscow, but was connected with an ideological debate in Washington and of course, Carter's Presidential election in 1980. The "cold warriors" had been successful in mobilizing the public opinion to such an extent that a majority opinion in the United States was in their favor. They believed that Carter administration was on the defensive in the nation's foreign policy against the Soviet Union. So the purpose behind a strong reaction after Afghanistan was to preempt domestic criticism of the administration.[75] As the Presidential Election Day was getting nearer, and Carter found that "tough words" were paying well to boost his popularity, and he continued on a course that the American public wanted to hear.

Otherwise, a rational American reaction could have been the joining with other nations in the United Nations to condemn the Soviet action and pressuring the Soviets by helping the Afghan resistance, as the Carter and later Reagan administrations did, along with all its high-sounding declarations. Without Iran factor, without Presidential elections, and of course, without the "victory of the hardliners," Carter might well have agreed with Kennan and others that Afghanistan really did not make all that much difference. By demonstrating the cold war rhetoric and the American military power, the United States not only returned to the "Dulles era" of confrontation, it also left no room for Moscow to fear Washington. In other words, barring a resort to war, the Soviet Union had already absorbed the worst of what the United States had to offer. Certainly, there was no point for the United States to go to such an extent, and surely, no Russian "master plan" had called for.

Notes and References

1. Henry S. Bradsher, *Afghanistan and the Soviet Union,* Duke Press Policy Studies, Durham, 1983, p. 191.

2. Anthony Lewis, "In the Afghan Wake," *The New York Times,* January 10, 1980, p. 23.
3. George F. Kennan, on Washington's Reaction to the Afghan Crisis: "Was This Really Mature Statesmanship?" *The New York Times,* February 1, 1980.
4. For example Louis Dupree, AUFS Reports, No. 37, 1980. Also see *East-West Relations in the Aftermath of Soviet Invasion of Afghanistan,* Hearing before the Subcommittee on Europe and the Middle East of the Committee on Foreign Affairs, House of Representatives, Ninety-Sixth Congress, Second Session, U.S. Government Printing Office, Washington: 1980.
5. Selig S. Harrison, "Dateline Afghanistan: Exit Through Finland," *Foreign Policy,* No. 41, Winter 1980/81, pp. 163-187. Also see Selig S. Harrison, "Did Moscow Fear An Afghan Tito?" *The New York Times,* January 13, 1980.
6. Cyrus Vance, *Hard Choices: Critical Years in America's Foreign Policy,* Simon and Schuster, New York, 1983, pp. 385-395.
7. *East-West Relations in the Aftermath of Soviet Invasion of Afghanistan,* p. 32-37. Also see Shulman's comment in *Defence/Space Daily,* February 12, 1980.
8. Raymond L. Garthoff, *Détente and Confrontation: American-Soviet Relations from Nixon to Reagan,* The Brookings Institution, Washington DC, 1985, pp. 928-974.
9. *The Guardian,* April 19, 1981.
10. A clear account of the Soviets decision-making processes, and their aims and objectives in Afghanistan (which were primarily defensive in nature) is available in *Journal of South Asian and Middle Eastern Studies,* Vol. 17, No. 2, winter 1994.
11. U.S. *Department of State Bulletin,* April 1980, p. 12.
12. Vance, *Hard Choices,* p. 388.
13. *Ibid.*
14. *Ibid.*
15. James Reston, "Kissinger On Afghan Crisis" *The New York Times,* January 4, 1980, p. 23.
16. Henry Bienen, "Perspectives on Soviet Intervention in Africa," *Political Science Quarterly,* 95 : 1, Spring, 1980, pp. 30-31. Also see Stanley Hoffmann, "Reflections on the Present Danger," *The New York Review,* March 6, 1980.
17. James McConnell, "Doctrine and Capabilities," in *Soviet Naval Diplomacy,* ed. Bradford Dismukes and James McConnell, Pergamon Press, New York, 1979, pp. 6-7.
18. James Schlesinger, "A Testing Time for America," *Fortune,* 106, February 1976, p. 76.
19. Robert Tucker, *Commentary,* January 1975, Walter Goodman, "Fair Game," *New Leader,* March 17, 1975, p. 15. Also see John Collins and Clyde Mark, *Oil Fields as Military Objectives: A Feasibility Study,* U.S. Congress, Committee on Internal Relations, August 1975.

20. James Schlesinger, "A Testing Time for America," p. 76.
21. Commenting on the membership and support of the Committee, Alan Wolfe wrote, "they in turn spoke for a broad-based coalition of 141 persons ranging from Commentary's editor, Norman Podhoretz, to erstwhile Presidential hopeful John Connally. Among the Committee's founders were ten labor leaders; also listed were numerous literary and academic figures, among them Nobel Prize winners Saul Bellow, Eugene Wigner, and W.F. Libby. A platoon of retired military commanders was led by Kennedy's adviser, General Maxwell Taylor, and Nixon's Chief of Naval Operations, Admiral Elmo Zumwalt. And as one might expect, a whole host of Cold War architects and long-time Presidential national security advisors, including Leon Keyserling, Gordon Gray, Charles Burton Marshall, Arthur Dean and Douglas Dillon . . .." See Alan Wolfe, "Resurgent Cold War Ideology: The Case of the Committee on Present Danger," *Capitalism and the State: U.S. Latin American Relations,* Stanford University Press, Stanford, CA, 1979, p. 41.
22. *The Wall Street Journal,* January 18, 1979.
23. Harold Brown's remarks were reported in *Middle East International,* March 14, 1980.
24. *Time,* May 14, 1980.
25. *Paul H. Nitze is diplomat-in Residence at the Paul H. Nitze School of Advanced International Studies, Johns Hopkins University. He has had a varied and distinguished career in government service. His positions include Deputy Director and Director, Policy Planning Staff, Department of States (1949-1953), more importantly, the coauthor of NSC-68, the secret paper in early 1950s that advocated a shift from political to military containment of the Soviet Union, Secretary of Navy (1963-1967), Deputy Secretary of Defense (1967-1969), Member, U.S. Delegation, Strategic Arms Limitation Talks (1969-1974, from which he had resigned in protest), Chief Negotiator for INF (1981-1984), and Special Adviser to President Reagan (1984-1989).*
26. Paul H. Nitze, "Strategy for the 80s," in *At Issue,* ed. Steven Spiegel, New York, St. Martin's Press, 1981, p. 315.
27. William Safire, "The Second Cold War," *The New York Times,* January 10, 1980, p. 23.
28. Zbigniew Brzezinski, *Power and Principle: Memoirs of the National Security Adviser, 1977-1981,* Farrar, New York, 1985, p. 427.
29. Jimmy Carter, *Keeping Faith: Memoirs of a President,* Bantam Books, New York, 1982, pp. 471-472.
30. Stanley Hoffmann, *The New York Review of Books,* March 6, 1980, p. 19.
31. Brzezinski, *Power and Principle,* p. 452.
32. *U.S. Department of State Bulletin,* February 1980, p. 4, and October 1980, p. 10.
33. U.S. Congress, Senate, *U.S. Security Interests and Policies in Southwest Asia,* Hearings before the Sub-committee on Near Eastern and South Asian

Affairs, 96th Congress, 2nd Session, U.S. Government Printing office, Washington D.C., 1980, p. 127. Also see Nancy Peabody Newell and Richard S. Newell, *The Struggle for Afghanistan,* Cornell University Press, New York, 1981, p. 14.

34. U.S. Congress, House of Representative, *East-West Relations in the Aftermath of Soviet invasion of Afghanistan,* Hearings before the Sub-committee on Europe and the Middle East of the Committee on Foreign Affairs, 96th Congress, 2nd session, January 24 and 30, 1980, U.S. Government Printing Office, Washington D.C., 1980, p. 1.
35. U.S. *Department of State Bulletin,* May 1980, p. 127.
36. *The Muslim,* January 20, 1986.
37. Cited in *Foreign Broadcast Information Service (FBIS)/Soviet Union,* January 14, 1980, pp. A22-26.
38. *Presidential Documents* 16 January 14, 1980, p. 41.
39. *Ibid,* p. 25.
40. *Ibid,* January 28, 1980, p. 196.
41. The White House, Washington DC, January 2, 1980. Zbigniew Brzezinski gave this top-secret document declassified/released on March 14, 1995, to this author.
42. "An Interview with Zbigniew Brzezinski," *The Wall Street Journal,* January 15, 1980.
43. The White House, Washington, *Special Coordination Committee Meeting,* January 14, 1980. Document obtained from Zbigniew Brzezinski.
44. *The Times,* December 31, 1979. Also see Brzezinski, *Power and Principle,* p. 444.
45. Carter's State of the Union Address of 23rd January as printed in *The New York Times,* January 24, 1980.
46. "An Interview with Zbigniew Brzezinski," *The Wall Street Journal,* January 15, 1980.
47. *Christian Science Monitor,* July 30, 1980, p. 2.
48. *Washington Post,* August 10, 1980, p. 2.
49. This nuclear gambit was leaked from the State Department to a *New York Times* reporter in February 1980. See *Tim Weiner, Blank Check: The Pentagon's Black Budget,* Warner Books, New York, 1990, p. 145.
50. The White House, Washington, *SCC Meeting,* January 14, 1980. Document obtained from Zbigniew Brzezinski.
51. *East-West Relations in the Aftermath of Soviet invasion of Afghanistan,* p. 32
52. The White House, Washington, January 14, 1980. Document obtained from Zbigniew Brzezinski.
53. Brigadier Mohammad Yousaf and Major Mark Adkin, *The Bear Trap,* Jang Publishers, Lahore, 1992, p. 25.
54. *The New Republic,* February 16, 1980, p. 14.
55. *The New York Times,* January 19, 1980, p. 8.

56. *Ibid.*
57. *Ibid.*
58. Brzezinski, *Power and Principle,* p. 449.
59. *The Wall Street Journal,* April 9, 1985.
60. *The Washington Post,* January 10, 1980.
61. *The New York Times,* January 17, 1980.
62. *Los Angeles Times,* January 23, 1980.
63. Jimmy Carter, *Keeping Faith: Memoirs of a President,* pp.473-75.
64. The White House, Washington, January 2, 1980.
65. Cited in Tim Weiner, *Blank Check: The Pentagon's Black Budget,* Warner Books, New York, 1990, pp. 145-147.
66. Bob Woodward, *Veil: The Secret Wars of the CIA 1981-1987,* Simon and Schuster, New York, 1987, p. 86.
67. *Presidential Documents* 16, January 14, 1980, pp. 25-27.
68. U.S. Congress, House Committee on Foreign Affairs, Subcommittee on Europe and the Middle East, *An Assessment of the Afghanistan sanctions: implications for Trade and Diplomacy in the 1980s,* 97th Congress, Ist session, April 1981, U.S. Government printing office, Washington D.C., 1981, p. 22.
69. For a clear view of the U.S. sanctions against the Soviets in the wake of Afghanistan, see, Henry S. Bradsher, *Afghanistan and the Soviet Union*, Duke Press Policy Studies, Durham, 1983, pp. 194-199.
70. *New Statesman,* Vol. 3, March 14, 1986, p. 18-19.
71. Zbigniew Brzezinski, *Game Plan,* The Atlantic Monthly Press, Boston/New York, 1986, p. 51.
72. *The Guardian,* March 2, 1980.
73. *Presidential Document,* 16, January 7, 1980, p. 12.
74. *Presidential Document,* 17, April 27, 1981, p. 466.
75. At a seminar organized by the Carnegie Endowment for International Peace on June 9, 1989, President Carter's Under Secretary of State David D. Newsom stated that the Soviet intervention in Afghanistan had put pressure on the Carter administration to make a demonstrably strident response. See Riaz M. Khan, *Untying the Afghan Knot: Negotiating Soviet Withdrawal,* Duke University Press, Durham, 1991, pp. 21-22.

4
Making a Policy

We are with you . . . you fight valiantly and your spirit inspires the world . . . the United States has, does, and will continue to stand with you. You can be sure—and I wish to state this with the greatest emphasis—that how best we can bring home to the Soviets the cost of their invasion of Afghanistan, will remain a top priority item for the U.S. government

—*Secretary of State George P. Shultz, addressing a cheering crowd of Afghan refugee at a camp near Khyber Pass, Pakistan, July 03, 1983.*

President Ronald Reagan assumed his office with a hard-line rhetoric on the Afghan question. He was a staunch anti-communist and committed to competing with the Soviets from a position of strength. His victory in the 1980 presidential elections not only marked the end of the post-Vietnam foreign policy "syndrome," which was often criticized as an American weakness, but also ended all doubts in the American mind that the U.S. needed to build up its military and strategic strength to deal with the Soviets. Once again, Reagan's foreign policy centered on the U.S.-Soviet relations. But interestingly, after a cosmetic changes, more or less, Washington pursued the same policy in Southwest Asia and especially towards Afghanistan, as did his predecessor after the Soviet invasion. He strengthens the American military position in the region, and very cautiously allowed to develop diverse policy options for the regions and towards Afghanistan. In fact, it was not towards Afghanistan, but Afghan resistance, since Afghanistan was under Soviet occupation. But an overall assessment of the American policy towards the Afghan resistance suggests that Reagan's high-keyed rhetoric on Afghan question did not match his action during his first term in office. This was because very few people in and out of the administration believed that the Soviets could be pushed back from Afghanistan. However, by the end of his term in 1984, certain policy options had developed in the different agencies of Reagan presidency, which believed in making Afghanistan a Soviet Vietnam.

What then were the obstacles on the way to an increased American aid to the Afghan resistance in the initial years? How did Washington formulate a policy that changed the course of history in a strategically important part of the world? In other words, what factors contributed to escalated American aid? And how did the regional scenario favour an American policy in Southwest Asia? This chapter examines the nature of American policy-making in the context of the containment of communism in Afghanistan, keeping account of the regional actors, most notably Pakistan. The study finds that several factors contributed to a cautious U.S. approach towards the Afghan resistance, most notable among them being the U.S. readiness for a protracted proxy war with the Soviets. It concludes that the strategic location of the country, and the determination of the Afghan people for their independence, favoured Washington more than any other factors in its policy-making. In fact, an unintended American policy emerged by the end of 1984, which later developed into a concerted U.S. effort to force Moscow to withdraw its troops from Afghanistan.

Initial Response

From the very beginning, the Reagan administration was dominated by the people who were known for their hard line stance and conservative views in America's foreign policy. Not surprisingly, 32 of the 182 members of the Committee on Present Danger (CPD) had been successful in entering the administration in positions dealing with the American foreign policy, national security, negotiations of arms control with the Soviets. etc. For obvious reasons, they intended to pursue a very hard line policy on overall Soviet-American relations. It is interesting to note that there was no place for the liberal minded people, and the whole administration was dominated by the conservative elements, especially in the context of their dealings with the Soviets in particular and American policy abroad in general. Also, it is interesting that a new "class of people" among the hard liners emerged in Washington, especially in their attitude and policy towards Afghanistan who were known as "bleeders,"—people who believed in taking revenge for the American defeat in Vietnam.

So, like the Carter administration, the Reagan administration believed that the Soviets must pay a heavy price for their invasion of Afghanistan. But in the initial years, it did not believe that the Soviets could be pushed back, and therefore, only continued a low-level aid program to the resistance forces who were fighting against the communist regime in Kabul. It felt that by giving limited aid to the rebels, the fighting would continue for an indefinite period, and eventually, the Soviet would negotiate with the resistance for a political settlement. Because from the very outset, the dominant positions of the conservative elements in the Reagan administration were successful in keeping the Soviets in the defensive in the context of the superpower relationship.

Initially, nothing was made public about the secret arms pipeline of the CIA. But administration officials believed that "the Soviets are not succeeding" in Afghanistan.[1] The United States wanted to keep the Afghan issue alive in the superpower relationship, and a limited secret operation of the CIA continued. The demarcation line of American policy remained to be the non-recognition of the Kabul regime and increasing condemnation and support in the United Nations. Basically,

American policy during the first four years of the Reagan Presidency was based on four fundamental principles: (1) demand for the unconditional withdrawal of the Soviet troops from Afghanistan, (2) mobilizing world opinion against the Soviets as an aggressor, (3) initiating United Nations condemnation, and, most importantly, (4) supplying arms and money to the resistance forces fighting the Soviet controlled regime in Afghanistan, and for that matter, improving the U.S.-Pakistan relationship. Besides this, the United States continued its military build up in the Indian Ocean and Persian Gulf region by upgrading the Rapid Deployment Force into a Central Command.

It can be stated that the Reagan administration's high-keyed rhetoric maintained in its commitment on Afghan issue did not match its response: it neither supplied large-scale aid to the Afghan resistance nor made Afghanistan as an issue in the U.S.-Soviet relations, viz. in arms control negotiation, etc. Instead, it lifted the grain embargo, and allowed to be lapsed subsequently to the other sanctions imposed by the Carter administration.

Among other issues, Ronald Reagan and his running mate George Bush won the 1980 Presidential election on the point what they called "fickle management" of American foreign policy by the Carter administration. Right from the outset, they believed in greater American strength and capability abroad, and need for an enhancement of defense budget to meet the Soviet threat. So far as Carter's sanctions against Moscow in the wake of Afghanistan was concerned, the Republican candidates severely criticized the Democratic agenda. For instance, during the campaign, the Republicans contended that the grain embargo imposed by Carter would hurt the United States more than the Soviet Union and that this export to the USSR made a significant contribution to the U.S. balance of payment. Reagan argued that one segment of the American population (i.e., farmers) should not be put under pressure and pay the price of U.S. policy abroad, while the Carter government could not even persuade other countries to deny grain to the Soviets.[2] Reagan lifted the grain embargo on April 24, 1981 followed by several other concessions related to the sanctions.

Strategic set up

Reagan administration was not whimsical in its response to the Soviets over Afghanistan. Rather, it moved slowly and developed a long-term strategy to compete with the Soviets in Southwest Asia. It seemed that Washington's policy against the Soviets over Afghanistan was not limited in supplying money and weapons to the resistance forces fighting against the Kabul regime. Instead, the administration "closed all doors" for Moscow during the first four years, and during the second term as President, Ronald Reagan increased pressure through Afghanistan by supplying adequate aid to the resistance, and started "talking" with the Soviets. As this chapter confines itself to the U.S. policy towards Afghanistan during Reagan's first term in office, it will only attempt to answer such questions as: how Washington's policy was designed to "close all doors" to Moscow? In other words, how the U.S.

"attacked" the Soviets from all fronts without fighting a war? And secondly, how this strategy strengthened U.S. position when it provided incremental aid to the Afghan rebels?

To answer these questions, it is necessary to look back to the Carter's responses to the Soviet move into Afghanistan which were subsequently followed by the Reagan administration with some cosmetic changes. Those are: (1) to deter further Soviet moves by strengthening Pakistan, and if possible Iran, and to improve relations with China to guarantee Pakistan's security; (2) to enhance U.S. military capability in the region by deploying RDF and seeking bases in the region; (3) to engage India diplomatically for the resolution of the Afghan problem and maintain an Indo-Pak "détente;" (4) to help stimulate political consciousness among the Soviet Muslims in the Soviet Central Asia by propagating the idea that the communists are anti-Muslim and that they are out to suppress Islamic culture, and most importantly; (5) to keep the Afghan issue alive by sustaining the resistance for an indefinite period in a protracted and prolonged war with the Soviet soldiers. By applying these strategies, Reagan administration not only kept the Soviet in defensive, but also indicated its readiness to fight with them if necessary. Once policies took its shape, the administration maintained an aggressive posture and confrontationist approach towards Moscow. For instance, within months of the assumption of his office, President Reagan had bluntly stated that if the Russians made a reckless move in the Gulf "they would be risking confrontation with the United States."[3] It was natural that Reagan's reaffirmation of the Carter Doctrine would be taken more seriously given his overall stand against the Soviets.

Firstly, Pakistan's security was given prime importance by the Reagan administration. The administration abandoned the idea of a "cooperative security framework" or a "woo" with the Indians advocated by its predecessor. Instead, Washington exclusively focused on Pakistan, and viewed the latter as strategically important in furtherance of its policy of containing communism. Administration officials insisted that there was a clear and continuing danger emanating from the Soviet occupation of Afghanistan.[4] Given the regional strategic environment, especially the hostile attitude of Iran against the U.S., Pakistan was considered as the only route to "deal" with the Soviets in the region. It was not only seen as a "front-line" state against Washington's strategy of containing communism, but also viewed as a country of considerable strategic importance to project American military power in the region and the sole way to supply arms to the Afghan resistance against the Kabul regime.

This strategic importance of Pakistan to the United States and the latter's commitment to the formers security in accordance to their 1959 defense agreement was reinforced by Washington's $ 3.2 billion package of military and economic aid extending over a six-year term 1982 through 1987. The United States also included 40 F-16s, the most advanced fighter aircraft of the time in the U.S. arsenal, 100 M48A5 tanks, recovery vehicles equipped with 1, 005 I-TOW missiles, howitzers, and attack helicopters. Washington justified this aid package on the ground that this was designed to meet Pakistan's air defense needs along its western front against the Soviets. But interestingly, "no realistic threat scenario (from the west) except India was ever envisaged in Pakistan."[5] It was also never credible both in India and Pakistan that even with the U.S. military aid and the sophisticated weaponry, Pakistan could withstand a massive attack by Soviet forces.

By rearming Pakistan, the United States not only furthered an arms race between India and Pakistan in an extravagant militarization of the subcontinent, it also indirectly allowed Pakistan to go ahead with its nuclear program. In fact, when in September 1981, $ 3.2 billion economic and military aid was agreed and announced; Reagan administration was left in no doubt that Pakistan would persist with its nuclear program. The U.S. was also well aware of Islamabad's opposition to the "strategic consensus" being promoted by Washington for the Middle East peace. Pakistan never stopped criticizing the Camp David Accords.[6]

Though the U.S. was interested initially to improve relations with Iran, the domestic turmoil and the subsequent war with Iraq left a very limited leverage to Washington to do so. Despite the fact that Iran was openly committed to anti-U.S. propaganda after the fundamentalist's revolution and the subsequent hostage crisis, and later involved in a war with its neighbour Iraq, Washington continued its efforts to normalize its relations with Teheran. As early as January 1980, even when the hostage crisis was at its peak, President Carter's National Security Advisor Zbigniew Brzezinski had expressed Washington's willingness to improve relations with Teheran.[7] When the war broke out between Iran and Iraq, the Reagan administration saw benefits in maintaining neutrality. Washington enhanced and strengthened its naval presence in the Persian Gulf and openly committed to protecting the flow of Gulf oil to its allies and friends in Europe. Administration officials stated that the U.S. was prepared to send even the ground troops to keep the Straits of Hormus open.[8] On the other hand, Washington hoped that the terrible cost of the war and the possibility of defeat would discredit the fundamentalist regime in Teheran and eventually lead to a pragmatic leadership there. The United States was also secretly assisting covert operation to the dissident elements in Teheran in the hope of the collapse of the Khomeini regime.[9] However, Washington could not succeed in overthrowing the government in Teheran and so, U.S.-Iranian relations remain tense throughout the Reagan Presidency. But it did not affect the American strategy in Afghanistan in any respect.

Strengthening Sino-U.S. ties was viewed by Washington as a crucial factor both for Pakistan's security as well as to supply arms to the Afghan resistance. In spite of their ideological and other differences in many international issues, Washington and Beijing were successful in working together in their stand on Afghanistan issue.[10] Over the years, China not only supplied adequate arms and money to the Afghan rebels through the CIA, it also supported Washington's stand in almost all international forum. So keeping Chinese in line on the Afghan issue was given much importance in the Reagan administration.

Secondly, as stated above, due to the Iran-Iraq war it was not possible for

Washington to improve relations with Iran. But the United States enhanced its military capability to a great extent so that it could meet the perceived Soviet threat in the region as well as any intimidation from Teheran. Officials in Washington felt that the best U.S. interests lay in an independent Iran from the point of view of possible Soviet incursion. Official position of Washington was maintaining neutrality in the Iran-Iraq war. However, "U.S. policy must rest primarily on a careful calculation of how Iran might affect vital U.S. interests in the region, and it must be clear to all that we cannot remain indifferent to the fate of Iran."[11] Washington had clearly stated that it would keep the Straits of Hormus open to oil traffic, and, in order to do so, was prepared to use sufficient firepower. By the end of 1983, the U.S. naval presence in the Persian Gulf area included nine warships, including the aircraft carrier *Midway,* with its formidable air power.

Besides this, the Reagan administration decided to strengthen the Rapid Deployment Force (RDF) far beyond than that was envisaged by his previous administration. According to the Defense Guidance Plan of May 1982, the RDF was to consist of five army divisions, two marine divisions and air wings, ten air force tactical fighter wings and two B-52 wings, and three navy aircraft carriers and escorts. It was estimated that the RDF could command a total of some 250,000 troops on an immediate basis and more in future. It was also placed under the direct command of the office of the Joint Chiefs of Staff from January 1, 1983. The Reagan administration also clearly pushed the regional actors to join in its own strategy in the region. It secured bases and military installations in Egypt, Somalia, Kenya, Oman and Spain.[12] The United States also improved its military capability in the Indian Ocean base of Diego Garcia and its air base in the Philippines. There was even a proposal from Washington to seek base facilities in the Pakistani ports of Karachi and Gwadar.[13] But Pakistan refused to agree to the U.S. proposal.

Thirdly, United States tried to seek Indo-Pak normalization of relations. U.S. diplomats believed that given the situation in the region after the Soviet invasion of Afghanistan, an Indian attack against Pakistan would "make things even worse" for Washington.[14] The visit of Indian Prime Minister Indira Gandhi to Washington in August 1982 helped improve Indo-US relations to a great extent and indirectly, put pressure to improve Indo-Pak relations. Pakistan made friendly overtures to India after prodding from the Reagan administration and offered no-war pact to New Delhi. Somehow, Reagan administration was successful in keeping both the countries in negotiations, which definitely served American interests. This was surely a "balancing act" of Washington against the perceived Soviet threat in the region vis-à-vis Pakistan's security.

Fourthly, Washington applied the idea, —that is, Clausewitz's theory of war— that the first offensive should be launched at the enemy's weakest link. And the Reagan administration rightly identified the communist ideology as the "weakest link" of the Soviet Union. So the administration's aggressive policy against the Soviets was not confined with its military buildup and containment of communism in the region. Its most significant "attack" against Moscow was probably the instigation of 55 million Muslim population of Central Asia. Washington helped set up or financed "Radio Free Afghanistan," "Radio Liberty," and news papers such as *Soldier of Fortune, Afghan News,* and *Afghanistan Times,* and continued anti-Russian propaganda in support of the Islamic religion and culture. The aim of all these radio broadcasts and newspapers was not only to stress an anti-Islamic character of Soviet policies in Afghanistan; it was also to generate a cultural awakening among the Soviet Muslim in Central Asia. Undoubtedly, it played a crucial role in portraying the war in favour of the resistance from the very beginning. But most important was the campaign against the Soviets for Muslim solidarity in its own territory, i.e. Central Asian Republics. So media propaganda was given a considerable importance by the Reagan administration. A major cause of the Soviet invasion of Afghanistan in 1979 was the fear of a "spillover effect" among its own Muslim populace. This was now pointedly targeted by Washington as a price for Moscow's invasion.

In addition, many private and non government organizations (NGOs) based in the United States played a crucial role in the war in Afghanistan as well as in supporting the Muslim solidarity in the region, including the Soviet Central Asian Republics. These groups also put pressure on the U.S. government from time to time, to increase the American aid for the resistance.[15] The most active private groups in the United States were: Committee for a Free Afghanistan (Washington DC); American Aid for Afghans (Portland, Oregon); and three New York-based groups: Freedom House, Afghan Relief Committee, Afghanistan Council of the Asia Society, and the Federation for American Afghan Action (Washington DC).

Finally, and most importantly, though an open secret, the United States policy towards the Afghan resistance was to keep the issue alive by supplying them limited aid and arms to fight against the Soviets. Like Carter administration, President Reagan also supported a low-level aid program, especially during his first term, though he assumes office insisting on the requirement for a hard-line on the Afghan question. In fact, during the first four years of the Reagan administration, Washington gave more importance to the U.S. strategic stake in the Southwest Asian region than to its arms supply to the Afghan resistance. It therefore gave more attention to the military buildup which was intended to "close all doors" to Moscow in the region, and then during its second term in office, the administration concentrated on arms supply to the Afghan rebels. So, in the early years, in spite of its pronouncement of commitment to the Afghan resistance in very strong and unambiguous terms, implementation of Reagan's policy did not match the words.[16] The administration very cautiously allowed to develop diverse policy options as regards to the question of arms supply to the Afghan rebels, and maintained a low level aid program just to keep the resistance alive against the Soviet soldiers.

However, during the first four years of the Reagan administration, the aid program to the rebels did increase each year: $50 million in the Fiscal Year (FY) 1981, $65m. in FY 1982, $75m. in FY 1983, and $122m. in FY 1984.[17] Up to 1984, the United States supplied the insurgents with light infantry weapons, rifles, light machine guns and grenades, most of which were either Soviet-built or designed, and provided by Egypt, China, the U.S., Saudi Arabia, and many other Muslim countries. There were also reports that the CIA—which had been assigned to carry out this covert mission—was supplying the resistance with British made radar-guided Blowpipe missiles and with Soviet designed heat-seeking SA-7s purchased in Poland. Intelligence sources believed that these missiles were attractive to the CIA because they could not trace to the United States. But the missiles "quite clearly weren't doing the job," i.e. not accurate in shooting the Soviet fighter aircrafts in Afghanistan.[18] However, by applying this low-level aid program, the Reagan administration became convinced that there was no more Soviet threat in the region, and during its second term in office, the administration went for escalated aid to the Afghan resistance.

Then what constraints did the administration face from within and without? And, more importantly, how did the United States evolve a policy to push the Soviets back from Afghanistan? This is to these questions that now we turn.

Constraints on U.S. Policy

Up to the end of the first term of Reagan Presidency, several causes are found as constraints on U.S. policy to an escalated aid for the Afghan resistance. First, in spite of its strategic location and what many experts said, "proximity" to the Soviet Union, Afghanistan had never been a focus of American foreign policy. Washington had not viewed this landmass as a Soviet sphere of influence (see Chapter 1) as it did recognize the Eastern Europe. What Washington's policy appeared over the years was a visible presence in Kabul until the Soviet invasion of that country in December 1979. After the Soviet invasion, many diplomats in Washington believed that it was naturally not a loss for the United States. Some people felt that Afghanistan was "a neighboring area of the Soviet Union, not of the United States."[19] So, from a historical perspective, the policy planners in Washington might have faced difficulty in changing its previous position of a limited aid program and "presence" to an active involvement and effective support to the resistance forces.

Secondly, it seemed that Washington's policy during this period was not to drive the Soviets out of Afghanistan, rather to pin them down in a protracted and prolonged war and to drain their economy. As such very few officials in the Carter, and later, Reagan administration believed that the Soviets could be pushed back from Afghanistan. Even Carter's National Security Advisor Zbigniew Brzezinski—who was known for his hard-line stand against the Soviets—also believed that the Afghan resistance "can never expect to defeat the Soviet Union militarily."[20] In accordance with Carter's policy of making the Afghan war costly for the Soviets, Washington was only trying to buy time by initiating a low-level aid program for the resistance. U.S. officials said that "there is little the U.S. and its allies could do to force Moscow to withdraw its force. All we can do now is to make it costly for the Soviets to stay there."[21] Carter's CIA Director Stansfield Turner, who initiated the covert operation, knew very clearly that the Afghan resistance was not going to win against the Soviets and that the U.S. policy was to "fight to the last Afghan." In the beginning, Turner thought, "whether it was permissible to use other people's lives for the geopolitical interests of the United States."[22] But the best American interests would be served if they were supplied with limited weapons to fight against the Soviets.

Reagan administration officials were equally skeptical about the military capability of the resistance to drive the Soviets out of Afghanistan. A retrospective remark of an U.S. official in 1986 best explains the Reagan administration's perception towards the Afghan resistance: "Six years ago a few of us could have imagined that today we would be talking about an Afghan resistance that has kept one of the most powerful armies of the world at bay."[23] Even William Casey, Reagan's CIA Director, initially assumed that "the Soviets will overpower and wear down the rebels."[24] It was argued that whether Washington helped or not, Afghan rebels would be pacified by the overwhelming Soviet military force. So, all that the U.S. could do was to play a negative role, i.e., bleed the Soviets by providing modest incremental aid to the Afghan resistance.[25] Congressional analysts observed "To a certain extent, broad U.S. policy objectives might be met by only a limited program of aid to the Afghan resistance."[26] So in the initial years of the Reagan administration, the United States did not believe that the Soviets could be pushed back by military force, and at the same time it was applying its own policy of bleeding the Soviets in Afghanistan by giving incremental aid to the resistance.

Thirdly, agencies of the U.S. government were wary about, and very cautious of the low-level aid program. They argued that if the U.S. escalated the aid program, the Soviets would retaliate against Pakistan, an important U.S. ally. And in that case, the United States would be forced to protect Pakistan against Soviet reprisals. This was a serious concern not only for the White House but also for the lawmakers in the Congress. American Senators worried that "if Russian troops chase Afghan rebels into Pakistan, do we want American boys up in the Khyber Pass trying to stop them?" "And if the Afghan rebels are armed too heavily, aren't we inviting the Soviets into hot pursuit?"[27] asked another Senator. The administration was also equally skeptical. Officials in the Reagan administration viewed that "what is good for the resistance there could be bad for Pakistan, an important US ally . . . if we escalate, then the Soviets might go after the Pakistanis."[28] From the Pakistani perspective, Islamabad feared that an escalated fighting would multiply the Afghan refugees in Pakistan and that Moscow could easily destabilize General Zia's narrowly based regime. This idea was further intensified by the repeated Soviet threats and warning to Islamabad. Moscow had categorically warned Islamabad that continued aid to the rebels would eventually result in war with Afghanistan, which the Soviet Union would support.[29] The periodical airspace violations, and occasional bombings and strafing attacks in the rebel bases inside Pakistani territory by the Soviet fighter aircrafts was obviously a military concern in Islamabad.[30] So, partly because of the Pakistani reservations, the U.S. had no other choice but to continue the low-level aid program to the resistance.

But critics alleged that Pakistan's military defense posture was quite different from its verbal concerns of a Soviet threat. It is assumed that Pakistan's reluctance against increased U.S. aid for the Afghan resistance had nothing to doing with the possibility of a Soviet retaliation than extracting more military and economic aid from the United States. Because, from the beginning of the Soviet invasion, Pakistanis, especially General Zia and his Inter Services Intelligence Directorate (ISI) had believed that Afghanistan was going to be Moscow's Vietnam, and that the "Afghan resistance must become a part of Pakistan's forward defense against the Soviets."[31] In fact, throughout the period of the Afghan war, Pakistan never considered the Soviets as their potential enemy. The real threat for Pakistan, what Islamabad perceived was India. Therefore, even at the height of the fighting between the resistance and the Afghan/Soviet forces, "Pakistan maintained only four under strength divisions (of its military) facing Afghanistan, while it had an estimated 11 full-strength divisions on the Indian border."[32]

Fourthly, there was institutional resistance in the U.S. government for an escalated aid program. Both the CIA and the State Department rigorously supported the low level program where as there was pressure from the Congress to increase aid. Some intelligence professionals in the CIA believed that the United States would be putting money into "a hopeless cause."[33] In spite of the incremental aid to the resistance, the CIA maintained "a no-win situation" in Afghanistan and, from time to time, they evaded the charges of shortcomings in its operation. The CIA and the State Department had been applying the former's strategy of bleeding the Russians through protracted war. So, in accordance with their policy, the CIA refused to address the need of the quantity and quality of weapons needed to "tailored to a winning strategy." They argued that "the Afghan were not to be trusted either with money or sophisticated weapons," and so, there was no need of "setting a policy toward Afghanistan more specific than one simply of delivering aid to the resistance."[34] Their only goal was to "keep the pot boiling," or "to raise the cost" to the Soviets. Even the CIA was successful in resisting the proposals that the Department of Defense be given the primary responsibility for channeling such assistance.[35] Not surprisingly, the CIA and the State Department strenuously opposed and delayed for about two years to the Tsongas resolution in the Congress, which was meant, for effective aid for the resistance to win. It aimed at changing the CIA's no-win strategy in Afghanistan.[36] The CIA was so cautious that it had assigned just three officers to Pakistan, and interestingly, none of who was a paramilitary expert, to manage the secret operation. So, to a great extent, the low-level aid program to the Afghan resistance did not rest with the Congress, rather it was a "consequence of bureaucratic inertia and deliberate obstructionism"[37] by some agencies of the U.S. government.

Fifth, it was argued that by pursuing an escalated aid program to the Afghan resistance, the United States would be investing its international prestige and image in a guerrilla war, which was not easy to win. Officials in the Reagan administration speculated that since the resistance could not win a war against the

Soviets, it would not only be a sheer wastage of money but also an embarrassment for the United States. For that reason, no one in the administration made a concerted effort to support an increased aid program. Fred C. Ikle, Under Secretary of Defense from 1981 to 1988 acknowledged that in the first three/four years of the Reagan administration, "there was a general shyness and hesitation, a reluctance to make a more concerted effort, to provide more instruments and tactics to freedom fighters in Afghanistan."[38]

Sixth, the Reagan administration argued that out of the seven prominent resistance groups based in Peshawar, Pakistan, four of them were Muslim fundamentalists and militarily more powerful in comparison with the other three groups who were known as the moderates. In fact, Washington acknowledged that the fundamentalists organizations were anti-United States and that they did not deserve the large-scale U.S. aid. In this regard, remark of a former U.S. ambassador to Afghanistan is very insightful when he said, "I personally would not like to see a fundamentalist Afghanistan. But that is for the Afghans to decide. If we start that game, it is going to end badly."[39] The administration wanted to support the moderates or the traditionalist groups, but since they lacked the fighting strength, Washington became reluctant to invest a lot of money propping up the fundamentalist organizations. The officials in Washington denied this, but throughout the decade, the moderates maintained far closer ties than the fundamentalists with the west, and many of their leaders had plush exile homes in the U.S. or Britain.[40]

An effective aid program to the resistance also suffered from American and Western differences in their responses to the Soviet invasion of Afghanistan. U.S. officials believed, opposing the Soviets would be a long-term adventure, and that the U.S. and its allies' differences on the issue might be an obstacle on the way to a concerted effort. The Carter, and later, Reagan administration officials feared that the domestic and international concern may soon fade and consequently that support for the long-term measures needed to counter the Kremlin may soon erode. Warren Christopher, Carter's Deputy Secretary of State had cited the short-lived Western response to Moscow's 1968 invasion of Czechoslovakia. In his view one of the lessons of Czechoslovakia was that the response needed to be determined and also the duration.[41] Secretary of State Edmund S. Muskie admitted that ". . . the public perception of the significance, gravity, and importance of the Soviet invasion will fade here, in Europe, and elsewhere around the globe, and our efforts to continue pressure on the Soviets—to continue to exact a price from them—may well begin to fade because of the lack of will."[42] So, in the beginning, aid program to the Afghan resistance largely depended on the Western responses to the Soviet action.

Some strategic analysts in the United States argued that providing aid to the Afghan resistance meant nothing but bringing them "closer to assuring the annihilation of much of the nation." Since it was impossible to dislodge the Soviets from Afghanistan, the argument goes, it would be morally justifiable for Washington not to escalate the aid program. The supporters of this argument believed that :

> *To aid the Afghans now is not to offer them a better chance of relief from oppression but rather to improve their prospects for near extinction. To intensify Afghan suffering in the hope of making the Soviet Union pay a price verges on a kind of racism.*[43]

Another pretext for the people who advocated low-level aid program was that the resistance groups were divided among themselves. Former U.S. ambassador to Kabul pointed out "the lack of a centralized organization, the lack of unity, contributes to the American difficulties in dealing with the resistance."[44] Some U.S. officials argued that the guerrillas' biggest problem was not lack of weapons, but "internal feuding."[45] Others were of the opinion that the tribal insurgents were without proper education and training to operate the sophisticated weapons given by the United States. However, American analysts concluded that the small arms and lower technology were more compatible with the low-intensity guerrilla warfare.[46]

Cost was another constraint on policy. This was especially true at a time of acute concern over the U.S. budget deficits and their effects on the economy and, so, opponents of higher levels of aid to guerrilla movements had a ready argument at hand. Some people in Washington were also concerned about the deterioration in U.S.-Soviet relations. They argued that increased American aid to the resistance would be an obstacle in the way to improving relations with Moscow. There was also an argument that "increasing arms aid to the resistance would jeopardize U.N.-sponsored diplomatic negotiations for a Soviet withdrawal."[47] So the officials in the Reagan administration in the first four years were reluctant to make a concerted effort to provide more instruments and tactics to the Afghan resistance forces.

Making a Policy

Like all other international upheavals and issues, Soviet invasion of Afghanistan had divided the Washington bureaucrats and policy-makers into two camps. There appeared two tracks of opinion with some believing that the Soviets would never leave Afghanistan. Afghanistan in this view was doomed to become a Soviet satellite, no matter whatever pressure Washington exerted against Moscow at bilateral level or through aid to the Afghan resistance. The other view was premised on the belief that military pressure could drive them out or even "a little covert military and financial support to the Afghan Mujahiddin can transform Afghanistan into a Soviet Vietnam."[48] Those who believed in the former, as identified in the previous chapter, came to be known as liberals or moderates, whereas the believers of the later hypothesis were termed as hard-liners, conservatives. By the end of the first term of the Reagan administration i.e. 1984, the hard-liners' view won out, and the American supplies to the Afghan resistance increased in both quantity and quality; thus the American policy turned towards a "winning strategy" intended to "bleed" more and more Soviet troops and ultimately drive them out from that country.

How did the United States evolve a policy towards that goal? It is to this question that now we turn.

Reagan administration had inherited a covert aid program for the Afghan resistance from its predecessor Jimmy Carter. From its very inception, the administration knew that the Soviets were in defensive position in Afghanistan and that they were already bogged down in a guerrilla war in a mountainous country. Clearly, the ball was in the Reagan's court, and Washington had two options. Should the U.S. press for a negotiated settlement intending a Soviet pull out and in exchange recognize the Babrak Karmal's puppet communist regime in Kabul, and stop supporting the resistance? Or should the U.S. keep on supplying covert arms and money to the rebels and continue to insist on unconditional withdrawal? According to a senior official of the Carter administration: "If you help Afghan insurgents who have no hope of winning, then you are sending them to slaughter? On the other hand, if you get over that moral hurdle, you can go all out and really bleed the Soviets, even if you can't beat them."[49] The Reagan administration had definitely been attracted to the second option of bleeding the Soviets, and for that matter, at the cost of the Afghan lives; crossing the "moral hurdle."

It seems that from the beginning of the Soviet occupation of Afghanistan, a small group of people in the Reagan administration had supported a low-level aid program for the rebels. But the real support for a moderate aid had essentially come from certain corners of the Congress. A diverse policy options were developed among the lawmakers and academia in the United States. But interestingly, up to 1983, nobody within or without the Reagan administration believed that the Soviets could be pushed back. Apparently, American policy was aimed at increasing the cost to Moscow of its invasion, so that in a certain point of time, they would negotiate with the resistance. As early as October 1980, a leading Senator argued that

> *United States inaction on Afghanistan is no guarantee that the Soviet Union would refrain from action against Pakistan. As their charge into Afghanistan demonstrated, the Russians would put pressure on Pakistan if they thought it were in their interest to do so and would manufacture the excuse of American assistance. Moreover, Soviet pressure on Afghanistan would be more effective if there were no American resistance to counter it. Significant military aid (would) show that we have emerged from the shadow of Vietnam as a confident, prudent power . . .* [50]

Similarly, other Congressmen argued that the international environment was not conducive to the much debated possibilities of Soviet retaliation against Pakistan because of the latter's role of channeling arms to the rebels. Senator John Heinz (R-Pennsylvania) wrote ". . . the situation in Poland makes a major military invasion of Pakistan strategically unfeasible. Soviet military planners are not fools. They are unlikely to intervene in Pakistan beyond minor border harassment—and increased military aid is unlikely to alter the situation either way."[51] So it is evident that in spite of a "no threat syndrome" to Pakistan, very limited aid was channeled to the rebels in the early years. The CIA's "no-win" policy was regarded as at best able to extract a heavy price from the Soviets. Political analyst felt that "the idea behind funneling international assistance to the insurgents was to make the Soviet Afghan expedition as prolonged and politically and militarily as expensive as possible."[52]

The year 1982 marked a "year of serious debate" mostly because of two major developments in Washington. Many people in the Reagan administration, and especially in the Congress, had started talking about the American aid and arms to the Afghan resistance. In a hearings of the Senate Committee on Foreign Relations on March 8, 1982, Thomas Goutierre's opinion was supported by many people in the United States not only as an American policy of increasing the cost to the Soviet Union, but also was seen as a major strategic advantage for Washington. Goutierre pointed out that to ignore the Afghan struggle was a foolish repudiation of American self interest because the Afghans are defending the Persian Gulf, which is vital to our security. At the moment, they are better than an American RDF because they are an instant deployment force, already fighting and successfully barring Soviet expansionism. They are pinning down nearly 100, 000 creak Soviet troops, thus restraining the USSR in Poland and relieving intolerable pressure on Pakistan and Iran.[53]

Another major development of 1982 regarding the U.S. policy towards the Afghan resistance was the introduction of a policy statement in the American Senate. In fact, it was the first sign of a bipartisan Congressional support for the people who were fighting against communist regimes throughout the world. This resolution was not inspired by "hawks" or "bleeders" within the Reagan administration, but rather by a Vietnam veteran, known in Washington circle as a liberal-Democratic Senator Paul Tsongas. The resolution clearly stated that the United States should give effective material assistance to the Afghan Mujahiddin "and that it was wrong to give them enough to fight and die, but not enough to prevail." But as the CIA and the State Department had their own agenda of a low-level aid program, they were successful in blocking and delaying this resolution for two years. Later in October 1984, the Congress passed this resolution contrary to the policies of some people in the CIA and the State Department.[54]

In the meantime, the United States stepped up the quantity and quality of aid and weapons to the resistance. A little more advanced weapons, such as bazookas, mortars, grenade launchers, mines and recoilless rifles were supplied. There was an internal debate between those who wanted to draw more and more Soviet troops into Afghanistan, and those who sought a more cautious approach. The two groups had reached a common ground and, accordingly, increased the U.S. aid. It is important to note that this decision was taken at a time when the Soviet leadership, especially General Secretary Yuri Andropov had started talking about the Geneva negotiation being pursued under Diago Cardovez, U.N. Under Secretary General. U.S. officials were also firmly convinced by this time that the Soviets were completely in a defensive in the war front and that the American intelligence reports had confirmed Moscow's intention not to increase the troop level in Afghanistan beyond 115, 000. One official remarked, "after more than three years, the Soviets find themselves embroiled in a counter-insurgency campaign that cannot be won with the current force level."[55]

The hard-liners in the Reagan administration were getting stronger by this time. Commenting on a Soviet official's remark of the increased American aid, a senior administration official had said, "Good, I'm glad they're feeling it." It is true that the stepped up American aid had increased the cost of war to the Soviets. But the "hawks" in Washington were never satisfied with the level of U.S. aid. They were always out to raise the cost to the Soviets more. One official's remark in this regard is very insightful when he said: "I couldn't believe that after all we had said about helping the guerrillas and being tough on the Russians, we weren't really doing much to help. It was outrageous."[56]

Among the U.S. government agencies, the most outspoken "bleeders" emerged in the Department of Defense. By the mid-1983, Elie Krakowski, the Pentagon's director of regional defense, became confident that the "Soviets could be forced by military means to withdraw their troops from Afghanistan." In an hour-long interview with the present author, Professor Krakowski claimed that from the very beginning he was advocating an escalated aid program for the Afghan resistance. But it was the State Department and the CIA who were very skeptical about this idea. The main issue confronting the Reagan administration was the fear that the Soviet might retaliate against Pakistan. In the State Department, a top intelligence officer, Morton Abramowitz was the first person to be pushed by the administration to review its policy towards the resistance and helped to initiate a strong lobby in the Congress and the White House. Now that it was Congress, the Pentagon, and the National Security Council (NSC) supported this idea. Krakowski acknowledged that the Assistant Secretary of Defense Richard L. Armitage played a crucial role in this regard.[57] In a previous interview with *The Wall Street Journal,* Krakowski had revealed that: "We moved from a typical containment approach in the 1980 to the first case ever since World War II of actually reversing a Soviet invasion."[58]

Since it was a covert operation, not much was known to the common people about the quality and quantity of money and arms supplied by the United States. But in 1983, several top officials of the Reagan administration visited Pakistan and talked about the American support to the Mujahiddin. On July 3, Secretary of State George P. Shultz, addressing a cheering crowd of Afghan refugee at a camp near Khyber Pass, Pakistan said:

> *We are with you . . . you fight valiantly and your spirit inspires the world . . . the United States has, does, and will continue to stand with you. You can be sure—and I wish to state this with the greatest emphasis—that how best we can bring home to the Soviets the cost of*

their invasion of Afghanistan, will remain a top priority item for the U.S. government.[59]

Within months, Defense Secretary Casper W. Weinberger visited Pakistan and reinforced the American stand by saying, "we will do all that we can."[60] In December 1983, in a conference in Washington, Zbigniew Brzezinski told the audience that the United States should step up its aid to the resistance. He argued that the continued reliance on Soviet-made or Soviet-designed weapons was causing them "operational and logistical problems."[61] In spite of all these high sounding wordings, most officials in the Reagan administration remained in a state of dilemma about a "winning strategy" in Afghanistan.

It was by the end of 1984; Washington had reached to a conclusion that the Soviet could be pushed back from Afghanistan. In fact, the last months of the year witnessed a "structural change" in the broader outlines of a policy framework of the Reagan administration's escalated aid program for the Afghan resistance. This policy not only emerged as a consistent and invigorated one in the coming years; it also subsequently developed into a winning strategy for the United States over the other superpower, the Soviet Union. So the making of a policy towards the Afghan resistance had a broader meaning for the U.S. and the world community as well. It had a greater repercussion in the international geo-political environment, which ultimately transformed the fate of Soviet Union and brought about a rapid change and by and large, a new world order. Then what were the factors that transformed the American perception of "making a costly war for the Soviets" to "an winning strategy," then making Afghanistan a Soviet Vietnam? In other words, what did the U.S. policy-makers see in Afghanistan that influenced them to invest lots of money and American prestige against a superpower, in a guerrilla war dominated by anti-American Muslim fundamentalists, and that too, in a distant tribal land in the heart of Asia?

Guerrilla Effectiveness

Perhaps the first and foremost cause of the U.S. escalated aid program was influenced by the guerrilla effectiveness. By the end of 1984, the Reagan administration had recognized the achievements of the resistance forces that were determined to fight against a superpower for an indefinite period. The Reagan aides had become convinced that even without substantial U.S. assistance, the rebels had proved their viability and potential to carry out an effective struggle. For the Afghan rebels, it was a *Jehad,* a "holy war to the last man." The Mujahiddin, during this period had not only kept the countryside under their control, but also showed "an impressive ability to carry the war into Afghan cities."[62] Washington recognized the resistance potential. President Reagan observed "for four long years the brave Afghan people have held the might of Soviet occupation forces at bay." The President remarked, "the Islamic fighters in a far away land have given new meaning to the words courage, determination and strength. They have set the standards for those who value freedom and independence anywhere in the world."[63]

In fact, from the beginning of the Soviet occupation, although they were not properly armed, the morale among the guerrilla was high. It was obvious that with the limited assistance of foreign aid and arms, their struggle would be more effective and at the same time they would be more organized; not as a political groups, but as a rebellion against the foreign domination. As such the Afghan people are by nature independent and fierce. In spite of their large-scale poverty, and the Soviets bombing on their villages, they were never discouraged. By 1984, the resistance proved that they were self-assured and determined to carry out their struggle against the Soviets for an indefinite period. Their strength in combat operation often amazed the foreign reporters who visited that country. The Western analysts of the war admitted that the Afghans have lived up to their tradition of independence, what the Viceroy of India, Lord Lawrence, said on the eve of the Second Anglo-Afghan War (1878-80): "The Afghan will put up with poverty and even insecurity of life but he will never tolerate being governed by foreigners." The Reagan administration had to recognize the resistance that had been growing stronger and cohesive enough to carry out a war with its own version of Dien Bien Phu. So it was the guerrilla effectiveness in the battlefield, more than anything else, which ultimately brought about a greater American involvement.

Role of Western Media

Role of Western media about the Afghan war was very critical throughout the 1980s. As very few people in the West understood Afghan politics, culture, and society before the Soviet invasion, it was the Western press that brought Afghanistan to the limelight and made it a "strategic storm center" between the East and the West. Undoubtedly, American reaction to the Soviet action was very sharp, and Moscow was taken by Washington as a test case only because of Afghanistan, but, had the Western media not bothered about it, American reaction would have been short-lived. And international community would have resumed business as usual within a short period of time.

As stated earlier, most parts of Afghanistan were under the control of the resistance, which by itself was not only appealing to the West, but also enabled the Western reporters to visit inside Afghanistan for a better coverage of the war. Many non-government and humanitarian organizations such as Medecins sans Frontieres, were encouraged by the United States and the West, which set up their networks in the resistance-controlled areas inside Afghanistan. These sources regularly pictured the war in the West and to a great extent helped mobilize the Western public opinion in support of the resistance.[64] It is interesting that several accounts of the Western correspondents' about the war tended to confirm one another. Several Western countries, including France and the U.S. also helped establish radio transmitters in the Afghan-Pakistan border areas and inside Afghanistan to mobilize Afghan people in support of the resistance.[65]

Wider publicity of the Afghan war was made in the U.S. academia, press, and the electronics media. In several press reports, resistance demands for the need for more and more sophisticated weapons were highlighted. In the U.S. Congress, Afghanistan became a priority agenda. The Reagan administration came under pressure from the liberals and more obviously, hard-pressed by the conservative elements. The quality and quantity of weapons increased, and the Congressional allotment for the Afghan rebels went up.

A War without American Troops

Many people within and without the Reagan administration were pleased by the fact that the Afghan war against the Soviets was being fought without direct involvement of the American troops. All that the U.S. had to do was to maintain a secret pipeline of arms by CIA, and invest some money in a proxy war. This was a policy first advocated by President Carter, and latter, the Reagan administration increased its involvement only through the CIA.[66] Reagan's CIA Director William Casey was committed to worldwide subversive networks against the Soviets. He insisted that the American policy had to be consistent: "the effort to aid anyone fighting communist had to be universal. The Soviet supported subversion worldwide; the United States could do no less."[67]

Since there was no direct involvement of American troops, and arming the Afghan rebels was paying off well in terms of making the war costly for the Soviets, the demand for an escalated aid program increased both from the liberals and conservatives in the Congress. It also to a great extent, counted on President Reagan's popularity at home. In fact, after Vietnam imbroglio, Americans had been increasingly sensitive about their troop involvement in a foreign land, especially in the far away Asia. So the Afghan war was considered as an opportunity not only to the intelligence apparatus in the U.S., but also to the common people. For many Americans, Afghanistan was a "God-given opportunity to kill Soviets, without any US lives being endangered."[68] Above all, the Afghans were ready to fight and die on their own against foreign usurpers. In fact, many of them had been fighting for years without outside assistance. As one Afghan put it, "It is not up to Washington whether we fight or not; it is up to Washington whether we will fight with reasonably good weapons or with stones."[69] These Afghan feelings naturally helped create an opinion in Washington to increase its aid for the resistance.

Taking Revenge

With the guerrilla effectiveness, many decision-makers in the U.S. Congress as well as some CIA officials felt that it was a great opportunity to take revenge of American defeat in the Vietnam War. The most outspoken supporter of resistance in the American Congress was the House member Charles Wilson, a Democrat of Texas. "I viewed this operation as an opportunity to defeat the Soviets in the battle field," Wilson said. "I looked at it this way: We lost 58,000 men in Vietnam. The Russians have lost maybe 25,000 in Afghanistan. I figure they owe us 33,000 dead." Charles Wilson had made several trips to Pakistan and once inside Afghanistan with the rebels. He had always pushed the Congress for an increased American aid.[70]

Among the CIA officials, Director William Casey himself was committed to "bleeding" the Russians in Afghanistan. In fact, Casey wanted to prove that the Agency under his leadership was clean and more effective than the image it had after the Vietnam humiliation, post-Watergate investigations, and a lots of firings and doubts. Afghanistan was seen by the CIA as an opportunity to test itself in a protracted war against the Soviets. Personally Casey hated communism. Like his other colleagues, "he regarded Afghanistan as the place where America could be avenged for its defeat in Vietnam. The Soviets must pay a high price in blood for their support of the North Vietnamese . . ."[71] It is evident that though the CIA was often criticized for not doing enough for the resistance, the hawkish elements in the Agency had supported more and more American aid to exact more and more price from the Soviets. The anger against the Soviets because of the latter's role in Vietnam was not confined within the governmental agencies. It was equally prominent in the Academia as well. An outspoken supporter of the resistance argued "the warmest years of détente were those during which the Soviet Union was providing very overt assistance to the Vietcong and North Vietnamese."[72] So the increasing aid to the Afghanistan guerrilla was partly a result of taking revenge against the Soviets for the latter's support to the insurgents in the Vietnam War.

Apart from these reasons, and most importantly, the conservative elements in Washington argued that by defending themselves and their families, the Afghan rebels were fighting "America's war," thus keeping the Soviet troops bogged down in a protracted war, exposing its vulnerability in terms of the limits of force in furthering Soviet foreign policy, and, above all, relieving unlimited pressures to Washington in other fronts, such as Central America. So, in this sense, the Afghan resistance served the American geopolitical interests in the region. Washington recognized that providing moral and material assistance to those fighting against the Soviets was the best way to deter Moscow's geopolitical encroachments.[73] Further, American analysts concluded that by failing to provide effective assistance to the Afghan rebels, "the United States was seriously undermining its credibility among other political groups resisting the Soviet imperialist ambition."[74]

In retrospect, some U.S. official reveals that the 1980s guerrilla war against the Soviets in Afghanistan was viewed as a strategic advantage for Washington in many ways. The Afghan resistance groups, most of who were dominated by militant Muslim fundamentalists, were regarded as an instant force against the Soviet troops. Given the United States' image of the Muslim fundamentalist, guerrilla casualties hardly mattered in Washington.[75] What the U.S. policy-makers saw was an opportunity to "use Islam against communism."[76] So without the involvement of the American troops, only by "spending some money," U.S. was in a position to severely drain the Soviet resources. So it was felt that with the increased aid to the resistance, increased price could be extracted.

Finally, the increasing bi-partisan support in both Houses of the American Congress paved the way for substantial aid to the Afghan rebels. In early October 1984, both the House and the Senate passed resolution saying that 'it would be indefensible to provide the freedom fighters with only enough aid to fight and die, but not enough to advance their cause."[77] This support of the legislators finally compelled both the liberals and conservatives in the Reagan administration to move towards the making of an American policy that witnessed since 1945: to reverse the Soviet's "gain" in different parts of the world.

Conclusion

The preceding discussion concludes that after looking at several pluses and minuses for supporting a guerrilla war in Afghanistan, the United States finally succeeded in making a policy. It can be stated that Afghanistan, with its geostrategic and geopolitical situation in the heart of Asia, offered the greatest advantage to the United States to get involved in a protracted war in a distant land. Undoubtedly, several factors counted for the American decisions, but the common features were the guerrilla effectiveness, non-involvement of American troops, and taking revenge against the Soviets in the context of the superpower relationship. Pakistan's role was also very critical in influencing American decisions towards the Afghan resistance. Because, without Pakistani support it was simply not feasible on the part of the United States to channel money and arms to the resistance.

However, by the end of 1984, the stage was set for an U.S. escalated aid to the resistance. The Soviets were already searching for a way out of the protracted war that was draining their resources. But the "bleeders" in Washington had already started "steering the wheel," who wanted greater Soviet involvement, more troops, and a prolonged war. The war continued.

Notes and References

1. Secretary of State Alexander Haig's remarks in the Department of State Press Release, 176, May 29, 1981. Also see Department of State *Bulletin*, July 1981, p. 15.
2. U.S. Department of State *Bulletin*, April 1981, p. 10.
3. *The Economist*, June 6, 1981, p. 3.
4. This idea is evident in several statements of the U.S. government officials. For instance, see "Developing a Cooperative Security Framework," *Current Policy*, No. 152, U.S. Department of State, Bureau of Public Affairs, Washington D.C., March 24, 1980, and United States Foreign Policy Documents, 456, 1981, p. 844.
5. Riaz M. Khan, *Untying the Afghan Knot: Negotiating Soviet Withdrawal*, Duke University Press, Durham, 1991, pp. 23-24.
6. Agha Shahi, Pakistan's Security and Foreign Policy, Progressive Publishers, Lahore, 1988, pp. 202-203.
7. See "An Interview with Zbigniew Brzezinski" *The Wall Street Journal*, January 15, 1980.
8. *Middle East International*, March 9, 1984, p. 14.
9. *The New York Times*, March 7 and November 17, 1982.

10. George P. Shultz, *Turmoil and Triumph: My Years as Secretary of States,* Charles Scribner's Sons, New York, 1993, p. 382.
11. Department of State Daily Press Briefing, January 20, 1982, in the *American Foreign Policy Current Documents,* 1982, pp. 782-783.
12. U.S. Congress, House Committee on Appropriations, Hearings before the Subcommittee in Foreign Operations and Related Agencies. *Supplementary Appropriations for 1982,* 97th Congress, 2nd session, May 13, 1982, pp. 1-77.
13. Admiral Thomas Moorer and Alvin Cotrell, "The Search for U.S. Bases in the Indian Ocean," *Strategic Digest,* New Delhi, January 1981, p. 30.
14. James Reston, "Kissinger on Afghan Crisis," *The New York Times,* January 4, 1980, p. 23. Also see, *American Foreign Policy Current Document,* 1982, p. 942.
15. For example, Rosanne Klass, Director of the Freedom House (and editor of *Afghanistan: The Great Game Revisited*), and Andrew L. Eiva, Federation for American Afghan Action, supported the "hawkish" elements in the Reagan administration and were always in support of the escalated U.S. involvement in the Afghan war. The role of the NGOs is evident in their writings in several newspapers, magazines, and a couple of Congressional Hearings.
16. For instance, see the statements of President Reagan and his officials in the *American Foreign Policy Current Documents,* 1981, pp. 835-849.
17. See the testimony of Andrew L.Eiva, Executive Director, Federation for American Afghan Action, to the Republican Platform Committee's National Security Subcommittee on August 13, 1984, at Dallas, Texas. Also see *The International Herald Tribune,* April 18, 1988, and John H. Lorentz, "Afghan Aid: The Role of Private Voluntary Organizations," *Journal of South Asian and Middle Eastern Studies,* Vol. 9, No. 1 and 2, Fall and Winter, 1987, p. 103.
18. *The Wall Street Journal,* February 16, 1988, p. 1.
19. George F. Kennan, on Washington's Reaction to the Afghan Crisis: "Was This Really Mature Statesmanship?" *The New York Times,* February 1, 1980.
20. Zbigniew Brzezinski, *Game Plan: A Geostrategic Framework for the Conduct of the U.S.—Soviet Contest,* The Atlantic Monthly Press, Boston, 1986, p. 225.
21. *The Wall Street Journal,* January 2, 1980, p. 3.
22. Bob Woodward, *Veil: The Secret Wars of the CIA 1981-1987,* Simon and Schuster, New York, 1987, p. 79.
23. U.S. *Department of State Bulletin,* February 1986, p. 2.
24. Bob Woodward, *Veil: The Secret Wars of CIA 1981-1987,* p. 295.
25. *The Washington Post,* January 10, 1981. For a comprehensive analysis of the U.S. perception on the Afghan war, see Robert L. Canfield, "Western Stakes in the Afghanistan War," *Central Asian Survey,* vol. 4, no. 1, 1985, p. 130.
26. Richard P. Cronin, *The United States, Pakistan and The Soviet Threat to Southern Asia: Options For Congress,* Report No. 85152F, Congressional Research Service, The Library of Congress, Washington D.C., September 1985, p. 21.

27. Hedrick Smith, "Tough Talk: Muscle Flexing Is Very Popular; But Its Effects May Be Less So," *The New York Times,* January 27, 1980.
28. *The Wall Street Journal,* April 9, 1984, p. 9. Also see Raymond W. Copson and Richard P. Cronin, "The Reagan Doctrine and its prospects," *Survival,* Vol. 29, No. 1, January/February, 1987, p. 45. For the Pakistani concern of the Soviet retaliation, see Marin Strmecki, "Can the Afghan Rebels Win?" *National Review,* Vol. 38, No. 12, July 4, 1986, p. 34.
29. J. Bruce Amstutz, *Afghanistan: The First Five Years of Soviet Occupation,* National Defence University, Washington DC, 1986, p. 356.
30. *Ibid,* p. 357.
31. Mohammad Yousaf and Mark Adkin, *The Bear Trap: Afghanistan's Untold Story,* Jang Publishers, Lahore (Pakistan), 1992, p. 25.
32. J. Bruce Amstutz, *Afghanistan: The First Five Years of Soviet Occupation,* p. 357.
33. *The New York Times,* April 18, 1988, p. 11.
34. For a sound argument of CIA's attitude to the arms supply to the Afghan resistance, see Angelo Codevilla, "The Reagan Doctrine—(As Yet) A Declaratory Policy," *Strategic Review,* Vol. 14, No. 3, Summer 1986, p. 25.
35. *Ibid,* p. 19.
36. *The International Herald Tribune,* April 18, 1988.
37. "Playing With Afghanistan," editorial, *Strategic Review,* Vol. 14, No. 4, Fall 1986, p. 8.
38. *The New York Times,* April 18, 1988, p. 11.
39. Former U.S. Ambassador Robert G. Neumann's comment in Ralph H. Magnus ed. *Afghanistan Alternatives: Issues, Options, and Policies,* Transaction Books, New Brunswick (USA) and Oxford (UK), 1985, p. 211.
40. *The Wall Street Journal,* December 27, 1984, p. 16.
41. *The Wall Street Journal,* January 7, 1980, p. 1.
42. Secretary of State Muski's statement in the *Current Policy,* No. 194, "Afghanistan Briefing," United States Department of State, Bureau of Public Affairs, Washington D.C., June 5, 1980.
43. James A. Nathan, "Don't Arm the Afghans," *The New York Times,* September 6, 1980, p. 21.
44. Ralph H. Magnus, *Afghanistan Alternatives,* p. 211.
45. *The Wall Street Journal,* April 9, 1984, p. 38.
46. Richard P. Cronin, *The United States, Pakistan and the Soviet Threat to Southern Asia,* pp. 20-21.
47. J. Bruce Amstutz, *Afghanistan: The First Five Years of Soviet Occupation,* p. 212.
48. Jagat S. Mehta, "Afghanistan: A Neutral Solution," *Foreign Policy,* No. 47, Summer 1982, p. 151.
49. *Time,* October 26, 1981, p. 47.

50. Bill Bradley, "Arming Afghan Rebels," *The New York Times*, October 1, 1980, p. 27.
51. John Heinz, "Helping the Afghan rebels—carefully," *Christian Science Monitor*, December 16, 1980, p. 23.
52. Bhabani Sengupta, *The Afghan Syndrome: How to live with Soviet Power*, Vikas, New Delhi, 1982, p. 181.
53. Hearing before the Senate Committee on Foreign Relations, *Situation in Afghanistan*, 97th Congress, 2nd session, U.S. Government Printing Office, Washington D.C., March 8, 1982, p. 71.
54. *The Christian Science Monitor*, April 1984. Also see Malcolm Wallop, "U.S. Covert Action: Policy Tool or Policy Hedge?" *Strategic Review*, Vol. 12, No. 3, Summer 1984, pp. 10-11.
55. *The New York Times*, May 4, 1983.
56. *Ibid.*
57. Interview with Professor Elie Krakowski, Harvard University, Cambridge, Mass, March 10, 1995.
58. *The Wall Street Journal*, February 16, 1988.
59. Quoted by Harmon E. Kirby in the Ralph H. Magnus ed. *Afghanistan Alternatives*, pp.150-151. Also see *The New York Times*, July 4, 1983.
60. *The Washington Post*, October 2, 1983.
61. *The Washington Post*, December 13, 1983.
62. U.S. Congress, Senate Committee on Foreign Relations. A Staff Report, *Hidden War: The Struggle for Afghanistan*, 98th Congress 2nd session, April 1984, U.S. Government Printing Office, Washington D.C., 1984, p. 19.
63. U.S. *Department of State Bulletin*, February 1984, p. 34.
64. For example reports by Edward Girardet of *Christian Science Monitor*, Aernoout Van Lynden, Gerard Chaliand and others who followed the several times inside Afghanistan. For a precise but insightful comments, see Thomas T. Hammond, *Red Flag Over Afghanistan: The Communist Coup, the Soviet Invasion, and the Consequences*, Westview Press, Boulder, 1984, pp. 164-165.
65. J. Bruce Amstutz, *Afghanistan: The First Five Years of Soviet Occupation*, pp. 215-217.
66. President Carter had ruled out any American military involvement in Afghanistan. U.S. Congress, House Committee on Foreign Affairs, Subcommittee on Europe and the Middle East, *An Assessment of the Afghanistan Sanctions: Implications for Trade and Diplomacy in the 1980s*, 97th Congress, 1st session, April 1981, U.S. Government Printing Office, Washington D.C., 1981, p. 22. A leading American scholar at the time supported the view that the U.S. and the West should provide arms to the resistance but "not men." See Louis Dupree, *American Universities Field Staff Reports*, No. 37, 1980, p. 7.
67. Bob Woodward, *Veil: The Secret Wars of the CIA 1981-1987*, p. 216.

68. Mohammad Yousaf & Mark Adkin, *The Bear Trap*, p. 63.
69. *U.S. News and World Report*, July 7, 1980, p. 27.
70. In fact, the CIA and Moscow's estimate of the Soviet deaths in the Afghan war was not more than 15,000. Again, Wilson's comment has been quoted from a 1988 interview. See Tim Weiner, *Blank Check: The Pentagon's Black Budget*, p. 158, and Bob Woodward, *Veil: The Secret Wars of the CIA 1981-1987*, p. 316-317.
71. Mohammad Yousaf & Mark Adkin, *The Bear Trap: Afghanistan's Untold Story*, p. 79.
72. Thomas E. Gouttierre, "The Role of Perceptions Concerning U.S. Interests in the Afghanistan Resistance," in Ralph H. Magnus ed. *Afghanistan Alternatives: Issues, Options, and Policies*, p. 19.
73. George P. Shultz, "New Realities and New Ways of Thinking," *Foreign Affairs*, Vol. 63, No. 4, Spring 1985, pp. 707-713.
74. Jiri Valenta, "To Halt Afghan War," *The New York Times*, December 29, 1983, p. 19.
75. For instance, see Selig S. Harrison, "Obstacles To Deal Over Afghanistan," *The Times of India*, December 24, 1983. When Harrison objected before a senior US intelligence official about Washington's policy of "fighting to the last Afghan," the official "shrugged," saying, "the Afghans love to fight."
76. Interview with Robin Raphel, Assistant Secretary of State for South Asia in the Clinton Administration, University of Illinois at Urbana-Champaign, February 23, 1995. In 1980s, Robin was in different positions in the American Embassies in New Delhi, Islamabad, and London.
77. *The International Herald Tribune*, April 19, 1988.

5
The Reagan Doctrine and its Impact on Afghanistan

You are not alone freedom fighters. America will support you with moral and material assistance, your right not just to fight and die for freedom, but to fight and win freedom.
—President Ronald Reagan, State of the Union Address, February 4, 1986

Afghanistan is considered as a covert operation success story in the attempts by the United States to roll back Soviet power in the Third World. While many believe that the huge Soviet domestic, political, and economic problems played a crucial role in Moscow's decision to get rid of Afghanistan, the massive U.S. military aid along, including sophisticated anti-aircraft missiles to the Afghan guerrilla, had enormous importance in determining the final outcome. For that reason, the Reagan Doctrine—designed not only for the containment of communism in the Third World, but also to compel Moscow to retreat from its own ideology and military philosophy—was thc final American politico-military and geo-strategic maneuver in the closing phase of the cold war. Naturally, it had a tremendous impact on the guerrilla war in Afghanistan, and the Soviets had only four options left: (1) to get out of the country, (2) to face a continual blood-bath for its troops, (3) to escalate its presence and (4) to initiate an offensive strategy, including hot pursuit or even an attack against Pakistan. Soviet leader Mikhail Gorbachev decided to pull the Soviet soldiers back. But pulling back from Afghanistan had a larger meaning for the Soviet Union and the world in terns of superpowers competition and carried fallout in the communist ideology. Therefore, withdrawal of Soviet troops from Afghanistan marked a turning point in the global balance of power and a triumph of American foreign policy.

What, then were the determining factors that shaped an American doctrine? And what were the results and consequences? This chapter shows that, very often, the decision-makers in Washington were guided by a conservative agenda meant to prolong the war. The Reagan doctrine was, undoubtedly, a combined response to the Soviets in international trouble spots such as Nicaragua, Angola, Mozambique, Ethiopia, Cambodia, but Afghanistan was the most prominent "strategic storm center" among all other "proxy-war" fronts. Because it was here that the United States was involved in a guerrilla war with the Soviet Union on its own border.

It may be stated that the Reagan Doctrine was the culmination of the hard-liners agenda in Washington. By the time in 1986 that the doctrine took shape, the conservative thinkers had already arrived at a conclusion that there was no way out for the Soviets in Afghanistan. They rightly believed that the only thing Moscow could do was to withdraw its troops. The Reagan doctrine provided them a valuable opportunity to play a very assertive and aggressive role against the Soviets. Like the "victory" of Zbigniew Brzezinski in the Carter administration that created a very sharp reaction against the Soviet occupation of Afghanistan in December 1979, the enunciation of the Reagan Doctrine left no one in doubt that Washington's policy of dealing with the Soviets was getting tough. It is, however, important to note that the Reagan Doctrine was not confined to the U.S. policy towards Afghanistan; rather, it was a global American strategy to contain and push the Soviets back from its recently acquired positions in the globe. In this sense, the new doctrine was one step beyond the previous American "doctrines"[1] of an earlier geopolitical era, which were only designed for the containment of communism. For Afghanistan, the message from Washington was quite clear: Moscow should reconcile itself to giving up recently acquired positions of influence in Kabul. Undoubtedly, Washington had a clear cut goal in Afghanistan: to drive the Soviets out of that country, and, therefore, the Reagan doctrine had a special implication on the American policy of arming the Afghan resistance forces. And since the enunciation of an American doctrine was viewed as a "victory" of the conservative elements in the United States, it is necessary to look into the contents of the doctrine as well as the role of conservative elements in the Reagan administration in the context of the developments in Afghanistan and the Southwest Asian region.

Doctrine Takes Shape

The Reagan doctrine was developed during 1985-86, but its origin can be traced back to the 1980 elections. Ronald Reagan's victory in the 1980 Presidential election was marked as the victory of the people who believed in greater American strength and power. It also marked the end of the Vietnam syndrome in American foreign policy. About two years later, on September 23, 1982, *The New York Times* stated that: "as administration officials explain the theory of prevailing, it means pushing Russian influence back inside the borders of the Soviet Union with the combined pressure of a military buildup along with diplomatic, economic and propaganda measures." Within the Reagan administration, officials felt the need of a "broad American strategy" to maximize pressure on the Soviets. In early 1983, President Reagan signed a National Security Directive, NSDD-75, which was designed in line with the conservative agenda. The directive primarily focused on economic pressure against and military competition with the Soviet Union, but, later, it was considered as a "step forward" on the way to making an American

Doctrine.[2] It means that the Reagan administration viewed the American-Soviet rivalry in terms of ideological stability and economic strength in the Soviet system. Few months before the signing of the NSDD-75, in a major address at London's Westminster Hall, on June 8, 1982, Reagan "hailed the inevitable triumph of democracy and the growing crisis of totalitarianism." The President emphasized that

> *. . . I believe we live now at a turning point. In an ironic sense, Karl Marx was right. We are witnessing today a great revolutionary crisis—a crisis where the demands of the economic order are conflicting directly with those of the political order. But the crisis is happening not in the free, non-Marxist west but in the home of Marxism-Leninism, the Soviet Union. It is the Soviet Union that runs against the tide of history by denying human freedom and human dignity to its citizens. It also is in deep economic difficulty. The rate of growth in the national product has been steadily declining since the 1950s and is less than half of what it was then. The dimensions of this failure are astounding . . . What we see here is a political structure that no longer corresponds to its economic base, a society where productive forces are hampered by political ones. The decay of the Soviet experiment should come as no surprise to us. Wherever the comparisons have been made between free and closed societies—West Germany and East Germany, Austria and Czchoslovakia, Malaysia and Vietnam—it is the democratic countries that are prosperous and responsive to the needs of their people.*[3]

In another occasion on March 8, 1983, for the first time President Reagan used the famous words "evil empire" to the Soviet Union and said: "I believe that communism is another sad, bizarre chapter in human history whose last pages even now are being written."[4] With the passage of time, Washington's perception of Moscow continued to change, making the Soviets more and more vulnerable in American eyes. Administration officials increasingly saw the Soviet "overextension in the developing world as a major strategic vulnerability."[5]

As early as May 7, 1983, an editorial of *The Washington Post* entitled "Reagan Doctrine," disclosed that the Reagan administration was committed to arming the guerrilla movements and that it would be based on "what kind of a government they are opposing." The editorial mostly focused on Central American insurgency, but so far as the administration's commitment to opposing the anti-communist guerrilla warfare was concerned, Afghanistan was the most distinct American agenda. Because within the administration, American policy goals towards Afghanistan were more clearly defined than any other resistance movements opposing the Soviet communism. Moreover, unlike divisive debates over the administration's desire to provide covert military aid to rebel groups fighting the Sandinista government in Nicaragua or Marxist rule in Angola, Congress had, by the end of 1984, achieved a sort of consensus on providing more assistance to the Afghan rebels.

But in spite of Congressional prodding for the Afghan resistance, it was viewed that the real threat to the U.S. interests essentially came from the Western hemisphere, rather than the distant land of Afghanistan. And that is what most directly influenced the emergence of the Reagan Doctrine. After the successful American invasion of Grenada in 1983, which was supported by neighboring democratic countries, advocates of forceful U.S. action to reverse the Soviet third world gains were greatly encouraged.[6] Then, during 1984-85, the Reagan administration increasingly started talking about the anti-communist guerrilla movements throughout the world and the American aid to the "freedom fighters." It was also felt by this time that the global balance of power what the Soviets had termed "the correlation of forces" was shifting against Moscow and that "American style democracy was once again ascendant as the wave of the future."[7]

Among administration officials, Reagan's Secretary of State George P. Shultz emerged as the most outspoken advocate of the Reagan Doctrine. In early 1985, Shultz had told the Senate Foreign Relations Committee that: "Experience shows we cannot deter or undo Soviet geopolitical encroachments except by helping, in one way or another, those resisting directly on the ground."[8] But his most explicit remarks were delivered at the Commonwealth Club in San Francisco on February 22, 1985 in which Shultz spoke on "America and the Struggle for Freedom," a speech, he claim, that came to be known as the Reagan Doctrine. He emphasized that the United States support to the anti-communist insurgencies throughout the world was "not only out of our historical sympathy for democracy and freedom but also, in many cases, in the interests of national security." Shultz's remarks was designed to reverse and challenge the very basis of the Brezhnev Doctrine which enunciated that "once you're in the so-called socialist camp, you're not allowed to leave," and which had been unwillingly conceded by the United States during the cold war years.[9]

The idea of "raising the temperature" in the Third World insurgency against the Soviets was not confined to the State Department and the White House. Many leading figures in the other governmental agencies also started talking about the need for an aggressive American policy as they looked at the problem from the point of view of increasing Soviet vulnerability on almost all fronts. It was viewed that "As anti-Soviet insurgencies are a problem for Moscow's foreign policy, so they are an opportunity for Washington's."[10] William Casey, Reagan's CIA Director, in a speech in New York on January 9, 1985, proclaimed:

There are over 100,000 Soviet troops in Afghanistan, 170,000 Vietnamese troops in Cambodia, and 40,000 Cuban troops in Africa. This is worldwide military aggression directly and proxy. That and the horror of it is the bad news. The good news is that the tide has changed. Today in Afghanistan, Angola, Cambodia, Ethiopia, and Nicaragua, to mention only the most prominent arenas, hundreds of thousands of ordinary people are volunteers in irregular wars against the Soviet army or Soviet supported regime. Whereas in the 1960s and 1970s anti-

Western causes attracted recruits throughout the Third World, the 1980s have emerged as the decade of freedom fighters resisting Communist regimes.[11]

In the meantime, bipartisan support in both Houses of Congress paid off well in providing a moral boost to the idea of the Reagan Doctrine. In many other national and international issues, Democrats were reluctant to accept Reagan's Republican's agenda. But in resisting communism in the Third World, even the liberal Democrats came forward to support the President. In mid-1985, a leading Democratic Congressman wrote that his party colleagues needed to be more forthright about expressing their "view of the inherent immorality of the Soviet system . . . Democrats need to recognize that Soviet repression and communist tyranny are not a distant memory but a living nightmare. It is a nightmare in the valleys of Afghanistan . . . in the jungles of Southeast Asia . . . in the street of Poland . . . It means resisting Communist expansionism in the third world by providing arms and aid to non-Communist forces, such as those in Afghanistan and Cambodia, resisting invasion and occupation of their countries."[12] In fact, this growing Democratic support enabled the Reagan administration to increase its aid programs for the resistance movements against the Soviets in various parts of the world. In the opinion of a former Reagan administration official, this increasing Democratic involvement in the Republican agenda helped "turning the Reagan Doctrine into an operational reality," without which, he emphasized, "the doctrine would have remained a rhetorical flourish, not a policy being implemented around the globe."[13]

But the most inspiring response for the anti-communist insurgents had come from the President Reagan himself. The President, in his February 4, 1986, State of the Union address, openly declared his willingness to support and aid guerrilla movements resisting Marxist regimes throughout the world—dubbed in certain circle in Washington as Reagan Doctrine or "roll back policy." The President said: "You are not alone freedom fighters. America will support you with moral and material assistance, your right not just to fight and die for freedom, but to fight and win freedom."[14] However, at this juncture, it is worthwhile to note that the Reagan Doctrine was not specifically meant for the rebels fighting the Soviets in Afghanistan. Rather, it represented Washington's policy of providing aid to guerrilla movements resisting Marxist regimes in the Third World. But significantly, as it had become a policy framework for the administration and aid to Afghan rebels was a part of it, policy-makers in Washington became tempted to put greater pressure to make the Afghan war more costly for the Soviets and, ultimately, to turn towards a winning strategy.

In another development, President Reagan told the Congressional Intelligence Committee early in 1986 that the United States' covert program of military aid to the Afghan rebels was aimed at removing Soviet forces from Afghanistan "by all means available."[15] In fact, by this time, the conservative lobby had become so strong in the Congress and elsewhere that it was a sort of necessity on the part of President Reagan to declare a kind of U.S. policy goals in Afghanistan. By declaring these American objectives, the President not only justified supplying more and better arms to the rebels, but also signaled to those in the Congress who wanted to do more that Reagan was on their side. It was obvious that the demand for a more concerted effort for money and arms would come from the hawks after a declaratory policy by the President.

The "Bleeders" Won

While the White House and the State Department officials were busy in promulgating a strategy to undo the Soviet "gains" in the Third World as a whole, a small group of officials in the Pentagon, and a group of legislators in the Congress focused on the implications of the Reagan Doctrine in Afghanistan. They believed that the rebel victory was eminent and that only military pressure could drive the Soviets out of Afghanistan. So they never attempted any political solution through negotiation. As such, many of them had been advocating a greater American involvement and investment in the Afghan war since the early 1983.[16] The changing environment and mood in Washington only provided them to reinforce their demands. These groups, in fact, did not want a deal or any political settlement over Afghanistan, rather they wanted to draw the Soviets deeper into that country so that the Russians could be made easy military targets.[17]

The main initiator of this policy was President Carter's National Security Advisor Zbigniew Brzezinski, who, even in the "Reagan era," was very much instrumental in policy making process.[18] His former student at Columbia University, Elie Krakowski, was by now a special assistant to the Assistant Secretary of Defense for International Security Policy Richard Perle, who never supported a political initiative in Afghanistan. Perle's other adviser on Southwest Asian Affairs was Harold Rhode, who was also known for his hard-line stand on the Afghan question. These three men represented the Department of Defense in an effort to take over and escalate the war by supplying sophisticated arms to the resistance in Afghanistan. Even these people, especially Rhode, did not believe in the reports of U.S. intelligence about the Soviet intentions in Afghanistan and the region. There were reports that Rhode depended, among others, on an Israeli consultant, Yossef Bodansky whose work on the Soviets, he would say was "superb."[19] The Rhode-Bodansky connection had also troubled Pentagon and U.S. intelligence officials who believed that they exaggerate Moscow's military intentions in Afghanistan. In 1984, Bodansky was even the target of a Pentagon security investigation.[20] In fact, this Pentagon group had its own agenda and they helped create a strong lobby in the Congress and the White House.

In the State Department, Morton I Abramowitz, head of the Bureau of Intelligence and Research, was the only person to support the Pentagon's view of an escalated aid to the Afghan resistance. In an hour-long interview, Elie Krawkoski revealed that Abramowitz not only supported the Pentagon's view, but also impressed many Congressmen and the National Security Council officials about the need for a strong U.S. stand against the Soviets in Afghanistan. Krawkoski observed that the war would have continued for some more years had the United

States not applied a "winning strategy." The CIA and the State Department were wary of Moscow's retaliation against Pakistan.[21] Morton Abramowitz had also helped the Pentagon officials to insert into the Presidential Directive 166, the language needed for an increasing American aid. Accordingly, they wanted to expand the aid program every year to force the Soviet leader Mikhail Gorbachev to decide whether he was willing to pay an ever-increasing price to keep Soviet troops in Afghanistan.[22]

It seems that by the mid-1985, a sort of consensus had been reached among the different agencies of the U.S. government and to implement the Reagan Doctrine with more vigor and zeal. Contrary to the popular opinion of the "dovish stand" of the State Department, Secretary of State George Shultz claimed that he was always in support of increasing American aid to the Afghan rebels. He wrote that by 1985, he felt that the United States "should help the freedom fighters in Afghanistan to be as effective as possible." He also argued that "there was no doubt why the Soviets wanted to leave: the war was bloody, and the resistance by the Afghan mujahiddin was fierce. In March 1985, with Bill Casey pushing hard and with me in full agreement, the President had stepped up sharply our level of assistance to the Mujahiddin."[23] Whatever the opinions and stands of different agencies of the U.S. government, one thing was certain, that is, the U.S. policy of increasing the price for the Soviets for their invasion of Afghanistan. This idea was exemplified in the various remarks and statements of the administration officials. For instance, in the late 1985, expressing the administration's determination and preparedness to increase aid to the Afghan rebels, Deputy Secretary of State said, "for our part, the rest of the world must exact from the Soviets a political price. They must pay for death and destruction they are wreaking daily in Afghanistan."[24]

In the Congress, many lawmakers increasingly supported the Defense Department's efforts to escalate the aid program. Among others, Senator Gordon J. Humphrey (R-N.H.) and Representative Charles Wilson (D-Texas) were the prime Congressional lobby from the very beginning. They not only fought vehemently for more money and arms for the Afghan resistance, they also visited Pakistan several times and helped create popular opposition against the Soviets both at regional and global level. In a press conference in New Delhi, Senator Humphrey stated that the ongoing superpowers relationship was not "normal" and that the United States needed to push harder against the Soviets in Afghanistan. He remarked, "the mujahiddin could be more effective if they were provided with better training, better weapons and better intelligence." About the Congressional support for the U.S. commitment of supporting the Afghan cause, Humphrey said, "they were vigorous and strong and bipartisan in their support of the Mujahiddin." He pointed out that the "Congress has been ahead of the administration in applying the Reagan Doctrine in Afghanistan." Senator Humphrey even went to the extent of saying that he had opposed the nomination of Arnold Raphel as the U.S. ambassador to Pakistan, because the latter had "shown no enthusiasm for applying the Reagan Doctrine."[25]

Similarly, Representative Charles Wilson, a Texas Democrat, was known as "an outspoken hawk whose Congressional district exemplified the Texas wildcat spirit." In 1986, Wilson made three trips to Pakistan to survey the situation and investigate the requirements of the Afghan resistance. In one of his trips, he also visited the rebel-controlled areas of Afghanistan. In fact, Wilson was thé only American lawmaker to have ever made a trip inside the Afghan border during the period of the Soviet occupation of that country. For him, "it was the right war at the right time."[26] Wilson, a member of the House Appropriations Committee, had pushed through a $40 million—virtually by himself—to buy anti-aircraft Oerlikon gun for the Afghan resistance in 1984. Undoubtedly, this sort of initiative had a great impact on the morale of the rebels on the one hand and the indication of the open support in the Capitol Hill on the other. But what is more significant was that the Congress could support and even get out ahead of the administration on the covert action. From the beginning, Wilson viewed the war in terms of defeating the Soviets. "It was a holy war from the very first day," Wilson said, "... I viewed this operation as an opportunity to defeat the Soviets in the battlefield."[27]

The Afghan rebels received nearly universal support from both American political parties. But the people in the Capitol Hill knew that arming or providing money to the rebels did not mean buying them. It had only become a stake for the lawmakers to defeat the Soviets in Afghanistan "by all means." Support was offered even though there was little likelihood that, if the rebels come to power in future, they would establish a democratic government respectful of civil liberties or necessarily pro-American. Human rights groups were never invited/allowed to testify in the Congress on massacres committed by the mujahiddin, even though there were reports from both the Soviets and the rebel's sides of the large-scale human rights violation.

In January 1985, Congress formed the Task Force on Afghanistan to investigate into the guerrilla needs and to put pressure on the administration for the increase of American aid. Senator Gordon J. Humphrey became the Chairman of this House-Senate Joint Task Force. As an ardent advocate of the guerrilla cause, Humphrey played a crucial role within and without the Congress. In spite of Washington's incremental aid program, he had charged the Reagan administration of not doing enough for the Afghan rebels and that the guerrillas "remain critically, tragically and scandalously short" of arms.[28] Now that he himself was the Chairman of the Task Force to see the guerrilla demands. In fact, several hearings of Humphrey's Task Force had embarrassed the Reagan administration by disclosing one shortcoming after another in Washington's military and humanitarian aid program to the resistance, and ultimately it had a great impact on the administration's decision to provide sophisticated weapons, including the Stinger missiles.

The "bleeders" started a "violent campaign" in support of more American arms and aid for the Afghan resistance as well as vigorous implementation of the Reagan Doctrine. They overcame almost all obstacles on their way to a winning strategy. By the early 1986, they initiated their last "struggle" for an appropriate anti-aircraft missile for the resistance by which they believed that the war could be turn into a winning strategy. The opposition to this idea came essentially from the CIA Deputy Director John McMahon. McMahon was worried that the weapons could fall into terrorists hand and, in that case, the U.S. would be compelled to pay heavier price than the idea of "bleeding" the Russians in Afghanistan. But nobody was prepared to listen to his argument. The bipartisan Congressional support and the U.S. public opinion were in favor of providing more arms, money, and intelligence to the resistance.

McMahon was seen as the only obstacle on the way to providing sophisticated anti-aircraft weapons including the Stinger missiles to the Afghan resistance. So, starting from mid-1985, a letter campaign against him continued until his resignation in March 1986. Thousands of letters were received by many Congressmen and different agencies of the U.S. government including the White House to take action against this Deputy Director of CIA. It was virtually became a public campaign. They complained that John McMahon had failed to "carry out effectively the Reagan Administration's policy of effective aid to the Afghan freedom fighters."[29] One of the letters, addressed to Reagan's White House Chief of Staff Donald Regan was very insightful and to some extent outrageous. The letter ask the administration to see "that John McMahon either—

> *Begins immediately to carry out that policy and provide effective weapons and supplies to the Afghan freedom fighters*
>
> *Or gets dismissed and replaced by someone who will carry out that policy.*
>
> *Congress and the American people strongly support the administration's mandate for effective aid to the Afghan freedom fighters. It is John McMahon's job to carry out that mandate.*
>
> *Yet for three years, McMahon has, in effect, pursued his own Afghan policy! He has effectively prevented decisive aid—crucial weapons and supplies—from reaching the freedom fighters.*
>
> *Then, he has covered up his bungled "aid" program by spreading disinformation—telling Congress that the CIA's performance in Afghanistan is "outstanding."*
>
> *Yet, this picture contradicts every independent assessment of CIA arms deliveries to the Afghans!*
>
> *If John McMahon cannot or will not provide effective aid to the Afghan freedom fighters, then he must go!*[30]

From the Congress side also, the conservatives attacked the CIA for what they called its "no-win policy." In retrospect, Congressman Wilson said, "from 1980 to 1984, the CIA was a little gun-shy. They had serious reservations. They did not want to step in another pile of shit. But in '83, '84, we were doubling their requests, insisting that they send anti-aircraft missiles . . . And we won. McMahon's departure was the key to the victory."[31] After about six years of the Soviet occupation, the United States had a clear-cut policy towards Afghanistan: "The bleeders had won. In spirit, and to a large degree in substance, American policy . . . was Charlie Wilson's policy: revenge for Vietnam."[32]

The Stinger

Demand for more and more sophisticated weapons started coming in from both the left and the right of the Reagan administration. Most people who studied the course of the war advocated that the most acute need of the mujahiddin was for a surface-to-air missile to shoot down the Soviet aircrafts. According to them, for years, a lack of effective air defense system allowed the Soviet aircrafts such as MI-24 to assault the insurgents almost at will. For about a year, the CIA had been supplying the rebels with the Soviet made SA-7 portable anti-aircraft missiles, which were said to perform unevenly. Then the next choice went for the British made, radar-guided Blowpipes, Swiss made 20mm Oerlikon, and Chinese built 14.5mm Ziguyac anti-aircraft weapons. These weapons were attractive to the CIA, because they could not be traced to the U.S. But the missiles "quite clearly were not doing the job."[33] Finally, in February 1986, breaking with the past rules of U.S. covert operation—never sending "made in America" arms to allow for "plausible deniability" of U.S. involvement—the Reagan administration decided to send the America made arms, including the Army's most sophisticated infantry anti-aircraft missile, the Stinger.

The Decision. Contrary to the popular opinion, Pakistan's President General Zia-ul-Haq had suggested the supply of the Stinger missiles to the Afghan rebels. Zia conveyed this proposal through a visiting Congressional delegation in Islamabad in summer 1985. The CIA station chief, who attended the meeting, relayed the request to the CIA headquarters, but it was reported that the senior officials decided, "to sit on it."[34] The real pressure against the administration was put by the conservative elements that demanded more money and more arms for the rebels.

The interagency debate over supplying "America-made" weapons had started in the mid-1983. The first proponent of this idea among the administration officials was Ronald I. Spiers, who, as ambassador to Pakistan in 1983, had proposed better arms for the mujahiddin and had sent a cable to then Under Secretary of State for Political Affairs Lawrence S. Eagleburger. This early initiative was stalled, but it had provided the hawks to rekindle the interagency debate over the issue. To the "good fortune" of the "bleeders," in the meanwhile, State Department internal reports warned that there was possibility of "declining battlefield fortunes of the mujahiddin in the face of an accelerated Soviet war effort." The report claimed that due to the introduction of new aircrafts, heavily armed Mi24/25 Hind helicopter gunship, and new tactics of elite *spetsnaz* commandos by the Soviets, the guerrillas were increasingly on the defensive.[35] For Washington, Hind's arrival seemed to demand an American answer.

In the late 1985, Morton Abramowitz visited Pakistan with Michael E. Pillsbury, an aide to a group of conservative senators, who had just become Fred C. Ikle's adviser at the Pentagon. Both of them studied the real guerrilla needs, and became the "proponent of Stingers."

> *Abramowitz came back 'beating the drums' for a strategy of 'shock therapy' to convince Gorbachev that Afghanistan was not, and should not become, 'his war'.*[36]

Again the subject centered in the small "bleeders" group around Fred C. Ikle, then Under Secretary of Defense for Policy, Morton Abramowitz, and the Perle group in the Pentagon, and a couple of Congressmen, including, of course, Sen. Gordon J. Humphrey and Rep.Charles Wilson. These people led the internal bureaucratic struggle against those opposed to sending Stingers to the Afghan rebels. After a couple years in early 1989, Ikle recalls that Congressman Charles Wilson was "a very important catalyst" because "he sort of kicked the bureaucracy," including the Pentagon. He said, "without him, I don't know, the Russians may not have started to withdraw yet."[37] It is true that the Congress was more aggressive than the administration in applying the Reagan doctrine in Afghanistan. In retrospect, Secretary of State George Shultz wrote in his *memoir* that it was Abramowitz who said, "I believe we are not putting significant pressure on the Soviets. We should put in an American weapon: the Stinger."[38]

This group rebutted every argument of opposition to sending Stingers to Afghanistan. For example, to overcome worries about shortages of the weapon, Pillsburry queried the General Dynamics plant in Pomona, California, where Stingers were made, to ask if production could be stepped up, only to get the answer that the plant could and would do so. But the most interesting development was the increasing bipartisan support from the Congress and several private organizations, which made things easier for the Pentagon hawks. In the meanwhile, Pillsbury, with the backing of Ikle, arranged two trips to Islamabad for the conservative members of the Senate and House Intelligence Committee. The purpose behind this was to convince the Congress that the Stingers were very urgently needed by the Afghan resistance and that President Zia of Pakistan was ready to risk the Soviet retaliation if the U.S. supplied them. Finally after recounting all pluses and minuses, on February 25, 1986, the interagency covert operations committee formally recommended sending Stingers to the Afghan guerrillas. It was reported that about 200 Stingers were supplied in September 1986, and 600 in summer 1987, which had proved decisive.[39]

The Constraints. Several obstacles came on the way to sending Stingers to the Afghan rebels. The first and foremost being the fear of "compromising American military technology." The fact was that the CIA ran the covert operation, but the Department of Defense controlled the Stinger missiles. A faction of the Defense as well as the CIA officials feared that the weapon might fall into the hand of the Soviets, and in that case it would have to compromise its own technology. Officials in the Joint Chiefs of Staff argued that if Stingers were supplied to the Afghans, that might reduce the U.S. Army inventories.[40]

Secondly, some officials feared that the missiles might fall into the terrorist's hand, and that they might target American civil airliners. This fear was especially intensified after the first batch of Stingers were sent, when, in 1987 it was reported that the missiles had already fallen into the Iranian Revolutionary Guards.[41] But later evidences proved that the Iranians had obtained the Stingers from the prominent mujahiddin leader Yunis Khalis. Whatever the truth, on October 8, 1987, a Stinger was fired from an Iranian gunboat to an American helicopter patrolling the Persian Gulf.[42] American weapons were finally aimed at the American soldiers. In Pakistan, General Zia-ul-Haq was worried about the possibility of Stingers getting into the hands of terrorist organization and is used against his own aircraft.[43]

Third, in the U.S. intelligence apparatus, a faction of the CIA officials led by the Deputy Director John McMahon were very skeptical about the mujahiddin victory in Afghanistan, and therefore, not in support of supplying Stingers to them. McMahon believed that each U.S. move would be "met with a Soviet counter move, an escalation." He questioned the U.S. policy of "bleeding the Russians" in Afghanistan, and doubted that Washington was putting enough diplomatic pressure to Moscow to leave Afghanistan.[44] In fact, McMahon had resisted the government's decision up to the end. Finally his resignation in March 1986 from the Agency paved the way for the Stingers.

Further, many people in the Reagan administration feared about the possible Soviet retaliation against Pakistan, the conduit for the Afghan resistance. Also from the Pakistani standpoint, the Soviet warning of June 1986 against the introduction of Stingers was taken very seriously. Because this time Moscow had expressed concern over Islamabad's nuclear program as a threat to Afghanistan's security.[45] Apart from this threat to Pakistan's security, officials in Washington were worried about the Soviet offensives in other strategic fronts such as Nicaragua, Angola, Mozambique and elsewhere. It was perceived that the supplying of U.S. sophisticated weapons to the Afghan rebels would encourage the Soviets to initiate "global anti-U.S. terrorism or sending anti-aircraft missiles to rebels in El Salvador for use against the Salvadoran army's U.S.-made military aircraft."[46]

The Weapon. Stinger is a "heat-seeking" radar guided missile, capable of engaging low altitude, high-speed jets, was first developed in the late 1970s by the General Dynamics Corporation. It was specifically meant for American foot soldiers who would use it as the last line of defense against attacking fighter planes in the theaters of war like Central Europe. A portable solder-fired missile, is weights 34.5 pounds when loaded, and is only 5 feet in length. The Stinger is capable of carrying high explosives to a range of 3 to 5 miles in a supersonic speed. It was first made operational in Germany in 1981, and in the following year by the 82nd airborne Division of the U.S. Army. When the United States invaded Grenada in 1983, the missile was considered as a "man-portable" weapon. But it was in Afghanistan that the Stingers were used for the first time against a real enemy of the United States. Describing the effectiveness of the missile, a Pakistani Army/ISI official, who was directly involved in the operation in Afghanistan wrote

> *The trigger was pressed, the missile fired, and the firer could immediately reload, take cover or move away. It is a 'fire and forget' weapon, with no need to remain exposed to guide the missile to its target. Nothing, short of a miracle, could stop the missile, traveling at over 1200 miles per hour, from homing on its target.*[47]

The Impact on Afghanistan. Soon after the mujahiddin received Stingers in the summer of 1986, the course of war changed dramatically in their favor. The Soviet jets and helicopters, which were known as the greatest obstacle to the resistance in air defense system, no longer lingered over attack areas, but made quick entries and exits. The U.S. State Department reported in December 1986 that the Stinger Missile shoot down, on average, one Soviet aircraft per day. Commenting on a State Department report marking the seventh anniversary of the Soviet occupation of Afghanistan, Deputy Assistant Secretary of State Robert Peck disclosed that the mujahiddin had achieved a "significant increase" in air-defense capability and inflicted "an unprecedented rate of aircraft losses."[48] This was however, an exaggeration. But, as nobody knew about the exact Soviet losses, and only the CIA had direct access to the U.S. satellite surveillance data, which could locate and identify aircraft wrecks in Afghanistan, the State Department's estimate was widely believed at that time.

Whatever the U.S. estimates of the resistance success with the Stinger missiles, nobody questioned the effectiveness of the weapon, which undoubtedly turned the tide of the battle. Because, before Stingers were supplied, other anti-aircraft weapons, such as the Swiss Oerlikon, Chinese SA-7s etc. had been only successful in downing no more than twenty aircraft a year.[49] With the Stingers in hand, it was estimated that the resistance were able to destroy at least 270 Soviet aircrafts per year, which included the most hated MI-24/25 gunship.[50]

The Soviet pilots, who had enjoyed complete air domination until Stingers arrived in the battlefield, had to fly much higher which restricted their accuracy and ability to operate in support of their ground troops. In fact, Stingers had a major effect on the war, improving the morale of the rebel forces and neutralizing Soviet air power. Each Stinger costs $75,000, and each Soviet Mi 24 it downs (and there was a success rate of approximately 70 percent) costs $8 million. For every dollar the mujahiddin had raised, the Soviets were compelled to spend approximately ten times more. Commenting on the success of Stingers in changing the course of the war, a Pentagon official observed: "The Stingers made it possible for the Mujahiddin to conduct large-scale combat and logistical operations in the country because the Stinger effectively neutralized the Soviet-Afghan tactical air power. While it was not the factor that turned the tide, it was certainly a key element."[51]

Pursuing an Offensive Strategy

With the increasing Mujahiddin success in the battlefield, on the one hand,

and the changing international environment after the Soviet President Gorbachev's advent to power, on the other, the United States pursued an offensive strategy in Afghanistan. It is true that no single factor was counted on for the American escalation of the war. But it cannot be denied that with Mikhail Gorbachev at the helm of affairs in Moscow, and his enunciation of *Perestroika* and *Glasnost,* along with his "openness" of saying Afghanistan a "bleeding wound," U.S. penetration of Afghan resistance was substantially increased. With the increasingly defensive posture of Moscow and Kabul, their rivals, Washington and Islamabad became more offensive. After 1985, resistance against the Kabul regime was getting stronger, and more organized day by day. The question was that what volume of "temperature" the superpowers would maintain with regard to their respective clients in the changing situation.

U.S. assistance to the Afghan rebels continued to expand after late 1984, reaching $250-280m. in FY 1985, $470m. in 1986, $630m. in 1987, and $600m. in 1988.[52] Up to this time the Chinese and the Saudi Arabian assistance also reached a fairly substantial level.[53] By contrast to the low level aid program of the Carter's and the first four years of the Reagan administration, the year 1985 marked a significant change in Washington's policy. More aid and arms poured in to the mountainous terrain of Afghan battlefields. "Allah and Stingers" became the slogan of mujahiddin, and the course of war changed dramatically in favor of the resistance.

By the time Mikhail Gorbachev came to power as General Secretary of the Soviet Communist Party in March 1985, Afghanistan meant stalemate. The Afghan/Soviet troops made periodic sweeps through the country-side controlled by the rebels, then pulled back to heavily defended base areas. By 1986 Moscow looked for a way to get out of the war through an international agreement of Afghan non-aligned status, but the American conservative lobby in Washington did not allow for an early settlement on these terms. With the changing international environment, Gorbachev understood that an unconditional withdrawal from Afghanistan would send a "contaminated message" to Poles, Estonians, Muslims in Central Asia, and others, intimidated by the Red Army. So, he wanted to carefully pursue a creative diplomacy to achieve a "graceful exit" from Afghanistan without crumbling the Soviet Empire.

But this did not coincide with the United States policy. Washington pushed the hardest to Moscow on all fronts, such as military, political, and diplomatic. And as stated earlier, Reagan Doctrine's goal was not only to contain communism, but also to see that the Soviets face a military defeat from its recently acquired strategic areas throughout the Third World. In other words, the Doctrine was designed to "roll back" the Soviet's gain of the 1960's and 1970's. To achieve this strategic goal, Washington pursued an aggressive posture aimed at the winning strategy.

In the meantime, on November 12, 1987, President Reagan met with the Afghan resistance leaders in the White House and expressed the administration's determination and commitment to their cause. Among the leaders who were honored in the White House were, the newly elected spokesman of the Afghan Resistance

Alliance Mohammad Yunis Khalis, Prof. Barhanuddin Rabani, Prof. Sebgatullah Mojadedi, Pir Sayed Gailani, and others. The President not only reaffirmed American support to the resistance leaders, he also put more emphasis on the need for "effective aid" to them. The leaders also met with several Congressmen and the administration officials.[54] Later, in a reply note dated February 18, 1988, to the Chairman of the Federation for American Afghan Action, President Reagan wrote: "I was delighted to receive the delegation of Afghan resistance leaders . . . The ideal of freedom burns brightly in the hearts of the Afghan people. They are engaged in a life-and-death struggle to throw off the chains of foreign domination and their heritage of independence."[55]

When the curve in U.S. policy towards the resistance started moving "upward," Reagan administration tried to expand supports from all possible channels. With the increasing U.S. aid and reports of more and more Soviet/Afghan casualties, Washington opened another supply "front" for the resistance. In 1986, America's staunch enemy Iran agreed to channel the CIA supplied weapons to the Afghan rebels. It was part of a secret deal. In May, Oliver North, a NSC official, and his old boss, former National Security Adviser Robert McFarlane visited Teheran and made arrangement for the arms shipment through Iran. According to the deal, if Teheran agreed to Washington's term of supplying weapons to the Afghans, the U.S. would provide arms for the Iranians. Iran, which badly needed arms for its continuing war with Iraq, readily agreed to such an American proposal. North and McFarlane gave a gloomy picture to their Iranian counterpart of the Soviet intensions in the region. They argued that their interests were identical, and that the presence of the Soviet troops in Afghanistan threatened them. Iran, which was previously providing a limited aid and arms to only Shiite groups, now agreed to be the conduit for CIA arms. Within weeks, they passed some 100 of the 2,008 TOW anti-tank missiles supplied by the CIA to the Afghans. Later, the National Security Adviser John Poindexter told Congressional leaders "one previously unstated purpose of the secret Iran operation was to open a new supply route to the hard-pressed Afghan rebels."[56]

Apart from this, the United States put more emphasis on the propaganda campaign so that the people around the world would know the Afghan cause. In 1986, the U.S. Information Agency signed a contract with the Boston University to train 30 Afghans about how to use TV cameras to report the war.[57] In fact, during this period, this sort of propaganda campaign had a major impact on world public opinion in favor of the resistance.

By pursuing an aggressive policy against the Soviets in Afghanistan, the United States had to ignore many aspects of the war, such as the Pakistani nuclear program and the "siphoning off" of money and weapons from the CIA pipeline, and, above all, promotion of Muslim fundamentalism in the region.

Overlooking the Pakistani Agenda. While Washington's policy was targeted at the Soviet soldiers in Afghanistan, Islamabad had its own agenda to be pursued. First, by the mid-1980s when the war came to a stalemated situation, Pakistan

President General Zia-ul-Haq started dreaming about establishing a fundamentalist regime in Kabul. Secondly, although Pakistan was active in the United Nation sponsored negotiation, at least "diplomatically," many officials in the military and Inter Services Intelligence (ISI) had second thoughts about the increasing American military and economic aid and Islamabad's own clandestine nuclear program, which the Pakistani feared, would create "misgivings" in their relations with the U.S. once the Soviet troops were withdrawn. U.S. policy towards this Pakistani objective was just to whitewash the truth in implementing the Reagan Doctrine.

One of the conditions the Pakistani authority had put forth before becoming the CIA conduit to the resistance in the early 1980s was that the Pakistani ISI would distribute the arms.[58] The fact that at least three of the seven mujahiddin leaders based in Peshawar—Gulbuddin Hekmatyar, Barhanuddin Rabanni, and Yunus Khalis—were being supported by Pakistan since 1974, long before the Soviets came to Afghanistan.[59] After the Soviet invasion and the subsequent flow of arms and money to the resistance, Pakistani ISI was the sole authority to distribute arms to the political leadership of the guerrillas. It decided which factions in the resistance received which weapons, and in what qualities and quantities. Islamabad had always supported the most militant fundamentalist party known as Hezb-i-Islami of Gulbuddin Hekmatyar.[60] Throughout the decade in the 1980s, including the "era of Stingers," Hekmatyar's party "received more than half a billion dollars' worth of the CIA's weaponry over the years, a heavily disproportionate share, despite his well-earned reputation as a brutal zealot. A man who stood for almost everything the West despises became the biggest beneficiary of the CIA's arms shipments."[61]

The reasons for Pakistani support to Hekmatyar were very much explicit in accordance with Islamabad's ambition of seeing an Islamic and pro-Pakistani, and Afghan nationalist regime in Kabul. The most important factor was that he seemed willing to settle the long-standing border dispute—the Durand Line—between Pakistan and Afghanistan on term favorable to Islamabad, i.e. to forget about the Pashtoonistan issue. More than that, Hekmatyar was suitable for the Pakistani leadership, because he was committed to ending Afghanistan's close relationship with India, an archrival of Pakistan.[62] Pakistan also viewed that a satellite regime in Kabul would open a great deal of opportunity for its trade and commerce as well as its political influence in the Central Asian Muslim Republics.

To the utter surprise of the people outside the world, Pakistani President General Zia-ul-Haq went on record by openly admitting Islamabad's objective in establishing a satellite state in Afghanistan. In an interview with Selig Harrison, weeks before his death, Zia said,

> *We have earned the right to have a very friendly regime there. We took risk as a front-line state, and we won't permit it to be like it was before, with Indian and Soviet influence there and claims on our territory. It will be a real Islamic state, part of a pan-Islamic revival that will one day win over the Muslim in the Soviet Union, you will see.*[63]

Secondly, many people in Pakistan, especially in the military and ISI began to see the Afghan war in support of their advantage partly in terms of the multi-billion dollars American military and economic aid including the highly sophisticated F-16 fighter bombers, and partly the "siphoning off" of weapons and money from the CIA pipeline which were meant for the Afghan guerrillas. The Pakistani military took this advantageous position to strengthen itself, whereas the United States wanted "to strengthen the Pakistani military as the eastern pillar of Western defenses in the Gulf."[64] Above all, the burden of three million Afghan refugees in the Pakistan's border provinces were largely covered by international humanitarian aid; thus without any pressure to Pakistan's economy.

Most importantly, so long as Soviet troops were there in Afghanistan, Pakistan did not have to worry about its clandestine nuclear program. In fact, it was a great opportunity for the Pakistani leaders to develop their nuclear program under the cover of the American support and aid, to Islamabad and to the Afghan resistance. In fact, at the time of the announcement of the American multi-billion dollar military and economic aid package to Pakistan, the Reagan administration was left in no doubt that Pakistan would not desist from its nuclear program.

Moreover, by 1987, United States was convinced that Pakistan had achieved a nuclear capability. In a March 1987 hearing before the House Foreign Affairs Subcommittee on Asia and Pacific, a nuclear proliferation expert of the Carnegie Endowment for International Peace, Leonard S. Spector, remarked that in the "last six years, Pakistan could possess a de facto nuclear arsenal of nearly 20 devices." Similarly, referring to the Pakistani denial of its nuclear program, a leading Senator said, "Quite frankly, we're tired of the Pakistani leadership looking us in the eye and laying us repeatedly."[65] Even, Reagan's Deputy Assistant Secretary of State Robert Peck had admitted that the United States could no longer obtain "reliable assurances" from Pakistan that it had stopped producing nuclear explosive material.

But in spite of these periodic criticisms of the Reagan administration's policy towards Pakistan, Washington bypassed it on the ground that that was the only country to be the conduit for the Afghan resistance. And, according to the lawmakers in Washington, the presence of the Soviet soldiers in Afghanistan was considered more important than the Pakistani nuclear program. They argued that the Congress was reluctant to punish the Pakistanis "too harshly" because of their support in funneling American aid to the Afghan resistance forces. In fact, by this time, nothing was more important to Washington than the presence of Soviet troops in Afghanistan. It was, however, a shortsighted policy given the view that, in the long run, Pakistani nuclear bomb could be a security threat to the United States, at least indirectly.

The "Fallout" of U.S. Policy. The "success" of the Reagan Doctrine in Afghanistan to "roll back" the Soviets came only when the United States bypassed all other limitations in the war. By providing unaccounted money from the CIA pipeline, Washington not only knowingly allowed its millions of dollars to be "siphoned off" both by the Pakistani ISI and Army as well as the resistance leaders, but also helped create "monster" among the mujahiddin in the form of militant Islamic fundamentalists. It has been reported that over the years, the "theft and diversion" from the CIA pipeline ranged from $600 million to $1 billion or even more. Among the U.S. government agencies, CIA estimated in 1986 that the loss was 20 percent; National Security Council (NSC) figured 30 percent and placed the amount roughly $900 million, State Department and the members of Congress accounted the loss as 50 percent.[66] However, the United States was prepared to pay this price in order to further its interests in the region, especially in implementing the Reagan Doctrine. But what "misfired" was that the legacy of weaponizing a people. When the CIA pipeline started shrinking, the veterans of the war multiplied. The "Arab Volunteers" created disturbances in turning up in the cadres of Islamic movements in Egypt, Algeria, Jordan, the West Bank and many other places. Many of them have been implicated in anti-Western and ant-U.S. activities including the bombing of the World Trade Center in 1993. A Federal News Service report of October 28, 1994, datelined London, found that the Afghans veterans were leading new "Islamic Holy Wars" in different parts of the world. It declared: "US authorities believe there may be as many as 200 Arab 'Afghans' in the New York-New Jersey area alone, all viewed as potential terrorist in the aftermath of the World Trade Center bombing (in 1993)."[67]

But what is more important is that the United States also ignored the human factor in the Afghan war. U.S. policy not only failed to create an Afghan leadership in the aftermath of the Soviet withdrawal, but also left the "weaponized land" to fend for itself; thus the result was an unending civil war and loss of unaccountable human lives. When the civil war broke out in the country, U.S. officials said, "once the civil war come to an end, Washington would consider some economic aid for the Afghans."[68]

The "Success" of the Reagan Doctrine

In his *memoirs,* Reagan's Secretary of State George Shultz claimed that the Reagan Doctrine was a victory over the Brezhnev Doctrine in the context of the superpowers rivalry in general and Afghanistan in particular. Shultz emphasized that the Soviet withdrawal from Afghanistan was a triumph over the Brezhnev Doctrine, which claimed, "Once a country was in the so-called socialist camp, it was not allowed to leave." He wrote, "if the Soviets left Afghanistan, the Brezhnev Doctrine would be breached, and the principle of "never letting go" would be violated. The stakes were high."[69] Undoubtedly, the Reagan Doctrine had a tremendous impact on the Soviet decision to withdraw its troops under the cover of U.N.-sponsored agreement concluded in Geneva in April 1988, but it was not the sole factor in Moscow's decision.

Moscow had never declared its occupation of Afghanistan in terms of Brezhnev Doctrine like it did in case of Czechoslovakia in 1968 and the Eastern

European nations and the Warsaw Pact countries in the late 1940s and early 1950s. So, since there was no implementation of the Brezhnev Doctrine in Afghanistan, there was no question of "breaching" it.

Secondly, the Soviets never attempted to occupy the entire Afghan territory. What they had planned to do was to protect the communist government from an ever-increasing offensive guerrillas being supported by Pakistan, United States, China, and many other Muslim countries. A Soviet expert on Afghanistan, Yuri Gankovsky outlined that from the beginning, the Soviets had "no need to control all Afghanistan territory" and therefore, about 100,000 troops were considered sufficient to control the "main administrative centers and two or three economic and strategic centers."[70] And since, Moscow did not have any "grand design" in Afghanistan, it neither attempted to attack the neighboring countries nor did it raise the Pashtoonistan issue in an apparent attempt to dismember Pakistan, as many people had feared at the time. In that case, the United States would have come under intense pressure to provide meaningful support to both Pakistan and the Afghan resistance—on conditions unfavorable to Washington.

American Sovietologists believed that Afghanistan was never covered under the Brezhnev Doctrine, which was only "applicable to Eastern Europe and to Warsaw Pact countries which were integrated inside the Soviet empire during the late forties." Dmitri Simes, a Senior Associate of the Carnegie Endowment for International Peace, said,

> The Soviets, from the very beginning, were saying two contradictory things about Afghanistan: first, that the revolution was going to be reversible; but, second, that the revolution was not necessarily Socialist and communist in nature, but rather national democratic—even despite the fact that the revolution was led by the Communist Party.[71]

It was argued that the Soviets had never focused on bringing Afghanistan under the Brezhnev Doctrine and that of late, they were "emphasizing that it is up to the Afghan people to determine their own fate." The expert concluded that he was "not persuaded it had a lot to do with Afghanistan to start with . . ."[72]

Third, in spite of repeated demands by the Red Army high command for more troops or an attack against Pakistan, the Soviet leadership in Moscow had refused to allow such a move.[73] Instead, the Soviet leaders gave several indications, especially after the death of Brezhnev, and more, after the advent of Gorbachev, that they were seeking a negotiated settlement over Afghanistan.

From this and other analysis of the Soviet aims and objectives in Afghanistan, it can be inferred that the war in Afghanistan was not a confrontation between the Reagan Doctrine and the Brezhnev Doctrine. Rather, from a pure American perspective, it can be argued that the Reagan Doctrine was a "success" in reversing the Soviets "gain" in the Third World countries in general and Afghanistan in particular. For President Reagan, Afghanistan was naturally a foreign policy victory greater than Grenada.

Conclusion

Afghanistan was considered a "success story" of the Reagan Doctrine, because the position was quite clear: there was Soviet occupation. And American policy was appropriately targeted at that. It was because of this position that the American Congress was always ahead of implementing the Reagan Doctrine than the administration itself did. No Soviet move since the deployment of missiles in Cuba had so united the Americans. Congress had even voted more money than the administration sought for the Afghan rebels. American policy-makers idea that a sustained pressure would convince Moscow that it "could not win and so must withdraw" came true. And the Soviet Union for the first time in history after the Second World War withdrew its forces, because it could not afford to fight a war economically, politically, and diplomatically against the will of a people, supported by a superpower, the United States.

What emerges from above is an example of American policy of opposing Soviet power successfully. In Vietnam, the U.S. policy resulted in failure. The United States had to withdraw, paving the eventual rise of Soviet influence. In Afghanistan, it was the opposite. The Reagan Doctrine proved a success against Soviet intervention in its own backyard. In this case, sustained American pressure with consistent local pressure assured American success. It was not just the victory of American power over the Soviet power. The American resistance in Afghanistan ultimately sealed the fate of the Soviet Union, with its ideological menace, political ambitions, and over arching military power.

Notes and References

1. For instance, the Truman Doctrine and the Eisenhower Doctrine.
2. Peter Schweizer, *The Reagan Administration's Secret Strategy That Hastened the Collapse of the Soviet Union,* Atlantic Monthly Press, New York, 1994, pp. 130-132.
3. Cited in Peter W. Rodman, *More Precious Than Peace: The Cold War and the Struggle for the Third World,* Charles Scribner's Sons, New York, 1994, pp. 262-263.
4. *Ibid,* p. 264.
5. *Ibid,* p. 266.
6. Stephen S. Rosenfeld, "The Guns of July," *Foreign Affairs,* Spring 1986, pp.700-01.
7. Angelo Codevilla, "The Reagan Doctrine—(As Yet) A Declaratory Policy," *Strategic Review,* Vol. 14, No. 3, Summer 1986, p. 17.
8. Secretary of State George P. Shultz, "The Future of American Foreign Policy: New Realities and New Ways of Thinking," Statement before the Senate Foreign Relations Committee, January 31, 1985, U.S. Department of State, *Current Policy,* No. 650, Government Printing Office, Washington D.C.
9. George P. Shultz, *Turmoil and Triumph: My Years as Secretary of State,*

Charles Scribner's Sons, New York, 1993, p. 525. Also see Shultz's address before the Commonwealth Club of San Francisco, February 22, 1985, U.S. Department of State, *Current Policy,* No. 659. Government Printing Office, Washington D.C. In a separate article Shultz wrote that, "The American people have a long and noble tradition of supporting the struggle of other peoples for freedom, democracy, and independence . . . If we turned our backs on this tradition, we would be conceding the Soviet notion that Communist revolutions are irreversible while everything else is up for grabs . . ." George P. Shultz, "New Realities and New Ways of Thinking," *Foreign Affairs,* Spring 1985, p. 713.

10. Mark N. Katz, "Anti-Soviet Insurgencies: Growing Trend or Passing Phase?" *Orbis,* Vol. 30, No. 2, 1986, p. 386.
11. William J. Casey, "Collapse of the Marxist Model: America's New Calling," speech to the Union League Club, New York, January 9, 1985, in Herbert E. Meyer ed., *Scouting the Future: The Public Speeches of William J. Casey.* Washington D.C., Regnery Gateway, 1989, p. 171; quoted in Peter W. Rodman, *More Precious Than Peace: The Cold War and the Struggle for the Third World,* p. 271.
12. Stephen J. Solarz, "It's Time for the Democrats to be Tough-Minded," *The New York Times,* June 30, 1985, p. 27. Also see, Christopher Layne, "The Solarz Report: Hawks, Doves, and Democrats," *New Republic,* May 19, 1986, p. 11.
13. Peter W. Rodman, *More Precious Than Peace: The Cold War and the Struggle for the Third World,* p. 270.
14. *The New York Times,* April 18, 1988, p. 11. Also cited in Raymond W. Copson and Richard P. Cronin, "The Reagan Doctrine and its prospects," *Survival,* Vol. 29, No. 1, January/February 1987, p. 42.
15. *The New York Times,* June 19, 1986, p. 7.
16. Interview with Prof. Elie Krakowski, Harvard University, Boston, March 10, 1995. Prof. Krakowski was a former Pentagon official.
17. Reagan's Secretary of State George P. Shultz wrote that the "hard-liners did not really want the Soviets to leave Afghanistan; they preferred to "bleed" them to death through the indefinite continuation of war." See George P. Shultz, *Turmoil and Triumph: My Years as Secretary of State,* p. 1092.
18. In a personal correspondence dated April 17, 1995, Brzezinski wrote to the present author: "I was involved in the critical Reagan administration's discussion regarding the Stingers."
19. *New Statesman,* Vol.3, March 14, 1986, p. 18.
20. *Ibid.*
21. Interview with Elie Krawkoski, March 10, 1995.
22. *The Wall Street Journal,* February 16, 1988, p. 1.
23. George P. Shultz, *Turmoil and Triumph: My Years as Secretary of State,* p. 692 and p. 1087.

24. U.S. *Congressional Record,* Senate, December 18, 1985, p. 37522.
25. Senator Gordon Humphrey's Press Conference, New Delhi, April 14, 1987.
26. Bob Woodward, *Veil: The Secret Wars of the CIA 1981-1987,* Simon and Schuster, New York, 1987, p. 79.
27. Tim Weiner, *Blank Check: The Pentagon's Black Budget,* Warner Books, New York, 1990, p. 157-158.
28. *The Washington Post National Weekly Edition,* February 20-26, 1989.
29. An incoming mail to the White House dated January 13, 1986. Documents obtained from the Ronald Reagan Library, Simi Valley, California.
30. *Ibid.*
31. Tim Weiner, *Blank Check: The Pentagon's Black Budget,* p. 159.
32. *Ibid,* p. 160.
33. *The Wall Street Journal,* February 16, 1988, p. 1.
34. *Ibid.*
35. *The Washington Post National Weekly Edition,* February 20-26, 1989.
36. *The Wall Street Journal,* February 16, 1988, p. 1.
37. *The Washington Post National Weekly Edition,* February 20-26, 1989.
38. George P. Shultz, *Turmoil and Triumph: My Years as Secretary of State,* p. 692.
39. *The Wall Street Journal,* November 30, 1987, p. 20.
40. *The Wall Street Journal,* February 16, 1988, p. 31.
41. *The Wall Street Journal,* October 14, 1987, p. 5.
42. Tim Weiner, *Blank Check: The Pentagon's Black Budget,* p. 151.
43. Mohammad Yousaf & Mark Adkin, *The Bear Trap: Afghanistan's Untold Story,* Jang Publishers, Lahore (Pakistan), 1992, p. 181.
44. Bob Woodward, *Veil: The Secret Wars of the CIA 1981-1987.* p. 104.
45. Pakistan had suspected a possible Soviet air strike against its nuclear facilities at Kahuta. See, Riaz M. Khan, Untying the Afghan Knot: Negotiating Soviet Withdrawal, Duke University Press, Durham, 1991, p. 175.
46. *The Washington Post National Weekly Edition,* February 20-26, 1989, p. 6.
47. Mohammad Yousaf & Mark Adkin, *The Bear Trap,* p. 175-176.
48. *The Washington Post,* December 17, 1986, p. 12. Also see Michael Jones, "The Lessons of Afghanistan," *Policy Review,* No. 40, Spring 1987, p. 32.
49. Aaron Karp, "Blowpipes and Stingers in Afghanistan, One Year Later," *Armed Forces Journal International,* September 1987, p. 38.
50. *Ibid,* p. 40.
51. *The Washington Post National Weekly Edition,* February 20-26, 1989.
52. John H. Lorentz, "Afghan aid: The Role of Private Voluntary Organizations," *Journal of South Asian and Middle Eastern Studies,* Vol. 9, No. 1 and 2, Fall/Winter, 1987, p. 1987, p. 103. Marin Stremecki, "Can the Afghan Rebels Win?" *National Review,* July 4, 1986, p. 54. *The New York Times,* February 11, 1989, p. 5. *The International Herald Tribune,* April 18, 1988.
53. Zia ul-Haq reportedly said that "the Chinese support is as important as the

U.S. support." See *The Washington Post,* January 24, 1980. In the first five years of the war Chinese assistance was estimated at over $400 million and up to 1986 Saudi support was totaled $500 million. See *The Washington Post,* June 20, 1986.

54. White House Documents obtained from the Ronald Reagan Library, Simi Valley, California.
55. *Ibid.*
56. *The Wall Street Journal,* November 24, 1986, p. 64.
57. *The Wall Street Journal,* August 22, 1986, p. 16.
58. The CIA had agreed to the Pakistani condition that all arms and money would be distributed by the ISI. Training programs for all sophisticated weapons including Stinger missiles were also conducted by the Pakistanis, not by the Americans. See Mohammad Yousaf & Mark Adkin, *The Bear Trap,* pp. 116-117.
59. For a vivid picture of the growth of resistance movements in Afghanistan, see Olivier Roy, *Islam and Resistance in Afghanistan,* Cambridge University Press, Cambridge, 1986. For the initial Pakistani support under Zulfikar Ali Bhutto, see pp. 75-76. Also see, Testimony of Bernett Rubin in the U.S. House of Representatives, *United States Policy Towards Afghanistan,* Hearing before the Subcommittee on Europe and the Middle East and Asia and Pacific Affairs, Committee on Foreign Affairs, 101st Congress, 2nd session, Washington D.C. March 7, 1990, p. 14.
60. For the extent of this Pakistani favoritism to Hekmatyar, see Marvin G. Weinbaum, "War and Peace in Afghanistan: The Pakistani Role," *Middle East Journal,* Vol. 45, Winter 1991, p. 78. Also see Marvin G. Weinbaum, *Pakistan and Afghanistan: Resistance and Reconstruction,* Westview Press, Boulder, 1994, pp. 33-37.
61. Tim Weiner, *Blank Check: The Pentagon's Black Budget,* p. 149.
62. Robert S. Greenberger, "Afghan Guerrilla Leader Armed by the U.S., Hekmatyar, Could Prove Embarrassing," *The Wall Street Journal,* May 11, 1992, p. 6.
63. Selig S. Harrison, "Avoiding Afghan Civil War," *The New York Times,* November 14, 1988, p. 19.
64. Testimony of Bernett R. Rubin, in a hearing before the Subcommittee on Asia and Pacific Affairs of the Committee on Foreign Affairs, House of Representatives, 99th Congress, 2nd session, The Situation in Afghanistan, Washington D.C., May 1, 1986, p. 83.
65. As quoted in *The New York Times,* March 15, 1987, p. 3.
66. Tim Weiner, *Blank Check: The Pentagon's Black Budget,* pp. 152-153.
67. Also see, Thomas W. Lippman, "Aid to Afghan Rebels Returns to Haunt U.S.," *The Washington Post,* July 26, 1993, p. 1.
68. Interview with Robin Raphel, Clinton's Assistant Secretary of State for South Asia, University of Illinois at Urbana-Champaign, February 23, 1995.
69. George P. Shultz, *Turmoil and Triumph: My Years As Secretary of State,* p. 1086.

70. *The Washington Post National Weekly Edition,* April 25-May 1, !988, p. 7.
71. Testimony of Dmitri Simes, in the Hearings before the Subcommittee on Asia and Pacific Affairs of the Committee on Foreign Affairs, House of Representatives, 100th Congress, 2nd session, *Developments in Afghanistan,* February 1988, Washington D.C., February 17 and 25, 1988, p. 63.
72. *Ibid.*
73. Testimony of Barnett R. Rubin in *The Situation in Afghanistan,* May 1, 1986, p. 81.

6

United States and the Geneva Accords

The obligations that we take at Geneva must be balanced by reciprocal obligations taken on by the other side . . . There will be no cutoff of support for the resistance under any other circumstances . . . It is only logical that non-intervention and non-interference provisions should apply to the Soviets too. The Soviets cannot claim a right to aid a faction in the Afghan civil strife just because that particular faction tries to call itself the government of Afghanistan.

—*U.S. State Department Press Report, March 11, 1988*

The Geneva Accords of April 14, 1988 between Pakistan and Afghanistan as two signatories, and the United States and the Soviet Union as two guarantors, were intended to bring peace to the war-ravage Afghanistan. But, not surprisingly, the accords failed to achieve its goal. All parties concerned violated the accords and left Afghanistan in a state of virtual anarchy. It seems, in retrospect, that Afghan peace was not the real purpose of the superpowers, but it was only a part of their game in broad international strategic context. Afghanistan was only made a scapegoat, and the only sufferers were the Afghan people, who are still paying a heavy price of a superpower game of the cold war. The only clause of the accords that was obeyed was the withdrawal of Soviet troops from Afghanistan.

For the United States, the main objective—the withdrawal of Soviet troops from Afghanistan—was achieved by signing an accord. Most people in Washington believed that the accords provided a way for Moscow to a "face-saving escape," and, for the United States, a geo-political retreat of the Soviet Union. Some even speculated that it was a military defeat of Moscow in a guerrilla war, supported by many countries including Pakistan, United States, and China. Whatever the truth might be, it cannot be denied that the United States' policy towards the Afghan resistance had a tremendous impact on both the military effectiveness of the guerrillas fighting the communist regime as well as in determining the Soviet decision to withdraw. U.S. policy over the decade was aimed at increasing the cost to Moscow of its invasion of Afghanistan in anticipating the view that sufficient military pressure could compel Moscow to come to the bargaining table. So, during the period of the Soviet occupation from December 1979 until April 1988, the United States policy towards Afghanistan was to increase the political, military, and economic cost to Moscow by supplying money and arms to the resistance forces. Therefore it was obvious that Washington paid a lip service or maintained at least a half-hearted approach to the United Nation's initiated Geneva negotiations.

Though the main aim of the United States was the withdrawal of Soviet troops, throughout the period during the United Nation's sponsored Geneva talks, Washington neither encouraged nor discouraged the negotiators. This is mostly because of two factors: (1) initially, most people in the U.S. government did not believe that the Soviets would ever leave Afghanistan (see chapter 4), and (2) by mid-1985, when the resistance became more effective after the supply of sophisticated weapons to them, and the Soviets were seen as increasingly on the defensive both on the Afghan war fronts and in the international trouble spots, the conservative lobby became so strong in Washington that the government had to move very carefully towards an accords keeping an eye on the hard-liner's agenda (see chapter 5). However, a section of the U.S. government, namely, the State Department, showed limited support to the ongoing United Nations sponsored negotiations under its various ambiguous terms and conditions from time to time.

It was when the Soviets openly showed their determination to withdraw their troops, even without a "face-saving accord," that the United States caved in. Undoubtedly, by early 1988, President Reagan was at the height of his bargaining power against Moscow; he had achieved everything on Afghanistan that he demanded from the Soviets and no card was left to play. Further, "the last minute" accords at Geneva were also considered as a milestone in President Reagan's role in the Afghan war and a Republican agenda in the upcoming Presidential elections of Vice-President George Bush.

This chapter attempts to show that the mainstay of the U.S. approach towards Afghanistan had not been the negotiations as much as the arms supply to the anti-government resistance forces. U.S. approach was termed as one-track policy of military assistance to the resistance with at best half-hearted support to the U.N. peace initiative.[1] Once the United States felt that the Soviet soldiers were bogged down in Afghanistan and that the fear of a march towards the Persian Gulf or the Indian Ocean had receded, as some officials had envisaged, Washington's policy was to make the war costly for the Soviets by supplying money and arms to the resistance fighting the Kabul regime. In spite of Moscow's periodical hints of a negotiated settlement over the Afghan problem, Washington never came up with a visible plan or showed any serious interests in the Geneva talks. A Congressional analyst observed that over the decade, "U.S. criteria for ending the conflict were never defined in detail. The United States called for a Soviet withdrawal and for the restoration of Afghanistan's independence and nonalignment, but would not, for instance, comment on its terms for an internal political settlement save for stating that the matter was for 'the Afghans to decide."[2]

The Soviet Position

From the very first day of the invasion, Soviets were willing to withdraw their troops under one condition: if Pakistan supported by several other countries, stopped aiding the resistance to the Kabul regime; that means the Soviet troops would be withdrawn if a communist regime in Kabul was secured. This Soviet position had been reflected from its various official and non-official statements.[3] In a major policy statement, soon after the Soviet troops crossed into the Afghan border, President Leonid Brezhnev categorically stated: "I want to state very definitely that we will be ready to commence the withdrawal of our troops as soon as all forms of outside interference directed against the government and people of Afghanistan are fully terminated. Let the U.S., together with the neighbors of Afghanistan, guarantee this and then the need of Soviet military assistance will cease to exist."[4] However, with the increasing opposition by the resistance in the subsequent years, Moscow tried its best to pacify the country with its military might.

After the invasion, Moscow's relentless war against the resistance continued. But it soon realized that there was no military solution to the problem and so, looked for some sort of political solution. Then up to the last moments in Geneva, the Soviet position was based on retaining their communist puppet in power in Kabul and a "graceful exit" from the protracted war. For that reason, they perceived that the outside aid to the resistance forces must stop and therefore, that be made a primary condition in the Geneva negotiations for their troop withdrawal. The Soviets leaderships believed that without outside support to the resistance, a communist regime would remain in power and that their political interests in the country as well as in the region would be protected.

The American Stand

American stand towards a settlement ranged from skepticism to one of "deliberate negligence." That is, Washington did not want to take a lead in the negotiation, rather it would welcome proposals by others. "But as a matter of policy," the State Department spokesman said, the United States believed that the first step "must be the withdrawal of Soviet troops from Afghanistan."[5] President Carter, in a letter to President Tito of Yugoslavia, wrote that after the Soviets pulled out their troops from Afghanistan, the United States would guarantee the neutrality of the country and pledge noninterference.[6] Carter administration officials privately said that it was not wise for Washington to seek talk with the Soviets on hints coming from Moscow because to do so would lend legitimacy to Moscow's allegation that it sent its troops into Afghanistan to counter American, Chinese, and other subversion.[7]

. However, in a major internal development, Carter's Secretary of State Cyrus Vance initiated a genuine proposal for the neutrality of the Persian Gulf and Southwest

Asian region in exchange for Moscow's withdrawal of all its troops from Afghanistan. Vance's proposal offered to join Moscow in an agreement "not to introduce combat forces or mutually threatening bases or facilities in Iran and Pakistan" in exchange for a complete withdrawal of Soviet troops from Afghanistan. But this proposal was blocked by the National Security Advisor Zbigniew Brzezinski, who later wrote that he did not want to "make the Soviet Union in effect the co-guarantor of neutrality in the Persian Gulf region."[8] Certainly, it would have served the interests of all parties concerned, and American interests would have been served the best in the Southwest Asian region with no direct presence of Soviet troops in Afghanistan. Within two months of its invasion, Moscow indicated that its action was a "mistake" and that the Soviets side was interested to talk to the Americans about Afghanistan. By then, Washington was not prepared to accept a "puppet government in place" even though Moscow withdrew all its troops.[9] It may be stated that before the invasion, the United States had never withdrawn recognition to the Afghan communist government of Taraki and A nin. Instead, American aid had continued to Afghanistan until Ambassador Adolph Dubs' kidnapping and murder in Kabul in February 1979. After the invasion, Washington was not prepared to accept a communist government in Afghanistan even in case of an eventual Soviet withdrawal. In fact, after the invasion, the hard-liner's view had gotten an upper hand in the Carter administration, and there was no room left for negotiation over Afghanistan.[10]

The Initial Phase

As the U.S. would not take any lead in negotiation with the Soviets about the possibility of troop withdrawal from Afghanistan, the countries mostly concerned about the problem were the European Community (EC) and Pakistan. The EC was mainly concerned about the phase of détente in the East-West relations, whereas Pakistan feared the presence of over 100,000 Soviet soldiers to their North as a security threat and millions of refugees as burden in its own economy that might make President Zia's narrowly based military regime more vulnerable. For that reason, both the EC and Pakistan opened the possibility of some sorts of political settlement to the problem. However, although they could not achieve anything substantial in the initial phase, they did open the long road to the Geneva negotiations by a United Nations Special Representative, Diago Cardovez.

The first proposal for a peaceful settlement of the Afghan conflict came from the EC. It was because, most of Europe was not in favor of President Carter's punitive measures and sanctions against Moscow in the wake of Afghanistan. For the Europeans, there was no alternative to détente, and, especially, France and the Federal Republic of Germany did not support the U.S. decision to freeze the arms control talks. The EC viewed the United States response as cold war rhetoric against the Soviet Union and believed that Moscow did not pose any threat to their interests in the Persian Gulf region. Carter's decision to arm the Afghan rebels was also severely criticized by the EC, especially by Great Britain. The British felt, from their own experience, that arming the Afghan tribesmen was no guarantee of controlling them. They viewed that "the longer the United States, and even more so China, Pakistan and the Arab States, continue to send arms to the rebels, the longer the Russians will be tempted to stay."[11] For that reason, Europeans wanted to bring about a solution to the Afghan crisis to ease the East-West relations. A proposal put forth by the British Foreign Secretary Lord Carrington stipulated international guarantees for Afghanistan's neutrality if Moscow withdrew its troops. But as the proposal specified free and fair elections, it sounded vague and the Soviets turned it down.[12]

The stakes on the part of Pakistan was not to recognize the communist government in Kabul and to initiate and lead the worldwide condemnation (including in the United Nations) of the Soviet invasion. Pakistan earned international sympathy mostly because it provided sanctuary to about three million Afghan refugees. Again, as described in previous chapters, Islamabad never believed that Moscow would attack Pakistan. Even so, the perception of threat remained, and General Zia-ul-Haq succeeded in popularizing the Afghan cause before the international community, mostly to exact money and sophisticated weapons from the West and the United States. So from the very beginning, Pakistan made it clear that it would not join in any negotiation with Afghanistan so long as Babrak Karmal remain in power in Kabul, because he was the person who came to Kabul "riding a Soviet tank."

Pakistan's Afghan policy was very much influenced by the first ever held extraordinary session of the Islamic Foreign Ministers, convened in Islamabad on January 25-27, 1980 to discuss the Soviet intervention in Afghanistan. The Organization of Islamic Countries (OIC) demanded "immediate and unconditional" withdrawal of the Soviet troops from Afghanistan. Though it was essentially meant to be a propaganda campaign to mobilize and agitate international opinion, it had a far-reaching impact on Pakistan's Afghan policy, especially regarding the question of channeling outside support to the resistance. The OIC resolution also intensified an internal debate in Islamabad on the implications of the Afghan situation and the former's policy towards Kabul. As Pakistan was under military dictatorship of General Zia-ul-Haq without popular support, Islamabad was very sensitive on the Afghan question, and had to develop a cautious policy towards Kabul. Pakistani military and the Inter Services Intelligence (ISI) Directorate felt that "Pakistan could not take the heat on its northern border with Afghanistan without rebuilding its relations with the United States, for which an opportunity seemed exist. The military thinking was partly influenced by its desperate need for modern equipment."[13]

For its part, Soviets never expected to occupy Afghanistan in the way they did the Eastern Europe and the Central Asian Republics in the aftermath of the World War II.[14] So, from the very beginning they showed their interests in a negotiated settlement of the Afghan crisis on which they could withdraw their troops under certain conditions that would allow to leave a communist regime behind.

With this hope, as early as May 1980, Moscow, together with Kabul, showed its first formal interests for negotiations. But they stipulated that the prerequisite for such negotiations must be direct talks between Afghanistan and Pakistan. Pakistan rejected the Moscow/Kabul overtures on the ground that such a dialogue would legitimize the Kabul regime before them. However, Pakistani Foreign Minister Agha Shahi encouraged U.N. sponsored talks on the condition that the Kabul government would not be represented.

Taking account of the Pakistani interests, American "hard-line stand," and the increasingly effective resistance against the Kabul regime, Moscow pressed the Karmal government to drop the idea of government-to-government talks. Moscow also declared that the U.N. could play a role in the ensuing conflict. But internal political development in Pakistan altered the proposed talks to some extent. Agha Shahi, who pressed for the U.N. talks, was severely criticized in Pakistan as well as in the conservative Arab capitals and the United States for failing to include the resistance in the projected talks. He complained that the State Department officials were "giving a hard time" to him. Later, when he was fired from his job, Shahi admitted that the State Department objected to his "encouragement to a U.N. mediating role."[15]

Selig Harrison, a senior associate at the Carnegie Endowment for International Peace quoted Richard Burd, then director of the Bureau of Politico-Military Affairs in the State Department as saying, "we don't trust Shahi at all, we route everything to Zia through General Akhtar."[16] A Pakistani Geneva negotiator later wrote that General Zia along with his Inter Services Intelligence (ISI) chief, Lieutenant General Akhtar Abdur Rahman was almost exclusively dealing with "material support to bolster the Afghan resistance."[17] This implies that even in the initial phase of the Soviet occupation, Washington was more concerned about the support to the Afghan resistance than in a Pakistani initiated negotiated settlement. However, in spite of the American indirect maneuver, Pakistani and Soviet interests led to a U.N. mediating role.

The first United Nations overtures were made by the then Secretary General Kurt Waldheim who sent Javier Perez de Cuellar, then Under Secretary General for Political Affairs, on two missions to Kabul, Islamabad, and Teheran. At the end of his mission, Perez de Cuellar declared that "the Russians want to do something." Since then, Waldheim became confident that the U.N. could play a good-offices role.[18] After Perez de Cuellar became Secretary General, he appointed Diego Cardovez as the Under Secretary General for Special Political Affairs and extended the charge of the U.N. mediation role to resolve the Afghan crisis.

Cardovez initiated first round of proximity talks between Pakistan and Afghanistan at Geneva in April 1982. In this round, "there was agreement on the objective of a complete withdrawal of foreign troops," but Cardovez did not raise the question of a withdrawal timetable. Instead, he decided to test the Soviet intention later.[19] Nothing-concrete came out of the first round talks, mostly because passion were high among the parties involved. No party was seen in a hurry. While Pakistan stood on the point of non-recognition of the Kabul regime, the Afghan side insisted on the government-to-government talks. The Soviet statements showed little flexibility, but firm on the "outside interference" in the affairs of Afghanistan, whereas, the United States was busy preparing a long-term strategy in the Southwest Asian region. On principle, Washington was kept informed by Islamabad on the developments of the Geneva negotiation, but by the time of the first round of talks, American officials were more concerned about the $3.2 billion U.S. economic and military aid to Pakistan and military build up in the Indian Ocean and Persian Gulf region than a sketchy United Nations negotiations.

In Washington, the Reagan administration's high-keyed rhetoric on Afghan question, and the conservative political lobby were getting stronger in support of the resistance. While the administration was divided on many questions relating to the issue, the popular opinion went in support of raising the cost to the Soviets of their invasion. In order to do so, Washington improved its relations with Pakistan and committed to the latter's security in the event of a Soviet aggression. The $3.2 billion aid package to Pakistan and the military buildup in the Indian Ocean and the Persian Gulf region were the clear evidence that Washington was paying more attention to its "strategic stakes" rather than to the United Nation's sponsored talks. The hard-liners in the Reagan administration also wanted to "avenge Vietnam" by raising the cost to Moscow in a prolonged and protracted war.[20] A Pakistani Geneva negotiator later wrote that U.N. special representative Diego Cardovez was mostly concerned about the U.S. attitude. Cardovez "feared growing support for the Afghan resistance and conservative backlash in the United States as a potential obstruction to his efforts; and he discerned in the press reports and leaks about military supplies to the resistance a calculated ploy to encourage hard-liners in Pakistan and to undercut the diplomatic process."[21]

When the question of U.S.-Soviet guarantee on non-interference in Afghanistan's "internal affairs" was raised, Under Secretary of State Lawrence Eagleburger gave a legalistic view by indicating U.S. constitutional requirement for ratification of international agreements.[22] The State Department not only refrained from any diplomatic initiative relating to the Geneva negotiations, but also "cautioned Pakistan against over commitment." Moreover, throughout 1982, Pakistani officials were very much skeptical about the U.S. approach to a political settlement. Much to the distress of the Americans, President Zia categorically stated that Pakistan would support to the Cardovez plan "much against the advice of our close friends. We are seeking a settlement at our own initiative because we know that political pressure must go with military pressure."[23] Pakistani diplomats believed that the U.S. State Department was "much too legalistic" in its approach to the idea of Afghan self-determination.[24] So, it is clearly evident that in the early years of the Afghan negotiations, Washington seemed to be not in a hurry for a quick solution to the Afghan problem and showed its reservation to accept a Soviet sponsored communist regime in Kabul.

Andropov Ignored

Many observers believed that the United States never bothered to test the Soviet intention during 1982-83, and that "the issue before the United States is no longer whether a settlement in Afghanistan is possible but whether this is the best time for one and whether the type of settlement envisaged in the U.N. negotiations would be acceptable."[25] Moscow, during this period had clearly indicated its willingness to bring about a political solution to the Afghanistan problem.

When President Zia-ul-Haq visited Moscow in November 1982 to attend the state funeral of Leonid Brezhnev, he was received by the new Soviet leader, Yuri Andropov. It was no surprise that Andropov was seriously willing to see an Afghan settlement as early as possible. Because, even at the time of the Soviet invasion, as the KGB chief, he had strong reservations about the Politburo's decision, and that over his doubts, the decision had been taken by Brezhnev and his close associates. After his meeting with Andropov, in a press conference in Moscow, Zia declared that he perceived a "new freshness and flexibility on the Soviet side, a recognition of the need for an early resolution of the crisis."[26] Moreover, Andropov emphasized the need for a political settlement disclaiming any Soviet intention to pacify Afghanistan. He also expressed desire to improve relations with Pakistan.[27]

Andropov's seriousness was also evident from the views of U.N. negotiators. After their visit to Moscow in early 1983, U.N. Secretary General Perez de Cuellar and Cardovez became more optimistic about a political settlement. Cuellar declared that he had received "renewed encouragement" from his meeting with Andropov. Andropov had assured that Moscow was ready for "definitive steps," but doubted that Islamabad and Washington would support the U.N. effort. Recounting his conversation with Andropov, Cardovez later described

> *He ended it by holding up his hand and pulling down his fingers, one by one, as he listed the reasons why the Soviet Union felt a solution had to be found soon to the Afghan problem. The situation was harmful to relations not only with the West, but also with socialist states, the Muslim world, and other Third World states. Finally, he said, pointing his thumb down, it was harmful for the Soviet Union internally, for its economy and its society.*[28]

Andropov was not only concerned about the Soviet economy and Moscow's relations with other countries; he was also worried about the Soviet troops who were being killed by the rebels in Afghanistan. For the first time since the invasion of Afghanistan, he recognized that the rebels were strong enough in mountain warfare to pin down the Soviet troops for indefinite period. He saw no benefit to Moscow by occupying Afghanistan. During 1983, a key Soviet official told Selig Harrison several times that "Andropov had been prepared to offer an 8-month timetable in the June round [of Geneva talks] until the Pakistani volte-face. If Yakub had been willing to sign a bilateral agreement with Kabul, the timetable could have been written directly into it."[29]

In retrospect, it seems that the period between April and June 1983 was very much crucial from the point of view of a "breakthrough" in Afghanistan. After the April 1983 round of Geneva talks, considerable progress was reportedly made, and Cardovez claimed that 95% of the agreement was in hand. This optimistic and encouraging statement echoed in several state capitals, and came as an alarm bell to the resistance forces fighting the Kabul regime. The greatest optimism was shown by Pakistani Foreign Minister Yakub Khan. In a press conference in Islamabad, Yakub revealed that Andropov was sincere about a political settlement and that the "Soviet Union seriously intends to withdraw its forces from Afghanistan."[30] Reiterating the Pakistani stand, he also told the Soviets and the U.N. negotiator Cardovez that Islamabad could go ahead with the settlement if Karmal was replaced in Kabul.

Regarding the cut off of "outside aid" to the resistance, Kabul had demanded that it be stopped even before Moscow made a commitment to withdraw. The Pakistani position was that aid would be ended with the stages of withdrawal. Maintaining a balance between these two parties, Cardovez was exploring the possibility that "cutoff would not be initiated until after the signing of the withdrawal agreement but would have to be completed by the start of the withdrawal itself."[31]

Soviet Union, for its part, had not yet given any stipulated timetable for its troops withdrawal, but their public statements and diplomatic activities indicated that they were hoping to reach to an agreement in the June [1983] round of negotiations. Moreover, on May 19, Vitaly Smirnov, then Soviet Ambassador to Pakistan, publicly confirmed Kabul's "willingness to give a timetable for the withdrawal of the total Soviet contingent."[32] Moscow hoped that after a protracted bargaining, the parties would reach to an agreement. Encouraged by the April round, and the "positive developments" aftermath, Cardovez reconvened another round of talks in June.

In the meantime, Yakub visited Washington to discuss the June round of talks. He held extensive consultations with the U.S. officials including Secretary of State Shultz, Under Secretary Eagleburger, and Vice President George Bush. Referring to the criticism of U.S. policy on Afghanistan, Shultz assured his Pakistani counterpart that Washington would not stand on the way of an agreement acceptable to Islamabad and that the United States policy was not to "bleed" the Soviet Union.

But the press "leaks" about the U.S. covert assistance to the Afghan resistance and Pakistan's complicity in facilitating the operation on the eve of Yakub's visit to Washington created a hostile atmosphere on the way to the Geneva process. Though American press was periodically reporting about the secret Afghan operation, it was for the first time that explicit acknowledgment was made of the CIA funneling mortars, bazookas, grenade launchers and other light weapons to the resistance. The timing of the disclosure was viewed as a deliberate effort of hard-liners in the Reagan administration to torpedo the U.N. process.[33] Because Yakub had to meet a hostile press in Washington and later, in the June round, nothing concrete came out of the talks, and Pakistan reversed its previous position and the words given to Cardovez three months ago. Yakub later admitted that Pakistan had to change its posture between April and June because Cardovez's statement of the "95 percent completed." He disclosed that this remark "made it necessary to slow down, in order to deal with the apprehensions among the Afghan refugees and our allies that we were going to sell them out behind their backs."[34]

During the June round of talks at Geneva, both Pakistan and Afghanistan maintained strong positions and the talks were stalled. This is mostly because of the Pakistani deviation from its earlier commitment to Cardovez which Yakub put before Gromiko on their June 9, 1983 meeting in Moscow, which was later described by Cardovez as a "disaster." Pakistani side not only differed about aid cutoff and understanding regarding the replacement of Karmal in Kabul, Yakub now demanded a non-communist government as the precondition for any settlement. Washington never came forward with any specific proposal or showed any interests during this period. Instead, it was widely believed that "a hidden U.S. hand" led Pakistan to differ its stand. Washington maintained that the June round of talks was stalled "on the crucial issue of the Soviets' unwillingness to provide a timetable for troop withdrawal from Afghanistan."[35]

It should not be surprising that the United States put pressure on Pakistan to stall the June round. After all, it was Moscow's problem, not Washington's. It was the Soviets, who were the guilty party, who had occupied Afghanistan with their military might, not the Americans. So it was obvious that Washington did not take any interests in the Geneva negotiations during this period even if there was possibility of a breakthrough. And the mainstay of the U.S. approach remained the arms supply to the resistance rather than negotiations. Referring to the covert CIA operation, Charles Cogan, then Director of CIA covert operation in Southwest Asia, told Selig Harrison on May 8, 1983, that "Pakistan would not conclude the projected settlement in June or ever." Quoting the Pakistani President, he said, "Zia knows how we feel about it. He recognizes that this will be a long, long war and he is committed all the way. He and General Rahman fully accept out view that Pakistan's security is best assured by keeping the Russians tied down there."[36]

In retrospect, it can be safely argued that the Reagan administration was divided over the Geneva talks. While some people surrounding the State Department "diplomatically" supported the U.N. initiative, others had a different agenda. In fact a small group of State Department officials were ready to abandon the resistance in favor of a settlement with the Soviet Union. But they "found themselves in the minority and totally ineffectual due to the anti-communist passion of the Reagan administration."[37] From time to time, many administration officials commented that the Soviets were using the Cardovez initiative merely to buy time to consolidate their control over Afghanistan. From the U.S. viewpoint, the Soviets were sticking to their standard position of withdrawing troops only after securing international guarantee of non-interference in Afghanistan's affairs. On the other hand, the hard-liners in the Reagan administration were believed to have convinced the White House that Washington was not really ready for a political settlement that would allow Moscow to make itself free from the Afghan entanglement.[38]

Reagan administration officials believed that there was no change of Moscow's approach towards a political settlement. Referring to Andropov's initiatives, a high-ranking official, who had been clearly identified with the hardliners in the Reagan administration, said, "that was essentially what Moscow had been saying for the last three years." He rather discreetly admitted that Soviet invasion of Afghanistan was viewed by Washington in terms of American-Soviet global strategy, and therefore, the Reagan administration felt that there was no point in talking to the Soviets over Afghanistan until they withdrew their troops unconditionally. He clarified that Washington never considered Andropov's revelations as something new and positive.[39]

U.S. policy during this period could be termed as one where an appearance of support for negotiations was maintained while actual policy obstructed the U.N. sponsored diplomatic process. Whether the Soviets under Andropov were willing to withdraw their troops or not, Washington never bothered to test Moscow's intention. After Andropov's death in February 1984, Soviets further hardened their positions on Afghanistan.

Maintaining Distance

After the June 1983 round of talk's failed, all concerned parties maintained a distance from each other. Although the parties had agreed that Cardovez should visit the region in September for further discussion, U.N. Secretary General Perez de Culler decided in late Summer that such a visit at that time would not be productive. However, Cardovez continued his efforts in spite of a virtual deadlock. He submitted a draft to Moscow and Washington for comments. By this time, both of them remained silent. Tension between the superpowers increased after September 1, 1983, when a Soviet fighter plane shot down a South Korean passenger airliner over Soviet territory.

In the meantime, Soviets further intensified their military activities in Afghanistan in a bid to suppress the militants. And after the death of their Geneva negotiator Gavrilov, with whom Cardovez had developed a "confident working relationship," Moscow appointed Vasily Safronchuk,[40] who was known as more obdurate and tough in his dealings. During the June round, when Cardovez had pressed Safronchuk to give a certain timeframe, he simply ruled it out saying "the negotiations had not reached the appropriate stage."[41] With the deteriorating health of Andropov, the hard-liners in Moscow began to insist on direct talks between Islamabad and Kabul on a bilateral non-interference treaty. Encouraged by the political developments in Moscow, Kabul also rejected the Cardovez proposal designed for the American aid cutoff in the beginning of the troop withdrawal. Babrak

Karmal demanded his regime's recognition by Pakistan before any negotiation with Islamabad.[42]

Looking at the deteriorating international environment and US-Soviet relations, Pakistan further back away from its earlier commitment of aid cutoff and understanding regarding the replacement of Karmal in Kabul. Explaining his country's Afghan policy, Yakub told the Asia Society in Washington on October 5, 1983 that the Afghan regime must be replaced by a more representative one, which would include an "important part of the resistance."[43] Pakistani public opinion, however, was in support of the continuation of the negotiation not because of an anticipation of a breakthrough, but because a major faction of the Zia government felt that a stalemated situation on negotiation would be perceived as a failure of diplomacy. Zia-ul-Haq also supported Cardovez initiative, mostly to defuse the domestic criticism of Pakistan's status as a front-line state.

The end of 1984 marked a turning point in the U.S. policy towards the Afghan resistance. The Reagan administration had come to a conclusion that more American aid could exact a heavy price from the Soviets and compel them to be more serious about the negotiation, which would end Moscow's occupation. In October 1984, Congress overwhelmingly passed a resolution calling the President to "render effective material aid to the freedom fighters." The administration then increased its annual secret budget for the Afghan resistance.[44] Main concern of Washington during this period was not the negotiation, but to put more and more pressure on Soviets by military means in Afghanistan.

Cardovez, for his part, tried his best to reactivate all parties to continue the Geneva process. He paid a visit to the region in April 3-15 1984 and completed the groundwork for the next round of talks scheduled to be held in August 1984. During this round, Pakistan somewhat "tilted," and without the knowledge of the U.S., Yakub agreed to begin discussions on the most vexed noninterference treaty. He told Cardovez privately that Pakistan was ready to accept his compromise on the timing of the aid cutoff, if Moscow stipulated an acceptable time frame. However, the tensed relationship between the superpowers did not produce any positive results in the Geneva process.

The Stalemated Situation

The year 1985 marked a turning point in the U.S. covert operation in terms of the increased aid and arms to the rebels as well as in bringing about a change in international environment after the coming to power of Soviet Communist Party General Secretary Mikhail Gorbachev in March 1985. It was also in this year that for the first time, the U.S. State Department agreed to join the Soviet Union, as an eventual "guarantor" of nonintervention in Afghanistan's internal affairs if other provisions of the U.N. sponsored Geneva negotiations were satisfactory.

When Gorbachev met General Zia-ul-Haq in Moscow soon after taking power, he warned the Pakistani leader sternly and personally about Islamabad's support to the resistance. Starting from early 1985, the Soviets intensified their military effort in

Afghanistan in what turned out to be one last effort to pacify the country. Gorbachev also appointed a prestigious former Soviet commander in East Germany General Zaitsev as the chief of Afghan operation. Rumor spread that Zaitsev had one or two years to win in Afghanistan. In an effort to intimidate the Pakistanis, the Soviets also increased their air and ground violations in the Afghan-Pakistan border by the Afghan forces. Most importantly, during this period, there were sharp increases in terrorist explosions inside Pakistani territory attributed to the Soviet and Afghan secret agents.[45] Most probably, to maintain a strong position in the Geneva negotiation, Gorbachev had intensified this military tactics. At the same time, he showed more flexibility in the U.N. talks.

Cardovez later recalled, "From the time Gorbachev came in, things began to change. Only two months after he took over, [the Soviets] came up with a number of ideas on how the negotiations should move forward."[46] Cardovez convened two rounds of Geneva talks in April and June 1985. These talks ultimately produced a proposed agreement on international guarantees of a negotiated cease-fire and withdrawal.

With the passage of the Cardovez talks, and the increasing flexibility of Moscow about the timetable to withdraw its troops stretching over years, the United States construed the Soviet offer as device to gain time to crush the resistance and achieve military objective before the Red Army was withdrawn.[47] On the question of troop withdrawal, Washington argued that Moscow must withdraw within logistical criteria.[48] However, after a long period of lack of interest, the U.S. State Department for the first time agreed to endorse the text forwarded by Cardovez in late 1985. Deputy Secretary of State John Whitehead wrote to Cardovez that the United States "could accept the draft guarantee provided, of course, that the central issue of the withdrawal and its relationship to other elements of the settlement is effectively addressed and resolved."[49] The right-wing elements in the Reagan administration, and especially in the Congress, criticized the State Department decision as prematured. Congressmen demanded that any negotiations over Afghanistan must include the mujahiddin as they were the "legitimate representative" of the Afghan people, and that without them, the United States should not support the Geneva talks. In a hearing before a Congressional committee, a leading lawmaker explicitly commented, "we should not go along with the talks unless in some way the wishes of the Mujahiddin are taken into consideration, and they buy off, at least for most of them, on whatever the solution is. Unless that happens, there will be no solution anyway."[50] But the State Department officials were able to defend the U.S. position to become a guarantor on the ground that the U.S. stand would be applicable only if the other pending clauses in the Cardovez's possible agreement were completed and that Soviets give a short timetable for their troop withdrawal. Moreover, many officials in the CIA and even in the State felt that since the "settlement isn't going anywhere, there was nothing to be lost in agreeing to guarantee."[51]

Around the same time when the State Department showed a little flexibility towards the U.N. negotiation, the White House was busy preparing its final testament to compel Moscow to face a military defeat in Afghanistan. In a National Security Planning Group meeting held in late January 1985, President Reagan sternly stated: "Do whatever you have to help the Mujahiddin not only survive, but win."[52] This followed the National Security Decision Directive (NSDD)-166, which the President signed in April 1985. The key elements of the new directive were the more effective supply and distribution to the resistance, a special consideration for supplying American made weapons, more vigorous collection of intelligence both from the war and the Soviet decision-making apparatus.[53] This decision also ultimately led to the supplying of Stinger missiles in mid-1986, an anti-aircraft missile that was often credited with turning the tide of war in favor of the resistance.

Long before the Summer of 1986 when the Stinger missiles landed in Afghanistan, the Soviets were desperate to withdraw their troops, of course without the knowledge of the United States. According to a report, the "political decision of principle" to withdraw was made as early as December 1985.[54] After about two months, on February 25, 1986, Gorbachev addressed the 27th Soviet party Congress where he declared that the Soviet Union wanted to bring its troops home "in the nearest future." Gorbachev also disclosed for the first time that an agreement had been reached between Moscow and Kabul on a "phased withdrawal" of troops when the U.N. sponsored political settlement ended the war and barred Pakistan from interfering in the Internal affairs of Afghanistan. It was here that the Soviet leader termed Afghanistan as "bleeding wound," saying "counterrevolution and imperialism has turned Afghanistan into a bleeding wound."[55] Gorbachev clearly implied that the "bleeding" must stop one-way or another. From this time on, Moscow allowed its people to know about the Afghan war by showing limited television coverage of the war, mostly in order to mould public opinion in favor of a "graceful-exit" under certain U.N. plans. The Soviets showed more flexibility in searching a political solution in the Geneva negotiation.

In mid-March 1986, the Afghan government under Babrak Karmal offered a timetable of 48 months to Cardovez for the Soviet troops withdrawal. But as it was too much a long period of time, Kabul was severely criticized by the other parties. Even Moscow pushed for a shorter timetable, and when Karmal resisted Moscow's new proposal, he was eased out and replaced by Najibullah on May 4, 1986.

Gorbachev convened a Politburo meeting in Moscow on November 13, 1986 to review the Afghan situation and take a realistic stand on the U.N. settlement. Coincidentally, this decisive meeting was held just after two months of the arrival of the Stinger missiles in Afghanistan. Gorbachev forcefully told his colleagues: "We have been fighting in Afghanistan for six years now. If we don't change approaches, we will be fighting there for another 20 or 30 years . . . We must finish this process in the swiftest possible time."[56]

A clearly desperate Soviet view for withdrawal was reflected in the Dartmouth Conference organized in Moscow in November 11-15, 1986. In this U.S.-Soviet discussion group, Soviet participants openly commented on the need for a "national reconciliation" and stated to their American counterparts that Moscow did not want to control Afghanistan. A senior advisor to Gorbachev bluntly said: "We know we have to get out, but we don't know how to get out. Please help us."[57] Within weeks of this conference, Soviet Deputy Foreign Minister Vorontsov invited Pakistan's Foreign Secretary Abdul Sattar to Moscow and sought Pakistani help for the Soviet troop withdrawal. Vorontsov also asked his Pakistani counterpart to work for a political solution to avert a possible bloodbath following their withdrawal.[58]

In the meantime, U.S. State Department's virtual acceptance of a more flexible time frame of Soviet withdrawal and cutoff of aid to the rebels at the beginning of the withdrawal ran into strong protest in the Congress. In early January 1987, Senator Gordon J. Humphrey and Congressman Jack Kemp registered their "strongest objections" to U.S. readiness to guarantee a "sellout." These lobbies dismissed the Geneva negotiations as a Soviet ploy and fully endorsed the resistance demand for recognition from the United Nations and international community as the legitimate representative of the Afghan people.[59] In a reply to the lawmakers, Shultz had to reconfirm U.S. support for the resistance. The Secretary of State pointed out that the U.S. would support Pakistan's position on a timetable for withdrawal, which was based on "logistical criteria" and "in months, not years." Shultz clarified that the United States "policy remained essentially unchanged since the Soviet invasion in 1979 and reflects the views Congress has expressed on this issue. Our objective is a negotiated settlement, consistent with U.N. resolutions, and predicted on the prompt and complete withdrawal of Soviet troops and full self-determination for the people of Afghanistan.[60] The dominant view in Washington, which was emerged in the Congress, was essentially to increase American aid to the resistance that would bring the Soviets to the bargaining table. It was felt that only diplomatic pressure was not enough to bring about the solution of the Afghan problem. Congressman Stephen J. Solarz wrote :

> *If the Soviets are to pay for their occupation and even contemplate withdrawal, and if they are to be deprived of a platform from which to threaten Pakistan or the Persian Gulf, it will be largely because the mujahedeen, as the Afghan resistance forces are known, sustain their nationalistic and religious struggle. Diplomatic pressure for a settlement has played a role, but is an insufficient means to achieve U.S. ends. The United States and other countries that share America's strategic concerns should therefore provide a range of assistance to the mujahedeen.*[61]

However, in the diplomatic front, the United States supported the United Nation's resolutions for any political settlement of the Afghan problem. Elements which were consistent with the U.N. resolutions in the U.S. eyes were immediate withdrawal of the Soviet troops from Afghanistan, preservation of the sovereignty, territorial integrity, political independence and nonaligned status, the right of the Afghan people to determine their own future and form of government without outside interference; and creation of necessary conditions enabling the Afghan refugees to return to their homes with safety and honor.[62] Starting from 1980 to 1988, the United Nations General Assembly (UNGA) had passed resolutions demanding the above conditions. The record of votes was as follows:

Year	*For*	*Against*	*Abstentions*
1980	104	18	18
1980	111	22	12
1981	116	23	12
1982	114	21	13
1983	116	20	17
1984	119	20	14
1985	122	20	12
1986	122	20	11
1987	123	19	11

In 1980, Emergency Special Session was convened.

Bringing the Russians to their knees

After the advent of Mikhail Gorbachev, when the Soviets showed more and more flexibility towards a political solution, the United States not only demanded more and more concessions from Moscow, but also switched its position nearest to the hard-liners' agenda. It was not surprising that a cold war rival for about fifty years, now facing a humiliating military defeat, could not expect any "strategic concessions." Naturally, for the Reagan administration, it was a matter of historic importance to expand American power and influence in the region by compelling Moscow to retreat itself from its geo-political gains.

As stated above, as early as December 1985, the United States had committed itself to the American aid cutoff to the resistance at the beginning of the Soviet withdrawal. As Cardovez had already obtained Moscow's concurrence to be an international guarantor, diplomatic pressure was put on Washington. The State Department had to "hesitatingly" give its approval. Moreover the hard-liners in the Congress had charged that the decision had been taken by the State Department without the knowledge of President Reagan.[63] However, later evidence proves that Secretary of State had briefed the President and that Reagan had accepted Shultz's recommendation.[64] But with the passage of the Geneva negotiations, American policy-makers found that the Soviets were increasingly on the defensive on the war front as well as in the diplomatic arena, and that their move into Afghanistan was defensive and limited, they pushed for a hard-line approach to the question of a political settlement. From now on "American motive was really to pay back the Soviets for our humiliation in Vietnam."[65] And therefore, the State Department "support" to the Cardovez's talks in 1985 was nothing but a "diplomatic move" of Washington.

Washington was also skeptical about the Pakistani position of the Geneva process. A high-ranking Reagan aide speculated that the United States "was peculiarly diffident in expressing its views on the evolving [Geneva] texts." Referring to the Pakistani acceptance of the U.N. terms, he wrote :

> *Some of these undesirable developments were allowed to occur because neither Pakistani nor American diplomats thought the Geneva negotiations ever produce any significant result. The Pakistanis were constantly responding to Soviet and U.N. pressures not to obstruct; they did not want to give the Soviets a propaganda advantage by seeming to block progress. Therefore, they went along with Cardovez's importuning. In any negotiation, mediators tend to put pressure on the side most likely to yield. Thus, Pakistan was induced to accept a formula that left the mujahedin's survival in jeopardy.*[66]

Keeping this idea in mind, the National Security Council did not "make a big fuss" over the terms of the Geneva negotiations and left the entire issue to be dealt by the State Department. For his part, President Reagan was very critical about the possibility of the success of an accord under the U.N. plan. His perception was that "this country had a commitment to the 'freedom fighters' and could not just look the other way if Pakistan someday decided to cut a deal with the Soviets against the wishes of the resistance."[67] Pentagon officials were equally skeptical about the Soviet motive. Indicating the Soviet interests over the Geneva talks, a senior official asked: "the question is not whether the Soviets are now in fact seriously contemplating withdrawal, but why they have chosen to make such a concerted effort at deception at this time."[68] He argued that the Soviets were using the U.N. sponsored talks "to lull the rest of the world into believing that the problem is solvable through negotiations alone, that if only 'moderation' were exercised by outside powers, that if only we could give the Soviets 'some help,' the problem would be solved."[69]

No doubt, for a long time, Moscow kept secret its withdrawal decision, but still, it was surprising that in spite of the American declaratory goal of a Soviet withdrawal from Afghanistan and increasing willingness of Moscow to that direction, many officials in the Reagan administration doubted Kremlin's motive. Officials even disputed with the State Department's assessment. An under Secretary for Policy in the Defense Department characterized the Soviet motives during this period as "a thinly disguised attempt at deception."[70] All Soviet initiatives and commitment regarding their withdrawal from Afghanistan were given little credence by the Soviet experts in the administration. Until Gorbachev's offer of February 8,

1988, to begin withdrawing by May 15 [if an agreement was signed in March], the CIA continued to take the position that Moscow was not serious about withdrawal. Even after that, the Soviet section of the agency continued to reject the reality of a pull out for several days.[71]

This was the state of American perception when the U.N. sponsored talks came to a central point. In the meantime, Cardovez initiated Geneva talks had dramatically reflected the Soviet's moves in the year 1987. From the Soviet-Afghan troop withdrawal of 48 months in the previous year, it reduced to 22 months, and, after some intense negotiation, to 18 months. By the end of the year Moscow offered 12 months time frame, which made the road clear to Geneva for ultimately 9 months. But in the meantime, the issue of "symmetry" came as a stumbling block on the way to the negotiation process.

Symmetry

By the closing phase of the Geneva agreement, it was the American Soviet dialogue rather than the U.N. sponsored proximity talks that helped make the final testament. Whether the United States would continue its aid to the resistance after the final accord or not was termed as "symmetry." If both the American and the Soviets would continue aid to their respective clients, namely the resistance and the Najibullah regime, that would be called "positive symmetry," and if both the superpowers stopped supporting their surrogates that would be called "negative symmetry." This issue was partially solved only in the U.S.-Soviet encounters.

About two months before the Reagan-Gorbachev summit meeting in Washington December 8-10, 1987, Soviet Foreign Minister Shevardnadze clearly and in unambiguous terms told his American counterpart that the Soviets wanted to leave Afghanistan; thus, clearing all doubts from the American mind. In a private meeting with George Shultz, Shevardnadze revealed: "We will leave Afghanistan. It may be in five months or a year, but it is not a question of it happening in the remote future. I say with all responsibility that a political decision to leave has been made."[72] For George Shultz, "this was a development of immense importance—and a dramatic moment." In his *memoir*, Shultz wrote that the Soviet Foreign Minister not only asked him for American help for a peaceful solution to the Afghan problem, but also expressed his deep concern over the spread of Islamic fundamentalism in the Soviet Central Asian Republics. Shultz quoted Shevardnadze as saying: "A neutral, nonaligned Afghanistan is one thing, a reactionary fundamentalist Islamic regime is something else." The Secretary of State accepted this as "confirmation of a huge breakthrough in the making." Shultz however, emphasized the need for a short timetable for withdrawal of all Soviet troops and expressed American interests in a nonaligned and neutral Afghanistan."[73]

But, in substance, the United States demanded more than the Soviet withdrawal from Afghanistan. Just before Gorbachev arrived in Washington,

Reagan squarely reversed the earlier U.S. commitment of the cutoff of aid at the beginning of the Soviet withdrawal. Prompted by the conservative agenda, the President now stated that Washington would not agree to stop its arms flow because that would leave the "freedom fighters" at a disadvantage.[74] After the summit meeting, Soviet Foreign Minister Shevardnadze sent a message to Shultz pointedly asking whether the President or the State Department was speaking for the United States.[75]

After a high level meeting in the White House, U.S. policy was termed: "it would stop supplying aid to the mujaheddin only if the Soviet Union stopped its aid to the Kabul government."[76] Explaining the United States position, State Department spokesman Charles Redman emphasized that

> *The obligations that we take at Geneva must be balanced by reciprocal obligations taken on by the other side . . . There will be no cutoff of support for the resistance under any other circumstances . . . It is only logical that non-intervention and non-interference provisions should apply to the Soviets too. The Soviets cannot claim a right to aid a faction in the Afghan civil strife just because that particular faction tries to call itself the government of Afghanistan.*[77]

In effect, Washington abandoned the earlier pledge of cutoff of U.S. aid to the resistance at the beginning of the Soviet withdrawal. Referring to the ongoing U.N. sponsored negotiations; a Reagan administration official later admitted that by this time the United States was "about to redefine what Geneva meant."[78]

Some officials in the Reagan administration predicted that the Soviet leadership would never accept the new American terms. But most aides rightly believed that Gorbachev was determined to withdraw from Afghanistan and he would accept any American terms in the last moment of the accord that would provide him an "international cover."[79]

What then compelled the United States to reverse its earlier position? First of all, it was the bipartisan Congressional support more than any thing else which was a constant pressure on the Reagan administration over the years to increase the U.S. aid. Senate Resolution 386 of February 29, 1988, and House of Representative Resolution 392 of March 1, 1988, expressed its "strong belief that the Government of the United States should not cease, suspend, diminish, or otherwise restrict assistance to the Afghan resistance or take actions which might limit the ability of the resistance to receive assistance until it is absolutely clear that the Soviets have terminated their military occupation, that they are not redeploying their forces to be inserted again, and that the mujahiddin is well enough equipped to maintain its integrity during the delicate period of a transition government leading up to new elections."[80] It was obvious that the administration could not act contrary to the overwhelming and bipartisan support of the Congress.

Secondly, Congressmen and Senators also put pressure on the administration by writing letters to President Reagan opposing the Geneva accords that did not make the resistance a party to it. The lawmakers not only criticized the State Department's approach towards the proposed agreements, they also feared that that would be contrary to the U.S. interests in the region, and the Reagan administration's declaratory policy in Afghanistan. On January 27, 1988, 25 bipartisan members of Congress wrote to the President that "there should be no cutoff of military aid to the Afghan resistance until all Soviet troops have been withdrawn and until a genuinely independent government is in place."[81]

Apart from this, many individual letters started pouring in into the White House criticizing the State Department's approach to the Geneva accords. One Congressman described the Geneva accords as "false settlements and sham agreements."[82] Such an agreement, it was argued, would allow the Soviets to achieve through diplomacy what they failed to achieve through several years of occupation. A few days before the signing in ceremony in Geneva on April 14, 1988, one Senator even urged the President "not to agree to these accords until Congress returns back to session next week . . .."[83] So the Congressional pressure was a major factor in the administration's decision to reverse its earlier pledge.

Thirdly, a former Pakistani Geneva negotiator wrote that Zia-ul-Haq sent message to Reagan to ask the Soviets to accept "symmetrical cessation of military supplies." Zia wanted to affirm that if Moscow disagreed, Washington would continue its supplies to the resistance.[84] Because he was worried about Pakistan's concerns that the refugees would not return to Afghanistan so long as a communist government was in power in Kabul and the resistance to the regime continued. President Reagan asked Zia how he would handle the fact that in that case Pakistan would be violating the agreement. Zia replied that they would "just lie about it. We've been denying our activities there for eight years." Reagan later recounted Zia saying: "Muslims have the right to lie in a good cause."[85] It is assumed that Pakistani factor had also a greater impact on the administration's decision to defer on the "symmetry" issue.

On their part, the Soviets were fed up with the American terms and conditions. In last minute efforts, Foreign Minister Shevardnadze took up the issue with his American counterpart Shultz. In a very emotional and strong way, he argued that Moscow had done everything that Washington had asked: "announced their intent to withdraw, set a date, and established a short, front-end-loaded withdrawal schedule." Shevardnadze wanted, forcefully, an American "yes" to the cutoff of aid at the beginning of the withdrawal. "This one last piece," the Foreign Minister argued.[86] But the American side did not see "any reason to change our position." Shevardnadze "paled, threw up his hands."[87] Finally the U.S.-Soviet position remained, what was called the "positive symmetry."

In the meantime, Afghan leader Najibullah came on the way and declared that he would not accept the "symmetrical terms," and unless that was finalized, Afghanistan would not sign in Geneva. Moscow's last diplomatic effort was Gorbachev's meeting with Najibullah in Tashkent on April 7, 1988, and the next day the Soviets accepted the American terms of what was called as "symmetry" and informed Washington of their approval.

Finally, the Foreign Ministers of the United States, Soviet Union, Pakistan and Afghanistan joined in Geneva on April 14, 1988, and signed the Accords, under which all Soviet troops would be withdrawn starting from May 15, 1988 and ending within 9 months period. In a statement after the signing in ceremony in Geneva, Secretary of State Shultz said:

> The obligations undertaken by the guarantors are symmetrical. In this regard, the United States has advised the Soviet Union that the U.S. retains the right, consistent with its obligations as a guarantor, to provide military assistance to parties in Afghanistan. Should the Soviet Union exercise restraint in providing military assistance to parties in Afghanistan, the U.S. similarly will exercise restraint.
>
> By acting as a guarantor of the settlement, the United States does not intend to imply in any respect recognition of the present regime in Kabul as the lawful Government of Afghanistan.[88]

Conclusion

In retrospect, a question might arise about why the United States accepted a peace agreement over Afghanistan while it was evident that the Soviet Union was ready to leave even without an agreement? Several factors contributed to the American decision.

First, an agreement on Afghanistan that was designed to "breach" the Brezhnev doctrine was considered as a greatest achievement of Reagan's two terms in office as the President of the United States. It was also considered as a "success story" in the Republican Party's domestic politics for its Presidential candidate Vice-President George Bush in the 1988 elections. Secretary of State George Shultz wrote that "the Soviet withdrawal from Afghanistan was a tremendous triumph, one of the biggest events of Ronald Reagan's two terms and a turn of seminal significance in Soviet internal as well as external policies."[89] So, retreat of the Soviets from Afghanistan had a larger meaning for the American domestic politics, for which the Reagan administration decided to "go ahead" to sign an accord that provided an excuse for the Soviet withdrawal.

Secondly, it was felt that the Geneva agreement satisfied a key U.S. and Pakistani objective—withdrawal of Soviet troops from Afghanistan. Again, the accord contained a "written, signed political commitment" by the Soviet Union to withdraw all its troops in a stipulated period of time, i.e. 9 months.[90] By these conditions, the administration became confident that "it was the first step, and critical to" achieve the common goal of restoration of independent Afghanistan and the safe return of refugees.[91]

The Reagan administration also viewed that without an accord the Soviet Union would be free to withdraw according to its own will, ultimately prolonging the agony of the Afghan people and resulting a civil war in the war-ravaged country.

There was also fear of cross-border reprisals against Pakistan. So, in spite of the strong opposition from the "hard-line right, who did not really want the Soviets to leave Afghanistan—they preferred to 'bleed' them to death through the indefinite continuation of war"[92]—the Reagan administration finally decided to become a guarantor of the Geneva accord along with the Soviet Union to end the war.

In spite of a strong opposition from the hard-liners in Washington, Geneva accords was a triumph of American foreign policy to be contrasted with its defeat in Vietnam in the early 1970s. In fact, the main goal was to force the Soviets to withdraw from Afghanistan, and that was achieved in Geneva. Washington's believe that sufficient military pressure in the battlefield would compel Moscow to withdraw came true at the end. So it was not unjustified argument that the United States, in the early years of the U.N. proximity talks, did not pay much attention to negotiations and kept its arms supply to the resistance forces. Had the United States taken much initiative in the U.N. talks, it would have to give many "concessions" to the Soviets. By compelling Moscow to withdraw from Afghanistan, Washington not only obtained greater strategic advantage in the region, but also sealed the fate of the Soviet Union [though it was not anticipated at that time] that ultimately led to the disintegration of the Soviet empire.

Notes and References

1. Munawar I. Noorani, "Afghan Negotiations: Implications for the U.S. of an Impasse," *Journal of South Asian and Middle Eastern Studies,* Vol. 9, No. 3, Spring 1986, p. 9.
2. Richard P. Cronin and Francis T. Miko, "Afghanistan: Status, U.S. Role, and Implications of a Soviet Withdrawal," Issue Brief Order Code IB88049, *Congressional Research Service,* Washington D.C., April 20, 1988, p. 7.
3. For example, see the statements of Leonid Brezhnev in *Pravda,* January 13, 1980.
4. Brezhnev's statement of January 22, 1980. Also see *Washington Star,* February 24, 1980.
5. *The New York Times,* February 29, 1980.
6. *Ibid.*
7. *Ibid.*
8. Cited in Selig S. Harrison, "Toward Afghanistan Peace," *The New York Times,* March 17, 1986, p. 19. Also see, Zbigniew Brzezinski, *Power and Principle: Memoirs of the National Security Advisor 1977-1981,* Farrar, New York, 1985, pp. 443-454.
9. See Zbigniew Brzezinski, *Power and Principle,* pp. 435-436.
10. See chapter 3.
11. Fred Halliday, "On Afghanistan, With Skepticism," *The New York Times,* March 4, 1980.

12. *The New York Times*, February 20, 1980.
13. Riaz M. Khan, *Untying the Afghan Knot: Negotiating Soviet Withdrawal*, Duke University Press, Durham, 1991, p. 18.
14. See Chapter 3.
15. Selig S. Harrison, "Inside the Afghan Talks," *Foreign Policy*, Fall, 1988, p. 36.
16. *Ibid.*
17. Riaz M. Khan, *Untying the Afghan Knot*, p. 51.
18. Selig S. Harrison, "inside the Afghan Talks," p. 37.
19. *Ibid*, p. 39.
20. *Far Eastern Economic Review*, June 9, 1983, p. 30.
21. Riaz M. Khan, *Untying the Afghan Knot*, p. 104.
22. *Ibid*, p. 105.
23. Selig S. Harrison, "Inside the Afghan Talks," p. 39.
24. *Ibid.*
25. Selig S. Harrison, "A Breakthrough in Afghanistan," *Foreign Policy*, No. 51, Summer 1983, p. 4.
26. *Ibid.* Also see Riaz M. Khan, *Untying the Afghan Knot*, p. 106. *Far Eastern Economic Review*, December 10, 1982, p. 14. *The New York Times*, November 21, 1982.
27. Riaz M. Khan, *Untying the Afghan Knot*, p. 106.
28. Selig S. Harrison, "Inside the Afghan Talks," p. 42.
29. *Ibid*, p. 47.
30. *Ibid*, pp. 43-44.
31. *Ibid*, p. 43.
32. *Ibid*, p. 44.
33. *The New York Times*, May 4, 1983. Also see Selig Harrison, "Afghanistan Stalemate: Self-determination and a Soviet Force Withdrawal," *Parameters*, Vol. 14, No. 4, Winter 1984, p. 38.
34. Selig Harrison, "Inside the Afghan Talks," p. 46.
35. "Afghanistan: Four Years of Occupation," *Special Report*, No. 112, United States Department of State, Bureau of Public Affairs, Washington D.C., December 1983, p. 8.
36. Selig Harrison, "Inside the Afghan Talks," p. 47.
37. Rasul Bakhsh Rais, *War Without Winners: Afghanistan's Uncertain Transition After the Cold War*, Oxford University Press, Oxford, 1994, p. 122.
38. Munawar I. Noorani, "Afghanistan Negotiations: Implications for the U.S. of an Impasse," *Journal of South Asian and Middle Eastern Studies*, Vol. 14, No. 3, Spring 1986, pp. 9-10.
39. Interview with Elie Krakowski, March 10, 1995.
40. Safronchuk had served in Kabul with a special status from 1979 to 1982.
41. Riaz M. Khan, *Untying the Afghan Knot*, p. 125.
42. Selig Harrison, "Inside the Afghan Talks," p. 48.
43. *Ibid.*

44. For the amount of American aid during this period, see Chapter 4.
45. Riaz M. Khan, *Untying the Afghan Knot,* pp. 172-176.
46. Quoted in Don Oberdorfer, *The Turn: From the Cold War to a New Era,* Poseidon Press, New York, 1991, p. 238. Also see *The Washington Post National Weekly Edition,* April 25-May 1, 1988, p. 7.
47. Stephen J. Solarz, "When to Intervene," *Foreign Policy,* No. 63, Summer 1986, p. 26. Also see, U.S. *Department of State Bulletin,* February 1986, p. 11, and June 1987, p. 88.
48. U.S. *Department of State Bulletin,* June 1987, p. 88. Richard P. Cronin, "Afghanistan: Issues for U.S. Policy" in *Contra Aid and the Reagan Doctrine,* A Major Issue Forum, Congressional Research Service, Vol. 8, No. 3, March 1987, p. 18.
49. *The New York Times,* December 14, 1985. Also quoted in Selig S. Harrison, "Inside the Afghan Talks," p. 52.
50. See the remarks of Congressman Lagomarsino, *The Situation in Afghanistan,* hearing before the Subcommittee on Asia and Pacific Affairs of the Committee on Foreign Affairs, House of Representatives, 99th Congress, 2nd session, May 1, 1986, U.S. Government Printing Office, Washington, 1986, p. 9.
51. Selig S. Harrison, "Inside the Afghan Talks," p. 52.
52. Peter Schweizer, *Victory: The Reagan Administration's Secret Strategy That Hastened the Collapse of the Soviet Union,* The Atlantic Monthly Press, New York, 1994, p. 213.
53. *Ibid,* pp. 213-214.
54. Don Oberdorfer, *The Turn: From the Cold War to a New Era,* p. 238.
55. *FBIS, Daily Report: Soviet Union,* February 26, 1986, D31.
56. Quoted in Michael Dobbs, "Dramatic Politburo Meeting Led to End of War," *The Washington Post,* November 16, 1992, p. A16.
57. Don Oberdorfer, *The Turn: From the Cold War to a New Era,* p. 239. *The Washington Post National Weekly Edition,* April 25-May 1, 1988.
58. Don Oberdorfer, *Ibid.*
59. See the remarks of Senator Gordon J. Humphrey in *The New York Times,* December 1, 1986.
60. For the text of the letter of Secretary of State George P. Shultz to Senator Gordon J. Humphrey, see Fiche # 01891, January 17, 1987, in *The Making of U.S. Policy: Afghanistan 1973-1990,* Chadwyck-Healey, The National Security Archive, Washington D.C., 1991. In response to a question about what the State Department considered "an acceptable short timetable for withdrawal," Shultz had replied, "they can't be in there for a year or more in a withdrawal process and have it be a kind of meaningful thing." See *The New York Times* of December 13, 1986 and January 7, 1987.
61. Stephen J. Solarz, "When to Intervene," *Foreign Policy,* No. 63, Summer 1986, pp. 26-27.

62. U.S. *Department of State Bulletin,* February 1987, p. 19. Also see, Jeane J. Kirkpatrick, "Afghanistan: Five Years of Tragedy," *Current Policy,* No. 636, U.S. Department of State, Bureau of Public Affairs, Washington D.C., November 14, 1984, p. 4.
63. Constantine C. Menges, *The Twilight Struggle: The Soviet Union v. the United States Today,* American Enterprise Institute, Washington D.C., 1990, p. 69.
64. Peter W. Rodman, *More Precious than Peace: The Cold War and the Struggle for the Third World,* Charles Scribner's Sons, New York, 1994, p. 332.
65. Richard J. Barnet and Eqbal Ahmad, "Bloody Games," *New Yorker,* April 11, 1988.
66. Peter W. Rodman, *More Precious than Peace: The Cold War and the Struggle for the Third World,* p. 333.
67. *Ibid,* p. 334.
68. Elie Krakowski, "A Negotiated Settlement to the Soviet Afghan War," Seminar presented at the Heritage Foundation, Washington D.C., January 16, 1986, p. 7. This document is available in Afghanistan: The Making of U.S. Policy 1973-1990, Fiche # 01686, January 16, 1986, Chadwyck-Healey, The National Security Archive, Washington D.C., 1991.
69. *Ibid.*
70. *The Washington Post National Weekly Edition,* April 25-May 1, 1988, p. 8.
71. *Ibid.*
72. George P. Shultz, *Turmoil and Triumph: My Years as Secretary of State,* Charles Scribners Sons, New York, 1993, p. 987. Also see, Don Oberdorfer, *The Turn: From the Cold War to a New Era,* Poseidon Press, New York, 1991, p. 235.
73. George P. Shultz, *Ibid.* Also see Don Oberdorfer, *The Turn: From the Cold War to a New Era,* pp. 234-235.
74 .Don Oberdorfer, *The Turn: From the Cold War to a New Era,* p. 269. For a more detailed statement of President Reagan, see, Peter W. Rodman, *More Precious than Peace,* p. 345.
75. Don Oberdorfer, *Ibid.*
76. *Ibid.*
77. U.S. State Department *Press Report,* March 11, 1988.
78. Peter W. Rodman, *More Precious than Peace,* p. 345.
79. *The Washington Post National Weekly Edition,* April 25-May 1, 1988, p. 9.
80. See the Senate and House Resolutions. Senate had adopted it 77-0.
81. Letter from Congressmen to President Reagan, January 27, 1988. Documents obtained from the Ronald Reagan Library, Simi Valley, California.
82. Letter from Congressman Jack Kemp to President Reagan, January 9, 1987. *Ibid.*
83. Letter of Senator Charles E. Grassley to President Reagan, April 8, 1988. *Ibid.*
84. Riaz M. Khan, *Untying the Afghan Knot,* p. 270.

85. George P. Shultz, *Turmoil and Triumph: My Years as Secretary of State*, p. 1091.
86. *Ibid*, p. 1090.
87. *Ibid.*
88. Statements released to the press in Geneva on April 14, 1988.
89. George Shultz, *Turmoil and Triumph: My Years as Secretary of States*, p. 1092.
90. A secret telegram from the Secretary of State to the American Embassy Islamabad and U.S. mission in Geneva, April 12, 1988. This document is available in fiche # 02183 in *Afghanistan: The Making of U.S. Policy*.
91. Ibid. Also see George P. Shultz, *Turmoil and Triumph: My Years as Secretary of States*. p. 1092.
92. George P. Shultz, *Ibid.*

7
Post-Soviet Afghanistan and US Policy

With more sweeping political change and prospect in Soviet Central Asia, with the Soviets rolled back in significant places and with the moral and economic bankruptcy of Marxist Leninism laid bare for the world to see, who cares who mans the Kabul outpost?

—*Charles Cogan, Director of Near East and South Asian Division of the Operations Directorate, 1979-1989*

With the withdrawal of the Soviet troops from Afghanistan, American policy towards the region also drastically changed. A major question for the U.S. policy was how much the United States should seek to shape the political outcome of the Afghan conflict, especially after a military victory against the other superpower. Now that from the strategic point of view, the Soviet troop withdrawal transformed the nature of the Afghan problem, though it did not completely resolve it. It also meant, for the Americans, an end to the threat to Pakistan and the Persian Gulf posed by the Red Army's thrust (if it had one) in 1979. So, within a very short period after the Soviet withdrawal, Afghanistan reduced to a low priority area in the American thinking and Washington did not pay much attention to either the political situation of the country, or to the issues like the return and rehabilitation of about five million refugees who lived in Pakistan and Iran for a decade, or to the much needed reconstruction of the country. The United States virtually left Afghanistan to anarchy and civil war although it had a strategic eye on the oil and gas routes to Central Asian Republics through Pakistan and Afghanistan. With the American disengagement, a power struggle among the regional players such as Pakistan, Iran and Saudi Arabia to further their own strategic interests greatly contributed to an uncertain situation in the country. This chapter will discuss this regional power struggle vis-à-vis the U.S. role, and focus on the American policy towards the resistance in the post-Soviet Afghanistan and factors that led to the dovetailing of U.S. engagement and aid to the rebels. It will highlight the American objectives and concerns in a post-Soviet Afghan scenario, which were partly responsible for the subsequent civil war in that country. Because initially, the situation became such that if dollars continue to flow to the resistance that would lead to more divisions among the rival parties, and if American support stops, Washington perceived, the Soviets would get some geo-political advantage in the region. It seems that the United States' support to the guerrillas continued (albeit in low-level) till Washington realized that the American policy was heading against its own national security interests. In fact, the United States could not follow a consistent policy after the Soviet troops were withdrawn, simply because there was no policy as to what the Americans would like to see happen in Afghanistan.

American disengagement and Regional Power Rivalry

Though the Afghan war had helped catalyze the dissolution of the Soviet Union and the end of the Cold War, this was an eminent case of there being no gratitude in politics. The United States, which had led the battle for the Afghans for about ten long years, abandoned their cause at the end without addressing their basic issues such as the formation of a strong interim government, repatriation of the refugees and their rehabilitation, and the reconstruction of the country, which should have been of paramount interest to Washington. Ironically, instead of the resolution of these issues, the United States decided to withdraw its diplomatic presence from Kabul on 'security reasons.'[1] U.S. disinterest and disengagement is reflected from the relinquishment of its role to the United Nations, whose efforts since 1988 had been singularly ineffective. This American detachment also created a vacuum in Afghanistan, and the regional actors like Pakistan, Iran, Saudi Arabia, and Uzbekistan since 1992, have individually or in combination, tried to influence the events in that country, which predictably led to disastrous results and civil war and took a strong geopolitical dimension after the Soviet troop withdrawal. The most significant aspect of this change was that in place of the competition between the superpowers, the new realities were based on the confrontation among the Islamic states which were fluid and disruptive by themselves and therefore, the likelihood of any positive results remained extremely slim. The remote control this time around was no longer laid in Moscow, Washington and Islamabad but in Cairo, Riyadh and Jiddah. That means, the confrontation was no longer between Islam and Communism, but among various Afghan factions (backed by ethnic and regional surrogates) to gain political legitimacy through the approval of Mullahs. This is one reason why the United States had not been able to pursue a coherent and consistent policy towards Afghanistan and the Southwest Asia region since the end of the Cold War in 1990.

A Policy Leads to Nowhere. Clearly, the administration was divided over whether the United States should play a more active and direct role in trying to influence Afghanistan's future. The policy options for the United States were also closely related to the changing nature of American political and security interests. Some people believed that there was no point in American engagement in the region after the Soviet withdrawal especially at a time when there is no more danger of Soviet threat to its south or to the Gulf oil. Also as per this view, as the cracks in the Soviet Central Asia began to appear and the "death" of the other superpower looked imminent, American concern and involvement in a war-ravaged country was considered less significant. The other view was based on the American concern about Afghanistan's future related to the establishment of a viable Afghan government. This school argued, "A civil war in Afghanistan will limit the magnitude of our success and make the success look less significant."[2] They were in favor of more American involvement in future political settlement of Afghanistan. Yet another view argued that United States should take a more direct role in its relations with the resistance, and that efforts should be made to prevent the resistance movement from being dominated by the fundamentalists. Some others even expressed their concern on humanitarian issues such as repatriation of the refugees and the rehabilitation of the country regardless of the specific impact on U.S. regional security and political interests.

But at the same time, American officials acknowledged that the United States did not have a plan either for the return of refugees or the reconciliation of the Afghan resistance forces. One State Department official declared that there was no "blueprint for Afghanistan" and that the only objective of the United States was for the people of Afghanistan to decide their own future. The official asked, "Superficially, who could disagree with that?" and continued, "But what it really means in practice is that this government does not have a plan on such issues as how to help return refugees and be explicitly supportive of the resistance." He described such statements as "cover phrases that mask a desire to do nothing."[3]

This aimless policy was widely criticized by many people on the ground that the U.S. administration had failed to address a number of key policy issues. Among the key issues, as stated above, the government took the position that while many forms of political compromise were possible, "a Communist-dominated regime in Kabul was still unacceptable."[4] Because it was viewed that the Kabul regime had been installed by the Soviet Union, and now facing a countrywide rebellion by its own people, and therefore, lacked legitimacy. One senior official of the Reagan administration who later participated in the Bush administration's decision-making top brass, argued that the communist government of President Najibullah in Afghanistan stilled embodied a strategic problem: "The defeat of the Soviet aggression was not complete as long as the political fruit of that aggression still survived."[5] However, after the Soviets left Afghanistan, this problem was confidently thought to be about to solve itself. Political and strategic pundits in Washington made several predictions about the imminent demise of Najibullah government that ranges from two to at best eighteen months. The Bush administration thought the rebels' victory was at hand, and therefore, it took some extra precaution such as pulling out of its charge d'affaires out of Kabul anticipating an imminent and bloody final siege of the capital.[6] American officials even speculated, "Najibullah may be on board one of the last Soviet troop planes heading north."[7] Washington was so confident about the fall of Kabul that it even dwelt on such strategic and geopolitical questions as how to convert a covert military assistance program into an overt program of economic aid in the middle of a fiscal year. The Bush team even went to the extent of thinking about the "legislative, technical, and tradecraft implications" attached to such a decision.[8] Also, of greater significance, was Washington's decision to withhold new weapons and equipments to the resistance beginning in December 1988 in anticipation of the war's early end.

This was, however, a total miscalculation as the final crisis was delayed for over three years and only in April 1992—four years after the signing of the Geneva Accords—the government fell, and Najibullah took refuge in a U.N. office in the capital. Later, President Bush and his national security adviser Brent Scowcroft admitted that the conventional wisdom on the staying power of Najibullah had proven wrong.[9]

For the Bush administration, it was a very critical and a remarkable period in many respects. Because, it was during this period that the whole world was passing through a momentous phase of history due to the imminent disintegration of the Soviet Empire and simultaneous democratic revolutions in erstwhile communist countries of the Eastern Europe and parts of former Soviet Central Asia. The Iron Curtain was crumbling. The Cold War conflicts between the United States and the Soviet Union through out the Third World, the Horn of Africa, in Central America and of course, Afghanistan were moving towards settlements favorable to Washington. It was also the time when the Gulf war was fought between a multi-national force led by the United States and Saddam Hussein's Iraq in early 1991, which marked the beginning of a new world order and a unipolar moment in the world. It marked the emergence of the United States as a more confident and prudent single superpower in the world, which was no longer hesitant to take unilateral decisions against any country or any trouble spot in the world. Obviously, these profound changes had far-reaching implications and strategic significance for the U.S. policy on Afghanistan. American interests shifted to focus on resolving Cold War issues rather than confrontation with an old enemy, and now, a strategically less significant Afghanistan. It seems that these developments also led the United States to exercise its power in a more arrogant manner and even without any proper policy alternatives Washington did not hesitate latter to pump money and arms to the Afghan resistance.

The American Aid

The day after the Soviet withdrawal, Mikhail Gorbachev proposed that the superpowers suspend their weapons shipments and work as guarantors of a cease-fire. The White House reflexively rejected the offer. Because by that time Washington had already taken a decision to accept the recommendations of an inter agency review to continue aid to the resistance even after the Soviet departure from Afghanistan. Several factors led to this U.S. decision.

The conservative elements in the Congress and elsewhere in the United States were yet to lose interests in Afghan affairs as they targeted the fall of the communist regime in Kabul. The Congressional support for the mujahiddin, still regarded as "anti-communist knights in armor,"[10] helped sway the Bush administration to maintain the arms pipeline. The Congressmen complained about the hiatus in military aid and successfully insisted that the U.S. aid program be continued, not terminated. While Secretary of State James Baker was negotiating on some political solution in Moscow, a high-powered bipartisan group of Senators, led by Majority Leader Robert Byrd and Minority Leader Robert Dole cabled Baker to warn that any compromise that left Najibullah in power even in a transitional government was unacceptable.[11] There were also so many influential voices in the Congress for the continuance of aid to the resistance. For instance, Representative Robert G. Torricelli said, "It would be an error to undertake a change in policy at this point. A traditional weakness of American foreign policy is a lack of patience. The best plans often fail because we don't have the patience to see them to conclusion."[12] In fact, Congress has often influenced the shaping of American policy towards Afghanistan by urging a hesitant executive branch to take new initiatives.

Secondly, the 1989 Jalalabad debacle[13] compelled Washington to continue the ongoing flow of aid and underscored the need for a new approach as some people in the U.S. were contemplating at the time. The United States continued to support the view that the mujahiddin had to be strengthened through continued arms supplies. This single military defeat of the resistance also convinced the Washington observers (of Afghan war) that a military solution any time soon was out of the resistance's grasp, and that it was necessary to maintain balance with the Soviet build up of weapons for the Kabul regime. Officials in Washington, thus, saw no reason to cut off arms supplies to the mujahiddin any time soon.[14]

Thirdly, as stated above, the presence of Najbullah government in Kabul was not only a problem for the hardliners in the Congress, it was also considered as the single most obstacle on the way to improved relations between Afghanistan and Pakistan on the one hand, and, the United States and the Soviet Union on the other. Because the cold warriors still looked at Afghanistan through their cold war lens and the presence of Najibullah regime as their incomplete agenda. Under Secretary of State Robert Kimmitt in a speech to the Asia Society in April 1990, clarified that "Soviet insistence on propping up the Najibullah regime is the single most important impediment to a peaceful settlement."[15] It was also viewed that before being elevated by his Soviet patrons, Najibullah was head of the "Afghan version of the KGB," and for that reason, he and his party cooperated over the last 10 years in a genocide against the Afghan people costing well over 1 million lives. In the words of Benazir Bhutto, Najibullah regime was "not acceptable to the Pakistan-based mujahiddin, the Iran-based mujahiddin, the Afghan commanders, and even ex-king Zahir Shah." So, the impediment to an Afghan settlement was "an obstinate refusal of the administration in Kabul to step down."[16] So, in order to get rid of Najibullah, the administration wanted to put more pressure on Afghanistan through its military aid to the resistance.

Fourthly, support to the resistance was also considered as a moral imperative for Washington as the Afghans had sacrificed a lot for the cause of the United States. One Senator, who led the Congressional support for the resistance throughout the decade argued that if the U.S. strikes any "deal" with the Soviets over Afghanistan that would be a "sell-out" of the mujahiddin and a "great tragedy for Afghanistan." The outspoken Senator categorically stated, "Let us not permit the Soviets to win through clever political maneuvering what they failed to win by force of arms . . . The struggle in Afghanistan is to overthrow a regime imposed by a foreign army of occupation."[17]

Fifthly, it was argued that the cutoff of the U.S. aid would divide the mujahiddin, and that would lead to civil war in Afghanistan. One State Department official viewed that it was the supply of arms over the years that had encouraged a greater degree of unity on the part of the resistance. Thus, in his view, the continuation of arms and ammunition into Afghanistan would not be the cause of the Afghan civil war, as some people envisaged, but limit or at least lessen the possibility of any civil strife. The official also observed that the amount of arms and the question of their continuing supply or not could have an impact on the amount of time it would take to bring about the expected collapse of the communist government in Kabul. He also opined that a cutoff of assistance to the resistance could possibly have a "deleterious effect" on their morale, on the ground that with or without support of their friends, they would be fighting as the crucial battle approaches.[18]

Sixthly, it appears that the Bush administration had come under certain pressure from the newly formed Benazir Bhutto government of Pakistan. During her visit to the United States in early June 1989, Bhutto was applauded in Congress when she declared that "we must not abandon" the Afghan rebels "out of impatience or fatigue" with the war.[19] In fact, after so many years of military rule in Pakistan, Bhutto as a democratically elected Prime Minister not only enjoyed good rapport among the Congressmen; she also successfully reestablished the traditional ties Islamabad was maintaining with Washington. Pakistani officials also urged their American counterpart that any attempt to substantially change the present arms distribution arrangements would severely disrupt the logistical support arrangements of the resistance, including assistance in operating and repairing equipment, and politically undercut Benazir Bhutto.[20]

Seventhly, initially the Bush administration decision in effect meant that the political goal of American policy in Afghanistan was to hasten the collapse of the Kabul regime. Administration officials argued that if Washington took the policy decision to cutoff aid because of Soviet good behaviour, it would be hard to get started again if the Soviets start up again. Therefore, officials acknowledged, "we have a practical approach and will supply them as needed." American policy remained one of positive symmetry.[21] Apart from this U.S. approach, the large-scale military aid was also intended to counter Soviet aid to the Afghan government. Because it was estimated that by the time the Soviets left Afghanistan, they left behind some $1 billion in military equipment and installations.[22] In addition to this, it was reported that after its troop withdrawal, the Soviet Union was supplying

$250—$300 million a month, i.e. $3 to $4 billion a year, including new systems such as hundreds of SCUD-B surface-to-surface missiles and more advanced aircraft. It was widely believed that these high-technology weapons and massive stockpiles created a new imbalance between the resistance and the Kabul regime. Later, a U.S. General, with jurisdiction over the theater, declared that the Soviet material flooding to Afghanistan was "absolutely unbelievable."[23]

Lastly, the presence of the communist regime under Najibullah was interpreted in terms of strategic significance to the United States. It was emphasized that if the American unilateral cutoff of assistance is the persistence or the survival of the Najibullah regime or its domination of a coalition over time, then history will judge the Soviets won in Afghanistan. Zalmay Khalilzad, a long time supporter of the Afghan resistance, reminded the Americans about why the Soviets came in. Then he argued, "It was because without their coming in, the communist regime wouldn't have survived. If they came in and then they left and the regime did survive . . . they would have won it." And in that case, "the Soviets would continue to have significant influence in Afghanistan, and Afghanistan would be made available to them, and in the regional context . . . things can change. Attitude of the states can change."[24] He finally emphasized that the resistance had been a popular movement and that a unilateral aid cutoff would appear that the United States had abandoned them. "We sort of won the war but lost the peace,"[25] he claimed. One Bush administration official also later wrote the U.S. strategic interest still required that "the Communist leadership in Kabul be removed to complete the symbolic defeat of the Brezhnev enterprise."[26]

The above factors influenced the American decision-makers to continue aid to the guerrillas in Afghanistan which were valued at about $600 million in 1989, $300 million in 1990, and $100 million in the fiscal year 1991.[27] Finally, in September 1991, Washington and Moscow agreed to halt the shipments of all weapons to both U.S.-backed guerrillas and the Moscow-backed Najibullah government in Kabul by January 1, 1992.[28] In addition to these yearly allotments, the United States was providing bilateral aid to the resistance held areas of Southern Afghanistan through its cross border program of non lethal aid valued at about $95 million for the fiscal year 1989. Washington also provided about $55 million in the same year to the United Nations High Commissioner for Refugees (UNHCR), largely in food aid, to support the Afghan refugees in Pakistan.[29] These aids, however, subsequently dovetailed with the changing situation and realignment of forces among the resistance.

Apart from the above aids to the resistance and the refugees, the United States was providing more than $600 million each year to Pakistan for its support and role as a front line state. Therefore, at least theoretically, Washington should have considerable influence over Islamabad's policy towards the resistance. However, in the past, it has often appeared that in matters of Afghan policy the U.S. was more dependent on Pakistan than the obverse.

The AIG and America's Declaratory Objectives

Throughout 1980s, seven principal mujahiddin groups had formed a loose alliance that headquartered in Peshawar, Pakistan. With an imminent Soviet withdrawal from Afghanistan, these groups were pressurized by the United States, Pakistan and other aid donors to form a government that would serve as an alternative to the Kabul regime. On February 10, 1989, they convened a Shura (special assembly) near Islamabad, and after two long weeks of deliberations the guerrillas formed an Afghan Interim Government (AIG) under the presidency of a moderate resistance leader Sibghatullah Mojadedi. Very shortly, this government was recognized by Saudi Arabia, Sudan, Bahrain, and Malaysia. United States put certain conditions for the recognition of this new outfit. Washington stated its policy that the AIG would first have to demonstrate (1) control of a substantial amount of Afghan territory, (2) the capacity for civil administration, and (3) the ability to fulfill international obligations, before it could accord recognition to the Mojadedi government.[30] However, at the same time, the United States did appoint an envoy to the AIG with the rank of ambassador but resident in Washington.

By the mid-1992, it appeared that the United States was following a two-track policy towards Afghanistan. First, Washington was seeking a reasonable political solution with Moscow about whether Najibullah should continue in power in Kabul till a transitional government takes over. In fact, James Baker, the US Secretary of State, had clearly stated in Moscow that the United States now accepted retaining Najibullah as President until a transitional process produced a new government. And, second, the administration continued to support the mujahiddin on both military and political fronts. However, according to the press reports, the United States advanced its own ideas on a process for establishing a transitional administration. As per the American proposal, the process of transition should take place in three stages. A) The AIG convenes a representative Council in which the supporters of the former king, the Iran-based groups and the commanders would participate. B) This council decides on a new AIG that would be much more broad-based than the current one. C) The new AIG convenes another council that should include delegates from cities that the regime controls. This council would, finally, decide the shape of the transitional administration for post-Najib Afghanistan.[31] This approach had so many pluses and minuses. But one central issue was whether the AIG would convene a truly representative council. And should it do so, it would strengthen the opposition against the Kabul regime and the balance of power might change in favour of the mujahiddin.

However, it was a well-known fact that from the very outset the AIG had been plagued with a number of deficiencies and contradictions. The biggest problem was its factionalism. It was too much weighted in favor of certain diverse ethnic groups and underrepresented others. The seven parties it comprised ranged the political spectrum from royalist to a desire to establish a strict Islamic regime. One noteworthy example was that of Gulbuddin Hekmatyar, who was seen as an opportunistic seeker of power lacking ideology and alleged of fighting other guerrilla forces. In fact, it was the killing of some commanders of Ahmed Shah Masud in northern Afghanistan in July 1989 that led the AIG President Mojadedi to condemn Hekmatyar, after which the latter withdrew from the Interim Government and his position as foreign minister. In fact, the disagreements between the moderate leaders of the AIG and Hekmatyar affected virtually every important issue for a long time. Another fatal weakness of this umbrella organization was that it left power on the ground in the hands of the field commanders operating inside the country of whom very few was present at the Shura. Even the leaders of Shia factions, who lived in Iran, were absent in the new formation. One more significant drawback of the AIG was that it suffered from the onus of being seen as a Pakistani-U.S. creation.[32] Moreover, due to lack of funds, offices, and other infrastructures of the ministers, many people including mujahiddin commanders, foreign donors, and even the common mass of Afghanistan did not take the AIG seriously or pay much attention to it. It remained as a fractured system, and was unable to bring about a political settlement in the war-wracked country.

Initially, Bush administration believed that the mujahiddin should be given some more time to organize themselves and put more military pressure on the Najibullah regime. The United States still showed its interests to march in close step with the Pakistani agenda. In November 1989, AIG President Mojadedi visited Washington and was received by President Bush in the White House. At the end of the visit, the White House stated: "President Bush reaffirmed our support for the Afghan resistance's efforts to achieve self-determination and also expressed U.S. interest in a political settlement. The President called upon the Afghan Interim Government to continue and increase its efforts to fashion a stable, broad-based government responsible to the needs of the Afghan people."[33] However, unofficially, administration officials admitted that they find themselves in a "difficult situation" about the American support to the AIG.[34]

In an attempt to maintain unity among the resistance factions, the United States told all the mujahiddin groups that cooperation with the interim government was a condition for receiving aid. It also decided to stop payments to the resistance parties for running their separate offices and to attempt to transfer weapons directly to effective commanders inside Afghanistan. This US policy only accentuated the existing differences among the different factions rather than create an alternative to the Kabul government. Because immediately after the American policy was known, the Hezb-i-Islami chief Gulbuddin Hekmatyar announced that he was "suspending participation" in the AIG as a result of the conflict with the Jamiat Party. This reaction of Hekmatyar revived the debate in Washington as to whether he should continue to receive American money and arms. The American attempt to channelize weapons directly to the effective commanders also faced many obstacles as the parties control the existing logistic channels, and the actual transfer would take place under the direct control and supervision of the Pakistani ISI. It was also wrong to assume that supplying arms directly to the commanders on the field without any political framework would help evolve a political way out of the ongoing mess.

As far as the military aspects are concerned, the year 1989 marked a watershed year for the resistance. One significant setback to the expectations of the Bush administration over Afghanistan was the Jalalabad fiasco. Jalalabad, in eastern Afghanistan, is just fifty kilometers from the Pakistani border and was known as a city close to the ISI supply line and in the fundamentalist-controlled part of the country. The resistance' assaulted Jalalabad mostly because of two reasons. The first was to provide a territorial base to the AIG in Afghanistan without which it was difficult for the new Interim Government to acquire recognition from the foreign countries. As stated above, even the United States had put this as one of its condition to extend political acceptance of the new setup. Secondly, it was conceived that the fall of a major city like Jalalabad would cause a devastating blow to the Soviet-backed Najibullah government in Kabul. But surprisingly, this decision was taken by the Pakistanis at their restructured Afghan cell under the leadership of the ISI chief Hamid Gul and foreign minister Yakub Khan. No Afghan resistance leader or mujahiddin commanders were consulted before taking such a fateful decision. American ambassador Robert Oakley was however, present in the meeting who had agreed and indicated that the United States would follow Pakistan's lead on the issue of recognition to the AIG.[35] Thus with the American tacit support, the Pakistani orchestrated the Jalalabad adventure. The war finally, was launched with continued presence of Pakistani army officers providing logistical and tactical advice to the field commanders. It began in a promising fashion, but soon the mujahiddin became bogged down. The field commanders and fighters from different factions "failed to coordinate their effort, frequently fought among themselves, and showed little skill in attacking fixed defensive positions."[36] The mujahiddin also failed to interdict the road between Jalalabad and Kabul, which was one of the most strategic supply. routes for the government forces. The differences between the ISI and AIG also contributed to this failure to a great extent. AIG president Mujaddedi had raised claims of continued interference by the Pakistan's military intelligence in his efforts in discussing a peaceful solution. But the most surprising thing was Mujahiddin's claim that the fighting in Jalalabad was started without the knowledge of the AIG.[37] Part of the problem was that the mujahiddin were not prepared to take prisoners, and this inevitably stiffened the defence. The fierce and effective government defences surprised the guerrilla and its backers, and the first military defeat from a post-Soviet Afghan regime immensely affected the political and military situation, rising important questions about the resistance strategies and its organizational ability. One result of this guerrilla defeat was that the United States immediately resumed arms supplies that had lapsed at the time of the Soviet departure in the expectation of a quick mujahiddin victory. But the situation in Afghanistan remained fluid and fragmented.

The declaratory American objectives in Afghanistan remained "consistent." In a speech to the Asia Society in April 1990, Under Secretary of State Robert Kimmitt stated that the American objectives were: "the establishment of a representative

Afghan government through a process of self determination, . . . the return of the refugees to a secure environment with dignity and honor, and . . . an independent and non-aligned Afghanistan at peace with its neighbors."[38] But the focus of the American policy shifted from Afghanistan to other trouble spots, and Washington did not pay much attention to the Afghan politics, resistance, or even Pakistan. Obviously, the American interests and influence over the AIG declined making it practically ineffective either to provide a viable political alternative to the Kabul regime or to capture any substantial territory in the country. The alliance, in effect was dissolved at the end of 1991. The military situation had frozen once again into a stalemate.

Backing Away From Afghanistan

By the time President Bush assumed office in the beginning of 1989, a number of regional conflicts around the world were heading toward solution. The communist influence in different trouble spots was down sliding and Moscow looked defensive everywhere. Obviously, it was Europe, rather than any regional proxy war, which seized the attention of the new administration. One significant difference of perception between the Bush and Reagan administrations was that the Bush team consisted of more pragmatic men whose emotional and ideological commitment to the resistance forces was much less than that of their Reaganite predecessors. This pragmatism and change of perception may have significantly complicated chances for resolving these regional conflicts including Afghanistan.

In certain quarters in the United States people could envision about the civil war situation in a post-Soviet Afghanistan. But nobody was interested to come forward to help the Afghans in a significant manner. One leading voice in this school of thinking was Elie Krakowski, a professor of international relations and law at Boston University, who acted as Pentagon's point men on Afghanistan during much of the war. He observed, "People are saying that the Soviet Empire is breaking up, and they can't send aid to Najib anymore, so everything will be hunky-dory. But that is probably wishful thinking." Krakowski emphasized that

> *The problem is, Washington has virtually abandoned Afghanistan. Our major concern was always getting the Soviets to withdraw, not who ultimately controlled Afghanistan or the welfare of the Afghan people. That is allowing outsiders with their own agendas – the Pakistanis, the Saudis, the Iranians – to come in and divide the resistance and weaken it. Without a more direct, positive role by the United States, anything could happen. Afghanistan could fragment, or civil war could drag on forever.*[39]

It was surprising that soon after the Soviet withdrawal, the United States sought ways to extricate itself from the responsibilities of reconstruction and rehabilitation programs in Afghanistan. Washington only declared that it preferred a moderate, independent state to emerge and civil war to be averted. But practically did nothing to bring about such a situation. It really mattered little in Washington which factions or faction come to power in Kabul so long as their infighting did not carry over into Central Asia and draw large Russian involvement. The Bush administration was so much obsessed with the superpowers geopolitical compulsions even after the Soviet withdrawal that it hardly paid any attention to other strategic aspects of the Afghan conflict. Even the desire to quash the drug trade from Afghanistan, the number two global source of heroin, had not drawn the U.S. attention, much less a commitment to stay politically engaged in the region which was no longer at stake in the American thinking. Washington also did not bother about a possible hostile regime in Afghanistan that might be uncooperative with the United States in trying to stop the spread of opium and heroin. Several factors accounted for this American policy.

As early as October 1990, there were some expression of concern about the duration of the American commitment and the seeming inflexibility of the American position in Afghanistan. The first major impatient expression came from the Congress itself when the powerful Senate Foreign Relations Committee Chairman, Senator Claiborne Pell urged the administration to push for the establishment of a "neutral" government in Kabul and the calling of a national assembly, possibly under the former king. He also clearly expressed that the Bush administration should explore with the Soviet Union "a mutual cut-off of military supplies to each side of Afghan allies."[40] Even there was media speculation in the United States that the U.S. strike a deal with the Soviets whereby Washington would cease military assistance to the Afghan resistance and the Soviets would cease such assistance to the Sandinistas in Nicaragua.[41]

It was viewed that the guerrillas were unreliable and many of them were Islamic fundamentalist who would not hesitate to go against their mentors. So, even if the United States tried to shape events, its enormous investment in the rebels would not necessarily bring a money-back guarantee of loyalty or a promise that whatever government eventually takes control of Kabul would be friendly. As such there were clear division among the mujahiddin and some of them had already expressed their opposition to the U.S. policy in the region.

It was increasingly clearer that a military victory by the resistance against the Kabul regime was no longer realistically possible. The government in Kabul was entrenched. The apparent victory in Khost of the Afghan forces, in fact, did not reflect the capabilities of the resistance that could lead to a military victory. So, if the United States did continue military aid to the resistance, needless bloodshed would be there without any help to anybody.

Some influential policymakers, such as the National Security Advisor Brent Scowcroft, held the view that the Afghan conflict was no longer a superpower clash by proxy. Instead, it was a civil war, and therefore American policy was harder to defend. American officials argued that the Soviet withdrawal from Afghanistan in conjunction with the end of the Cold War and the collapse of the Soviet Union had all but eliminated the strategic aspect of the superpower game, i.e. from the

American perspective – Soviet threat to the Persian Gulf.

American experts had their own viewpoints. Some of them argued the question of U.S. aid to the Afghan rebels in terms of broader US–Soviet relations in the global context. In a Congressional Hearing, Selig Harrison of the Carnegie Endowment for International Peace viewed that it was not in the American interest to prolong a confrontation with the Soviet Union in a country adjacent to its borders especially at a time when the United States was seeking to improve its relations with the Soviet Union worldwide, and when the Soviet Union was withdrawing from many of its forward positions in the Third World and cooperating with Washington in creating a new environment in the Third World countries.[42] Harrison cited several examples where the Soviet Union cooperated or did not oppose the United States. Among them, he cited Soviet position in the Gulf War against Saddam Hussen, Soviet removal of their military facilities from Dahlak Island off Ethiopia, their air forces were no longer based in Cam Rann Bay where they had disengaged to a considerable extent, in Nicaragua and Angola they had cooperated in political solutions etc. Finally, he said that it was time for reciprocal gestures on the part of the United States in an area that was obviously more vital to Moscow than Washington.

Harrison forcefully put forth that the U.S. was supporting fundamentalist groups that were attempting to destabilize Central Asia with the encouragement of the ISI in Pakistan.[43] As far as the question of a communist regime was concerned, Harrison argued, the United States should take notice of the efforts of the Najibullah who was desperately bringing about so many changes in Afghanistan. In fact, the Afghan ruler lifted the state of emergency, called for the loya jirga and multi-party system, and invited the foreign investment and the private enterprises. The Peoples Democratic Party of Afghanistan (PDPA or the Communist Party) was reformed as the Hezb-i-Watan (Homeland Party) where communism was soft-pedaled, and Islam and nationalism emphasized. Besides, Najibullah had sent many signals to Washington expressing his readiness to cooperate with the United States in almost every respect except the provision of intelligence bases that would be addressed to the Soviet Union. He had sent secret emissaries to Washington, and that was one of the reasons why Moscow was unhappy with his continuation in Kabul.[44]

Again, Harrison viewed that "discontinuing aid would strengthen the moderate elements in Pakistan who are now attempting to move toward a political settlement and a policy on the part of Pakistan in which the civilian elements are dominant and the ISI is subservient." It was hoped that phasing out of the U.S. aid would pave the way for a political settlement under the United Nations auspices.

One significant aspect of the Afghan war after the departure of the Soviet troops was that it changed the political nature of the war. It reignited the old social and political fragmentation on ethnic lines and took an explosive dimension. Intra-groups fighting among the mujahiddin became the order of the day. They were no longer freedom fighters, but warlords. As an expert on the field put it: "The Soviet withdrawal undermined the common ground among the Mujahiddin. No longer were they waging *jihad* [holy war] coupled with a war of national liberation against non-Muslim invaders, but civil war, in which traditional social segmentation was now superseding the ideological dimension."[45] The United States simply wanted to walk away from this fluid situation and paid little attention to the internal civil war in the country. This situation also led to the curtailing of U.S. aid to the resistance.

The most important factor that compelled the Americans for a reassessment of their policy towards the Afghan resistance was Washington's disenchantment with the leadership of the fundamentalist parties, particularly Gulbuddin Hekmatyar and Abdul Rasul Sayaf who supported Saddam Hussein in the 1991 Gulf War. Although the traditionalist groups sent a small force of 300 mujahiddin to protect the Islam's holy place in Saudi Arabia, the fundamentalists' support to America's enemy re-ignited bureaucratic disputes between the CIA and the State Department. With Afghanistan in a virtual civil war, division and fragmentation among the resistance, and the fundamentalists open support to Saddam Hussein, many people both within and without the Bush administration were now questioning the rational of continuing U.S. support to the guerrillas. Ultimately, it led to the dovetailing of the U.S. aid. In fact, immediately after the Gulf War, both the United States and Saudi Arabia decided to cut off aid to Hekmatyar and Sayaf and made an attempt to strengthen the moderate parties that continued to receive limited aid. But after a short break, Hekmatyar continued to receive Saudi money, and even dollar flowed to the fundamentalists through different routes.

The Soviet failure in Afghanistan could have been a significant factor in the ultimate disintegration of the empire, but the success of the effort against them (led by the United States) could not bring peace to Afghanistan. The collapse of the Soviet Union at the end of 1991 compelled Moscow to cease its support to the communist government of Afghanistan. As per the agreement signed by the two superpowers, from January 1, 1992, the flow of aid were stopped by the United States and Russia to both their clients – that is the resistance and the Najibullah regime in Kabul respectively – and Afghanistan was left to anarchy and civil war. The death of the Soviet Union and communism as a political ideology left hardly any option for Moscow to come to the assistance of any country including Afghanistan. And since that was the ultimate target of the United States, and Afghanistan was merely a means to that end, Washington's attention was obviously diverted to the aftermath of the Cold War and to the realignment of forces around the globe. From a strategic angle, Afghanistan no longer remained a buffer between the contending empires or alliance systems. It also lost its intrinsic value to receive aid from the out side powers including the United States. Instead, the fourteen years of war and superpowers game had spread modern arms to every corner of this otherwise technologically backward country. During the first few months following the mujahiddin victory over Kabul in April 1992, while Sebghatullah Mojadidi briefly held the presidency, the US ambassador to the Afghan resistance, Peter Tomsen, and his deputy, Richard Hoagland, made the last significant visit of a US official to Kabul. After that, the entire international community had no political strategy for Afghanistan up to 1994.

The Afghan war also facilitated the spread of opium production through out a cash-starved and economically devastated society. What the superpowers left in Afghanistan was the huge quantity of modern sophisticated arms and millions round of ammunitions that were used to kill each other. Afghanistan got very little attention on the global scene after 1992, and the United States left the Afghan issue with the United Nations, which was again increasingly an ineffective institution after the end of the Cold War. Moreover, the United Nations' humanitarian efforts were also limited by danger of the security of the personnel, lack of a viable and stable government in Kabul, and failure of the United States and other Western countries to fund most of the programs they had proposed. Surprisingly, the decline of the American humanitarian assistance had been the most dramatic, amounting to around $6 million in 1993-94.[46]

The Aftermath as the Unintended Consequences

With the end of the flow of the American aid to the resistance, Pakistani and Saudi Arabian military support and aid did not end. They continued to provide money, arms and other logistics support to the Afghan war veterans to recruit and train Muslim volunteers from other Islamic countries in various training camps in North-West Frontier Province, Baluchistan and the tribal areas of the long Pakistan-Afghanistan borders. Much to the dismay of the Americans, thousands of these recruits known as the 'Afghanis' belonged to Algeria, Egypt, Morocco, Sudan and Indonesia later implicated in anti-Western and anti-American terrorist incidents. The veterans of the Afghan war later spread to India, Egypt, Algeria, and other countries and increased their terrorist activities. During 1992-94, many countries protested to the United States about Pakistan having emerged as a training ground for all these terrorists. Then it was rumored that the United States might include Pakistan in its list of countries sponsoring terrorism. Pakistan immediately started expelling these 'foreign Afghans' to their countries largely to avoid being branded by the U.S. State Department as a country that sponsored terrorism, which automatically disqualifies it for US economic aid.

There is no doubt that the partnership between the Central Intelligence Agency (CIA) and the Pakistani Inter-Services Intelligence Directorate (ISI) proved highly successful in serving American strategic interests in the 1980s in ousting the Soviet troops from Afghanistan. But one of the unintended consequences of this strategic alliance had nurtured a new breed of terrorists in Pakistan and Afghanistan, the best known of whom is Osama bin Laden.

The enormous inflow of arms from the CIA's arms pipeline into the region under the American covert program was also responsible for transforming the whole Pak-Afghan border's tribal territories and parts of Pakistan itself into what is called a Kalashnikov culture. Even the most sophisticated small arms became accessible in the bazaars of Peshawar and different semi urban centers in the North West Frontier Province and Baluchistan. This became a very important cause of violence and lawlessness in Pakistan and Afghanistan throughout the 1990s and exacerbated Islamic extremism and fundamentalism in the whole region.

The American covert aid and arms also strengthened the hand of the Pakistani intelligence agency (ISI) which not only began to behave something of a law unto itself and framed its own policy under the leadership of the Mullah supported Generals, but also deliberately (and continued to?) fan the flames of Islamic extremism since the Soviet withdrawal from Afghanistan. This also allowed the ISI a free hand to have its own Afghan policy where the American money and arms were used to set up terrorist camps and perpetuate international terrorism.

For more than a decade in the 1980s, the United States (and the West) lavishly and unquestionably financed and armed fundamentalist, reactionary armed bonds in order to make the Soviet Union pay a heavy price for its intervention. That was perhaps understandable as long as the fundamentalists were fighting against the Red Army. But strangely enough, American support continued directly or through Pakistan, even after the fundamentalist factions that benefited most from the U.S. money supported Saddam Hussen in the 1991 Gulf War. The United States could not realize that an Afghanistan under a thoroughly reformed (see above) Najibullah would make more sense than one under a militant fundamentalist Gulbuddin Hekmatyar. Washington gradually dovetailed the aid program and finally walked away from Afghanistan; thus leaving the country to the mercy of regional powers and fundamentalist warlords. Neither the United States press harder for a peaceful settlement of the Afghan conflict nor opposed the ISI's policy of emphatically supporting the Islamic extremists. A little more forceful, well planned, and concerted American effort might have averted the tragic civil war that spawned the Taliban and provided a heaven for the Saudi terrorist, Osama bib Laden. The United States did not pay any heed to the Afghan civil war, because it could not "discover" any strategic interest at stake in the region after the death of the "Evil Empire."

In fact, it was during this period that Pakistan became the breeding ground of global terrorism that later haunted the United States as a worldwide phenomenon. In retrospect, American officials admit that the United States made a mistake in continuing to support the "largely ISI-driven Pakistani policy on Afghanistan and in failing to shift gears sooner after the Soviet pullout." Richard Armitage, a former Assistant Secretary of Defence for international security affairs commented, "We drifted too long in 1989 and failed to understand the independent role that the ISI was playing."[47] But it is not that all the American policy making top brass were 'blind' about the Pakistani agenda on Afghanistan. One exception in this regard was the American ambassador to the Peshawar based mujahiddin, Peter Tomsen. Within a very short period of his appointment, friction quickly developed between Tomsen and the CIA, which did not like his interference in an area that had been a CIA preserve for a long time. The Pakistani ISI also disliked Tomsen as the new ambassador openly criticized its support to the fundamentalist leader Gulbuddin Hekmatyar and instead urged increased help for the moderate elements like Ahmed Shah Masud.[48] Unfortunately, these kind of voices were not given due importance at that time, which only temporarily fulfilled the Pakistani agenda, but created a monster against the long term strategic interests of the United States. So great were the implications of the US Afghan policy by 1994 that, in the words of Carpenter:

> *. . . the United States, together with its Pakistani and Saudi allies, has helped bring to power in Afghanistan political forces that are nearly as odious as the communists they overthrew. Today the people of Afghanistan are ruled by a collection of authoritarian warlords and sectarian fanatics. A Soviet puppet regime has been replaced by an assortment of Pakistani and Saudi puppets, and Afghanistan has become a breeding ground for terrorists. If that outcome is a US policy triumph, one shudders to contemplate what a policy failure would look like . . . the United States was not merely a relatively passive accomplice in the destructive agenda pursued by Islamabad and Riyadh-it was an active collaborator in foisting an oppressive political system on the people of Afghanistan, the result of that policy is a damning enough indictment of American action.*[49]

Notes and References

1. American Embassy in Kabul remained open throughout the 1980s despite U.S. covert aid to the mujahiddin. With the closing of the embassy by the new Bush administration, Washington would now be deprived of a useful listening post as well as a possible point of contact with the Afghan government after the Soviet withdrawal.
2. *The New York Times,* March 1, 1989.
3. *Ibid,*
4. Peter W. Rodman, *More Precious Than Peace: The Cold War and the Struggle for the Third World,* Charles Scribner's Sons, New York, 1994, p. 350.
5. *Ibid.*
6. Poland and Hungary also closed their embassies in Kabul, presumably for the same security reasons.
7. Elaine Sciolino, "What Was Lost In Afghanistan," *The New York Times,* February 5, 1989.
8. *Ibid.*
9. George Bush and Brent Scowcroft, *A World Transformed,* Knopf, New York, 1998, pp. 134-135.
10. Denis Kux, *The United States and Pakistan 1947-2000: Disenchanted Allies,* Woodrow Wilson Center Press, Washington DC, 2001, p. 299.
11. Elaine Sciolino, "Legislators Send Letter to Baker on Kabul Shift," *The New York Times,* February 9, 1990, p. A9.
12. Robert Pear, "Why the U.S. Is Urged To Think Again About Afghanistan," *The New York Times,* June 11, 1989.

13. For details of the battle for Jalalabad, see a later section of this chapter.
14. Marvin G. Weinbaum, *Pakistan and Afghanistan: Resistance and Reconstruction*, Westview Press, Boulder, 1994, p. 118.
15. Cited in Theodore L. Eliot, Jr., "Afghanistan in 1990: Groping Toward Peace?" *Asian Survey*, Vol. 31, No. 2, February 1991, p. 132.
16. Statement of Senator Gordon J. Humphrey before the Subcommittee on Asian and Pacific Affairs of the Committee on Foreign Affairs, House of Representatives, 101st Congress, 1st session, February 21 and June 14, 1989, U.S. Government Printing Office, Washington, 1990, p. 29.
17. *Ibid*, p. 28.
18. Comments of Howard B. Schaffer, Deputy Assistant Secretary of State for Near East and South Asia, in *Ibid*, p. 16.
19. Robert Pear, "Why the U.S. Is Urged To Think Again About Afghanistan," *The New York Times*, June 11, 1989.
20. *The New York Times*, February 26, 1989.
21. *The New York Times*, February 11, 1989.
22. Rosanne Klass, "U.S. Must Reassess Afghan Policy," *The Wall Street Journal*, October 18, 1989.
23. Patrick E. Tyler, "Soviets Said to be 'Pouring' Arms, Equipment into Afghanistan," *The Washington Post*, February 9, 1990.
24. Comments of Zalmay Khalilzad before the Subcommittee on Asian and Pacific Affairs of the Committee on Foreign Affairs, House of Representatives, 101st Congress, 1st session, February 21 and June 14, 1989, U.S. Government Printing Office, Washington, 1990, p. 125.
25. *Ibid*, p. 126.
26. Peter W. Rodman, *More Precious Than Peace*, p. 355.
27. Barnett R. Rubin, "The Fragmentation of Afghanistan," *Foreign Affairs*, Winter 1989/90, p.164. *The Wall Street Journal*, December 1, 1989, p. A16. *The New York Times*, September 30, 1990.
28. *The New York Times*, September 14, 1991.
29. Richard P. Cronin, "Afghanistan After The Soviet Withdrawal: Contenders For Power," *CRS Report for Congress*, Congressional Research Service, The Library of Congress, Washington D.C., March 2, 1989, p. 31.
30. Theodore L. Eliot, Jr., "Afghanistan in 1989: Stalemate," *Asian Survey*, Vol. 30, No. 2, February 1990, p. 160.
31. Zalmay Khalilzad, Testimony on *The United States Policy Toward Afghanistan* before the Subcommittee on Europe and the Middle East and Asian and Pacific Affairs of the Committee on Foreign Affairs, House of Representatives, 101st Congress, 2nd session, March 7, 1990, U.S. Government Printing Office, 1990, pp. 74-75.
32. Charles G. Cogan, "Shawl of Lead: From Holy War to Civil War in Afghanistan," *Conflict*, Vol. 10, 1990, p. 196.
33. *The New York Times*, November 29, 1989.

34. *Ibid.*
35. Denis Kux, *The United States and Pakistan 1947-2000: Disenchanted Allies,* p. 298.
36. *Ibid.*
37. Marvin G. Weinbaum, *Pakistan and Afghanistan: Resistance and Reconstruction,* p. 131.
38. Cited in Theodore L. Eliot, Jr., "Afghanistan in 1990: Groping Toward Peace?" *Asian Survey,* Vol. 31, No. 2, February 1991, p. 132.
39. Quoted in Rob Schultheis, "In Afghanistan: Peace Must Wait," *New York Times Magazine,* December 29, 1991, p. 38.
40. U.S. Senate, Committee on Foreign Relations, *press release,* October 1, 1989.
41. Theodore L. Eliot, Jr., "Afghanistan in 1989: Stalemate," p. 164.
42. See the statement of Selig Harrison in *Recent Developments in U.S. Policy Toward Afghanistan,* Hearing before the Subcommittee on Asian and Pacific Affairs of the Committee on Foreign Affairs, House of Representatives, 102nd Congress, 1st session, June 20, 1991, U.S. Government Printing Office, Washington, 1993, p. 30.
43. *Ibid,*
44. *Ibid,* p. 31.
45. Olivier Roy, *The Lessons of the Soviet/Afghan War,* Adelphi Paper No. 259, London, Brassey's/International Institute for Strategic Studies, Summer 1991, p. 24.
46. Zalmay Khalilzad, "Afghanistan in 1994: Civil War and Disintegration," *Asian Survey,* vol.XXXV, No. 2, February 1995, p. 152.
47. Quoted in Dennis Kux, *The United States and Pakistan,* p. 299.
48. *Ibid,* p. 296.
49. Ted Galen Carpenter, "The Unintended Consequences of Afghanistan," *World Policy Journal,* September 1994, p. 84.

8
United States and Taliban

The question of the Afghan refugees is not just another large-scale insolvable humanitarian problem; it is also a security problem. By 1997, the first baby born in those camps will be 18 years old, and it is probable that that generation will from that time on begin to pose some kind of a terrorist problem if they are not resettled under a government they can support.

—Barnett Rubin, an American expert on Afghanistan[1]

The United States had a very clearly visible hand in the growth and sustenance of the Taliban as a formidable force in Afghanistan. Once the Americans found that a new out fit was in place and that could serve their strategic interests in the region, they initially extended tacit support and then gradually came out openly. The 1980's honeymoon between the American Central Intelligence Agency (CIA) and the Pakistani Inter Services Intelligence (ISI) was given a new colour in the mid-1990, and the brainchild produced was named Taliban. In fact, a popular perception emerged in the whole region that the United States was allied with Pakistan and Saudi Arabia in this effort, as in channeling aid and arms to the mujahiddin during the 1980's war against the Soviets. The sudden surfacing of this new organization and continuous military successes in Afghanistan changed the course of political configuration of the country and redefined the American policy towards the whole region including Pakistan, Iran, and newly emerged Central Asian Republics. America discovered some kind of benefit in supporting the Taliban, which obviously led to a realignment of forces within the country and the region. Initially, two important factors motivated the American decision. First, after the disintegration of the Soviet Empire and the independence of the Central Asian Republics, American strategic eye caught the oil and natural resources of the region. Afghanistan's strategic location was seen as a conduit for expanding American influence in the new Republics and extracting the regions vast oil, gas, and natural resources to the world market. Second, in conformity with its strategic interests, Washington would be in a position to show to the world that it was doing a moral duty by amending for the problems that it had created during the Afghan War of 1980's and 1990's (although its real intention was different). On this ground, it was being seen as an obligation on the part of Washington to bring about peace by supporting a powerful force, which could provide political stability to the war-torn country. However, the Americans soon realized their folly of supporting an Islamic fundamentalist regime, and withdrew their support although internally through Pakistan, they continued to look for a moderate leadership in the existing Taliban set up. But it was already too late to check the "warriors of Allah" from exporting terror to different corners of the world, including the United States.

This chapter will discuss the emergence of Taliban as a political and Islamic fundamentalist force in Afghanistan, and the American role and interests during its rule in Kabul. It intends to dwell upon the Pakistani role in order to understand the strategic dimensions of U.S. policy and proposes to analyse how Washington's policy was trapped by Islamabad's agenda. In fact, a retrospective analysis of the US involvement in Afghanistan tends to suggest Washington's great confidence in Pakistani assessments of the developments in Afghanistan including the Taliban movement. Moreover, the study finds that the indecisive American policy towards Pakistan and Afghanistan seemed to have boomeranged in the form of its former allies becoming the sources of largest terrorist networks worldwide, which led to the attack on America on September 11, 2001.

Emergence of an Ultra-fundamentalist Force

The term taliban is the plural form of talib that means religious students brought up in Islamic madrasas (religious schools or seminaries). The system of madrasa is an age-old tradition in Pakistan and Afghanistan. But it was during the war in the 1980's, hundreds of new madrasas were set up in the tribal territories of the Pak-Afghan borders and Pakistan's North West Frontier Province and Baluchistan state to train fighters for the jihad against the Soviet Union. Most of these religious boarding schools were established and maintained by the fundamentalist political out fit of Pakistan called Jamiat-e Ulema-i Islam (JUI) led by its flame buoyant leader Maulana Fazlur Rahman. From the very outset, this political party, which subsequently played a very critical role in Pakistani politics, had a strong anti-American stance. And yet, Americans did not oppose anything about these Islamic fundamentalists, because the role of JUI in training talibs in Madrasas was in conformity with America's 1980s anti-Soviet policy, and later (on the eve of Taliban takeover), considered as part of its regional strategy.

Most Taliban fighters grew up in Afghan refugee camps in a very unhealthy economic environment and got educated in madrasas. The students belonged to the landless and weakest sections of the Afghan society, who naturally preferred to live in religious schools for free meals and shelter. According to one estimate, "the students lacked official subsidies, but rather lived on the charity of the community, often virtually as beggars obtaining a bowl of rice at one house and tea and bread at another, and washing their own clothes in the village stream (something no ordinary male villager would ever do on his own.)"[2] Several JUI sponsored madrasas offered an opportunity to the poor refugees (and many of them orphan) of a free education. They were taught the Holy Koran and Islamic Law, and also given military training. Run by barely literate mullahs (many of them untutored in Islamic law), these institutions indoctrinated Taliban as per the Islamic orthodoxy and the dominant role of the ulema. Obviously, they developed a very strong believe in Islam and the concept of Jihad or holy war. So, among others, the socio-economic factor holds the talibs together to constitute a formidable force in future.

With the Taliban movement on, bulk of the rank and file of the new militia constituted these products of radical Pakistani religious schools. The movement was radicalized further by thousands of Arab Afghans (veterans of anti-Soviet war) still in the region, who were happy to join its ranks and fight what they saw as a continuing religious war.

There is a story about the origin of the Taliban movement in Afghanistan. As per the story, a guerrilla leader in Kandahar region raped and killed three women in July 1994. A little known mujahiddin leader from the frontier area called Maulvi Mohamed Omar[3] was asked by the local people to do something about the incident. Mohamed Omar then recruited a group of religious students who executed the guerrilla commander and dispersed his militia. The group of students then called upon to deal with other atrocities and gradually gained reputation in the region. The effect of this incident was electrifying to public opinion, and other local commanders rallied to Taliban. This induced and made them confident for more recruitment of fighters and to fight with the people, whom they considered, had betrayed the country.[4] A movement was born, in the rare words of Omar, as "a simple band of dedicated youths determined to establish the laws of God on Earth and prepared to sacrifice everything in pursuit of that goal."[5]

Then they proceeded to clear the roadblock from Quetta to Kandahar, and captured the Afghan border town of Spin Baldak in October and Kandahar in November and entered the war.[6] Then the Taliban had moved further up and broken the Hizb-i-Islami forces in the neighboring Ghazni and Maidan-shahr provinces. By February 1995, they had captured Gulbuddin Hekmatyar's headquarters, Charasyab base, which is just 16 kilometers south of Kabul. Then for a quite some time they had to face resistance and temporary retreat from the combined government forces led by the famous General Ahmed Shah Masud, and finally on September 27, 1996, the Taliban took over the capital, Kabul.

There is no doubt that the very foundation of this new militia had a fundamentalist orientation from the outset. But they emerged in the Afghan scene as a reaction to the collapse of the state. A civil war broke out in 1992 when the Mujahiddin overthrew the pro-communist government of President Najibullah. The political vacuum left by 20 years of war led to the fragmentation of Afghanistan and the country was divided into several fiefdoms ruled by warlords, most of who had fought against the Soviets in the 1980s.[7] In late 1994, the Taliban organized a campaign to cleanse the country from fiefdoms and warlords, and promised to bring peace to the country, disarm the population, establish law and order and impose Islamic law (Sharia). Initially the movement was quite popular, especially among the Pashtun dominated areas in Southern Afghanistan mostly because of the militia under Mullah Omar's successful melding of religious fervor with the tribal patriotism of this largest ethnic group. It was also seen as a reimposition of Pashtun domination over the ethnic minorities–Tajik, Uzbek, Turkmen, Hazara and Baluch–that constituted the Northern Alliance forces of President Burhanuddin Rabbani and the legendary commander Ahmed Shah Masud. As Pashtuns had ruled the country since 18th century, and the country was under non-Pashtun since 1992, the emergence of Taliban was welcomed by the predominantly Pashtun belt, especially in Southern Afghanistan. People also wanted to get rid of the lawlessness and anarchy in the country and hoped that the new militia would bring peace to the country.

But as they marched up and captured Kabul in 1996, the Taliban emerged as just another warlord party. Its draconian interpretation of Islamic law and a profound belief in never-ending jihad isolated it from the international community, and even the Afghan themselves began to question the credibility of the new rulers. Mullah Omar, the supreme Taliban leader, shown little knowledge of or concern for the outside world. When the Taliban officials and clerics, under international pressure, debated whether to destroy the 1,500-yearold Bamiyan Buddha statues early in 2001, Mullah Omar is said to have issued the order: Go ahead; it's only breaking stones. The initial American coddling of Taliban came under intense pressure and forced Washington to review its own policy.

But this was not the whole story. While the story could have been a fact at the local level, it is just unbelievable that a small group of mafia goons would conquer a country of Afghanistan's size in a four/five month's period without any outside support. Thus, here comes the question of an undeclared "strategic partnership" between Pakistan and Saudia Arabia and a strong distant hand and tacit approval from the United States. In fact, it is the convergence of interests of these three countries that played a vital role in the origin and survival of this new fundamentalist force in Afghanistan. The American-Saudi-Pakistani support to the Islamic militants in Afghanistan was not new,[8] what was strategically significant around this time was, however, the realignment of fundamentalist forces in the region and their attempt to "Talibanise" the whole region and exporting Islamic extremism to other parts of the world. The interesting part was that even such a regime continued to receive support from the United States and two of its important allies in the region.

Pakistan. Like the U.S. support to the 1980s Afghan war against the Soviets, around this time also Washington relied heavily on the Taliban's backers in Pakistan. Even fully knowing that the new militia constituted an Islamic fundamentalist force and openly being supported and perpetuated by the fundamentalist elements of Pakistan, United States did not hesitate to collaborate with them. It is because of the fact that the Pakistani agenda and the American strategy had the same objectives in Taliban controlled Afghanistan. These objectives were mostly driven by the Pakistani ambition of establishing an economic foothold in the Caspian area by setting up a trade route to Central Asia through Afghanistan and simultaneously giving access to the American policy which aimed at the containment and encirclement of China, and not allowing the ambitious Iranians to increase their relations with their Muslim brethren in the Islamic republics of Central Asia.

One of the major objectives of Pakistan's (and American) foreign policy after the disintegration of the Soviet Empire and the emergence of the Central Asian Republics was the opening up of a trade route to Central Asia. This aim, Pakistan wanted to achieve by fulfilling General Zia-ul-Haq's dream of establishing a fundamentalist satellite state in Afghanistan. Even after Zia's death in 1988, his ghost continued to hunt in Pakistani Army and intelligence, and Islamabad was looking for an opportune time to proceed with its own intensions. That is why Pakistan supported fundamentalist Hezb-i -Islami leader Gulbuddin Hekmatyar for a long time, and when the later could not succeed, Islamabad carefully crafted a semi-religious movement in the name of Taliban and shifted its stand towards it. In fact, there was a 'clash' between Pakistan's official policies under the Ministry of Interior and its intelligence, ISI. In the beginning, at a time when the ISI were still backing Hekmatyar, the Taliban were sponsored by Interior Ministry under the leadership of General Naseerullah Babar, who was personally determined to the opening up of an overland trade route to Central Asia. Within weeks of the emergence of the Taliban, it was General Babar who headed a group of Islamabad-based ambassadors from the United States, the United Kingdom, China, Italy and Korea on a flight from Quetta to Kandahar and Herat to drum up support for a US $300 million project to upgrade the trans-Afghan highway. This indicates the importance Taliban was given by the Pakistan government and demonstrates the interests of several outside powers including the United States. Within a few days, it was General Babar again, who led a convoy of thirty trucks, guarded by Taliban fighters, across the border towards Kandahar, and demonstrated that the venture was practicable. Whoever blocked their way, the Taliban proceeded to deal with the militia responsible and, to everyone's surprise, they seize Kandahar immediately within days.[9] These events not only show the determination and personal commitment of Pakistan's Interior Minister and the government of Pakistan towards the cause of the Taliban and the opening up of a trade route to Central Asia through Afghanistan, it also demonstrates the strategic interests of the United States and willingness on the part of Washington to support the Pakistani initiative.

Another significant area of Pakistani support to the militia was clearly evident from Taliban's military capability across Afghanistan where the cadres were equipped with tanks, APCs, artillery and aircrafts, the operation of which was not possible without proper military training and logistic support including fuel and maintenance from outside. It was also inconceivable that within six months period, the Taliban successfully mobilized some 20,000 fighters without any support from Pakistan.[10] In fact, Pakistan left its border open for these militants who were not only given training in the Southern Afghanistan, but also in several training camps and madrasas in different parts of Pakistan.

The most significant support to the Taliban, however, came from the Jamiat-e Ulema-i Islam (JUI) under Maulana Fazlur Rahman who played a very critical role in the emergence of the fundamentalist militia itself. JUI had a powerful political base in the Pakistan's Northwest Frontier Province and Baluchistan and a strong support and sympathy for the Taliban. At the time of the emergence of the militia in 1994, JUI was a part of the coalition government of Pakistan People's Party (PPP) led by Benazir Bhutto. Maulana Fazlur Rahman was the Chairman of the National Assembly's Standing Committee for Foreign Affairs—a position that enabled him to influence foreign policy and establish close links with army, ISI and the Interior Ministry under General Naseerullah Babar.[11] In this capacity, Maulana Rahman visited Washington and European capitals to lobby support for the Taliban, and often went to Saudi Arabia and Gulf states to mobilize their financial and military assistance for the Taliban, which was forthcoming.[12] The JUI remained the most vocal supporter of the Taliban even after the fall of the Bhutto government in November 1996 and continued to fight for the cause of the fundamentalist militia.

All these developments lead to the conclusion that the Taliban were openly assisted by the powerful Inter Services Intelligence agency (ISI), the Pakistani fundamentalist religious party JUI and radical Arab Muslims, including members of Osama bin Ladin's terrorist network. Together, these forces unleashed a powerful coalition, but they were closely operated and coordinated by the Pakistani army and intelligence. The Pakistani connection had given the Taliban the muscle to turn its aspirations for law and order into a quest for national power. Jane's Intelligence Review reported in December 1996:

> *That semi-literate Afghan mullahs could have been capable of such planning and execution defies belief. Nor is it any more credible to suggest that ex-officers of the former communist regime now in the Taliban ranks could have put together such a plan. In the two years since it emerged, the Taliban movement has never achieved anything approaching this degree of military sophistication. In short, circumstantial evidence points strongly towards Pakistani involvement at the planning level, and reliable reports of cross-border logistics support this. Pushtu speaking ex-Pakistani military personnel operating on the ground suggest Islamabad's backing was not confined to the map room.*

Saudi Arabia. It was however, not feasible on the part of Pakistan's poor economy to finance such a costly adventure in Afghanistan backed by the luxury of a major foreign policy issue and a big advantage of the "strategic depth" for the Pakistani military against its arc rival India. No doubt, Taliban were able to raise money from tolls on transport and the drugs trade, but obviously that was a meager amount if it is measured with such an expensive military expedition that needed sustained warfare and logistic support for such a long period. And that is where the Pakistanis gave way to the Saudis to cave in, and acted as a conduit for substantial financial assistance from another powerful regional ally of the United States. In fact the triangular strategic relationships among the United States, Pakistan and Saudi Arabia over their policy on Taliban have been affirmed by former Prime Minister

Benazir Bhutto of Pakistan when she told BBC on 14 October 1996 that "the United States and Britain supplied weapons to the Taliban on money provided by Saudi Arabia," and that the Taliban movement "met the interests of Pakistan, too." The Pakistani Prime Minister, during whose tenure the Taliban was extended all support by Islamabad, was certainly a reliable source of what was hither to undeclared information.

Although Saudi Arabia did not have very strong economic and strategic interests in Central Asia, it considered the United States and Pakistan strategic allies and Iran a regional rival. Like its heavy financial backing to American and Pakistani efforts in the 1980s Afghan war, Taliban was also extended adequate support by Riyadh. In fact, Saudi financial support to the fundamentalist elements in Pakistan's Afghan policy never stopped. Riyadh's policy only shifted with the changing situations and shifting of alliances, but always favored the fundamentalist elements. Throughout 1980s, major portion of the Saudi aid had gone to the Hezb-e–Islami of Gulbuddin Hekmatyar who was known for his hard line stance and anti-Americanism since early 1990s. One report suggests that during 1991-93 alone, Saudi Arabia had spent two billion dollars in Afghanistan, with Hekmatyar as a major beneficiary.[13] But when Pakistan lost its confidence on Hekmatyar and shifted its policy favoring Taliban, Saudi Arabia also did the same, and Saudi money began to flow towards the Taliban and Afghanistan. It came in a larger scale after the secret visit of Prince Turki al-Faisal Saud, head of the Saudi General Intelligence Agency, to Pakistan in July 1996; making Saudi Arabia the principal financial backer of the Taliban. Later the Saudi Intelligence Chief visited Afghanistan for talks with the Taliban and assured his country's support to the fundamentalist militia.[14] Saudi Arabia continued to supply heavily subsidized fuel to the Taliban through Pakistan until 1998, when under US pressure Riyadh was compelled to dovetail its financial pipeline.

Saudi Arabia's policy towards Taliban converged with that of its American counterpart at least in three aspects: support for the Taliban was consistent with its rivalry with Iran, long-term strategic cooperation with Pakistan, and interests of some Saudi companies and individuals over the various pipeline proposals under consideration. In addition to these strategic and economic interests, the Taliban also provided some kind of ideological support to the Saudi policy as the latter felt some affinity to the former interpretation of Islam.

This convergence of interests were however, challenged by the activities of the Saudi dissident Osama bin Laden, the millionaire businessman, who has supported militants and terrorists in Afghanistan, Saudi Arabia, the United States and elsewhere through his global Al Qaeda network. The United States considers him as the man behind several terrorist acts against the Americans including the September 11, 2001 attacks on World Trade Centre and Pentagon.

Osama bin Laden was one of the first Arabs to join and finance the mujahiddin's war against the Soviet Union from early 1980s that stayed throughout the war and worked in collaboration with the Saudi intelligence agency and its

Pakistani and American counterparts. He turned against his erstwhile sponsors at the time of the 1991 Persian Gulf War when he opposed the invitation and presence of American troops in what he called the sacred land of Allah [Saudi Arabia]. Then he lost his Saudi citizenship in 1994 and lived in Sudan for some time, and finally came to Afghanistan in 1996. In exchange for a haven in Afghanistan's switchback valleys and rugged passes, the Saudi millionaire offered the Taliban money and fighters. Many people—both in Afghanistan and the Western world—believe bin Laden had given some $3 million that helped push the Taliban into control the Afghan capital in September 1996. Then he settled down in the country and revived his global terrorist network and declared a jihad (holy war) against the United States. It is interesting to note that it was another American ally's (Pakistan) intelligence agencies that assisted his entry to Afghanistan in return for his agreement to help train fighters for Kashmir, where Pakistan supports a guerrilla war against India.[15] That is the reason why several Pakistanis were killed in 1998 American missile attacks in Bin Laden's terrorist camps in southern Afghanistan, and hundreds killed and captured through the 2001—war against the Taliban regime causing much embarrassment to Pakistan and its supporters in the United States.

With these supports of Pakistan and Saudi Arabia in the origin and sustenance of the Taliban and support to international terrorism, it is indeed imperative to assess the American policy towards Taliban, especially in the context of the initial American reaction and the hand-in-glove relationships of U.S. officials with the Taliban leadership.

Role of the United States

Most American officials deny it emphatically that Washington had extended any material support to the "student militia" at any point of time. They also deny that the United States had any role in the emergence and growth of the new movement that had its origin in an "ideologically supercharged environment against a background of pervasive violence and deprivation . . .which gave them the only occupation for which they were qualified."[16] A retrospective analysis, however, suggests that the tacit American support to the Pakistani and the Saudi initiative in extending all kinds of support to the fundamentalist militia, and the hand-in-glove relationships of some American officials with the Taliban leaderships had greatly propped up the student militia. Had there not been Taliban's sanctuary and support to terrorist mastermind Osama bin Laden, and especially attacks on the U.S. targets, Washington would have very easily embraced the new dispensation in Kabul; notwithstanding its other domestic dimensions such as the imposition of Sharia law and the atrocities on women etc. The new strategic configuration among the United States, Pakistan and Saudi Arabia could well have been the precedent to the 1980s strategic alliance after the Soviet invasion of Afghanistan. Like the early 1980s, in mid-1990s also the United States was slowly trying to reconcile itself to the realignment of forces and a new set up within Afghanistan. The only visible difference was that in case of the former, the strategic stakes were against a superpower, whereas in case of the later, economic interests in Central Asia and containment of a regional power, namely Iran. Therefore, it is only naïve to say that the U.S. policy was not meant to acquiesce the ultra-fundamentalist Taliban. However, with its origin, growth, and the change of policy, American policy also altered.

On February 20, 1995, *The New York Times,* reported in a front page news item describing Taliban as "a new and mysterious Afghan force," whose "lull is more astonishing because it succeeded, in province after province, with barely a shot fired." At the same time, it also reported that "in areas already under their control, the Taliban have ordered women not to leave their homes unless accompanied by a male relative, and only with their heads completely covered by a burka, an enveloping headdress with a net mesh over the eyes. Although they have said they will not impose Iranian-style social restrictions on Afghans, the Taliban have banned alcohol, smashed television sets and pulled the tape out of videocassettes."

So, when the American officials and the Congressmen claimed their ignorance about the Taliban's Islamic orthodoxy and extremism, it was meaningless. As during the period of the US-Pakistan coddling of the Taliban, they had already known the real face of the militia outfit. Among the first foreign visitors to their base in Kandahar, Talibans had the opportunity of receiving the U.S. ambassador to Pakistan John Monjo, and Pakistan's Interior Minister General Nasrullah Babar.[17] Other American officials including the assistant secretary of state for South Asian affairs, Robin Raphel also paid several visits to Kandahar and Kabul and met with several Afghan leaders. The State Department spokesperson declared that the United States could see "nothing objectionable" in the steps the Taliban had taken to impose Islamic law in the areas under their control and called on the Taliban to "move quickly to restore order" and to form "a representative interim government."[18] As far as the American official position was concerned, Raphel stressed, 1. establishment of peace and security through a political process under the United Nations auspices, 2. support for reconstruction and the return of the refugees, 3. combating of narcotics trafficking, and 4. an end to the harboring of radical groups.[19] It is surprising that the whole Taliban movement started in July 1994, and by the end of August 1994, hardly the militia had organized itself as a jihadi force in Afghanistan, yet Raphel had her statement supporting the fundamentalist group. From this statement of the U.S. assistant secretary in charge of the region, one could be very sure about the American involvement in the creation of this new political force. Later at a Congressional hearing, Raphel spoke favorably and defended the Taliban on the ground that the new militia leaders support for a political process, in contrast to "factional leaders" (indicating President Rabbani) who were not interested to relinquish their personal power for the over all good of Afghanistan.[20] Raphel apparently believed that the militia constituted a force that was completely under Pakistani control, and could serve U.S. interests in the region.[21] Some influential Congressmen and certain elements in the Central Intelligence Agency, who were known for their close links with the Pakistani ISI, also supported these views.[22]

Then what made the United States renewed its interests after a period of relative disengagement? What were the American objectives in supporting an Islamic fundamentalist regime in a land-locked Afghanistan? The available evidences suggest that like the past American engagement in the 1980's, Washington's ambition was largely motivated by some strategic factors in the region and not necessarily the political stability of the Afghan state or any humanitarian ground to help the people of Afghanistan.

The geo-strategic argument was that since the Taliban was pro-Pakistani, and at the same time anti-Russian and anti-Iranian, the United States ought to accept it. As per this argument, it was not an American affair how the Taliban treats its own people, and "better a stable Afghanistan with an aesthetically challenged government than a convulsed Afghanistan that offers a playground for Iranian and Russian devilments."[23] Containment of Iran had become an American strategy in the region specially, after the Teheran government declared its readiness to extend port facilities to the newly independent Central Asian Republics. American interests in Afghanistan also increased when it became clear that the Rabbani government in Kabul had been drawn closer to Teheran, after the killing of Iran-backed Shia leader Abdul Ali Mazari by the Taliban in early 1995. What was more alarming for the Americans and the Pakistani intelligence agencies was the Iranian diplomatic success in bringing together of the erstwhile enemies of the Afghan war, Rabbani and Hekmatyar in an agreement in June 1996.[24] Right from the very beginning, the Iranians correctly perceived the Taliban as an organization propagating Sunni Islam. Iranian clerics even branded the Taliban as "narrow-minded."[25] Similarly, the United States was also anxious about a possible Taliban-Iranian nexus in the initial phase of the rise of the fundamentalist militia. So, Washington decided to pre-empt any deal between them and instead sent its own assistant secretary of state for the region Robin Raphel along with a very influential Senator Hank Brown[26] to Kabul to directly interact with the Taliban leaders.

After the Soviet disintegration, a very remarkable systemic change took place in the newly independent Central Asian Republics (CAR), which was ethnically defined, and hence, had strong ethnic links with Afghanistan. At the same time, the discovery of huge quantity of hydrocarbon and mineral resources including oil and natural gas in the CAR attracted the attention of the United States and its allies. This was especially relevant in view of the CAR's impel drive to accelerate their economic development through the export of these items. Afghanistan's strategic importance had increased because of its being a transport junction and land approach between the landlocked countries of Central Asia and the littoral countries on the Arabian Sea and the Indian Ocean. The United States, Saudi Arabia and Pakistan wanted exclusive access to these resources and to the markets of these countries for investment and export purposes. Therefore, competition over control of trade and pipeline routes from Central Asia to the Arabian Sea (Indian Ocean) transformed relations between Iran and Pakistan, and Teheran's initiative in this respect was openly supported by Russia and India. Taliban's ability to provide security for trade, and the projected pipelines was considered strategically advantageous to both Teheran and Islamabad. Significantly, around this time, in the spring of 1996, a partnership between the American company UNOCAL and the Saudi Company DELTA had concluded plans for a multimillion-dollar ($2 billion) oil and gas pipelines from Turkmenistan to Pakistani Baluchistan via Herat and Qandahar.[27] Pakistan with the American backing (as an American company got involved) and Saudi Arabia considered the deal very lucrative since it was not just the trade route, but potential oil and gas pipelines were at stake.

As Kabul was still under the control of Rabbani and Masud, and a large portion of the country including Qandahar and Herat and the entire Southwestern region were under the control of the Taliban, both the companies had to conclude separate agreements with the commanders all along the projected pipeline route. No doubt, Taliban had become their major partner as the militia controlled the entire route. But it became apparent that the billions of dollars of financing required for this route would not be available without the agreement of a legitimate government of Afghanistan. So the Pakistani military and logistics support to the Taliban had been mostly aimed at the removal of the "strategic obstacle" (i.e. Rabbani government) to Islamabad's goal of reaching Central Asia and Saudi Arabia and American goal of containing Iran. Obviously, the United States had looked at its larger strategic interests in the region by supporting the Taliban. The pipeline project would serve the economic interest of a U.S. company and a Saudi company, would serve the American goal of isolating Iran, and might provide funds needed for the reconstruction of Afghanistan.

American policy of supporting Taliban also motivated by the feeling that the new militia's "conservative, tribal brand of Islam was also hostile to the radical, revolutionary Islamic movements involved in international terrorist activities, some of which had training camps in Afghanistan."[28] Taliban Information Minister Amir Khan Mutaqi had declared, "We don't want subversive actions to be launched from here against any other countries. In areas under Taliban control, there are no terrorists."[29] In fact, the initial activities and statements of the Taliban created a positive image in the United States. American officials described the new militia as "anti-modernism" rather than "anti-Western," and also noted that they were keen on restoring a "traditional society" rather than "exporting Islam."[30] The United States was even contemplating on such issues as whether the diplomatic representative of the Rabbani government in Washington should continue or not. Regarding Washington's close association with the student militia, the State Department spokesman confirmed that the United States had contacts with the Taliban "regularly in the years past but also this year."[31] He acknowledged that the United States had a national interests involved in supporting the Taliban and added that "we may not like everything that they are doing, but that does not mean we should just cut them off from all contacts with the United States." Even the editorial comments in *The New York Times* said, "The Islamic fundamentalist movement that gained control over much of Afghanistan with a recent string of military victories has brought a measure of stability to the country for the first time in years." The over all assessment of the time shows that the United States welcomed the fundamentalist Taliban regime as a moderate force and a symbol of peace and stability in the region. It looks very naive and benign that the United States could visualize and treated such a fundamentalist organization to keep under its control although it had a (not so distant) past experience of Gulbuddin Hekmatyar's Hezb-i-Islami which took the lion's share of the CIA money in the 1980's Afghan war and finally very conveniently went against the United States.

Another strange "good fellows" the United States found in Taliban was the militia's assurance that it would stop drug trade in the country once it comes to power in Kabul. But once they controlled a portion of Afghanistan's opium producing areas, they had rather profited from it, as had the previous governmental authorities. In fact, U.S. federal narcotics agents based in Pakistan had a very high aspiration from the Taliban whom they called "students." They had a high hope that the Taliban would bring an end to the booming opium trade out of Afghanistan. In addition to this drug trade, American officials believed that the Talibans would (a) serve as a bulwark against Russian and Iranian interests, (b) restore order to all of Afghanistan as they had done in Kandahar and other regions, (c) get rid of terrorist training camps, (d) pave the way for the return of the former king, Zahir Shah, and (e) provide a US ally, Pakistan, "an overland link to the immense profits to be made from trade with the Central Asian Republics." In addition to this, Washington had no reason to disagree with the Taliban leadership when they declared that their opposition to schooling for girls was based on the absence of appropriate curricula and requisite number of female teachers, and they also promised to work on these matters once the war ends. Most significantly, the new militia promised to open doors for the construction of giant oil and gas pipelines facilitating the route from Central Asia down through Afghanistan to Pakistan and world market. It was visualized that the Talibans most important function was to provide "security for roads, and potentially, oil and gas pipelines that would link the states of Central Asia to the international market through Pakistan rather than through Iran."[32]

In the summer of 1996, Senator Hank Brown chaired hearings on Afghanistan. A remarkable presentation was made by Marty Miller, the UNOCAL Vice President, rather than by an Afghan or an important high-ranking U.S. official, in charge of the proposed pipeline project. Miller explained and displayed the proposed routes and argued that the project could, on day one, start pumping a million barrels of oil per day, and in few years, once linked to the oil fields of Central Asia, the pipeline could pump 5 million barrels a day.[33] When the Taliban captured Kabul, UNOCAL official applauded the arrival and spoke in glowing about the immediate prospects of doing business with them.[34] In light of such stakes involved, "it is easy to understand how it became accepted wisdom in Afghanistan that the United States backed, supported or even financed the Taliban."[35]

Surprisingly, a good deal of support, the administration got was from the Congressional leaders and even from the leading experts in the academia. For instance, Senator Hank Brown (R-Colo) convened a conference in Washington where he invited many Afghan groups except Hekmatyar and Sayyaf because of their links to "radical organizations outside Afghanistan."[36] Thomas E. Gouttierre of the Afghanistan Studies Centre at the University of Nebraska was quoted as commenting on the Taliban that, "The fact is, they are not out there oppressing people."[37] Gouttierre also headed a body which reportedly received as much as $1.8 million from 1997-1999 to complement UNOCAL in its Afghan operation i.e. to create goodwill in Afghanistan by establishing vocational and educational training programs.[38] UNOCAL put so much importance to Central Asia, because of its enormous potential for profit. Analysts believe that Central Asia may be the next Middle East.[39] Turkmenistan has 21,000 billion cubic meters of gas, the third largest reserve in the world, Uzbekistan has also comparable amounts of gas, and the prospective reserves of oil in Kazakhstan and Azerbaijan are what have been called "legends in the industry."[40]

Similarly, a former State Department official who dealt with the U.S. Afghan policy, Zalmay Khalilzad, said that the U.S. should actively assist the Taliban because even though it is fundamentalist, it does not practice the anti-US style fundamentalism of Iran.[41] Khalilzad, an Afghan-born senior analyst at Rand Corporation, a Los Angeles-based research organization, argued that the Taliban were Sunni Muslims like those in Saudi Arabia, not Persian Shites like the followers of Ayatullah Khomeini, and "are not into exporting revolution. Nor are they hostile to the U.S."[42] If the regime not led by international radicals, the U.S. cares little who governs Afghanistan as long as it is governed. Similarly, another expert on Afghanistan, Bernard Rubin very confidently viewed that "the Taliban do not have any links to Islams international radicals. In fact, they hate them."[43] In some other quarters Taliban were described as traditionalist. At a seminar held in Washington DC on 6 November 1996, former US Ambassador to Pakistan Robert Oakley suggested that what the Taliban represented was the arrival of "village" values and attitudes in the cities."[44]

The irony in the case of Afghanistan is that the attempt to exclude Iran by means of the expansion of Taliban power had had the opposite effect: more and more Iranian involvement in Afghanistan, largely as a result of the heightened fears in Teheran for the safety of the vulnerable Shiite minority in Afghanistan. After the election of the 'moderate' President Khatami in May 1997, U.S. officials shown some interests in engaging Iran, but such an idea was kept in backburner under the pressures of its "allies" in the region.

The United States seemed somewhat more engaged in Afghanistan in 1998, with United States permanent representative to the United Nation making a one-day trip to the country in April. Richardson was the highest United States official to visit Afghanistan in over 20 years. However, Washington's policy of "being in contact with all Afghan factions," which allowed the American officials to be in "touch" with the Taliban at least up to August 1998 when the U.S. intelligence traced the American Embassy bombing of Kenya and Tanzania to Osama bin Laden. Even beyond that as late as October 1998, certain elements in the Clinton administration accepted the notion that "Taliban policies might moderate"[45] and the American officials were in "touch" with the Taliban regime over the bin Laden issue right up to the 11th September 2001. That is why the big question was: if the ultimate aim of U.S. policy was to undermine the Taliban, as the American officials later claimed, why the United States was not open to support the elements who could weaken the Taliban?

The Bin Laden Issue

After the bombing of two American Embassies in Africa in August 1998, terrorist mastermind Osama bin Laden (OBL) became a hot topic between the United States and Afghanistan. Once the Americans realized that it was not possible for them to kill Osama directly through cruise missiles, they initiated secret dialogue with the fundamentalist regime regarding the possibility of extradition of the Saudi fugitive to the United States. Unfortunately, they greatly relied on the Pakistani leadership to mediate this secret dialogue, and depended on Islamabad's assessment about the developments in Afghanistan. But the Pakistani rulers had their own 'style' of censoring the facts. Indeed, it is clearly evident that General Musharaf never shown any interest for the extradition or capture of Osama bin Laden. Rather, clandestinely, Pakistani ISI was giving all support to the terrorist mastermind and his Al Qaeda cadres.

As per some documents obtained in Kabul following the collapse of the Taliban, a European journalist found that Pakistan played a very mischievous role on the question of OBL and the Taliban regime vis-à-vis the United States.[46] Pakistanis were doing something with the fundamentalist militia, but saying something else to the Americans. As a result, Americans seemed to be getting a wrong picture about the intention of both the Kabul regime and Pakistan over the Bin Laden issue. One of the documents revealed how the then Pakistani ISI Chief General Mahmood Ahmed—acted as intermediary between Mullah Omar and the U.S. administration —had gone to Kandahar, the Taliban headquarters and conveyed various American messages to Mullah Omar, and got back the latter's views to the Americans through the Pakistani leadership. As per the Pakistani 'talking points' prepared for the 26 May 2000 meeting with the US Under Secretary of State Thomas Pickering in Islamabad, the highest ranking (only next to the Secretary of State) official of the State Department was to be told about General Ahmed's trip to Kandahar. One of the messages was that: "Nothing short of the extradition of Osama bin Laden to a place where he could be brought to justice could satisfy the US," and that "Washington wanted immediate results. This meant that Osama should either be handed over to the US or sent to a place where he could be picked up. If the Taliban did not comply, the US wanted Pakistan to end all support for them." The Pakistani intelligence chief also passed on US concerns about the "export of religious extremism, terrorism and separatism, and laboratories near Kandahar producing heroin." The document recorded that "in the event that the Taliban did not cooperate in addressing these issues, severe measures could be taken by the US and the international community against them." This could include "greater" or "total sanctions" and "Afghanistan could be declared a terrorist state. This might entail missile attacks targeting the Taliban's military assets, Osama and even Omar himself could be targeted."[47] However, it is interesting to note that even at this point the United States was not contemplating direct military action against the fundamentalist Kabul regime. Rather, Washington was thinking of unleashing that of Russia's. According to the documents, the Taliban supremo was told that if he failed to comply with the US demands:

> Russia and its allies could be given the go ahead to embark on hot pursuit against terrorists. They could bomb strategic targets north of the Hindu Kush thereby eliminating the military potential of the Taliban to the complete advantage of [Northern Alliance military leader] Ahmed Shah Massoud . . . The US and Russia could coordinate their actions in pursuance of the above measures.[48]

This is what exactly happened when the United State began bombing the Taliban targets on 7 October 2001. The difference was that in the changed scenario, the air strikes just happened to be the American rather than Russian, and with this, the Taliban defence line collapsed and the Northern Alliance, equipped with Russian weapons, began to sweep the whole country into their control.

As far as Mullah Omar's responses to the American demands were concerned, the Pakistanis were censoring them according to their convenience and suitability before passing the same to their American counterparts. In consonance with their declared policy towards the Taliban regime, the Pakistani messages indicated that the United States should engage the Taliban in dialogue rather than initiating a confrontationist approach including on the issue of bin Laden. As per the documents, the Pakistanis would report the Americans that the Taliban leader Mullah Omar "wanted to get rid of Osama but did not know how," and that "the Taliban themselves were willing to punish Osama if proof was provided about his terrorist activities." The same Pakistani 'talking points' for the same May meeting with Thomas Pickering, only few days before the U.S. Secretary arrives in Islamabad, Musharaf told the visiting Afghan interior minister the same things they had heard from the ISI chief, "except that Musharaf had not demanded that bin Laden actually be handed over." Later, in his conversation with the Taliban's first Deputy Foreign Minister, Mullah Abdul Jalil Akhund, Musharaf said he would revive the proposal (with Pickering) of an Islamic Court for bin Laden saying that "perhaps the U.S. would now be amenable to it."[49] Another document revealed how Pakistanis had told the Americans only a few months earlier about their incisiveness demanding a resolution of the OBL issue. But when the Pakistani Foreign Minister Abdul Sattar met his Afghan counterpart Maulvi Mutawakil, he (Sattar) told his Afghan host that, "the Government of Pakistan admires the Afghan government's efforts on OBL."[50] Right up to September 11, 2001, Pakistan played a double-edged game, and neither discouraged the Taliban to even reduce its staff in its embassy in Islamabad nor the Musharaf government restraint itself from mobilizing international support to engage the fundamentalist militia. Clearly, Pakistan's policy towards the Taliban appeared tough when it was necessary to impress the United States, but very cool while dealing with the Afghan officials.

The Taliban regime did not show any sign that it was willing to handover bin Laden to the Americans, but U.S. officials (convinced by their Pakistani counterparts) said the Taliban had sent a clear signal that their desires to protect bin Laden was waning. One report suggests a senior Taliban official as saying "His (Osama's) presence is not a benefit to the people of Afghanistan," because it contributes to the nation's pariah status. But at the same time bin Laden poses "a puzzle for the Afghan leadership," because the Islamic Taliban cannot be seen to betray a fellow Muslim that is totally against the Afghan character.[51] The Taliban had even sent an emissary to the United States asking how to deal with the bin Laden issue "without seeming to double-cross him." Taliban's representative-designate at the United Nations Abdul Hakim Mujahid declared: "Our leadership decided to cut all communications from him, and even his telephone set has been taken from him. He has been told no foreigner can talk to him. Ten bodyguards were provided for him. The duty of the bodyguards was to supervise him and observe that he will not contact any foreigner or use any communication system in Afghanistan. He is now isolated."[52]

This statement of a Taliban representative might have been an exaggerated one. This could have been made with an intension to appease the United States since it came only a week after the Assistant Secretary of State for South Asia, Karl F. Inderfurth met Jalil Akhund, the Taliban's deputy foreign minister in Pakistan and repeated American demand to turn over Osama bin Laden. Senior American officials had stipulated that the Taliban leadership had at least three ways to deal with the issue that would be acceptable to Washington. First, they could arrange secretly for members of another nation's intelligence service to learn of his whereabouts in Afghanistan. Second, they could deliver him discreetly to a neighboring country, where American law-enforcement and intelligence officers could try to apprehend him. And third, they could keep bin Laden incommunicado in the hope that he might fade as a source of anti-American terrorism.[53] American officials were divided about their views regarding the bin Laden issue. Some thought the last solution was the best, since it holds no risk of making bin Laden a martyr, which could inspire fresh attacks against the United States from his followers. Others wanted to see him apprehended, whatever the risk. However, for the Saudi fugitive, Afghanistan remained as the "safest place in the world" at least up to the September 11 terrorist attacks on the United States. Neither the Taliban complied with the American demands, nor the United States could initiate any military action against Afghanistan to force the Taliban regime to handover bin Laden. The politics of sanctions did not work in case of Afghanistan, and the Americans failed to come out with any clear-cut policy alternative. Had the Americans taken the kind of military action what they did after October 7, 2001, the history of 'war against terrorism' would have been altogether different and the catastrophe of 9/11 would not have happened.

Evolving a Policy Framework

After the capture of Kabul by the Taliban in September 1996, a new military stalemate between the militia and their opponents emerged in Afghanistan. But this stalemate was virtually broken by the Taliban capture of the northern city of Mazar-e-Sharif on 25 May 1997.[54] Immediately after the capture of Mazar, Pakistan, Saudi Arabia and the United Arab Emirates recognized the Taliban government. It also came as a victory for the Taliban supporters in Washington, and the United States signaled that it would accept any Taliban-appointed diplomat to Afghanistan's mission in Washington DC.[55] But the United States neither develop a concrete policy towards Taliban, nor took any initiative to contain the spread of Islamic militancy in the region and beyond. Unintentionally, it allowed its allies in the region to play their own game that proved disastrous in future. After the 1998 attacks on the U.S. embassies in Kenya and Tanzania, Washington's only agenda vis-à-vis Taliban was to "get bin Laden."

Afghanistan under Taliban was the documented training and inspirational base for worldwide Islamic terrorist operations ranging from the United States to the Middle East, Central Asia, South Asia, and the Philippines. The growth of these terrorist networks took place with open support of Pakistan, and financial backing from Saudi Arabia, and of course, with the tacit consent and blessings of the United States itself. A former U.S. Ambassador to the Peshawar based Mujahiddin in the aftermath of the post-Soviet Afghanistan writes: "Just as the Soviets tried saving their communist asset in Kabul by invading Afghanistan, Islamabad has been funneling more troops and military resources to save its own asset, the Taliban. More than 10,000 Pakistanis (and one "brigade" of radical Muslims from Arab states) now fight alongside Taliban forces in what many Afghans describe as a "creeping" Pakistani invasion of Afghanistan. The ISI, the JUI, Arab extremists such as Osama bin Laden, and the Taliban leadership all cooperate closely. The ISI has long orchestrated this Islamist coalition."[56] Under these circumstances, the U.S. policy of "get bin Laden" was bound to be a failure. What the United States failed to understand (or accepted the reality?) was the intensity of its ally's involvement in the 'problem' and chalked out a comprehensive broad based strategy to solve the Afghan problem.

Like other foreign policy issues confronting the United States, Washington's policy towards the Taliban rule in Afghanistan suffered from some kind of intra-agency differences in the U.S. government, especially between the White House and the State Department. Even after the July 06, 1999 economic sanctions on Afghanistan,[57] barring Americans from trading with or investing in that country (a step short of declaring the Taliban a terrorist movement), which was reportedly favored by the White House, the State Department had a different idea. The State Department still believed that the U.S. should have a channel of communication with the fundamentalist regime in Kabul in hopes that it could eventually extradite bin Laden, whose exact whereabouts was known to only a few Taliban leaders.[58] This kind of "policy hurdles" are not new to the government agencies in Washington, what was horrifying this time around was the State Department's assessment of the ground situation in Afghanistan where the Taliban leadership defied all hopes of the Americans and ready to do anything and everything to harm the United States. Probably, their Pakistani cohorts misguided the Americans once again.

Some reports suggest that the CIA—which helped arm the mujahiddin—should have armed Taliban moderates with the aim of overthrowing Mullah Omar, and alternatively, the United States should have supported the return to power of Afghanistan's former king Zahir Shah, who ruled the country for four decades before being ousted in 1973. But given "Washington's policy flip-flops and general incompetence on Afghanistan, it would be disastrous if the CIA tried to fund anti-Taliban groups."[59] Yet some UN officials suggested serious American pressure on Afghanistan's neighboring states to halt supply of arms to that country— beginning with Pakistan. Burhanuddin Rabani of the Northern Alliance said, "The Americans hold the key to stop the external interference in Afghanistan, but they don't seem to have the will or determination to do so." In the words of a European diplomat: "Until the U.S. has a coherent Afghan policy rather than just a 'get bin Laden policy,' the war will continue."[60]

The Afghan civil war had obviously shaken up American strategic interests in the region. But as a very shortsighted, half-hearted stopgap measures, the United States tried its best to isolate the threat of terrorism from the Afghan conflict. In the absence of a clear cut strategic policy for the region that could have helped mitigate the Afghan problem to a certain extent, Washington only depended on sanctions as a weapon to teach the Taliban a lesson. Under US leadership, the United Nations imposed two rounds of sanctions in November 1999 and December 2000 with dramatically isolating the Taliban. The December 2000 sanctions were particularly more significant because it took some drastic measures against the Kabul regime. It gave 30 days to Taliban to close down all terrorist camps and hand over bin Laden to the United States. It also reinforced air embargo on the Taliban, froze their overseas assets, and restricted the travel of officials abroad among others. As expected, the sanctions went into effect on 20 January 2001, and supposed to last for at least one year. But it did not have any positive impact on the Taliban regime, and instead, led to a negative repercussion in Afghanistan and its supporters in Pakistan, and enhanced the Taliban's prestige among Islamic fundamentalists in the region and outside. With the support of all the fundamentalist elements and terrorist groups, Taliban became more stubborn in their resistance to the UN sanctions and US pressure.

The United States never developed a new strategic framework for Afghanistan and the region and "dealt with issues as they came up in a haphazard, piecemeal fashion, pursuing constantly changing single-issue agenda that were driven more by domestic American politics than the goal of ending the civil war."[61] Unfortunately, the United States could not learn any lesson and failed to create a policy more congruent with American interests in Afghanistan and the surrounding area. In stead, Washington allowed whatever typically incoherent policy it had, to breakdown.

Breakdown of the U.S. Policy

The shift in America's Afghan policy came amidst mounting international criticism against the Talibans appalling policies. It actually began shortly after the capture of Kabul by the Taliban.[62] Within a month, it was noticed that the United States abandoned the plan to send an envoy to Kabul. It also ended the Taliban hopes of the U.S. recognition of the new regime. Several factors led to this American disengagement.

With the unfolding of events along with various harsh directives issued from the Afghan supreme leader Mullah Omar, the United States could come to know about the real picture of the fundamentalist militia. Soon the United States realised the Taliban was not the type of government with which Washington could have mutually beneficial dealings. Leading experts on U.S. foreign policy issued opinion that "these people detest us, not for what we do but for who we are – and we cannot change that."[63] The pro-Taliban argument of some U.S. officials could not gain any ground when it was clear that the new regime was unlikely to moderate its attitude toward women in the public realm. It happened specially after capturing Kabul, when the Taliban quickly made clear that women should remain at home, men should grow beards, videos were banned etc, etc, and any deviation from their strict interpretation of the Koran would be sternly punished. Mullah Omar proclaimed that his country would become a "completely Islamic State" where a complete Islamic system will be enforced."[64] With these proclamations from the Taliban authority in Afghanistan, the U.S. State Department wanted to rapidly change its tune. A senior official explained, "the least thing we wanted to do was to fuel this total misperception that we were recognising and embracing the Taliban."[65] The Talibans barbaric treatment of women and children such as denial of work to women and even basic school education to girls, were championed by no less a person than the First Lady Hillary Clinton herself.[66] This was also backed and supported by the powerful American Feminist Movement and National Organization for Women that completely overshadowed the other problems in Afghanistan. Secretary of State Madeleine Albright dubbed the Taliban decrees 'medieval and impossible to justify or defend,'[67] and later she deplored the fundamentalist militia's "despicable" treatment of women and children and their lack of respect for human dignity. Albright made no secret that the U.S. was opposed to the Taliban militia.[68] A State Department spokesman very categorically warned that the Taliban should not expect recognition or any international assistance unless they showed respect for women's rights.[69]

Taliban harbouring of the terrorist mastermind Osama bin Laden also emerged as a stumbling block on the way to any rapprochement between the new militia and the United States. Osama bin Laden, described by friends as a "devout philanthropist" and the U.S. State Department as "one of the most significant financial sponsors of Islamic extremist activities in the world today,"[70] returned to Afghanistan immediately after the Taliban takeover of Kabul in mid 1996. In fact, it was reported in 1997 that bin Laden had been one of the significant financial sources that funded the Taliban's final thrust to Kabul.[71] This also explains why the Taliban extended the Saudi millionaire with so much of support and hospitality in subsequent years. The Taliban proved less sensitive to the American political interests than some in Washington had hoped, and it was soon became apparent that by the Taliban's definition, "bin Laden was not a terrorist but an Islamic brother-in-arms." When the Americans complained about the Saudi millionaire's terrorist activities elsewhere, Taliban leadership defended their Saudi guest vehemently. A senior Taliban leader Mullah Mohammad Sadiq told Time magazine: "Until we are sure that he committed crimes, how can we proceed against him? All we know is that bin Laden is a good Muslim and has taken part in the Afghan jihad (holy war) against the Soviets."[72] After August 1998 terrorist attacks on U.S. Embassies in Nairobi (Kenya), and Dar es Salam (Tanzania), that killed more than two hundred people, the U.S. intelligence community concluded that the attacks were organised by Osama bin Laden. The Clinton administration took a serious view of this incident and wanted extradition of bin Laden to the United States. But the Taliban categorically denied that their Saudi guest had anything to do with the U.S. embassy bombings, and hence the question of extradition did not rise. Then the United States ordered its Navy warships floating in the Indian Ocean to launch cruise missiles against bin Laden's terrorist training camps in Afghanistan and also targeted a factory in Sudan supposedly linked to Osama. As a reaction to the American missile attack, the Taliban warned that the "U.S. indictment of bin Laden would endanger Americans in the Muslim world and spark a storm of anger against the United States."[73] In fact, for a quite some time, Osama bin Laden had become the focus for Washington's Afghan policy as the U.S. administration concentrated on his containment and elimination, rather than focusing on other dimensions of the Afghan problems such as reconstruction, demining etc. or on bringing about peace to the country.

The United States also soon realised that the Taliban would not be able to unite and govern Afghanistan on its own and that the ongoing civil war there was likely to continue indefinitely. Because neither it was successful in capturing the whole of Afghan territory nor was it in a position to bringing about the chronic law and order problem to an end. An unstable Afghanistan inside and a fundamentalist Mullah dominated image to the outsiders did not make any sense to serve U.S. interest in the region. Taliban proved a sad disappointment to their supporters in Washington who had hoped that the new militia would disarm the armed guerrillas and warlords and reunite the country under a single stable government, and establish peace nationwide. Instead, the Taliban takeover of Kabul resulted in the establishment of an obvious police state in the capital, ethnic cleansing of the areas of its immediate north, and the spread of violence in areas which had long been relatively quiet."[74] This also came as an embarrassment for the Clinton team, especially in the backdrop of the Presidential election in the United States, to support such a regime that had only contempt for human rights. The United States changed its tune, and one official asserted, "as far as U.S. policy is concerned, we have always maintained that peace and security in Afghanistan can only be achieved through the establishment of a broad coalition government."[75] Secretary of State Madeleine

Albright made it clear when she said the United States believed that the Taliban were not in a position to occupy all of Afghanistan. She categorically stated "there are other parties who need to be recognised and there needs to be a government that is composed of them."[76] Finally, in a testimony to the Senate Foreign Relations Subcommittee on Near East and South Asia on 22 October 1997, Assistant Secretary Karl Inderfurth gave a clear statement of official U.S. policy towards Afghanistan and especially Taliban regime. He described the latest Taliban attempt to capture the northern city of Mazar-e-Sharif as 'stymied' and expressed his disbelief that any side could "win a military victory resulting in a peaceful and stable Afghanistan." Inderfurth identified Washington's objective as "an Afghan government that is multi-ethnic, broad-based, and that observes international norms of behaviour."[77] In fact, there was no doubt that the Taliban inability to capture the whole Afghan territory led the United States to confirm that Washington does not recognised 'governments' but only to 'states.'[78]

Another significant factor that compelled Washington to maintain distance with the fundamentalist militia was the latter's policy on opium poppy cultivation in Afghanistan. In fact, the American hope of making Taliban a partner in the 'war against drugs' proved to be an illusion. By the end of 1996, the Taliban-controlled areas were producing about 95 percent of Afghanistan's opium crop.[79] Instead of banning the opium cultivation, as the militia had promised, it turns out to be beneficiaries of the poppy trade. The advent of the Taliban regime had facilitated the growth of opium in rural Afghanistan. Poppy farmers were benefiting from the relative peace and security that the militia had brought about in its own controlled areas.[80] Taliban had set up model firms where farmers learn the best methods of heroin cultivation. As per one estimate, Afghanistan produced 4,600 metric tons of opium in 1999-twice as much as in the previous year. The country produced three times more opium than the rest of the world put together and ninety six percent of which was cultivated in Taliban-controlled area, making the militia the largest heroin producer in the world.[81] By the early 2001, the fundamentalist regime had raised a war budget of about $100 million of which about 40 percent revenues came from the drug trade.[82] It collected 20 percent tax from the opium dealers and transporters that directly went to the war chest of the Taliban.[83] After the U.S. embassy bombings in Africa in 1998, when the United States frozen most of Osama bin Laden's bank accounts, American officials claimed that bin Laden had begun to finance his terrorist operations through opium trade.[84] Thus the large-scale drug trade in Afghanistan ultimately had taken a security implication for the United States and Washington had no option left but to contain the Taliban regime along with the terrorist mastermind, Osama bin laden. One more significant area of confrontation relating to drug trade was that the Taliban went to the extent of making this a bargaining chip to gain international recognition. As a Taliban official reportedly demanded, "If the west support the Islamic demands of the Taliban and recognise our government then we can stop the poppy cultivation."[85] However, the United States did not come to consider such type of narcotics blackmail to recognise the Taliban regime.

Another American hope which apparently believed that the Taliban constituted a force under Pakistan's control which could serve U.S. interest in the region also belied, and rather had a negative impact on the U.S. policy. The militia could not be kept under Pakistan's control, and contrary to Washington's expectations, its extremist ideology spread to Pakistan – a reliable American ally – and created anti-Americanism to a great extent. Some Pakistani supporters, namely Maulana Fazlur Rahman of the Jamiat-e-Ulema-e Islami, has made several anti-American speeches since the days Washington came out openly against the Taliban. The large-scale Pakistani support, both in the government and the people, had also alarmed Washington. Each American move against Taliban has led lots of debates in Islamabad and made the Pakistani leaders unsettled. Pakistani officials have been openly critical of the change in the U.S. approach.[86] Instead of any change in their attitude and behaviour, the fundamentalist militia had also begun to Talibanizing parts of Pakistan. There were evidences of "the neo-Taliban parties" banning television and videos, imposing Sharia punishments such as stoning and amputation etc. in Baluchistan and North West Frontier Province.[87] What was alarming to the United States was that Pakistan – a key American ally in the region – was/is reluctant to help the Americans capture Osama bin Laden only due to excessive pressure from the fundamentalist parties and supporters of the Saudi fugitive and Taliban within Pakistan.[88] After persistent American diplomacy for quite some time, it appeared in September-October 1999 that Washington was making some progress over the extradition issue with the Pakistani Prime Minister Nawas Sharif who for the first time came out openly accusing the Taliban of fuelling Islamic extremism and supporting sectarian violence in Pakistan. However, after a short interlude of this statement, the Prime Minister was overthrown in a military coup led by the Army Chief General Pervez Musharaf and the people who had been the real shapers of Pakistan's Afghan policy since 1980s (the military and the ISI) assumed power. It appeared that Pakistan was heading towards a point of no return, and that the chances of Islamic revolution in the country were not so much impending ever before. Due to this kind of situation, American officials felt that there was no alternative to maintaining distance from the fundamentalist regime and containing the terrorist mastermind Osama bin Laden as well as the Taliban.

With the continual Taliban defiance, American officials were horrified and ashamed of the Pakistani ISI's ill-conceived plan that they had supported. Washington's over dependence on Islamabad's assessment and analysis of Taliban also evoked mounting criticism as it proved naïve and misleading. One official observed that "the United States' initial embrace of the Taliban, which proved to be an embarrassment, was prompted by Pakistan, which had misled Washington into thinking that the Taliban could stem narcotics-trafficking from Afghanistan and close down all the exports-oriented terrorist camps in that country. We soon realised that the Taliban could do neither and more so we found that they were to a large extent funding their own operations with the profits from drug trafficking.[89] This kind of opinions had an impact on the American decision to disengage with the

Taliban regime, which no longer had a good image before the United States or its allies.

A clear change in the direction of American policy took place with the appointment of Madeleine Albright as the new Secretary of State in early 1997. With this, so many important changes in the rank and file were brought about including the replacement of the Taliban supported Assistant Secretary of State for South Asian Affairs Robin Raphel with a cautious Karl F. Inderfurth. The new team could not comfortably embrace the Taliban either politically or ideologically.[90] In fact, with the assumption of office by the new team, the Taliban movement came to be seen as untouchables from Washington.

In addition to the above, the geo-strategic argument that since the Taliban was anti-Iranian and anti-Russian, as well as pro-Pakistani, the United States ought to embrace it, became meaningless. It made some sense so long as relations between the United States and Iran were highly antagonistic, with Washington determined to contain Iran, and that Iran was deeply engaged in regional power rivalry with America's allies. But with the advent of President Mohammed Khatami to power in mid-1997, American perception began to change. In fact, the new President's reform measures such as the steps towards bringing about an "Islamic democracy" and "Islamic civil society" attracted several good will overtures by the Clinton Administration, especially by the Secretary of State Madeline Albright. Although these positive American gestures did not lead to any concrete rapprochement between Teheran and Washington, at least it resulted in the participation of U.S. secretary of state and the Iranian foreign minister in a meeting on Afghanistan chaired by the U.N. Secretary-General in September 2000. This development also led to a new look in Iran's foreign relations towards America's friends and allies in the whole region including the members of Gulf Coordination Council (GCC) such as Saudi Arabia, UAE, as well as South and Central Asian states. Significantly, the Islamic extremism and medievalist behaviour practiced by the Taliban and parts of Pakistan came under severe criticism by Khatami's reformist government. Viewed from Washington, it seemed that it was in the American interests to support Teheran's reforms and work towards a friendly relations with Iran, and oppose the Taliban's brand of Islam as well as continual Pakistani military and political support to the fundamentalist militia.

As far as Pakistan's policy towards the Taliban regime was concerned, the United States became increasingly sceptical about Islamabad's role. Within months of the military coup in Pakistan in October 1999, it was clear that the new military ruler was not going to contain the Taliban under U.S. pressure or oppose the fundamentalist forces within Pakistan that constituted the real constituency for both General Musharaf and the rulers in Kabul. American officials were convinced that it was virtually impossible for the Taliban and their guest Osama bin Laden and associates to carry out "off-shore" operations without the consent of Pakistan, their only outlet to the world. Washington was left in no doubt that Pakistani intelligence was directly involved in providing all possible military and logistic support to the fundamentalist militia and helping the Taliban and Al Quaeda of supporting international terrorism. Interestingly, the military leadership in Pakistan also came out openly in support of the Taliban regime in Afghanistan. In continuation of the policy objectives framed by General Zia ul Haq in the 1980s, General Musharaf openly argued that it was in Pakistan's national security interest to support the Taliban as a cross-border force dominated by ethnic Pashtuns on both sides of the long Afghan-Pakistan border. In a BBC interview on August 2, 2000, the Pakistani ruler declared, "we have a certain national security compulsion and our national security compulsion as far as Afghanistan is concerned is that the Pashtuns of Afghanistan have to be on Pakistan's side." With regard to Osama bin Laden, he urged the United States to enter into direct dialogue with the Taliban, a stand through which Pakistan intended to gain broader international recognition for the fundamentalist militia in Kabul.

These factors led to American disengagement in Afghanistan, but ironically, the hand-in-glove policy of Pakistan did not lead to a clear-cut reaction from the United States. The small and insignificant steps such as permitting the Afghan opposition to open an office in Washington on behalf of the Rabbani government[91] was of no help in bringing about any significant change on the situation. Lack of sufficient resources had deterred the opposition from expanding its territorial control beyond the North Eastern provinces or providing any substantial support to local uprisings elsewhere in the country. American policy remained ambivalent towards Afghanistan and Pakistan, or for that matter towards the whole region, which had little incentive for any kind of negotiated settlement through the United Nations or by any initiative by the ex-Afghan King Zahir Shah. Only after the 9/11 terrorist attack on the United States that the Americans woke up to the ground reality in Afghanistan and Pakistani role thereof again in a more unconvinced manner.

Conclusion

An ambivalent US policy towards Afghanistan and its allies in the region had transformed the Afghans from the Cold War victors to tragic victims that ultimately led to the collapse of the Afghan state, its traditional society and the economy, and allowed all the disruptive and destabilizing forces to expand their network worldwide. American Cold War strategy of declaring sanctions or rouge status—a short term punishments to a state that does not comply to its own terms—to a country did not work in case of Afghanistan as it comes about in other political societies. America's initial support to Taliban was mostly based on the assessment of its close ally in the region, Pakistan that was pursuing its own longstanding agenda in Afghanistan. Ironically, the United States continually repeated the same mistakes despite having bitter experiences of their blind support and closer relationship with the Islamic fundamentalist leaders backed by the Pakistani ISI.[92] Whenever there is a political upheaval in any country in the region, or the Americans perceived any strategic threat to their interests, Pakistan is brought to the limelight and the U.S. strategists behave as if there is no alternative to Pakistani support in the whole of South and Southwest Asia. This American tendency has given raise to more anti-Americanism in Afghanistan and the surrounding region, rather than furthering some short-term American strategic interests. In a recent exposition, Nobel laureate V.S. Naipaul, opposing the post 9/11 wars against terrorism has said America's biggest enemy are its great allies like Saudi Arabia and Pakistan.[93] American failure to develop a viable Afghan policy during the Taliban era and blindly supporting its allies in the region ultimately proved disastrous to the United States which led to the terrorist attacks in New York and Washington DC on September 11, 2001 and brought about another catastrophic phase of war and tragedy for the Afghans. It is to this phase of study and analysis that now we turn.

Notes and References

1. Barnett Rubin's statement on "Recent Developments in U.S. Policy Toward Afghanistan," Hearing before the Subcommittee on Asian and Pacific Affairs of the Committee on Foreign Affairs, House of Representatives, 102nd Congress, 1st session, June 20, 1991, U.S. Congress Printing Office, Washington DC, 1993, p. 67.
2. Ralph H. Magnus and Eden Naby, *Afghanistan: Mullah, Marx, and Mujahid,* Westview Press, Boulder, 1998, p. 179.
3. Mullah Omar, a Durrani Pushtun, was a local mujahiddin commander in the 1980's jihad against the Soviet Union. Reportedly, he was operating from his base in the Arghestan district with a few hundred fighters. In course of fighting, he was wounded and lost an eye and then known as a "Rund" (one-eyed). This incident had enhanced his credibility as he personally had sacrificed for the cause of jihad.
4. Martin Ewans, *Afghanistan: A New History,* Curzon Press, Richmond, 2001, p. 182.
5. As cited in Johanna McGeary, "The Taliban troubles," *Time,* New York, October 1, 2001.
6. *Ibid.* Also see Ralph H. Magnus and Eden Naby, *Afghanistan: Mullah, Marx, and Mujahid,* p. 181.
7. Barnett R. Rubin, *The Fragmentation of Afghanistan,* New Haven, Yale University Press, 1995.
8. This undeclared strategic alliance played a vital role in the 1980s Afghan war against the former Soviet Union.
9. Martin Ewans, *Afghanistan: A New History,* p. 183.
10. *Ibid.*
11. Ahmed Rashid, "Pakistan and the Taliban," in William Maley ed., *Fundamentalism Reborn? Afghanistan and the Taliban,* Hurst & Company, London, 1998, pp. 75-76.
12. *Ibid,* p. 76.
13. *The Middle East,* June 1993, p. 22.
14. *The New York Times,* July 27, 1998.

15. Barnett R. Rubin, "Afghanistan under the Taliban," *Current History*, February 1999, p. 86.
16. Barnett R. Rubin, "Women and pipelines: Afghanistan's proxy wars," *International Affairs*, Vol. 73, No. 2, April 1997, p. 190.
17. *Ibid.*
18. Michael Dobbs, "Analysts Feel Militia Could End Anarchy," *Washington Post*, September 28, 1996.
19. Robin Raphel explained this in course of a lecture at the School of International Studies, University of Illinois at Urbana-Champaign in February 1995. Also told this author in a separate interview on the same day at the Program in South Asian and Middle Eastern Studies. For more details, see Robin Raphel, "U.S. Policy toward Afghanistan, Bangladesh, Nepal and Sri Lanka," *U.S. Department of State Dispatch*, Vol. 5, No. 35, August 29, 1994, pp. 582-583. Also see *Ibid*, p. 184.
20. Robin Raphel, "U.S. Policy Toward South Asia," U.S. *Department of State Dispatch*, Vol. 6, No. 13, March 27, 1995, p. 248. Also cited in Ralph H. Magnus and Eden Naby, *Afghanistan: Mullah, Marx, and Mujahid*, p. 184.
21. John Jennings, "The Taliban and Foggy Bottom," *Washington Times*. October 25, 1996.
22. Elements in Washington were so mad about the new militia that three months after the fall of Kabul to the Taliban, the State Department declared that the United States intended to establish contact with the new regime, despite its unacceptable policy toward women. See Ralph H. Magnus and Eden Naby, "Afghanistan: Mullah, Marx, and Mujahid, Westview Press, Boulder, 1998, p. 191.
23. Adam Garfinkle, "Afghanistanding," *Orbis*, Vol. 43, No. 3, Summer 1999, p. 415.
24. P. Stobdan, "War in Afghanistan," *Asian Strategic Review: 1996-97*, Institute for Defence Studies and Analysis, New Delhi, p. 259.
25. *US News & World Report*, November 11, 1996.
26. Brown was the first elected US representative to visit Afghanistan in 16 years.
27. Barnett R. Rubin, "Women and pipelines: Afghanistan's proxy wars," *International Affairs*, Vol. 73, No. 2, April 1997, p. 288.
28. *Ibid.*
29. *Time*, December 16, 1996, p. 22.
30. As cited in *World Press Review*, January 1997, p. 23.
31. *Hindustan Times*, October 10, 1996.
32. Barnett R. Rubin, "U.S. Policy in Afghanistan," *Muslim Politics Report*, No. 11, January/February 1997, p. 6.
33. Richard Mackenzie, "United States and Taliban," in William Maley ed., Fundamentalism Reborn? *Afghanistan and the Taliban*, p. 96.
34. *Ibid*, p. 97.
35. *Ibid.*

36. "Washington Conference Enhances State Position," *Afghan News,* Vol. 12, No. 6, June 30, 1996, pp. 1, 8. As cited in Ralph H. Magnus and Eden Naby, *Afghanistan: Mullah, Marx, and Mujahid,* p. 191. Later in August, Hekmatyar, then Prime Minister, replied by refusing to meet with Senator Brown during his visit to Kabul.
37. Richard Mackenzie, "United States and Taliban," in William Maley ed., Fundamentalism Reborn? *Afghanistan and the Taliban,* p. 98.
38. *Ibid.*
39. Rosemarie Forsythe, *The Politics of Oil in the Caucasus and Central Asia,* Oxford: Oxford University Press, Adelphi Paper No. 300, International Institute for Strategic Studies, 1996; Ahmed Rashid, *The Turkmenistan – Afghanistan – Pakistan Pipeline: Company – Government Relations and Regional Politics,* Washington DC, Focus on Current Issues, The Petrolium Finance Company, October 1997, as cited in *Ibid*, p. 99.
40. *Ibid,* p. 99.
41. As quoted in *The Times of India,* October 12, 1996.
42. Christopher Ogden, "Good News/Bad News in the Great Game," *Time,* October 14, 1996, p. 22.
43. *Ibid.*
44. As quoted in William Maley, "Interpreting the Taliban," in William Maley ed., *Fundamentalism Reborn? Afghanistan and the Taliban,* p. 19.
45. Adam Garfinkle, "Afghanistanding," *Orbis,* Summer 1999, p. 415.
46. A very interesting study about the Pakistani role regarding the Taliban regime vis-à-vis the United States is available with Tim Judah, "The Taliban Papers," *Survival,* Vol. 44, No. 1, Spring 2002, pp. 69-80.
47. *Ibid,* p. 70.
48. *Ibid.*
49. *Ibid,* p. 71.
50. *Ibid,* p. 73.
51. Tim Weiner, "Terror Suspect Said to Anger Afghan Hosts," *The New York Times,* March 4, 1999.
52. Cited in *Ibid.*
53. *Ibid.*
54. For details see Anwar-ul-Haq Ahady, "Saudi Arabia, Iran and the Conflict in Afghanistan," in William Maley ed., *Fundamentalism Reborn? Afghanistan and the Taliban,* p. 133.
55. *The Washington Post,* May 29, 1997.
56. Peter Tomsen, "A Chance for Peace in Afghanistan: The Taliban's Days Are Numbered," *Foreign Affairs,* January/February 2000, p. 181.
57. This was followed by the UN Security Council sanctions in November the same year.
58. Ahmed Rashid, "Afghanistan: Heart of Darkness," *The Far Eastern Economic Review,* August 5, 1999.

59. *Ibid.*
60. Quoted in *Ibid.*
61. Ahmed Rashid, "The Taliban: Exporting Terrorism," *Foreign Affairs*, November/December 1999, p. 35.
62. Elaine Sciolino, "US to Distance Itself From New Kabul Regime," *The New York Times*, October 23, 1996.
63. Adam Garfinkle, "Afghanistanding," p. 416.
64. Barbara Crossette, "Kabul Falls to Islamic Militia: Afghans Accuse Pakistan," and "Afghan Fundamentalists Sweep into Kabul," *The New York Times*, September 26 and 27, 1996.
65. Quoted in Elaine Sciolino, "State Department Becomes Cooler to the New Rulers of Kabul," *The New York Times*, October 23, 1996.
66. In a meeting of the Physicians for Human Rights, Hillary Clinton echoed the 1998-1999 Annual Report of Freedom House that said, "The Talibans violent, arbitrary rule has imposed order through terror. Its dehumanisation of women and girls has turned educated women into beggars; left widows, mothers and daughters to die of illness that have been treatable for decades; and denied a generation of girls access to basic education." *Voice of America*, April 30, 1999.
67. U.S. Condemns human rights abuses in Afghanistan, *The Nation*, October 26, 1996.
68. Ian Brodia, "Albright attacks Taliban oppression of women," *The Times*, November 19, 1997.
69. U.S. warns Taliban over Women's rights, *Dawn*, October 8, 1996.
70. *Time*, December 16, 1996, p. 22.
71. Steve Levine, Helping Hand, *Newsweek*, October 14, 1997.
72. Cited in *Time*, December 16, 1996, p. 22.
73. Adam Garfinkle, "Afghanistanding," p. 416.
74. Richard Mackenzie, "United States and Taliban," in William Maley ed., *Fundamentalism Reborn? Afghanistan and the Taliban*, p. 100.
75. "U.S. Claims it was Misled on Taliban," as reported by IANS, *The Pioneer*, November 23, 1996.
76. As quoted in Amin Saikal, "Afghanistan's Ethnic Conflict," *Survival*, Vol. 40, No. 2, Summer 1998, p. 121.
77. See the testimony of the Assistant Secretary of State for South Asia in the Subcommittee on Near East and South Asia, Senate Committee on Foreign Relations, Washington D.C. U.S. Information Agency, October 22, 1997.
78. "U.S. Treading Warily on Afghanistan," *The Hindu*, May 29, 1997.
79. "Opium Poppy Production in Afghanistan: High But Stabilised, New U.N. Survey Finds," *UN Information Service*, Vienna, September 1996.
80. Ahmed Rashid, "Drug the Infidels," *Far Eastern Economic Review*, May 1, 1997, pp. 25-26.

81. Ahmed Rashid, "The Taliban Exporting Extremism," *Foreign Affairs*. November/December 1999, p. 33.
82. Ahmed Rashid, "Afghanistan: Ending the Policy Quagmire," *Journal of International Affairs*, Vol. 54, No. 2, Spring 2001, p. 404.
83. Ahmed Rashid, "The Taliban Exporting Extremism," p. 33.
84. *Ibid.* Also see Ahmed Rashid, "Afghanistan: Ending the Policy Quagmire," p. 403.
85. Ahmed Rashid, "Drug the Infidels," pp. 25-26.
86. For example see, "Gohar Warns of New Arms Race in Region," *Dawn*, March 12, 1998.
87. Ahmed Rashid, "The Taliban Exporting Extremism," p. 27.
88. A very useful study about Taliban's fundamentalist influence outside Afghanistan is found in *Ibid.*
89. Quoted in P. Stobdan, "War in Afghanistan," *Asian Strategic Review, 1996-1997*, Institute of Defence Studies and Analysis, New Delhi, p. 262.
90. Amin Saikal, "Afghanistan's Ethnic Conflict," p. 121.
91. Although this office was not a replacement for the Afghan Embassy that was closed down two years ago because of an internal dispute over whether it should represent the Taliban or the Rabbani government, it did signal a change in the U.S. approach.
92. For example, the American support to the extremist fundamentalist leader Gulbuddin Hekmatyar who benefited most from the CIA pipeline in 1980s, and when the money dried up, he opposed the American policies and became anti-American. Similarly, during 2001-2002 Afghan war, Pakistani ISI allowed the Al Qaeda and Taliban leaders to enter into Pakistani territory and disappear unnoticed. And yet Pakistan is a "close ally of the United States in its war on terrorism."
93. "US allies are worst enemies: Naipaul," *The Times of India*, August 8, 2002.

9

America's Afghan War: The Success that Failed

On my orders, the United States military has begun strikes against Al Qaeda terrorist training camps and military installations of the Taliban regime in Afghanistan. These carefully targeted actions are designed to disrupt the use of Afghanistan as a terrorist base of operations, and to attack the military capability of the Taliban regime . . . The United States of America is a friend to the Afghan people . . . We will not waver, we will not tire, we will not falter and we will not fail. Peace and freedom will prevail.

—*President George W Bush, Address to the Nation, October 7, 2001*

Beginning with the attack on the United States on September 11, 2001, it took the United States, the sole superpower on earth, 27 days of war preparation before it dropped the first bomb over the Taliban/Al Qaeda forces, their infrastructures and establishments in Afghanistan. The innovative and war fighting strategy of the National Security team, code named as Operation Enduring Freedom (OEF)[1], began on October 7, 2001, and within two months it achieved a spectacular victory for the United States and its allies. It successfully overthrew the Taliban government and deprived Al Qaeda of its sanctuary within Afghanistan and left its surviving leaders running for their lives. Washington also helped establish a government under a new leadership and tried to bring peace and calm to this war-torn country. Under its initiative, international donors' conferences were held and marginal aid began to flow to Kabul from different quarters. Nearly two years after September 11, Afghanistan could be said to be sailing along, and the American policy has paid off well.

But despite all these 'successes,' the United States has failed to accomplish the main objectives of the war. 1. It has failed to kill or capture top leadership of Taliban and Al Qaeda, including Osama bin Laden (OBL), Mullah Omar, and associates, and to demolish their terrorist infrastructures and networks. 2. America has failed to bring about any real reconciliation among different Afghan factions, ethnic groups and warlords, or to eliminate the Taliban and Al Qaeda from the Afghan land. 3. United States has not succeeded to prevent poppy cultivation to check narcotic trade originating in Afghanistan which finances international terrorism. 4. Washington has also failed to fulfill its undeclared objective of transforming the events of 9/11 and the subsequent Afghan war into a geo-political and strategic advantage for the United States. Since the first three have not been achieved, obviously, the last one has remained an unfinished agenda. The sporadic attack by the Taliban/Al Qaeda terrorists still going on, and the chances of their regroupings and counter attacks still exists. Even after nearly two years of the launching of Operation Enduring Freedom, Afghan society remains fragmented politically, socially and economically. American policy has failed to initiate a nation building process. It has shown more interests on obscure military operation aiming at terrorist outfits and a half-hearted stopgap approach towards bringing about real peace in the country. As a result, there is a remote possibility of peace in the country, and the chances of American troops getting bogged down seem more.

All this happened because of four important factors that are more or less interlinked to each other. (1) A flawed American policy of over-dependence on Pakistani army and intelligence (ISI), which clandestinely supported the Taliban and the Al Qaeda in allowing Osama bin Laden, Mullah Omar and other top leaders to escape unnoticed; (2) US disinterests in ISAF; (3) Washington's policy of weaponizing the warlords; and (4) American geo-political ambition and shift in policy. The first one helped the Taliban and Al Qaeda leaderships to hide them, and the rest three factors are misleading the Afghan campaign to a state of chaos and confusion. Since Al Qaeda and many other anti-American elements back the Taliban, leaders and their terrorist outfits could always regroup themselves to pose a constant threat to the United States and its allies. The American offensive against Taliban/Al Qaeda has been, therefore, turned out to be a mere momentary respite, and the United States might have to stay back in this otherwise fiercely independent country for a long time to come. The search for Taliban and Al Qaeda leaders in the mountainous terrain of Afghanistan for an indefinite period may ultimately lead to ethnic and geo-political entanglement of Washington and invite Afghan resentment against the "occupying forces." It seems that Americans have won the war but lost the peace. After a phase of protracted war, Americans might be painfully learning the hard way that it was one way to bomb a country and conduct ground operations to oust an unacceptable regime, but it was quite another thing to fight the force that created and sustained that regime.

The 'Success' Story

The Destabilization Process

As far as the removal of the Taliban from power and the destruction of the Al Qaeda training camps and other infrastructures within Afghanistan are concerned, it was a simple walkover for the Americans. The United States did it very smoothly in a shortest possible time and, virtually without casualty to its troops.[2] This was possible mostly due to the working of four important determinants: (a) mobilization of American military forces, (b) international support, (c) use of high technology gadgets, and (d) indigenous allies. In addition, the support extended (coercively acquired?) by Pakistan and Central Asian Republics made the American war efforts easier and brought about a quicker than expected military victory for Washington.

Mobilization of Military Forces

America had a massive war preparation before it launched its air operation in Afghanistan. In addition to its permanent facilities in the Indian Ocean island of Diego Garcia, and floating aircraft carriers in the Arabian Sea, and Naval base off the coast in Oman, Washington used base facilities in Pakistan as well as Central Asian Republics. This was the biggest mobilization since the 1991 Gulf War. The U.S. arsenal included B-1 and B-52 bombers, dozens of fighters and support aircraft that were ordered to the Gulf and the Indian Ocean region along with elite Special Operations troops. The aircraft carrier USS Kitty Hawk, which was already in the Indian Ocean, was now fully loaded with helicopters and special operation forces for combat use and commando raids. American Navy planes, flying from carriers stationed in the Indian Ocean, also began patrolling specified "kill boxes" for what the Pentagon more precisely said was "engagement zones." With the unfolding of events, the United States increased the number of special operation forces and CIA teams, and engaged them in working with various opposition elements.

From Diego Garcia, B-52 and B-1 bombers; from Oman, F-15Es, and AC-130 gun ships; and from the three aircraft carriers based in the Arabian Sea came the rest "combat punch." It was also stipulated that reconnaissance and refueling flights would originate from Diego Garcia and the Persian Gulf region, and air support and relief missions to come from Central Asia where the Tenth Mountain Division of the US Army soldiers helped protect airfields. At the pick of the war, about 60, 000 American forces were involved in this operation, out of which about half were in the Persian Gulf. In addition to this, America's friends and allies added no more than 15, 000 troops. Also about 15, 000 Northern Alliance fighters mostly from Tajik and Uzbek ethnic groups, and thousands of Pashtun soldiers joined in the winning side in November 2001. So compared to Afghanistan's military capability, it was a huge preparation by the United States to remove the Taliban regime from power in the shortest possible time.

International Support

One of the immediate needs of America's war against the Taliban regime and Al Qaeda networks in Afghanistan was the mobilization of international public opinion. On this score, United States' first priority was the UN sanction. The Bush administration successfully maneuvered the Security Council Resolution 1373 adopted on September 29, 2001 and then centered around formation of a coalition against its "war on terrorism." Within days, the United States claimed that 48 countries had declared their support for the military campaign in Afghanistan.[3] Though all of them are not direct participants in the exercise, such a political support of so many countries on U.S. war efforts is a rare event in the American diplomatic history. All the major powers of the world supported the creation of a coalition against the terrorist campaign in Afghanistan. The countries, which directly participated in the war at some point of time or the other, included United Kingdom, France, Australia, Canada, Denmark, Norway, and Germany. Japan, Itâly and the Netherlands showed their support to the United States by deploying their warships in the Arabian Sea. In fact, the Europeans were so forthcoming about their support to the Americans that on the very next day of the terrorist attacks on the U.S., the French news paper *Le Monde* proclaimed on the front page, "We are all Americans now." A few days later NATO declared its full support to the American war efforts. The most powerful military alliance of the world rapidly invoked article 5 of the North Atlantic Treaty: an attack on one is an attack on all. As a token goodwill gesture, NATO demonstrated its unstinted support by sending five AWACS to help petrol U.S. airspace. However, regional support was more important in terms of the American war preparation and actual operation on the ground. In this connection, the role of Uzbekistan, Tajikistan, Saudi Arabia, Pakistan and Oman were very critical and worth noting. These countries provided the most essential logistical facilities as well as their respective territorial waters and transit facilities on their territories. Shortly after the American campaign began, President Bush appeared on television and claimed that the United States enjoyed wide support for its action both in the western hemisphere and the Arab and Muslim world. The President declared: "We are supported by the collective will of the world."[4]

Use of High Technology Weapons

High-technology weapons played a crucial role in this war. When the war was intensified in different strategic points in Afghanistan, it was intensified not in terms of fighter planes and bombardments, but in terms of the use of American high technology weapons such as Advanced Unmanned Aerial Vehicles (AUAV), Joint Surveillance and Target Attack Radar System (JSTARS) aircraft, use of Global Positioning System (GPS) technology, which bounces signals off of satellites to pinpoint a user's location, and laser range finders.[5] A special-forces soldier with a pager-sized battery-powered GPS device knows where he is to within 10 meters. Combined with new communications gear, he also knows where his fellow soldiers are. Such interconnectedness helped the American troops overcome the disconcertingly vast Afghan landscape. It was the use of high technology that gave them back the sensation of being part of a group. A special operation soldier on surveillance could use his GPS device through sighting a target with a laser spotter, comparing the readout to his GPS and to call in pinpoint strikes from far off bombers. Then the pilot programmes the coordinates into a 2000-pound smart bomb, and a few minutes later the target is smoke. Laser range finders are also equally wonder weapons. Laser illumination and guidance give heavy gravity bombs greater accuracy. Their sheer speed and weight drives them deep into the ground to penetrate bunkers.[6] Apart from this, the uses of night vision goggles were considered as standard equipment for many frontline troops. Users could see farther, clearly and with only the barest minimum of moonlight or even starlight as a source. The elite and secret squads among the special operations soldiers also used thermal imaging devices, which require no light at all and can see through fog, smoke and even some walls by picking up the slightest heat sources. All these new technology equipments helped the United States maintain continuous reconnaissance of the Taliban and Al Qaeda forces in the different parts of the country and put the enemy in the defensive from the beginning.

Indigenous Allies

Within weeks of this detalibanization process, it was observed that one significant development was getting momentum in the South and the Southeastern region of the country. A fraction of the Pashtun tribes who had welcome the Taliban six years ago, and continued to support the regime, had now begun to oppose it openly. In fact, this region of Afghanistan was considered as the stronghold of the fundamentalist militia, and therefore, once Pashtuns backtracked from their support. it implied that the days of the Taliban were numbered. To the chagrin of the Taliban, by mid November, these people began to accept help from the United States Special Forces. The present Prime Minister of Afghanistan, Hamid Karzai, who was trying to organize a pro-king revolt against the Taliban, led one of the Pashtun groups. Another significant support came from Gul Agha Shirzai tribal factions within the Pashtun populated areas in mainly Southern Afghanistan where the Americans played a very critical role in supporting the Afghan leaders. American policy and diplomacy towards the Pashtun populated South was just accurate and up to the mark. It helped quickly galvanize the mostly hitherto Taliban supported Pashtun forces to effectively fight against the militia itself, making the American efforts much easier. In the opinion of an American analyst, "Had these Pashtun forces decided that they feared the Northern Alliance and the United States more than the Taliban, Afghanistan might have become effectively partitioned, with Al Qaeda taking refuge exclusively in the South and the war effort rendered largely futile."[7] But the most crucial military support the Americans obtained was from the Northern Alliance of the assassinated commander Ahmed Shah Masud and former President Barhanuddin Rabbani. In fact, once the war started, it was Northern Alliance that began to capture one after another city and states in direct consultations with the Americans. They not only played a very critical role in providing intelligence inputs to the Americans but also made a clean sweep in the ground operation, making the things much easier for the U.S. forces.

In addition, one reason for the swift collapse of the Taliban could have been the "partial withdrawal" and "curtailment of overt support" of the Pakistani military advisors and regulars over the weeks following the American attacks began.[8] Western intelligence officials said at the time that the Pakistani move "may have been a crucial factor" in the surprisingly quick withdrawal of Taliban forces when confronted by the Northern Alliance. One Western diplomat commented, "We did not fully understand the significance of Pakistan's role in propping up the Taliban until their guys withdrew and things went to hell fast for the Talibs."[9] Thus, presumably, the lessening of Pakistani military support to the Taliban cost dearly to the fundamentalist militia and led to the fall of the regime.

Military Victory?

These entire American offensive put the Taliban forces on the run from the very beginning. It looked a very massive and systematic planning to achieve quick military victory with least allied casualties. Within weeks of the American air strikes, the Taliban/ Al Qaeda forces were on the run. The Taliban lost their large physical/ military assets such as aircraft, radar and command and control systems. Many Al Qaeda headquarters and training camps were also destroyed and their communication systems cut off. American air attack was so massive that within the first week itself, most of the immovable assets worth striking had already been hit. So right from mid-October, the allied bombers targeted only Taliban/Al Qaeda ground forces.

By the end of the second week of November, the Northern Alliance Forces began to clean up the Taliban troops, first in Mazar-i-Sharif and then in Taloquan. Thus two extreme northeastern states fell, which led to the fall of one after another towns, cities and states. After the fall of two states, Mullah Omar, the Taliban leader, broadcast a demand that his troops stop "behaving like chickens."[10] Kabul fell soon afterwards. There were reports of large-scale killings of Taliban and Al Qaeda troops including a top aide of Osama bin Laden, Mohammed Atef.

Meanwhile, about 1000 American marines of the 15th and 26th Marine Expeditionary Units established a base called Camp Rhino, which was just 6o miles southwest of Kandahar, still under Taliban occupation. The purpose of this deployment was to carry out support missions for special operational forces.

Northern Alliance moved speedily to fill the gap created by the implosion of the Taliban regime. Even as efforts were on to work out the contours of a post-Taliban coalition, the Northern Alliance served a fait accompli by waltzing into Kabul.

By December 8/9, 2001, Mullah Omar fled Kandahar with some of his bodyguards and few fighters, thus bringing an end to the six years of Taliban rule in Afghanistan. What the allied forces and the erstwhile Northern Alliance troops had to clean up were the small pockets of Taliban and Al Qaeda forces in different parts of the country including Kabul, Kandahar, Mazar-i-Sharif, etc.

One of the significant operations was launched at the Tora Bora Mountain, where it was suspected that Bin Laden might be hiding with most of his 1000 to 2000 elite foreign fighters. Afghan opposition forces, CIA, and special operation forces were deployed in the vicinity of the mountain, and air strikes continued. Within few days the fight for Tora Bora was over, only with the killing of a few Al Qaeda fighters. But it was presumed that before the operation started most of the Al Qaeda fighters with their leader Osama bin Laden had fled the mountain. A well-planned war by the United States against a fundamentalist regime in Afghanistan ended with these operations although sporadic bombing and small-scale ground operations were continued.

Within the first four months of the war, i.e. up to the end of January 2002, American fighter planes had flown about 25, 000 sorties in the air campaign and dropped over 18, 000 bombs, including some 10, 000 precision munitions. Again, during Operation Anaconda in March 2002, more than 3, 000 American and French bombs were dropped on the surviving enemy troops.[11] Thus, a combination of several determinants pushed the America led coalition to a military victory. In the words of US Defence Secretary Donald Rumsfeld, what won the battle was "a combination of the ingenuity of the US special forces; the most advanced, precision-guided munitions in the U.S. arsenal, delivered by U.S. Navy, Air Force, and Marine Corps crews; and the courage of valiant, one-legged Afghan fighters on horseback . . . on the plains of Afghanistan, the nineteenth century met the twenty-first century and defeated a dangerous and determined adversary—a remarkable achievement."[12]

But the main objective of the war, i.e. to capture Osama bin Laden and Mullah Omar and their top lieutenants, and to bring about a reconciliation among the different Afghan factions remained as unfinished agenda. The US public and Congressional opinion will find it difficult to accept that the war against Al Qaeda and the Taliban had been won without their leadership being brought to book. And as the trends of terrorism go, there is a remote possibility of bringing these fugitives to justice.

How did it happen? How was it possible for the top leadership of Taliban and Al Qaeda to deceive the world's most sophisticated intelligence agency (CIA) with its well-equipped reconnaissance aircrafts and all latest technologies? This is where the role of Pakistan comes in and the Afghan operation began to fail. In order to understand the present American 'failure,' it is necessary to have a glance at how it all came about.

Towards a Failed Policy

Over Dependence on Pakistan

On the eve of the Afghan operation, the United States probably underestimated the Pakistani involvement in the Taliban/Al Qaeda establishments. American leadership could not properly comprehend the bond of religious camaraderie that had been ignited in the form of extremism and terrorism across the Durand Line for quite a longer period of time. The situation around this time is that while there was large-scale Afghan resentment against the repressive Taliban regime of Mullah Omar, majority opinion in Pakistan, especially in the army and intelligence deeply supported the fundamentalist government of Kabul. In the North West Frontier Province and Balochistan states, people had even demanded the most orthodox sharia law and its implementation in the Pakistani society. Ironically, at this juncture, the Bush administration went by the promises of the Pakistani dictator, which are traditionally made to be broken and deceive people. The Pakistani leadership not only misguided the Americans to make war efforts a total failure, they also conceived well planned strategies to extract maximum benefit from the United States in the form of economic and military assistance. From their own previous experience,[13] Pakistanis knew that their main aim was to linger the conflict to the maximum possible extent so as to keep the country in the international limelight and gain diplomatic support from others. Therefore, in order to understand the Pakistani role vis-à-vis the U.S. policy in Afghanistan about how Washington was betrayed by Islamabad, it is necessary to look at the issue of terrorism and extremism in a proper perspective.

The Self-Made Menace

In a larger perspective, the present American failure in Afghanistan is mostly the outcome of the 1980s CIA's war against the former Soviet Union. Under an illusionary cold war policy, the American CIA and Pakistani ISI wanted to turn the Afghan jihad into a global war waged by all Muslims states against the Soviet Union. With the American money and the Pakistani logistics support, they trained some 35, 000 Muslim radicals from 40 Islamic countries who joined Afghanistan's fight between early 1980s and early 1990s. Tens of thousands more came to study in Pakistani madrasas from different quarters of the Islamic world. Eventually more than 100, 000 foreign Muslim radicals were directly influenced by the Afghan war.[14] Hundreds of training camps set up in Pakistan and Afghanistan became virtual university for promoting pan-Islamic radicalism in several Muslim countries including Egypt, Sudan, Yemen, Algeria, Jordan, the Philippines, and Bangladesh. Even a secular face like Benazir Bhutto once said "because of the Afghan war, people were taught that to be a Muslim means to spread Islam by armed struggle."[15] It was in the beginning of this decade-long war that in order to construct bunkers and set up training camps, the CIA recruited and brought in one Mr. Osama bin Laden to Peshawar, Pakistan. As the Saudi billionaire was having a lot of experience, especially in construction business, the ISI, CIA, and Saudi intelligence heavily patronized him.

After the anti-Soviet war, Bin Laden had left Afghanistan in 1990 but returned in May 1996. With the clandestine support and blessings of Pakistani army and intelligence, soon he established his headquarters at Khost, not far from border with Pakistan, rearmed and reunited all Arab and Pakistani militants, created the "055" brigade, and turned on his former patron and issued his first "Declaration of Jihad" against the Americans and the Saudi royal family whom he considered to be occupying his homeland. Within a very short period of time, Taliban, including its leader Mullah Omar, was radicalized by bin Laden and turn Afghanistan into a training ground for terror. Bin Laden's men infiltrated the Taliban's top ministries, especially Virtue and Vice, where they are said to have argued vigorously for the destruction of the 1,500-yearold Bamiyan Buddha statues in 2001. U.S. officials believe that bin Laden masterminded the September 9, 2001 assassination of the leading military commander of the Northern Alliance, Ahmed Shah Masud, the Taliban's chief rival for national power. In return, the Saudi terrorist leader was guaranteed sanctuary, plus room to set up camps to train their supporters and help to recruit fresh talent.[16] It is believed that it was bin Laden who brought anti-Americanism to the nationalistic Taliban ideology, and vociferously attacked the United States.

While fighting a Cold War against Soviet Union very little thought was given to the long-term consequences, and the likelihood that these militants, "now trained, experienced and self-confident," might later turn against the United States. Americans woke up to a considerable shock when they realized that bombing of the World Trade Center in 1993, killing six people and injuring 100, was the work of terrorists with an Afghan background. Then a more shocking attack for the United States was the bombing of the American Embassies in Kenya and Tanzania on August 7, 1998, killing over 250 people and wounding more than five thousand others. The United States traced Bin Laden as responsible and launched some 75 Tomahawk cruise missiles against his bases in eastern Afghanistan, killing 20 militants but leaving his network unharmed. Then comes the bombing of USS Cole in October 2000 that claimed 17 lives. Finally comes September 11, 2001, when more than 3000 people are killed in New York and Washington, and America declares "war against terrorism" and hunts for Bin Laden, Al Qaeda, Mullah Omar, and associates.

While the Taliban and Al Qaeda organized terrorist attacks, the big political, and military support they received from Pakistan, which had its own geo-political agenda vis-à-vis the fundamentalist regime in Afghanistan. As a strong U.S. ally in the region, Islamabad had hardly anything to worry about perpetuating its goal. It is doubtful that without such support from a neighboring Muslim country, the Taliban regime would have done so many nuisances against the world community. Therefore, it is only worthwhile to look at Pakistan's Afghan policy in a proper perspective.

Pakistan's Domestic "Compulsions"

Washington has so far been ambivalent and rather sluggish to understand the fact that what is known as terrorism to America and the world is a part of Pakistan's foreign policy, which has a very strong domestic root. The ISI deliberately fashioned Taliban as a military and political force basically for three reasons. First, Islamabad perceived that the creation of an Islamic fundamentalist regime in Afghanistan would provide Pakistan with a "strategic depth" during times of conflict with India.[17] This need became particularly acute in the 1990s as the Pakistan-supported insurgency escalated in the Kashmir Valley. After the creation of Taliban in 1994 and their capture of Kabul in 1996, (the year when Osama bin Laden returns to Afghanistan) the new militia and their friends in Al Qaeda were used by the Pakistani military and ISI to provide facilities and expertise for training Pakistani,

Afghan, Arab and Kashmiri terrorists in the jihadist ideology who were then infiltrated into the Line of Control into India to create mayhem in the Kashmir valley.[18] Second, since the independence of the Central Asian Republics, Islamabad wanted to ensure some clout for Pakistan as an important player in the region. As one of the leading Islamic countries, it has always been Pakistani policy to play a leadership role in the Muslim world, which impelled Islamabad's drive to establish good relationship with the newly emerging republics. This drive was also partly motivated by the policy of opening up of the trade route to Central Asia not only for Pakistan itself but also for its friends and allies including the United States. Third, Pakistan wanted to bury the long-standing Pashtunistan issue in the Pak-Afghan relations once for all and for that they needed an Afghan government, which would see eye to eye with them on the issue.[19] ISI found that the Taliban had closer links with Pashtun tribes in both sides of the border than any previous Afghan government.

Another domestic 'compulsion' for Islamabad was the emergence of Jamiat-i-Ulema-i-Islami (JUI) under Maulana Fazlur Rahman as a formidable force in Pakistani politics, especially in terms of its relations with Afghanistan as well as its management of madrasas and support to Taliban and Al Qaeda. It is also equally significant to note that the JUI had a strong anti-American stance from the very beginning although it successfully used the anti-Soviet war in setting up of hundreds of madrasas in Pakistan's Pashtun belt, which produced CIA-sponsored militants. Its political isolation ended in 1993 when it allied itself with Benazir Bhutto's Pakistan Peoples Party and became part of the ruling coalition. Then it established close links with ISI, army and the interior ministry. But the most radical step was that the Taliban handed over the control of training camps in Afghanistan to JUI in 1996, thus enhancing their image among the new generation of Pakistani and Arab militants studying there.[20] The JUI had become the main recruiter of Pakistani and foreign students to fight for Taliban. Ahmed Rashid has reported that between 1994 and 1999, an estimated 80, 000 to 100, 000 Pakistanis trained and fought in Afghanistan.[21] In this way, with ISI's backing, the JUI radicalized and transformed thousands of militants into fundamentalist terrorists. These militants also enjoyed considerable influence in Pakistan's North West Frontier Province and Baluchistan and aim at Talibanizing Pakistan itself. Significantly, they were now increasingly influential in non-Pashtun belt also. Of the 6, 000 – 8, 000 Pakistani militants who joined the Taliban for July 1999 offensive against the Northern Alliance, the majority were, for the first time, non-Pashtun but Punjabis.[22] Due to this attachment between Pakistan and Taliban/Al Qaeda, Islamabad has been reluctant to help Washington capture Osama bin Laden and Taliban leaders. Moreover, when there was talk of extradition of bin Laden to the US in 1999,[23] the JUI had issued death threats to all Americans in Pakistan, to be carried out if Laden was extradited to the United States.[24] Among several reasons for the October 12, 1999 military coup, where General Musharraf overthrown Nawaz Sharif, one was the Pakistani military and intelligence feared that the Prime

Minister might buckle to American pressure and reverse Pakistan's policy toward the Taliban. Similarly, one of the first priorities of the new military ruler was to cancel a top-secret mission being planned with the United States to send commandos using Pakistani intelligence information into Afghanistan to capture Osama bin Laden.[25] It implies that there is mass support in Pakistan for the JUI and ISI's policy towards Taliban/Al Qaeda. Therefore, Pakistan's support to the Pashtun Taliban in power in Kabul reinforced Islamabad's image as the main supporter of the Pashtun cause. In continuation of this policy, until very recently the Afghan bureau of the Pakistani ISI was something of a command post in supporting the Taliban. Also as part of a policy of "Islamic debts," a campaign to buttress its defenses against India, Pakistan used the Taliban's support to project power in the north. There were reports that Pakistani pilots often carry out air raids on behalf of Taliban forces, and that the Pakistani special forces take part in military operations inside Afghanistan. It was believed that around 30 percent of Pakistani military were sympathetic to the Taliban cause: something the Americans had to be painfully aware of. Obviously, General Musharraf did not pay any heed to the continuing American pressure and even sanctions against Afghanistan by the United Nations, and held fast his country's support of the Taliban until the terrorist attacks on the United States on September 11, 2001.

Policy After 9/11

Under these circumstances, when Pakistan President Musharraf was literally forced by the Americans, following 9/11 attacks, to take a U-turn in Islamabad's relations with Kabul, and withdraw support to the Taliban, it came as a rude shock to the Pashtun population and the fundamentalist political parties in Pakistan. Because these elements espouse militant fundamentalism within Pakistan and a jihadist foreign policy abroad, especially in relation to the United States, Israel and India.[26] In course of time, some of them also constitute a part of the Al Qaeda network, and supported the terrorist organization openly. In continuance of this policy, Musharraf, as he is, behaved a die-hard militant fundamentalist during the American operation in Afghanistan beginning October 7, 2001. First, he pleaded to shorten the bombing campaign to not bomb the Taliban frontlines. Second, he desperately requested the Americans to prevent the Northern Alliance from entering Kabul.[27] Third, he was equally desperate to figure out 'moderate' Taliban willing to join the new dispensation. And finally, when the Pakistani fighters and army officers fighting alongside the Taliban were trapped in Afghanistan, the Pakistani President had to request the Americans for their smooth evacuation to Pakistan.[28] In other words, Musharraf tried his best to have the fundamentalist regime in place in Kabul and so also the Al Qaeda network, its infrastructure, and terrorist training camps etc. And when the General failed on all counts, it was considered as a grave insult on Pashtuns and the Pakistani people and led to large-scale protests and demonstrations in the nook and corner of the country. Around this time, an opinion poll predicted that some 87% Pakistanis supported the Taliban and Al Qaeda.

The whole Pakistani intelligence, fundamentalist political parties such as the Jamiat-ul-Ulema-i-Islam and their followers are so much entangled with the Taliban that it was virtually impossible for General Musharraf to directly go against his own creation, although he himself had to declare support to America's war efforts. *World Street Journal* reporter Daniel Pearl's brutal murder indicates that the American journalist could not measure how much America and Americans are hated by religious extremists and ISI in Pakistan who felt thrashed by the United States in Afghanistan and betrayed by the Pakistani government at home. Also, it is interesting to note that the Organization – The Nationalist Youth Movement for the Sovereignty of Pakistan, – which claimed to have kidnapped and killed Pearl, had demanded, among others, the resumption of F-16 sales to Pakistan. How can terrorists, jihadi group that supposedly regards the Musharraf regime as treacherous, was putting forward a 20-year-old demand of the military and state bureaucracy? It has to be recognized by the international community that the ISI has always been something of a law unto itself. The agony, which patronized and funded Taliban, was livid at "the betrayal of the Taliban." Being forced to unravel the only victory they had ever scored – the Taliban takeover of Kabul – created enormous tensions inside the army and the ISI. In most of the cases, for obvious reasons, ISI's action does not match Musharraf's words.

The United States has now reconciled with the fact that its strategic partner in its war on terrorism is providing sanctuary to the Al Qaeda and Taliban leadership, and at the same time successfully extracting political support and financial assistance from Washington. The middle-level officers in the Pakistani army and intelligence who are sympathetic to the terrorist groups are becoming increasingly confident that they will be able to manage the situation without Washington being able to close in on the terrorist leadership. Similarly, the more time the leaders of Taliban and Al Qaeda get to consolidate within the safety of Pakistan, the higher the chances of their being able to merge with the local populace. It seems that General Musharraf finds it advantageous to permit Al Qaeda and the jihadist Taliban to function in his country since without that threat looming large, Washington will have no use for him. It is in Musharraf's interests to ensure that there are no rivals who could offer help to the United States and that he becomes as dispensable as he can. In this way, America's Afghan war benefited General Musharraf the most. From being virtually isolated by the international community and under increasing domestic pressure to prove his legitimacy, he became the toast of the "free world." Ironically, this metamorphosis from 'villain' to 'natural ally' was brought about by the United States, which gave millions of dollars in assistance, readjusted billion dollars loan, waived sanctions and strengthened diplomatic ties with the General's regime because it needed Pakistan to fight the war in Afghanistan.

This kind of American approach to Pakistani policy and massive support of the people for the Taliban/Al Qaeda elements is bound to make the US task of cleaning the region from terrorism far more difficult. It also highlights the fact that the main battleground against terrorism is Pakistan and not Afghanistan. Therefore, the United States and the global alliance will not only have to clean up the remnants of Al Qaeda and Taliban, but their mentors and supporters in the Pakistani ISI, army, government and political parties.

In addition to the above, the Americans should have asked themselves the following questions with the unfolding of events after September 11: Why Pakistan feared American strikes against its nuclear sites and shifted its nuclear weapons from the laboratories and plants to "more secure places"? Why there was talk of destroying Pakistani nuclear bombs and establishments through a non-nuclear means by employing American high-tech weapons? Why the Pakistani nuclear scientists, who had links with Osama bin Laden and Taliban, were arrested for interrogation? Why there was speculation in the United States for a back-up plan to deploy American troops to remove Pakistan's nuclear weapons? And as far as Musharraf is concerned, why he scuttled a US-Pak joint commando operation to get Osama bin Laden in October 1999? These are but a few questions out of hundreds, where the Americans need to dwell upon. Clearly, Islamabad is pursuing a policy of running with the hare and hunting with the hound.

American Failure in the Battlefield

Given this background, it was a kind of strategic miscalculation on the part of the United States that at a time when the whole of Pakistan supported the Taliban and Al Qaeda, Washington fully relied on Islamabad in its war against terrorism. Ironically, throughout the war, Americans and the Northern Alliance soldiers had to fight with both the Taliban/Al Qaeda cadres as well as thousands of Pakistani regulars in disguise. One significant American mistake was its expectation of Pakistani help during the operation of the Tora Bora Mountain. Washington wanted Islamabad to close off all possible escape routes for Osama bin Laden and associates from the Tora Bora region. Obviously, given the linkage between Pakistan and Taliban, and a six years old Pakistani policy toward the Taliban regime, the 4000 Pakistani regular army deployed along the border would not have the same incentives as the United States to conduct the effort with "dogged persistence."[29] In fact, Pakistani troops were not fully committed to the mission to prevent the Al Qaeda and Taliban forces that freely entered into Pakistani territory and fled elsewhere. So rather than relying on Pakistani forces to do the job near Tora Bora in December, the United States should have deployed American troops to prevent Al Qaeda fighters from fleeing into Pakistan. This is not to mean that the Tora Bora operation was the only fault-line during the American operation. This is just an example of the ongoing Afghan war. In March 2002, when 50 Al Qaeda men – including Abu Zubaydah, a top aide of Osama bin Laden – were arrested in Faisalabad, Pakistan, it was only FBI show. It was possible because the FBI intercepted their communication, and did not seek any assistance from the local authority. Otherwise, in most of the cases, the Pashtun and tribal chieftains, backed by the ISI, were helping the Al Qaeda and Taliban fighters' escape, while the American forces were endeavoring to catch them. Decapitating the terror threat, therefore, depend on Pakistan being willing to root the fugitives out, or to let others do so.

It is however, understandable, why the United States did not take such a decision. It would have invited anti-Americanism in Pakistan (which was already there anyway) and Afghanistan, would have the logistics problems, and would have led to more American casualties. But given the enormity of the stakes in this war, deploying US troops would have been more appropriate option. As per one estimate, to close off the 100 to 150 escape routes along the 25-mile stretch of the Pak – Afghan border closest to Tora Bora would have required 1,000 to 3,000 American troops.[30] Maybe real job would have been done with a little more concerted effort by the United States. But once the leaders of the Taliban/Al Qaeda escaped, they will continue to be the stumbling blocks to bring about peace in the country. In certain 'pockets' of Afghanistan Taliban/Al Qaeda cadres are very much active, and as per the American sources, the war in Afghanistan would continue for some more time, as the rebels were still loose in Afghanistan. The purpose of "Operation Condor" in the summer 2002 was aimed at hunting down a "substantial" force of suspected Al Qaeda and Taliban militants in the Khost-Paktia region of the country. The purpose of launching "Operation Dragon Fury" and "Operation Dragon Fury II" in June 2003 in the Shahikot mountain valley of Paktia province was also the same. These forces would continue to keep the fragile Afghan regime destabilize for a long time to come, and it is doubtful that the Americans would be successful in hunting down these terrorists with their current policy.

ISAF and American Troops

The United States seems to lack a clear-cut objective as far as the role of the multinational force in Afghanistan is concerned. Unless it is handled carefully, it might prove a futile exercise, and the force may get entangled in another civil war like situation. The International Security Assistance Force (ISAF), representing 15 nations and operating under the United Nations mandate constituted 4,700 troops. The main task of the force is of showing flag, sending troops on petrol on foot and in jeeps. The idea is to be seen by Kabul's one million residents to enlist help against the armed gangs who have exploited a power vacuum that followed the flight of the Taliban. It has been widely accepted that the ISAF has made an important impact, sharply reducing crimes like murder, housebreaking and car hijacking in just weeks. John F. Burns of *The New York Times* has reported that the "force has begun to help rebuilding roads, schools and clinics, restoring power lines and getting the garbage trucks back in service. Perhaps most important, the soldiers have reopened Kabul air-port assigning teams to remove unexploded bombs, shells and mines; blow up the wrecks of fighter planes left by Soviet occupation forces; and fill craters on the run ways and taxiways."[31] But unfortunately, Kabul is the only city to have the steadying influence of the international force, and thus improved to an extent unmatched anywhere else.

As per the United States, the administration was divided over whether the ISAF should be expanded to other sensitive parts of the country or confined to Kabul. The State Department was in favor of the enlargement of the troops. Its version was that no Americans would serve in the ISAF. But the United States would fly the other nation's troops to Afghanistan and the supplies for them, provide intelligence and offer a commitment that it would whisk the foreign security troops to safety if they were endangered, measures that Washington already provides for the Kabul-based international security force. The State Department's version was based on its concern that there were a few other places outside of Kabul where the ISAF could assist the Afghans in providing security.[32] Defense Secretary Donald H. Rumsfeld and his deputies, on the other hand, challenged the State Department's approach. The Pentagon officials argued that the expansion of the force was unnecessary and would "divert resources, including aircraft, from the broader American campaign against terrorism." Alluding to the State Department approach, Rumsfeld asked: "the question is, do you want to put your time and effort and money into the International Security Assistance Force—go take it from, say, 5,000 to 20,000 people? There is one school of thought that thinks that's a desirable thing to do." Rumsfeld continued, "another school of thought, which is where my brain is, is that why put all the time and money and effort in that? Why not put it into helping them develop a national army so that they can look out for themselves over time?"[33]

The opinion of the Pentagon has prevailed so far and the United States has resisted any expansion of the force beyond Kabul. The task of maintaining political order, the Bush administration insisted, was one for the Afghans to solder largely on its own. Administration officials have viewed that Afghanistan's future security lies in building a new national army, which Washington and London have pledged to help finance and train in the coming months. This cautious American approach reflects a determination not to be drawn too deeply into Afghanistan's internal affairs, and thus risk making a much larger force hostage to a new political breakdown or, in a worse scenario, to another civil war. The United States is afraid of the Force becoming entangled in the domestic politics of Afghanistan.[34] The American cautiousness is especially significant in view of the latest C.I.A. assessment that the "seeds of civil conflict" are still present in Afghanistan.[35] Second, the Pentagon had objected to enlarging the peacekeeping force largely because American soldiers are still (by mid 2003) trying to root out Taliban and Al-Qaida soldiers in rural areas. Having the ISAF troops operating in the same region could lead to conflicts between friendly forces. Third, Americans are facing some kind of strategic inadequacy in the sense that the power of the warlords themselves has been enhanced by the money and weapons funneled by the United States to regional leaders who have helped Washington to root out Al Qaeda fighters and the former Taliban government. Therefore, U.S. officials believe that the deployment of more multinational troops in rural Afghanistan would create more tactical problems for them then actually solving them. Fourth, the Bush administration is also skeptical about the feasibility of controlling such a vast country through the international troops. It has been viewed that scaling up the ISAF to cover a country the size of Afghanistan would pose significant logistical and command burdens, even if focused solely on other major population centers. Finally, it is also perceived in terms of Afghanistan's poor roads, high mountains and wide expenses, which posed different problems from international peacekeeping operations.

Well, the Pentagon and its boss Donald Rumsfeld may be right from their judgment and perspective, and the United States is wisely helping Afghans build a national army. But as the proposed Afghan National Army (ANA) will not be fielded until late 2004 or even 2006, they must find an way out of the on going mess as to who will maintain law and order beyond Kabul where only the law of the jungle prevails? Who will make this stopgap arrangement? Hence, for the time being, until the ANA takes over, the expansion of the ISAF may be the only solution to check the power of the feuding warlords, who control most of the country, and to give the fledgling government a chance to extend its authority. It has been a top priority of President Hamid Karzai as well as the United Nations' representative in Afghanistan Lakhdar Brahimi. In his September 2002 speech in the United Nations, Karzai warned about spreading disorder and urged the expansion of peacekeeping operations to at least three outlying cities to enhance the central government's authority. The Afghan leader forcefully insisted before the world body: "The Afghan delegates, that regularly visit us in Kabul from various provinces to exchange ideas with our administration, strongly request the expansion of the ISAF to other parts of the country. They want to be certain that Afghanistan will not be once again left alone by the international community."[36]

But neither the U.S. nor any other nation has offered any additional soldiers to the 4,700-member multinational force, which is now (at the time of writing this chapter) being led by a Turkish general.

The United States, however, seems very sensitive to the expansion of the ISAF whose operations are completely separate from those of the 4,000 odd American troops who are currently engaged in the country as part of the hunt for remnants of the Taliban and the Al Qaida. American policy indicates that the US soldiers should be used to kill the enemy, not keep the peace, and that the United States did not really bother about the task of nation building in the country. But without expansion of the ISAF, it may not be possible for the Americans to maintain a smooth sailing in achieving its objective of hunting down the terrorists and bringing peace to the country. As such the latest reports show that the U.S. troops have begun to face a rough weather in the Afghan countryside. As the action-hungry US soldiers continue the hunt for Taliban and Al Qaeda leadership, they risk inciting more anger towards the American forces that could imperil Washington's long-term goal of creating a stable Afghanistan where terrorist will not take refuge.[37] Another report suggests that after various special operations (such as "Operation Mountain Sweep" in August 2002 in the Shahi Kot valley of eastern Afghanistan), the steady stream of friendly intelligence from locals has nearly dried up, and that the incidents of harassment by US troops had increased.[38] The scale and dangerousness of the ongoing war in Afghanistan has been reinforced with the latest news that Osama Bin Laden was still alive and that the Al Qaeda leader has threatened to attack the United States and Great Britain very soon. United Nations Secretary General Kofi Annan also gave a gloomy view of the Afghan situation recently. Pointing out the absence of a functional Afghan security forces and yet allowing only a limited action of the ISAF, the head of the world body cautioned "Afghanistan will stay hostage to this prevailing insecurity. Lack of tangible improvement in the security situation could seriously undermine the political and reconstruction efforts.[39] Under these circumstances, the debate now is over how much of an effort Washington needs to make to keep the country from slipping back into chaos and provide security for international efforts to rebuild the country, and how long Afghans would not hesitate to turn their guns against the Americans as they have done with the foreign invaders and occupiers for centuries.

Weaponising the Warlords and its Larger Implications

In Afghanistan, an estimated 700,000 men remain armed,[40] and efforts to disarm them have barely begun, which is undoubtedly a very important step towards bringing peace and stability to the country. But instead of working towards that direction, the United States continue to pump weapons and money to the warlords to use them to fight Al Qaeda and the Taliban. In many parts of the country, US Special Forces have provided warlords and commanders huge amount of money, vehicles and sophisticated weapons. In a sense, the U.S. has become simultaneously a staunchest supporter and a greatest opponent of the Afghan government. On the one hand, Washington aims at stabilizing the central authority, and at the same time weakening the regime by working with the provincial warlords. The situation is exactly the same as during the 1980s, when the CIA supported even Osama bin Laden. Then, it was a fight against a super power (former Soviet Union), and now, the fight is within, among the Afghans but again with American money and weapons. American forces argue that it was necessary for them to support the "influential people" to get information about the terrorists, as well as to uphold local support. The advocates of this idea contend that they are only trying to make the best of an age-old Afghan tradition. Yet the notion that Afghanistan has always been a nation of feuding tribes and warlords is a myth popularized by the West which did not hesitate to walk away from the country once their geo-political interests were fulfilled. The present strategy could repeat the old American game in the country and a small spark in the whole Afghan society could ignite a terrible explosion in the form of civil war in future.

Warlords like Ismail Khan, who controlled much of western Afghanistan and General Rashid Dostum, who controlled Mazar-e-Sharif and much of northern Afghanistan had expressed their strong displeasure immediately after the constitution of the interim government under Hamid Karzai. They had complained that their regions and provinces were under-represented and that the Northern Alliance had retained control of important portfolios like defence, interior, and foreign affairs. Several other areas of rifts and disagreements among the warlords were noticeable at the time of Loya Jirga. One significant aspect was regarding the leadership issue itself. While Zalmay Khalilzad, the Afghan born U.S. special envoy to Afghanistan, was persuading the ex-king to issue a statement that he had no desire to accept any government post, Pashtun warlords—the majority of whom were being funded and armed by Washington to hunt down Al Qaeda members—demanded the ex-king be elected President.[41] So from the very outset, the coalition government in Kabul looked fragile. The Karzai government somehow succeeded in mollifying the situation temporarily, but such bickering suggests that the seeds of confrontation are very much there, and that could surface any time in future.

The intermittent civil war and bloodshed of the past two decades have entrenched ethnic and tribal animosities to such an extent that the present American policy is unlikely to provide a healing touch to the people. Rather, that will create more vested economic and political interests and help prolonging civil war in the country. Most of the warlords are directly or indirectly indulged in the illegal trade and business like poppy cultivation, drug trafficking, gun-running, protection money and control of scarce resources in the context of acute shortage in drought, famine and civil strife situations, and that they are the people who benefited the most by perpetuating insecurity in the country. As in "Somalia, Liberia, Sierra Leone and the Congo, the major warlords in Afghanistan have been, and continue to be, the principal economic beneficiaries of fragmentation and civil war. It is unlikely that they will be willing to relinquish this role and its benefits any time soon."[42] As such CIA is also not a new entrant in this game, and there are reports that the world's largest and the most powerful intelligence agency has been connected to drugs and illicit trade in the past.[43]

Therefore, by supporting the so-called influential people and warlords and commanders, United States is certainly undermining the very purpose of the war. Firstly, this effort to enlist local support has undermined the authority of the Hamid Karzai government that is already weak and, in the process of legitimizing itself. Strengthening the local commanders and warlords means weakening the central authority. Secondly, by supporting warlords, the United States is contributing to the further fragmentation of Afghanistan rather than promoting the development of a mature and stable state. American money and weapons in the hands of warlords have proved very explosive in the past, and that may do so in future also. This will only bring about more and more political and military fragmentation to the Afghan society. Thirdly, it has been pointed out that while hunting down Al Qaeda and Taliban in the Afghan countryside, U.S. troops are dismissive about their backing to the people and groups with very bad human rights abuses. The Americans maintain that it was not the time to raise the issue of human rights, and that the main concern was going after Al Qaeda and Taliban terrorists. Fourthly, as Karzai is considered as a U.S. backed ruler in Kabul, he has to witness the American operations to locate and eliminate Taliban/Al Qaeda remnants in parts of his territory. In the process, Karzai is indirectly and unintentionally making more enemy than friends, because the warlords and people who are being opposed by Washington are (in most cases) increasingly opposing the Karzai administration. Fifthly, American policy of supplying weapons to the warlords is also undermining the all out efforts of the ISAF, and diverting their attention from the original mission. For instance, the British forces had a great sense of accomplishments when they seized an important stockpile of arms believing that the same was the left over by the terrorists. But later they came to know that the arms captured did not belong to the Taliban/Al Qaeda terrorists but was part of CIA consignments for the warlords in Eastern and Southern Afghanistan. Obviously, the international peacekeepers would feel let down by such one-dimensional American policy. Finally, by supplying weapons and money to the warlords in different parts of Afghanistan, the United States, in a sense, is indirectly encouraging the regional power rivalry in the country. Americans are giving money and weapons to the people who are already receiving such assistance from Pakistan, Iran, Saudi Arabia, Uzbekistan, Tajikistan, Russia and other sources, and all these countries have vested strategic interests under which they firmly believe that if they cannot get a regime in Kabul favorable to them, they would rather have the country divided into fiefdoms so that they can dominate the Afghan territory they consider strategically and politically important.[44] As such sporadic fighting are not uncommon among different warlords even after two years of the assuming of power by the Karzai government. As late as in December 2002, there are reports that fresh fighting erupted between troops belonging to two rival commanders near an air base in western Afghanistan.[45] The recent fighting began when commander Amanullah Khan launched an attack on positions held by the powerful governor of the Herat province Ismail Khan. It is a well known fact that Ismail Khan, an ethnic Tajik, and Amanullah Khan, who is from Afghanistan's main Pashtun group, have been bitter rivals for years. Again, warlord like Gulbuddin Hekmatyar is reportedly plotting to kill U.S. troops in Afghanistan and has offered rewards for killing of any American.[46] Washington, in turn, wants Hekmatyar dead. This is just a case how the American troops are hard pressed before the rival power centers in Afghanistan. In such a situation, American money and weapons to the warlords are only encouraging the regional powers to expand their sphere of influence in the country and help bring more chaos and divisions. This attitude and policy of the United States shows they have failed to learn from the past.

Most of the political murders, since the Taliban/Al Qaeda were thrown out—including those of the Vice President Haji Abdul Qadir[47] and Civil Aviation Minister Abdul Rahman—have been variously attributed to residual Taliban antagonism, local tribal rivalries, and links with drug trade. It shows that the Afghan nation is again heading towards more fragmentation rather than any reconciliation, and the peace process is getting a serious setback with each incident like this. This is significant especially in view of the fact that Qadir and his brother Abdul Haq—executed by the Taliban during the early stages of the America's war—were among a handful of Pashtun warlords who had actively backed the U.S. war efforts, and that they had assumed the role of a bridge between the Tajiks and Uzbeks of the Northern Alliance and the Pashtun majority. It has got an additional relevance because a majority of the Pashtuns is still under Pakistani influence and they continue to sympathies with the Taliban and harbour a strong sense of resentment against the Karzai government in Kabul. As per Abdul Rahman, he was killed even as he tried to reason with stranded passengers waiting for the next flight to proceed on Haj. It is noteworthy that at the time of the incident the ISAF commandos were only a short distance away. It still remained a controversy whether Rahman's killing was simply a case of irate passengers taking the law into their hands or a result of a factional fight. There have been subsequent attempts on several other leaders including the Defence Minister Mohammed Fahim and even plans unearthed about attempts on Karzai himself.[48] These incidents have strengthened the apprehensions that the Taliban/Al Qaeda has been active under cover and trying to eliminate key elements in the Karzai government.

This kind of situation indicates that there lies bigger problems with far more worrying implications for the U.S. war efforts. The U.S. reluctance to provide adequately for law and order and for the expansion of the ISAF beyond Kabul has led to a situation where vast tracts outside the capital have once again fallen prey to the power of dominant local warlords. These warlords are calling the shots in their respective strongholds, collecting revenue and providing safe passage, thus keeping the Karzai government weak and impoverished. They are mistrustful and competitive among themselves, and their private militias are the source of their strength. Therefore, they are unlikely to give them up without a fight. As per the American policy, the proposed Afghan National Army and police force will disarm these warlords, and takeover the law and order situation in this 23 years war-ravaged country. Given the present state of fragmentation, it is highly doubtful whether the new forces would be at all effective in the absence of radical political changes in the countryside and a substantial disarming of the warlords, especially in view of the culture of strong and often antagonistic tribal loyalties.

The war on terrorism should not come at the expense of a strong and stable central authority in Afghanistan. Eliminating Al Qaeda and the Taliban must remain the priority and may, from time to time, require dealing with the people with unsavory reputation. But at the same time, American forces, while dealing with them must differentiate the useful warlords from the useless ones. In fact, if necessary U.S. troops should not hesitate to cut off ties with the unruly warlords and the United States should initiate steps to contain and eliminate them politically. Washington must come out openly and heavily with those forces who have outlived their utility in the war on terrorism, as well as who serve as obstacles to unifying the Afghan nation. It is true that deposing warlords means creating a kind of power vacuum at local levels. In such a situation only the ISAF or a well armed Afghan police or national army could fill the gap. Therefore, the primary American strategy should be, rather oriented towards the creation of professional, nonpolitical, and ethnically balanced police and military services. This would require a long-term strategy and concerted effort on the part of the United States.

The 'Failed' Objectives and Shift in Policy

Has the Taliban/Al Qaeda been a completely decimated force? From all indications, it is not. While it may be true that their air force, armour, and almost all immovable infrastructures were destroyed, more than half of the Taliban/Al Qaeda cadres could not be captured who slipped into the countryside with all their arms and ammunitions.[49] This happened because the Taliban did not fight a major battle with the Northern Alliance or with any American/multi-national forces except at Kunduz and Kandahar. Obviously, they fled with all their arms intact. Many of these fighters, including leaders of the fundamentalist militia also fled to Pakistan, a country where they command tremendous support from the people as well as from the governmental authorities.[50] The increase in number of terrorist attacks in different parts of Afghanistan, Consulate offices, Christian Community, etc. in Pakistan, in the temples, Parliament Building, and other significant targets in India, and various Western targets in different countries starting from Indonesia, Saudi Arabia, the Philippines to Mombasa in Kenya are examples of the same. One former Pakistani ISI chief, who was directly responsible for Pakistan's Afghan operation, and one of the leading voice in support of the Taliban said, "They (Taliban) are not going to go away. They are integral, organic, historic."[51] Later in January 2002, addressing a seminar in Islamabad, General Hamid Gul said that the jihadi forces would carry on their agenda of terrorism despite U.S. presence in this region. Even American officials are not sure about the elimination of this jihadi forces and terrorists. As late as July 2002, the United States saw "all kinds of signs that they (Taliban/Al Qaeda) continue to try to regroup and reorganize, and we've got to keep them on the run." U.S. Deputy Secretary of Defence remarked that this war was as big as any fought by the United States and that "victory is going to be measured by what doesn't happen as opposed to what does happen."[52] So the stakes were very much there. Given their worldwide network, they could always regroup themselves and pose a threat to the United States and its allies. In the long rugged terrain of the Pak-Afghan border they cannot be completely eliminated due to the local support extended by the mullah infested Pakistani army and the intelligence. Taliban government is not there in Afghanistan, but Mullah Omar's as well as Osama's followers along with the Pashtun militants of the out law organizations are very much visible. A Western commander of the coalition forces recently insisted, "The enemy remains dangerous. Although it had difficulty massing its forces, recruiting new members and moving freely in Afghanistan, it could still carry out operations."[53] From all accounts, it could be inferred that the United States government is conscious of the fact that their forces have failed to smoke out cadres of the Taliban and Al Qaeda.

Secondly, as far as the question of preventing the poppy cultivation and checking of narcotic trade from financing terrorism are concerned, it is almost the business as usual. There is no doubt that with the removal from the government, the Taliban hands are tight. They have to operate clandestinely. But since no state authority, so far, has initiated any serious measures to contain this drug menace, most of the areas are under the control of the warlords, who have links with the Taliban, and a bulk of the proceeds from this trade go to weapon purchasing. In the Afghan countryside and tribal territories of the Pak-Afghan borders many people who had strong linkage with the former Taliban regime, and present supporters and sympathizers of the fundamentalist forces, still control a bulk of the country's drug trade. Analysts expected production in Afghanistan to range from 1,900 to 2,000 tons in 2002, slightly lower than 2000's output, and about half the 1999,s size.[54] If the present status qua continued, and the Karzai government remains ineffective, the opium growers may ignore the fresh ban and lured by the high price of the Afghan opium in the international market. The continuation of drug powered politics and economics in the context of arms market and terrorism could spell disaster for not only the Karzai government but also for the over all attempts of the U.S. government to bring peace to the country.

Thirdly, the undeclared American objective of promoting its geopolitical interests in the backdrop of the 9/11 tragedies has led to strong disapproval and resentment among the countries in the region. They look at Washington's motive, as if the events worked as an alchemist for the U.S. foreign policy towards the region. U.S. geo-political drive is motivated by twin objective of the containment of China and extracting Central Asian oil and gas to the world market. For a long time, American strategic eyes are focused on China's economic and military strength, and its claim on Taiwan in the Pacific, which tends to confront U.S. interests. American strategists believe that it would be convenient for them to deal with an unruly China while based in Pakistan, Afghanistan, and Central Asia. Washington can have a close watch on the developments of the communist China and the position would give access to more strategic mileage to the U.S. foreign policy interests in the geo-politics of the region. The second objective is to extract oil from the Caspian region to the world market. Through its military presence and economic and political support in the Central Asian Republics, Washington hopes to get access to the regions tremendous untapped reserves of oil. One study suggests, "It would account for up to a quarter of the world's total reserves." The strategic significance of these oil resources are estimated in view of the depleting oil reserves in the Middle East, and the energy security of America's allies and friends—especially the West European countries and Japan. And in that case, "Central Asia will become the biggest oil supplier to the world in the foreseeable future and Afghanistan will become a transit for the supply of the oil to the rest of the world."[55]

These strategic and geo-political ambitions of the United States have led to considerable resentments among the countries surrounding the region. Russian, Chinese, and Iranian unhappiness is particularly visible in this context. In order to keep the Americans away from their "dirty games" in the region, these countries will continue to support the ethnic and tribal groups through whom they consider to promote their own geo-strategic interests. For instance, Chinese will continue to be perturbed by expanding U.S. presence on its southwestern frontiers and support the anti-US forces, Russians to Tajiks and Uzbeks, and Iranians to their Shia minority ethnic group in the northwestern part of the country. Because these countries perceive that through its military presence in the region, the United States is unduly interfering in their "sphere of influence." In this sense, the overarching American geo-political objective in the region will be kept off balance by the regional powers, and that will continue to keep Afghanistan fragile and fragmented. In the process, America might get bogged down militarily in this landlocked country that has a long history of fighting against the foreigners.

Another significant reason, for which American operation would be considered a 'failure,' is the lack of consistency and persistence in the U.S. policy towards a post-Taliban Afghanistan. President Bush, who once put the capture of bin Laden and Mullah Omar "dead or alive" at the top of his war aims, later said his main priority was a stable Afghanistan (even on this score, Bush has failed anyway). But within a year since the Afghan campaign began, Washington's foreign policy focus shifted from Afghanistan to Iraq, leaving behind a pale of uncertainty and perplexing future in this war-torn country. Without successfully bringing the 9/11 culprits into justice, without disarming (rather rearming) hundreds of warlords, without any check on poppy cultivation and drug trade, without doing any harm[56] to the country (Pakistan) which is primarily responsible for most of the ongoing uncertainties in Afghanistan and which is itself the real epicenter of international terrorism, the shift in U.S. policy indicates that America's priority was to fulfill its geo-political ambition in Afghanistan and Central Asia, rather than "hunting down" the terrorists. Washington's policy shift exposes that the 9/11 incident and the subsequent "war on terrorism" came as a catalyst for the United States to enhance its military presence to further its geo-political and economic interests in the region. But as the study shows unless Washington initiates some radical steps to help bring peace to the country, its highhanded dream will remain unfulfilled.

The US Aid

Despite declaratory American policy to help revive the Afghan economy and infrastructure, it is yet to be seen how willing the present U.S. administration is to rescue this near-moribund state[57] from reverting to anarchy and civil war. Compared to the magnitude of the horrifying Afghan economy and the situation of state collapse, the Bush administration's commitment of a paltry $300 million in economic assistance in the year 2002 is certainly an insignificant amount. Along with other donors (European Union, Japan, Saudi Arabia, etc.), the United States maintains that Washington would contribute substantial, long-term assistance, but that was subject to the interim government maintaining peace. It shows American disinterest in reviving Afghan economy and society and isolating the cause of terrorism.

Stephen Hadley, deputy national security advisor for President Bush said in a meeting that the "recovery and reconstruction of Afghanistan is an area where the interests of Afghans, the United States and the international community coincide." By the end of July 2002, Hadley declared, that the Bush administration had delivered over 90 percent of the $300 million it had pledged at the Afghan Donors Conference in Tokyo, and that Congress had approved an additional $150 million.[58] Afghanistan's Minister of Reconstruction Mohammad Amin Farhang complained in the same gathering that in terms of honoring its commitments, "the world has not delivered yet," and declared the fact that only a small percentage of the $4.5 billion pledged in Tokyo had reached Afghanistan was putting much needed recovery projects on hold.

In the February 2003 meeting with the Afghan President Hamid Karzai, President Bush reaffirmed United States' commitment as a full partner in Afghanistan's reconstruction and continue with a comprehensive program of U.S. assistance to the country. But in reality American aid is very limited, and restricted to few areas like transportation, agriculture, education and health.[59] With the American attention diverted to Iraq, Washington is also taking very little initiative to push other international donors to come forward generously.

This inexcusable delay by the West in providing funds for reconstruction, failing to help the Afghans improve security and take a firm position against warlordism were all criticized by elected Afghanistan representatives in the Loya Jirga which was convened in Kabul in the second week of June 2002.[60] In fact, many representatives pointed their fingers at Washington, which still runs its Afghan policy out of the Defence Department and treats the country as a war zone rather than one needing an economic and political strategy. The problem of lack of funding, in a sense, is the result of "Afghanistan fatigue" of the international community and particularly of the United States. U.N. Secretary General Kofi Annan's Special envoy Lakhdar Brahimi, who also heads the UN Assistance Mission in Afghanistan (UNAMA), said, "Afghans are impatient, very understandably—we are all because the country which has been neglected so dramatically for 23 years, needs everything today, not tomorrow."[61] In the words of a European ambassador in Kabul, the Americans have to "treat the Afghans better than just surrogates for hunting Al Qaeda."[62]

Conclusion

While the U.S. campaign against the Taliban and the Al-Qaida was successful in replacing the regime in Afghanistan, the gains have been offset by the lack of a comprehensive political strategy in preventing the defeated fundamentalist forces from regrouping in Pakistan. The unprecedented international support to the U.S. led coalition for the Afghan campaign did not have any clarity of objectives about what was to be done in Afghanistan after the detalibanization process and the military phase was over. This led to several contradictions in approach towards the post-Taliban Afghanistan. The stability of this region, vital to the United States as well as for global energy security, cannot be successfully handled by Washington alone, certainly not through a combination of high technology weapons and excessive dependence on Pakistani army and intelligence. A more concerted efforts on the part of Washington with clear approach to the root cause of the problem is required for long-term peace in the country that will also go in consonant with the American interests. The United States must put together a broad-based and comprehensive military and political strategy to eliminate the terrorist threat emanating from a land that has proved to be the graveyard of every previous foreign invader. Washington's approach, so far, has been one of short-term expediency. Unless it chalked out long-term politico-military strategy of fighting against the values and mindsets that generate terrorists, the war against terrorism may prove to be yet another Afghan disaster.

Whatever the stability of the Karzai government, (and at least so long as U.S. presence is there), it is doubtful that the Taliban/Al Qaeda will control the country again. But if they were successful in killing more U.S. troops and international peacekeepers, situation would be different altogether. Or, in a worst-case scenario, if the country again descends into civil war, neither Afghanistan would be considered a 'victory' for the U.S. or Washington's geo-political ambition in the region shall be realized. That would be a dangerous situation for Washington where Americans would have to think about civilian casualty through its operation, loss of their own troops through terrorist attacks, and at the same time, its own image through out the Islamic world. To prevent such outcomes, Washington must take some calculated but risky steps: 1. The United States must ensure that the Taliban/Al Qaeda elements are not given sanctuary in Pakistan, 2. It must review its policy towards the role of ISAF, 3. Washington must push hard to other donors to expedite reconstruction and aid programs, 4. It must donate generously to the relief efforts in Afghanistan, and 5. U.S. must figure out a strategy putting its weight with the government rather than dividing it between the warlord and the government.

There can hardly be any doubt that with the removal of Taliban and demolition of Al Qaeda networks and infrastructures in Afghanistan, the terrorist organization is weaker without sanctuary and training base. At the same time it cannot be underestimated that the Taliban/Al Qaeda leaderships, who continue to evade capture, could still inspire followers and strike back. American intelligence agencies are said to have intercepted a series of messages among terrorist operatives that hint at attacks on the United States target. US Vice-President Dick Cheney said in 2002 that another terrorist attack (on America) was "almost certain." Top U.S. military commanders have agreed that America's military campaign against Taliban and Al Qaeda fighters in Afghanistan still has a long way to go despite the recent relative peace in the war-ravaged country. Tommy Franks, the U.S. military commander said that the country remained dangerous and would require U.S. military help for the foreseeable future. In a recent interview, General Franks cautioned: "This is a dangerous place, we are all reminded daily of that fact. There is a lot of work to be done before we quit."[63] Defence Secretary Donald Rumsfeld has already revealed that U.S. troops could remain in Afghanistan into 2003. Americans are possibly entering into a period of chaos and confusion, and it may be difficult situation for them to either escalate the war efforts or to withdraw from the country. Washington might face a protracted conflict in Afghanistan. America has the military power, but Mullah Omar and Osama have followers who will continue to be inspired by him and hear the call for martyrdom and respond. Armies (like that of Taliban) can be defeated. Martyrs are another matter.

Notes and References

1. In the words of President Bush this war was codenamed 'Operation Enduring Freedom' because "we defend not only our precious freedoms but also the freedom of people everywhere to live and raise their children free from fear." See the address by George W. Bush, President of the United States, delivered to the nation, from the treaty room, Washington D.C. October 7, 2001. "We Are At War Against Terrorism: The Attack on the Taliban," *Vital Speeches of the Day,* Vol. LXVII, No. 1, October 15, 2001, p. 3.
2. As per one estimate, by the middle of March 2002, U.S. forces lost about 30 personnel. For details see Michael E. O'Hanlon, "A Flawed Masterpiece," *Foreign Affairs,* Vol. 81, No. 3, May/June 2002, p. 55.
3. General Tommy Franks, commander-in-chief of the U.S. and coalition military effort in Afghanistan, claimed in course of an interview that the international coalition, as on August 21, 2002, stands at about 70 nations. For the details of the interview see, "Franks Says Stability is Long-Term Issue in Afghanistan," *Washington File,* International Information Programs, U.S. Department of State, August 22, 2002.
4. See the address by George W. Bush, President of the United States, delivered to the nation, Washington D.C. October 7, 2001. "We Are At War Against Terrorism: The Attack on the Taliban," *Vital Speeches of the Day,* p. 2. Also see *The Times of India,* October 8, 2001.
5. Greg Schneider, "High-tech devices could help U.S. score in Afghanistan," *The Times of India,* October 16, 2002, p. 9. Also see Michael E. O'Hanlon, "A Flawed Masterpiece," p. 51.
6. GBU-28 is among the largest laser-guided bombs in the US arsenal at the time of the Afghan operation. For details about this wonderful technology see *The Times of India,* October 13, 2001.
7. Michael E. O'Hanlon, "A Flawed Masterpiece," pp. 55-56.
8. There is no doubt that the military and logistics support from Pakistan Army continued up to the last day of the Taliban rule in Kabul. Even hundreds of Pakistani regulars were killed in the U.S. bombardment and so many were captured in Kundus and elsewhere. For the first time this kind of report appeared in mainstream Pakistan print media after more than a year of the war. See *The Friday Times,* Lahore, December 13-19, 2002. An authentic analysis of the event is found in C. Uday Bhasker, "Lifting the Smokescreen: Terror

Tales from Pakistan's Army," *The Times of India,* January 3, 2003. But one important dimension of the Pakistani support was that Islamabad had to cease overt military support to the Taliban under U.S. pressure once the American bombardment started, although its intelligence agency (ISI) was directly involved in the operation, and even continue to support these forces.

9. Douglas Frantz, "Pakistan Ended Aid to Taliban Only Hesitantly," *The New York Times,* December 8, 2001.
10. Quoted in Michael E. O'Hanlon, "A Flawed Masterpiece," p. 52.
11. This was one of the major offensives against the Taliban/al Qaeda hideouts in the mountainous region of eastern Afghanistan. See *Ibid,* p. 48.
12. Donald H. Rumsfeld, "Transforming the Military," *Foreign Affairs,* May/June 2002, p. 21.
13. For example, their role during 1980s Afghan war against the Soviets.
14. Ahmed Rashid, "The Taliban: Exporting Extremism," p. 31.
15. "Pakistan not backing Taliban says Bhutto," *Dawn,* March 18, 1995.
16. Johanna McGeary, "The Taliban troubles," *Time,* New York, October 1, 2001.
17. Zalmay Khalilzad, "Anarchy in Afghanistan," *Journal of International Affairs,* Vol. 51, No. 1, Summer 1997, p. 48. Also see Kamal Matinuddin, *The Taliban Phenomenon: Afghanistan 1994-1997,* Oxford University Press, 1999, p. 180.
18. Johan Blank, "Kashmir: Fundamentalism Takes Root," *Foreign Affairs,* Vol. 78, No. 6, November/ December 1999, p. 36-53.
19. Martin Ewans, *Afghanistan: A New History,* Curzon, Richmond, 2001, p. 197. The two neighbours came to the verge of war over this issue more than once in the 1950s and 1960s. Even the Taliban, although they were Pakistan's protégés, did not officially endorse the Durand Line as the border with Pakistan.
20. Ahmed Rashid, "The Taliban: Exporting Extremism," *Foreign Affairs,* Vol. 78, No. 6, November/December 1999, p. 26.
21. *Ibid,* p. 27.
22. *Ibid.*
23. In September 1999, the Director General of ISI, Lt. Gen. Ziauddin and Prime Minister Nawaz Sharif's brother, Shehbaz Sharif, were summoned to Washington and were told by the American officials that Pakistan should force the Taliban to moderate their positions and turn over Osama bin Laden to the United States. See Gouglas Frantz, "Pakistan Ended Aid to Taliban Only Hesitantly," *The New York Times,* December 8, 2001.
24. Ahmed Rashid, "The Taliban: Exporting Extremism," p. 33.
25. Gouglas Frantz, "Pakistan Ended Aid to Taliban Only Hesitantly," *The New York Times,* December 8, 2001.
26. Mohammed Ayoob, "South-west Asia after Taliban," *Survival,* Vol. 44, No. 1, Spring 2002, p. 57.
27. Incidentally, some American officials had assured Musharraf that the Northern Alliance would not be allowed to takeover Kabul.

28. *The Times of India,* November 29, 2001. Around this time, the jihadi groups in Pakistan had even threatened to kill Afghan refugees in Pakistan if the Pakistani personnel trapped in Afghanistan were not given a safe passage. See *The Times of India,* November 25, 2001.
29. Michael E. O'Hanlon, "A Flawed Masterpiece," p. 54.
30. *Ibid,* p. 57.
31. John F. Burns, "Peace troops get back the streets of Kabul," *The Times of India,* February 23, 2002.
32. *The New York Times,* February 21, 2002.
33. *Ibid.*
34. Sumit Ganguly, "India and Pakistan in the Shadow of Afghanistan," *Current History,* April 2002, p. 149.
35. The CIA has already predicted that any short-sighted US policy might invite more chaos and disorder in Afghanistan. See Michael R. Gordon, "C.I.A. Sees Threat Afghan Factions May Bring Chaos," *The New York Times,* February 21, 2002.
36. As quoted in *The Times of India.* September 19, 2002. Also during his January 2002 visit to Washington, the Afghan President emphasized the need of the expansion of the ISAF, and suggested the multi-national security force to go on duty beyond Kabul and the U.S. troops must be part of this force. See the *Asian News Digest,* February 11-17, 2002. The January 28, 2002 visit was the second visit by an Afghan head of state after King Mohammed Zahir Shah, representing a radically different Afghanistan, was received by President John F. Kennedy in 1963.
37. Margaret Coker, "US operations leave bad blood in Afghanistan," *The Times of India,* January 25, 2002.
38. See *The Times of India,* October 1, 2002. The incidents like the 'mistaken' American bombing of a wedding party in October 2002, which resulted in dozens of civilian casualties, is bound to vitiate the atmosphere further.
39. The overall picture of the Afghan situation is available from a report of the UN Secretary General Kofi Annan to the Security Council and General Assembly released at the UN Headquarters in New York on July 17, 2002. See the *UN Weekly Newsletter,* July 20-26, 2002.
40. Michael Massing, "Losing the peace?" *The Nation,* New York, May 13, 2002.
41. Ahmed Rashid, "Freedom Isn't Easy," *Far Eastern Economic Review,* June 27, 2002, p. 16.
42. Mohammed Ayoob, "South-west Asia after the Taliban," *Survival,* Vol. 44, No. 1, Spring 2002, p. 53.
43. A very interesting study is available in John K. Cooley, *Unholy Wars: Afghanistan, America and International Terrorism,* Pluto Press, London, 1999, especially see chapter 7 "Poppy Fields, Killing Fields and Druglords, pp. 126-160.

44. Ahmed Rashid, "Afghanistan: Ending the Policy Quagmire," *Journal of International Affairs*, Vol. 54, No. 2, Spring 2001. Also see Michael Massing, "Losing the peace?" *The Nation*, New York, May 13, 2002.
45. *The Times of India*, December 2, 2002.
46. See *The Asian Age*, New Delhi, May 10, 2002.
47. Qadir's elder brother and the governor of Nangarhar province, Haji Deen Mohammad has announced that he will never go to Kabul because his brother was invited there by Karzai and then assassinated—implying that Kabul is controlled by some unseen hands that may treat him in the same manner. An updated assessment of the recent developments in the country is available in Sohail Abdul Nasir, "Afghanistan: The More it Changes . . ." *Bulletin of the Atomic Scientists*, Vol. 59, No. 2, Chicago, March/April 2003.
48. President Karzai, instead of depending on the interior ministry's security guards, uses U.S.-supplied guards for his personal security.
49. As per one estimate, as many as 8,000 to 12,000 Taliban/Al Qaeda cadres were killed—roughly 20 percent of the Talibans initial fighting capability and approximately two wounded for every person killed, and about 7,000 were taken prisoner. See Michael E. O'Hanlon, "A Flawed Masterpeace." p. 55.
50. *The Economist*, June 1, 2002.
51. Quoted in Douglas Frantz, "Pakistan Ended Aid to Taliban Only Hesitantly." *The New York Times*, December 8, 2001.
52. See the interview of Deputy Secretary of Defence Paul Wolfowitz with Greta Van Susteren of Fox News Channel, as available in *Washington File*, International Information Programs, U.S. Department of State, July 10, 2002.
53. *The Economist*, May 18, 2002, p. 36.
54. Todd Diamond in "After the Taliban, Afghan Opium Resurges," eurasianet.org, July 17, 2002.
55. V.D. Chopra, "Strategic Role of Afghanistan," in his own edited book, *Global Challenge of Terrorism*, Gyan Publishing House, New Delhi, 2002, p. 223. The author emphasizes how oil is "attractive" to the U.S. and how American oil giant Unocal is waiting for a stable government in Afghanistan to construct the pipeline from the Caspian area to the Arabian Sea through Afghanistan and Pakistan. See pp. 221-225.
56. Instead of containing Islamabad and destroying terrorist infrastructures within Pakistan, the U.S. is providing millions of dollar economic assistance to the country, and adjusting billion dollar loans perceiving that Pakistani role was crucial in its war against terrorism.
57. According to Afghan Finance Ministry, only $80 million reaches the central government in Kabul, where as the country's annual budget is $550 million. See eurasianet.org May 21, 2003.
58. Stephen Kaufman, "Afghan Reconstruction Conference Draws Afghan and U.S. Officials," *Washington File*, International Information Programs, U.S. Department of State, July 26, 2002. In early 2003, Washington allocated $60

million to be used by the national police force, to improve judicial system's capabilities to combat drug trafficking etc. See eurasianet.org February 27, 2003.

59. See the joint "statement between the United States of America and Afghanistan," Weekly Compilation of Presidential Documents, Washington D.C., March 3, 2003.
60. Ahmed Rashid, "Freedom Isn't Easy," *Far Eastern Economic Review,* June 27, 2002, p. 18.
61. *UN Weekly Newsletter,* April 6-12, 2002.
62. Quoted in Ahmed Rashid, "Freedom Isn't Easy," p. 18.
63. *The Times of India,* October 20, 2002.

10
Towards Enduring Engagement

President Bush and President Karzai reaffirm their common vision for an Afghanistan that is prosperous, democratic, at peace, contributing to regional stability, market friendly, and respectful of human rights. They affirm their ironclad and lasting partnership in pursuit of this vision, and will work together to ensure that Afghanistan is never again a haven for terrorists and that no resurgence of terrorism threatens Afghanistan.

—Joint Statement between George W Bush and Hamid Karzai, Washington D.C., February 27, 2003[1]

The presence of American troops to hunt down the remnants of Taliban/Al Qaeda elements in Afghanistan have changed the political and military situation in the country to a great extent. American policy has so far failed to achieve the result what the leadership had apparently hoped for. Instead of killing or capturing the leaderships of Al Qaeda and Taliban, and preventing Afghanistan from the menace of terrorism, the presence of American troops seems to have opposite effects. What had probably seemed to President Bush like a very short high tech military operation to de-Talibanize Afghanistan became an endless chronic problem for Washington. Their indefinite presence in the country is leading to Afghan traditional opposition against the "occupying forces," and also helping in regrouping the defeated elements in the post 9/11 wars. As a result, the United States faces a no-win situation in the country. Neither can it contemplate to withdraw its troops nor can the present level be increased. Since it has only a relatively small (although effective) contingent of troops in the country, there is also no risk for the United States of entering into a Vietnam-like situation at least in the current situation. Moreover, through its deep involvement in the internal politics—within the Karzai government as well as among the warlords—Americans have sufficient scope to maneuver the emerging events in favour of their own interests. But at the same time, Washington has so far failed to chain up a clear-cut strategy to contain the Pakistan sponsored Al Qaeda terrorists alongwith an amalgam of anti-American warlords and Taliban cadres which seems to pose the biggest challenge to the U.S. presence in the country. Lack of a coherent policy towards the region, especially towards

Pakistan has made the American presence difficult and the Afghan peace process derailed. It appears that Washington will remain contented with a slow political process, limited aid, limited but long-term presence, and a very cautious approach towards the country. Because it understands that the country is an economic and political basket case that will take years, if not decades, to sort out. And since the United States cannot afford to leave Afghanistan to anarchy and civil war, its policy is going to be one of a long-term engagement.

Looking at the sources of terrorism, America's military strategy and operations, Washington's policy towards the internal and external forces including Pakistan, the study does not provide an optimistic picture for Afghanistan as well as smooth sailing for the ongoing presence of the United States. It concludes by acknowledging that the Americans are going to stay in Afghanistan for a quite some time to come. It attempts at some prescriptive solutions for Washington to at least partly over come the current Afghan entanglement, but anticipates a period of uncertainty and instability in the country.

The Reborn Terrorists

Since the beginning of the "Operation Enduring Freedom," Americans aimed at the killing or arresting Osama bin Laden, Mullah Omar and their terrorist's networks, and accordingly they chalked out their military strategy. Their focus was to punish the culprits of 9/11. But in course of their operation, Washington left so many "fault lines" that before accomplishing their mission, they landed up in endless quagmire and unforeseen war games.

First, in the beginning of the anti-terrorists war, American campaign suffered from some kind of "military ambivalences."[2] While President Bush and Secretary of Defence Rumsfeld declared their objective to remove the Taliban from power, they did not give sufficient operational and military support to the Rabani led Northern Alliance to quicken the capture of major urban centres including the capital, Kabul. This American policy, partly motivated by the Pakistani pressure, not only confused the whole Afghan campaign, but also gave more time for the terrorist's leaderships to reorganize their defence positions and simultaneously arrange their escape routes. Here the Pakistani strategy worked well. Because the Pakistani Army and ISI officials engaged in Taliban/Al Qaeda decision making apparatus as well as in the battlefields got more time to ensure a safe passage for "their leaders" to their own country. American officials took time to understand the fact that Musharraf's basic objective was to protect and nurture the remnants of the fundamentalists militia as much as possible and to induct them in the proposed new dispensation in Afghanistan. U.S. intelligence assessments might have been detrimental to such a strategy, and that might have led to the Americans to give covert signals to the Northern Alliance forces to move forward. The fundamentalist regime was defeated, but this strategy subsequently helped General Musharraf to play the "Pushtun card" to perpetuate terrorism inside Afghan territory.

Second, there is no doubt that the American GPS technology, with precision bombs annihilating enemies at a considerable distance, and the role of other high tech weapons surprised the Taliban, but at the same time it cannot be denied that the militia fighters quickly adapted to the U.S. methods. They successfully adopted countermeasures that allowed many Taliban/Al Qaeda cadres to elude American surveillance and survive air strikes.[3] As the war progressed, the militia defenses were well "camouflaged, dispersed and making use of natural terrain for expedient cover." They did not just passively suffer under frenzied American air strikes: they adapted their own methods to try to reduce their vulnerability. With this, "the war changed character."[4] Some of these surviving, however, had to be engaged in close-quarters fighting, but most of them fled to the jungles with all their weapons intact. It should also be remembered that except at Kandahar and Kunduz, the Taliban/Al Qaeda fighters never fought a major battle with the Northern Alliance forces. So with the progress of the war, when many of them disappeared into the countryside, they were not without their arms and ammunitions.

Third, even during the war, United States did not want to kill so many enemy troops out of hope that they might show the road to their leadership. Ostensibly, American soldiers were misled and deceived in the war fronts itself in the name of tracking Osama bin Laden. During the war, an American official said that the United States Central Command was considering how the U.S. and its partners might deal with non-Afghan prisoners, "especially those who might have valuable intelligence about the Taliban regime on Al Qaeda." The official observed that the United States was not interested in a large number of prisoners of war, "but clearly, we'd be interested in interrogating the prisoners."[5] In the process, the Taliban/Al Qaeda cadres backed by the Pakistani ISI began to manipulate the situation from the very beginning.

Fourth, when thousands of Pakistani fighters and army officers fighting alongside the Taliban were trapped in Kunduz, Mazar i-Sharif, Kabul and Kandahar, the Pakistani President requested the Americans for their smooth evacuation to Pakistan. According to the Northern Alliance as many as 16,000 Taliban soldiers—many of them refugees from battles lost across northern Afghanistan—had been encircled only in Kunduz. Of those, as many as 6,000 were Taliban troops from foreign countries.[6] A top official of the Alliance said that "Fifty trucks left Kunduz full of foreign Taliban, and they did not come back."[7] In addition to this, alongside Pakistani personnel, hundreds of hard-core Al Qaeda and Taliban cadres were also airlifted to Pakistani cities. Despite several American requests, US agents were not allowed access to these evacuated personnel after their nighttime Pakistani airlift.

Fifth, under the secured cover of the Pakistani dictator, the Taliban/Al Qaeda has regrouped in Pakistan and allied itself with Gulbuddin Hekmatyar, the fundamentalist anti-US extremist. Hekmatyar, who was known as one of America's anti-Soviet 'heroes' of 1980's became a 'terrorist' when he began to oppose the Americans during the 1991 Gulf War. He is known for his anti-American stance and close relations with the Pakistani ISI. As per one assessment Gulbuddin Hekmatyar, along with the "non-elected" part of the Iranian leadership, has been behind the coup attempt against the Karzai government in Kabul.[8] As a protégé of the ISI, Hekmatyar will continue to play a larger role in Pakistan's Afghan policy and a source of terrorism, especially against the American interests in Afghanistan.

Sixth, at a time when Americans and the Northern Alliance soldiers were fighting both the Taliban/Al Qaeda cadres as well as thousands of Pakistani regulars in disguise, President Bush sought assistance from Musharraf to close off all possible escape routes for Osama bin Laden and associates from the Tora Bora region into Pakistan. General Musharraf did deploy 4,000 Pakistani regular army along the border to please his Big Boss, but he was equally confident of doing just the opposite of what the US President had asked for, i.e. he ensured free entrance of the Al Qaeda and Taliban forces into Pakistani territory and to disappear unnoticed. CIA latter confirmed that Bin Laden paid $15 million to Pakistan army and "bought his way out" of Afghanistan during the US siege of Tora Bora. While the army and ISI were helping the Al Qaeda and Taliban fighters' escape, the American forces were endeavouring to catch them.

Seventh, General Musharraf—after being wined and dined at Camp David and granted aid worth $3 billion by President Bush—appears to have strengthened perceptions within the Army and ISI that they can do anything since the United States, now militarily bogged down in Iraq, badly needs them in the war against terrorism. The direct result of this mindset is clearly visible in Pakistan's current policy (as of August 2003) towards Afghanistan, where the authorities in Islamabad do bother, and openly allow the free movement of Taliban/Al Qaeda terrorists in Pakistan, especially in Baluchistan and North West Frontier Province. According to US officials thousands of Taliban are living in Quetta, the capital of Pakistan's Baluchistan Province, studying in Islamic schools and being recruited to fight US forces. Taliban leaders are openly giving press conferences and talking to reporters on mobile phones[9] and yet Islamabad is doing nothing to stop these Islamic radical activities despite repeated requests by President Hamid Karzai and other Afghan leaders (and also U.S. officials) to take action.

And finally, perhaps the greatest source for the continual instability so far is the "security vacuum" caused by the Karzai government's feeble hold over the country, and the American unwillingness to station international peacekeepers outside Kabul. This "vacuum" is preventing promised aid and developments reaching large parts of the south and the east, mainly to the Pashtun populated areas. The Pashtuns, who as such feel disenchanted due to what they perceive as their under-representation in the present governmental structure in Kabul, think very much insecure and frustrated. Into that vacuum of frustration and state of insecurity has stepped the Taliban. Mullah Omar, Gulbuddin Hekmatyar, and hosts of other renegade warlords along with some Taliban remnants are trying to fill the gap by not only mobilizing the people in the region in support of a "Pashtun cause" but also challenging American forces searching the leadership of the ousted government. Recently, Hekmatyar issued a taped message calling on Afghans to unite "to oust the foreign troops and cut the hands of the foreign meddlers."[10] They are not considered as any major political force, "but they can have a massive nuisance value."[11] As a diplomat rightly commented, "I don't think the Taliban can win, but they can set things back a longway,"[12] Afghan as well as American officials have expressed concern about an increase in the movements of the Taliban since the beginning of the war in Iraq.

To check and prevent these sources of terrorism and forces of instability from the Afghan scene, the United States is initiating several measures, but only on piecemeal basis. Even those steps are being diluted before its implementation at the ground level. As a result, a cohesive U.S. policy regarding the formation of the Afghan National Army vis-a-vis the role of warlords and America's military strategy has not been feasible to develop. The messy situation is leading to more bewilderment, and that in turn, dragging more American involvement.

The Politics of National Army, Warlords and Military Strategy

President Bush has rejected repeated calls by the United Nations, several NGO's working in the country, military generals, and President Hamid Karzai to deploy foreign peacekeeping troops around Afghanistan. Instead, the US administration has said a new Afghan army will do a better job patrolling the provinces—even though such an army is not expected to reach its projected full strength of 70,000 until 2006 at the earliest. Americans have no answer as to who will control eventual high-intensity guerrilla warfare, or in a worst-case scenario, a civil war? American commanders are also silent about the future of warlord's militias, whether that would join the new army or cede to it. At the same time US officials have their own style of military strategy to capture terrorists leaders and their remnants in the countryside, in many cases encouraging the anti-government warlords who are opposed to a large national army. In this untidy politics about the creation of Afghan National Army, maintaining balance with their own military strategy vis-à-vis the warlords, and denying more strength for the ISAF, Washington seems to be confusing its own objectives in Afghanistan and not interested for a comprehensive strategy. In July 2002, the United Nation's Special Afghan representative, Lakhdar Brahimi told the Security Council that "It is indispensable that plans are in place for the phasing out of those who currently call themselves soldiers and police."[13] But warlords are still strong enough with substantial military strength, and not willing to give up their weapons. Interestingly, some of them are still being pay rolled by the Americans through the prism of Washington's own game plan of hunting down the terrorists.

Under the United Nations and key Western nations (donors) auspices, the Afghan government does have a working paper for the national army. Accordingly, "Establishing an affordable, effective and efficient modern armed forces will require down-sizing of current force levels over time."[14] As per the working paper, Afghanistan would have 60,000-strong army, a border guard of 12,000, and an Air Force of 8,000 at a price of $289 million. Provisions are also there for a Quick Reaction Corps based in Kabul with 6,000 soldiers on alert to threats which would be the first division to operate, and backed by a combat support division and a service support division of 6,000 men each.[15] It also addresses the need for nationwide security by providing for seven 6,000-soldier corps around the country, each with a rapid action brigade and two light-infantry brigades. Acknowledging the country's ethnic problems and troubled neighbours, the working paper defines the army strategic goals in terms of "international security cooperation in the region . . . dealing with internal and external security needs and helping civil society with emergencies and rescue services."[16] This would ultimately lead to the formation of a National Security Council with the President as the Chairman and ministers of Defence, Interior, Finance and Foreign Affairs, as members. It is also mentioned in the paper that the proposed council would ensure uniformity in terms of military recruitment and management on a 'multi-ethnic basis, free from interference" and that the present Vice-President and Defence Minister Mohammed Fahim (Tajik) would head a Kabul-based Defence Council of the corps commanders.[17]

If on "multi-ethnic basis, free from interference" the Afghan National Army (ANA) is trained, even by the end of 2006, Afghan peace would be a reality. But that is where the question of ethnicity and warlordism comes in, and the Afghan society remains fragmented. As discussed elsewhere in this chapter, not only many warlords are being supported with money and weapons by the regional states on the basis of ethnic linkages, but also they are unwilling to give up their weapons, and work towards the formation of the ANA. But the worst part of all is that some warlords are still being lured with American money in the name of their support to America's war against terrorism. This American strategy goes contrary to Washington's stated goal and support for Karzai's efforts on the creation of the National Army. As per an estimate of the Afghan government, 75,000 armed soldiers worked for warlords, over 100,000 armed irregular combatants and war veterans have dispersed around the country, and unknown number of other fighters remains armed.[18] The idea that most commanders would "lay down their arms" in exchange for "reasonable economic alternative," has not worked, and that Washington, so far, does not look like coming out with a well-planned strategy to do this job. So the biggest fault line lies with the Americans. While President Bush is seeking Congressional approval to finance the new ANA, CIA is paying for warlord armies to help locate Al Qaeda/Taliban elements. This American stance leads to more confusion among the common people as well as foreign aid workers, most of who are in support of the expansion of ISAF, now (from August 2003) being taken over by NATO.[19] It also appears that Americans are unwilling, disinterested, or incapable to play an active role in terms of putting adequate pressure on the Tajik dominated Afghan government to maintain ethnic uniformity in the new Afghan National Army. This situation is hindering the flow of international aid—especially from the western donors who are concerned about the internal politics of the country—vital for reconstruction of this economically devastated country.

In fact, Americans have done very little to unify the warlords who are the actual and unbridled power holders in their respective occupied areas.[20] Most of their political prominence derives from their history either as mujahiddin commanders during anti-Soviet war of the 80s, or as leaders of militias. They control and police specific areas of territory within the state where the writ of the central government does not run. Their political ascendance is inextricably linked to their military power. Through trade and commerce, or levying taxes and duties, they exercise degrees of economic and political power. On this basis, the entire country has been fragmented into fiefdoms. Former Northern Alliance commanders control entire northern Afghanistan and capital Kabul. Defence Minister Mohammad Fahim, Uzbek leader Dostum and his rival Ata Mohammad, and former Afghan President Burhanuddin Rabbani are the real rulers of this region. In the southwest, Ismail Khan controls Herat, and Gul Agha Shirzai controls Kandahar (and parts of neighbouring provinces). Commander Hazrat All controls most of the eastern regions, while Paktika province is under Badshah Khan. And so long as these warlords remain powerful, the central authority of Karzai will bound to be weak. But it appears that Americans will continue to support the warlords as the U.S. depends on them for intelligence[21] and various operations for the capture of Taliban/Al Qaeda leadership in the mountainous terrains of the country. Therefore, the role of the warlords will remain critical as long as the United States continues its military in Afghanistan, and the country will remain fragmented for quite a considerable period of time.

Since the beginning of 2003, the United States appears to have developed some renewed interests in Afghan internal affairs, especially in terms of military strategy and reconstruction. Three reasons of these interests could be cited. First, Washington wanted to show that with the American and world attention focused on Iraq, Afghanistan is not forgotten land in their scheme of things. Secondly, Americans have been rightly convinced that without a substantial change in their military strategy vis-à-vis reconstruction, security situation in the country would not improve. Third, through this strategy, Washington has also sent a tough message to everybody, especially to regional warlords, that they are not going to go back soon and that their support to President Hamid Karzai would continue indefinitely. Americans also wanted to mitigate the growing criticism that the United States was not doing enough to help the Karzai government begin reconstruction of the country and dilute warlords' power in the provinces.

In view of that, American commander of Special Forces in Afghanistan Lieutenant General Dan K. McNeill declared in early January 2003 that he was planning to expand security and reconstruction related missions beyond the capital. As per the plan, Mc Neill prepared Joint Regional Teams (JRT) of 70 soldiers, civil affairs officers, engineers, medics and State Department officials to travel to selected areas, especially in Taliban/Al Qaeda strongholds, to set up base and begin reconstruction projects. The purpose is to help President Karzai to extend his still dormant authority in different parts of the country. "Our prediction was that most parts of the country will soon begin to realize some reasonable degree of security and stability,"[22] said the American commander. The commander declared that he reached to this decision after consulting the American and Afghan military officials,

United Nations, NGOs, officials from Britain, Germany and France, and officers of the ISAF. According to the plan, reconstruction "would pull an improvement of security along," which will enable coalition forces to foil "the residue of Al Qaeda and those who support it," and simultaneously "pursue support for the central government." Initially, the plan was to send JRT to Gardez and Kunduz, but afterwards expanded to other areas such as Bamiyan, Mazar-e-Sharif, Herat, Jalalabad, Kandahar and other significant areas.[23] According to the United Nations officials, the strength of McNeill's plan laid in its apparent flexibility, and that it had no "Donald Rumsfeld-designated model," "instead, McNeill is modifying the plan along the way as stakeholders like the UN or Karzai have questioned some parts of it."[24] The American General also promised that the JRTs would receive backup, including "rapid deployment of troops," air cover and potential airlift, and "need not worry about funding or attention." The JRTs, however, would not substitute for the ISAF or get involved with the local conflicts, or attempt to end disputes between national troops and warlords. That is for the central government. But the JRTs would have some flexibility on how to deal with local warlords in cooperation with central government officials. Once more troops for the new Afghan National Army are trained; the government troops could accompany the JRTs.[25]

American forces plan to expand the number of Joint Regional Teams (JRTs)—subsequently renamed as Provincial Reconstruction Teams (PRTs)—to 16. With its progressively expanding jurisdiction, Pentagon has indicated that in addition to the current level of conglomeration of soldiers alongside civilians from State Department, the Justice Department, and the Agency for International Development, staff from the United States Department of Agriculture would soon join the team. "PRTs are an innovative means to extend central government authority to the regions, enmesh local government with the central government and help with reconstruction"[26] said General F.L. "Buster" Hagenback, the current acting commander of US forces in Afghanistan. Britain, New Zealand and Germany are working on the same direction to expand the number and role of PRTs. North Atlantic Treaty Organisation (NATO) officials have also raised the idea of cooperating more closely with the teams once they took over the ISAF on August 11, 2003.[27]

So far, the PRTs are doing well with their limited jurisdiction and stipulated nature of job, but their progress is very slow. In a country of Afghanistan's size, it may take years to feel any visible results of this innovative reconstruction teams. Secondly, since they do not intervene in "green or green,"[28] or local infighting among various armed factions, maintenance of law and order at the local level is still a big problem where factional fighting, backed by different warlords, are the order of the day. Thirdly, the teams are heavily relying on the people who do not have adequate knowledge about Afghanistan's ethnic and tribal complexities, which may lead them to wrong place and people. PRTs have also found that the influence of warlords in the provinces will not be easily reduced,[29] which is presumably, the single largest obstacle to American efforts in the country.

America's Operation "Operations"

The U.S. and coalition military campaign against Al Qaeda training camps and Taliban military installations in Afghanistan began 7 October 2001. The campaign, code named "Operation Enduring Freedom" achieved a spectacular "victory" in a very short period of time as the Taliban regime crumbled almost overnight and the counry was quickly liberated. Commenting on military action in Afghanistan, President Bush said, "In four short months, our nation ... destroyed Afghanistan's terrorist training camps, saved a people from starvation, and freed a country from brutal oppression. Terrorists who once occupied Afghanistan now occupy cells at Guantanamo Bay. And terrorist leaders who urged followers to sacrifice their lives are running for their own [lives]."[30] But this proved to be a too much oversimplified statement, and that, much have changed in the military situation of the country since President Bush declared victory over the Taliban regime. Despite several "operations" and mop-up battles with Al Qaeda and Taliban remnants in the various mountainous terrains and caves in different parts of the country (especially in the south and east), Americans have not been successful in eliminating the terrorist threat. The recent increase in the numbers of terrorist's incidents reflects the impunity with which they believe they can now operate and make a difference in the Afghan security situation. America's military operations continue with different code-names, but with no avail.

"Operation Anaconda" was launched on March 1, 2002 in a 155 sq. km. area south of the provincial capital Gardez. The purpose of this operation was to rout hundreds of enemy fighters believed to have regrouped after the Taliban fell on December 7, 2001 from their spiritual base in Kandahar. U.S. officials declared that about 2000 coalition forces, divided almost equally between the US and Afghan troops participated in this operation. Special operations forces from six allied nations also participated. One significant event during this operation was that the terrorists bullets brought down one Chinook helicopter and damaged another, killing seven US troops, the worst casualty toll in a single offensive operation of the 5-month-old war.[31] Another important development on the eve of this operation was that the Americans, through the Gardez intelligence unit, declared a $ 4,000 reward for the capture of any Al Qaeda warrior. The leaflet offering the reward was an enlarged 10,000 Afghani note with the figure of 150 million Afghanis emblazoned on the front. On the back is the reward offer: "Dear countrymen: The Al Qaeda terrorists are our enemy. They are the enemy of your independence and freedom. Come on. Let us find their most secret hiding places. Search them out and inform the intelligence service of the province and get the big prize."[32] American officials later claimed that the operation resulted in the elimination of the Shai-Khot and Chumarra Valleys as sanctuaries for concentrations of Al Qaeda and Taliban. It was considered as a major success where "significant enemy pocket was destroyed, and notice was served to terrorists that there would be no safe harbor in Afghanistan."[33]

Similarly in June 2002, United States and coalition conventional and special operations forces started conducting "Operation Mountain Lion". The purpose was to demonstrate to terrorists and terrorist's sympathizers that they have nowhere to hide, and that this operation would root out remaining terrorists as long as it takes.[34]

In January 2003, the US military launched "Operation Mongoose" in a cave complex in the Adi Ghar Mountains that killed all of 18 rebels.

In February 2003, the US forces launched "Operation Eagle Fury" and "Operation Viper" with similar objectives.

In March 2003, "Operation Valiant Strike" was launched in southern Afghanistan avowedly to flush out extremists linked to the Al Qaeda.

In early June 2003, around 500 US-led coalition troops launched "Operation Dragon Fury" in the Shahikot mountain valley of neighbouring Paktia province in a search for suspected Taliban and Al Qaeda fighters. In the mid-June 2003, "Operation Dragon Fury II" was launched in the same area for the same purpose.

All these "Operations" have proved futile, as they could not help contain the growth of terrorist's threat. By the end July 2003, it was reported that the Taliban forces based in Pakistan were intensifying on US and Afghan government forces.[35] One notable clash occurred in July 18-19. On the night of July 19, US warplanes launched air strikes on a Taliban position close to the Pakistani border. The bombing raid came in response to a Taliban attack on a government checkpoint near the border town of Spin Baldak. As per one estimate, over 120 Afghan soldiers and civilians have been killed in Taliban attacks since the start of the year upto July 2003.[36] Increasing numbers of attacks and counter-attacks go on. Is the country slipping back into a protracted guerrilla war?

Quagmire

Like the anti-British protests of an earlier geo-political era, and anti-Soviet struggle of the 1980's, an increasing number of Afghans have begun to raise their voice against the American presence. The nature of Afghan resentment is also not quite different from what it was before. With the increasing numbers of clashes between the American/Afghan government forces and the emerging Taliban/Al Qaeda elements, Afghanistan seems to be again slipping back into chaos and confusion, and that the U.S. troops face a clear prospect of a protracted war. "I think the security situation in eastern Afghanistan is going to be a problem for some time to come just because of the freedom of operating back and forth from the Pakistan border,"[37] said US Joint Chiefs of Staff Chairman Richard Myers on December 21, 2002.

In early May 2003, about 300 Afghans chanted anti-American and anti-British slogans in Kabul in the first such protest since the U.S. led forces overthrew the Taliban in 2001. The protesters, who included government employees and university students, complained of growing insecurity, slow post-war reconstruction and delay in payment of state salaries by Hamid Karzai's US-backed government.[38] Terming the presence of American troops in their homeland as "American invasion," they shouted slogans like, "We don't want Brits and the Americans!" "Death to Bush, death to America!" "The time has come to beat the nail in the White House's coffin." "If we had dogs instead of these Jews and Christians, we would have security," etc. etc. The protest was organized by the "Scientific Centre" headed by Sediq Afghan, a prominent Afghan philosopher known for his outspoken criticism of the successive Afghan governments since 1980's. The protesters were however, seemed more concerned about the security situation in the country, improvements in the economy, and progress in post-war reconstruction.[39] This was relatively a small demonstration, but its significance cannot be underrated as it helped mould people, and developed tendencies of the masses to come to the streets in anti-government as well as anti-American protests through its wide publicity and propaganda.

The circulation of shabnamas ("night letters") has always marked the beginning of an internal resistance movement in Afghanistan.[40] Shabnam is a Persian word that means "message delivered at night." This is normally the secret massages conveyed about the enemy and operational strategy, urging jehad or holy war. Traditionally, it has come in the form of a poster, hand written in Pushto or Dari. It has been reported that in almost all the Pushtun belt of Afghanistan, the circulation of shabnamas has become a daily affair. One shabnama says: "By the grace of God, *jihad* once again has started, the enemy is fleeing. Keep your morale high and prepare yourself to fight against intruders and their local agents and motivate your brothers for the sacred cause."[41] It is widely believed that the Hezb-i-Islami leader Gulbuddin Hekmatyar and the Taliban have joined hands and formed a joint war council consisting of six to eight persons from each side to launch resistance against the U.S. presence in the country. Accordingly, Hakmatyar will direct the guerrilla war because the Taliban are not "sufficiently trained in the technique."[42]

The increasingly organized terrorist activities and growing opposition to the U.S. backed Kazrai government might have been the immediate result of the "new resistance alliance" and is certainly the cause of concern for the Americans. According to General F.L. Hagenback, the acting commander of the US-led coalition force in Afghanistan, Taliban fighters and affiliated Islamic militants have divided eastern Afghansitan into three zones for launching attacks and that Al Qaeda is offering bounties for killing or capturing US troops in order to undermine the Afghan government.[43] Captured Taliban have confirmed that bounties range between $5,000 and $100,000, depending on the target. One Taliban interviewed by reporters in mid July said he had been offered $2,000 to kill a civilian and $5,000 to kill an American soldier. Speaking at his headquarters located at the main US base at Bagram, about 25 miles outside Kabul, General Hagenback acknowledged an increase in Islamic radical activity in several key Afghan regions—mainly in the south and east of the country, along the country's long border with Pakistan. Hagenback said that in north eastern Afghanistan, also close to the Pakistan border, forces under renegade commander Gulbuddin Hekmetyar, who is allied to the Taliban, are "operating on the Jalalabad road moving up and down." The US commander emphasized that "there are second- or third-level Al Qaeda leaders trying to establish cells on the road between Khost and Gardez." He however, insisted that the terrorists have very little local support, and that the anti-terrorism coalition had the resources to contain the security threat.[44]

Recent developments indicate the stabilization efforts in Afghanistan remain fragile. People in many parts of the country still live virtually in a Hobbesian state of nature. American as well as Afghan security forces have arrested dozens of suspects who allegedly conspired to overthrow the Karzai government in May 2003. U.S. officials have pointed their fingers at exiled warlord Gulbuddin Hekmatyar behind the coup attempts. Hekmatyar, alongwith Al Qaeda and Taliban militants has become very active in recent days. Even after two years of the fall of the Mullah Omar's Taliban regime, remnants of the militia continue to launch regular attacks on American and pro-government targets. Killings and clashes are the order of the day mostly in Pakistan's neighbouring provinces. Of late, fighting is largely focused in southeastern Afghanistan, especially in Nangarhar, Paktia, Paktika, and Kandahar provinces.[45] The clashes are of such intensity that in most of the cases. US warplanes have to launch heavy air strikes in support of their forces (alongwith Afghan government troops) fighting on the ground. Another puzzling development for the Americans is that when thousands of US troops continue to surround and search homes in Pashtun heartland, in most of the cases their style of operation—without regard for local customary norms—is viewed as extortionists, which in turn, produce more resentment against what they call occupying forces. In this way, "a vicious circle is being created where insecurity prevents development, and that in turn breeds more insecurity."[46]

The problem of controlling outside interference in Afghanistan's internal affairs has also not been possible so far. Regional support to their ethnic brethren and warlords continues. Russia is arming one warlord, Iran another and India and Pakistan are secretly backing different claimants to power, Saudis are funding Islamic extremists and some Central Asian Republics are backing their ethnic allies. The Afghan government of President Karzai seems practically handicapped about the assertiveness of the warlords although he said, "We are not going to be a political football for neighbours in the region as we were in the 1990s. The soil of Afghanistan cannot be used by any country against a third country. We are watching the emerging situation very closely." Similar hollow warnings come from the American ambassador to Kabul Robert Finn. The ambassador said, "We have made it clear to all of Afghanistan's neighbours that the country should be allowed to develop without interference."[47]

The recent Pakistan-Afghanistan tension is likely to be stumbling block in the Afghan peace process. This will halt the aid and reconstruction efforts in southern Afghanistan along the Pak-Afghan border. Reports from the border areas confirm that there are frequent exchanges of fire from both sides, and that according to some western analysts; Islamabad was seeking to take advantage of the undemarcated border to extend itself. As per the reports, for the first time in decades, the dominant Pashtun majority was beginning to actually believe the thesis that

"Pakistan was not so easily going to give up its strategic depth in Afghanistan. That Pakistan's ISI and even a large section of the Army continued to consider Afghanistan its fifth province."[48] According to Ahmed Rashid, an expert on Afghan affairs, "... once extremely friendly to Pakistan such as Vice-President Hedayat Arsala and the Afghan Pashtuns—believe that President Pervez Musharraf, the Army, the ISI and the MMA are directly supporting the Taliban as a matter of Pakistani state policy and not through rogue elements."[49] It also places the United States in a delicate situation, frustrating its attempts to promote better coordination between the two governments to curb Taliban/Al Qaeda incursions. Despite a Triparite Commission among the United States, Pakistan and Afghanistan, promise to jointly verify the ground situation, Pakistan is continuing interference. The United States military and civilian officials are now swiftly moving from a position of ambiguity on this issue to one of direct and public criticism. Afghan leaders have been urging Washington to reign in Taliban supporters in Pakistan, but the Americans have so far not done anything on the ground, which would stop Islamabad from its perpetual interference. As a result, there is free movement of terrorists in the long-Pakistan-Afghanistan borders. According to an Afghan intelligence officer, "There is no hindrance for the Taliban in crossing the border. They just walk into Afghanistan and provide arms for their fighters. It cannot be done without Pakistan's security agencies' blessings."[50]

American and Pakistani cooperation with armed regional warlords also exacerbated the fragility of post-Taliban Afghanistan. One leading journalist, who has worked on the field points out that it was "untrained" American military officials and diplomats, and Pakistan's "state sponsored" policy towards Afghanistan creating more problems in the country. "Warlords... are not allies of convenience in an effort to stamp out insecurity, they are the single greatest threat to stability... It is in their interest that a certain level of instability exist,"[51] warned former NPR correspondent Sarah Chayes. She also criticizes American officials for their wrong policy. By choosing to deal with some leaders, she said, US military officers on the ground were essentially making policy by recognizing the legitimacy of certain tribal chiefs over others. "They were not trained to make policy, they were not trained to be diplomats," Chayes said. She also singled out Islamabad for its role in provoking Afghan unrest, saying Pakistani army officers worked in guerrilla training facilities near the southern Afghanistan border and that it was an essential part of Pakistan's foreign policy to "obstruct Afghanistan's efforts at establishing some kind of viable statehood."[52] The United States has to be little more cautious about the ground realities in this war-torn country.

The recent upsurge in terrorist activity has coincided with US military operations in Iraq. Many Taliban and Al Qaeda supporters believe that the United States' attention is focused on Iraq, and that Americans would not pay too much attention to the Afghan problem out of their big strategic catch in Baghdad. This belief is emboldening them to mount attacks against President Hamid Karzai's government troops and the American forces. It seems that they have already recovered from the shock of their defeat at the hands of US forces and are renewing armed operations. The significance of the ongoing "small-scale operation" of the Taliban/Al Qaeda cadres and Hekmatyar's militia is that the continuing attacks might grow into a large-scale well-organised resistance forces, exactly the way opposition grew up against the Soviet troops in the 1980's. And that would be increasingly supported by more and more anti-American elements within the country and the region.

Recent developments in Afghanistan's security situation indicate that the country is passing through a very thin edge of civil war. In a bold move to gain public confidence, President Hamid Karzai fired three governors and six regional security chiefs on August 14, a day after more than 50 citizens died in ambushes and a bomb attack.[53] The unrest is increasing in the south and the east because the senior Taliban commanders are capitalizing on popular discontent, and (their) long-time allies now govern the Pakistani provinces bordering Afghanistan. Several reports suggest security woes may force more reconstruction delays, potentially ballooning the need for aid. Already the United Nations has delayed work on road projects in the country's eastern provinces twice since May 2003, both times in response to bomb attacks.[54] So, security and reconstruction are interlinked and complimentary to each other, and therefore, without the former, the later cannot be achieved. So, before the present situation goes out of control, the United States must take adequate preventive measures soon.

What the Americans Should do about it

Given such a clumsy and perplex scenario, it would be unrealistic to suggest any immediate solutions to the Afghan problem. But the United States, with its huge economic resources, political leadership in the world, and military capability; can certainly influence people, institutions, and nations to its own democratic ideals and values judiciously in terms of a long-term strategy to contain the menace of terrorism. The Americans need to reassess their perception, and give up hegemonic and cold war mindset in their dealings with other countries, especially with the Islamic world. Then only Washington would be in a position to deal with Afghanistan and its neighbours fairly and firmly. The following observations may be seen as part of long-term Washington strategy towards Afghanistan.

The Taliban/Al Qaeda cadres have complete freedom of mobility in Pakistani territory with much of the supports and instigations coming up from the Army and ISI. The situation is such that General Musharraf will continue to be in the saddle with liberal doses of American aid and favour, and in turn, the indefinite search for bin Laden and Mullah Omar will continue. If the "body bag" conscious Americans withdraw from the country, that will ensue a vacuum which will allow the Taliban and Al Qaeda to return with as usual Pakistani auspices. And so long as American presence is there, Musharraf's clandestine support to terrorists will continue which the Pakistani leader knows, would ensure an American long rope for his survival. US Special Envoy to Afghanistan, Zalmay Khalizad has observed that Pakistan must provide "100 per cent" assurance that the Taliban would not be allowed to use Pakistani territory to regroup and destabilize Afghanistan, as they seem to be planning in Quetta.[55] So the prime requirement is that the United States must ensure that there is no undue Pakistani interference in the internal affairs of Afghanistan, and that the military strategists in Islamabad must stop their masquerading intension of making their neighbour a satellite state. Unless terrorists, their infrastructures, and their organisations are dismantled within Pakistani territory, Afghan peace is unimaginable.

Soon after the commencement of military operation in Afghanistan on October 7, 2001, President Bush announced that the campaign against terrorism would be a long-term exercise against terrorist organisations, individuals and states and entities which give them support and sanctuary. But the administration is not ready to prevail upon the states that have direct complicity in the 9/11 events as well as malicious records of supporting terrorism. This is happening despite sufficient evidence in hand.[56] The U.S. administration is seemed to be opting desperately whatever immediate cooperation it can squeeze, cajole or buy, even from a country like Pakistan. The Bush decision so far is mostly influenced on the stand taken by the CIA and the Pentagon who face the day-to-day demands against their failure to capture the Al-Qaeda/Taliban leadership. "A skilful political alchemist" like General Musharraf will continue to hoodwink Washington by manipulating the situation in the region, and will be successfully "transforming a record of failure, extremism and betrayal in to gold from the US treasury."[57] Clearly, the current U.S. policy wouldn't work, and needs immediate review in the interest of the Afghan peace.

United States must work towards a viable political alternative in Kabul. It does not mean an alternative to the Karzai government. It means reorientation and readjustments of governmental forces aiming "stability and security" as the immediate requirement. If the US continue to only focus on the "hunt down" of Osama bin Laden and Mullah Omar, and does not extend a helping hand to the Kabul government, that would not help in Afghan peace. "Afghanistan's attempt to draft a new constitution could prove a meaningless exercise without concurrent efforts to improve security in the country's provinces," said Barnett Rubin, an Afghanistan expert who helped draft the 2001 Bonn process for Afghanistan's political reconstruction. "The most important thing outsiders can do is to create the conditions that will make it possible for the constitution to mean anything,"[58] said Rubin. What is required is a concerted and sincere effort on the part of Washington, not only to help mobilize public opinion within the country, but also to strike a strategic balance among the internal forces.

America's troops deployment and military operations abroad also willy-nilly perceived as anti-Islamic exercise by increasing numbers of Muslim countries all over the world. So the United States should work towards minimum and short-term troop deployment in case of genuine necessity, and should stress on political stability of the nations. Washington must understand the fact that the current trends in the US foreign policy has a direct bearing in Afghanistan and its Muslim neighbours. Through their commitments and actions, Americans must prove that they want genuine peace in the country and that they are not anti-Islam. Such an effort would look credible if the United Nations is allowed to play a more pro-active role in the reconstruction of this war-ravaged country.

As the sole superpower in the world, the United States should act as a "coordinator" among the regional actors. Without active participation of the neighbours of Afghanistan long-term peace and stability cannot be achieved. United States has the potential to influence people and leaders of the region to work towards some kind of regional security or cooperative framework, which would reflect the security as well as prosperity of the entire region. While framing such a strategy, historical, cultural, sociological, economic and more significantly, religious aspects must be taken into consideration since all these factors will ultimately determine the final outcome of any Afghan peace process. Some U.S. officials seem to have positive vision in this context when they say that in the international arena, there should be no "nineteenth century style zero-sum game, but rather a cooperative arrangement" that fosters multilateral cooperation.[59] They also indicate that the United States would work to convince Russia, Iran and Pakistan. But how this idea will be worked out depends on Washington's will and determination.

Washington also has to make some changes in its policy towards the warlords in the domestic politics of Afghanistan. During the anti-Taliban war in the Autumn 2001, American and allied forces did not hesitate to accept support from even the most notorious and "serial turncoat" warlords like Rashid Dostum.[60] Indeed, many Afghan commanders and warlords who helped American led forces are now considered the main threat to the Karzai government's peace building efforts. Experts believe that American money still pays salaries to warlords' troops in the name of fighting Al Qaeda.[61] A senior aide to Karzai said, "The US needs a new strategy putting its weight with the government rather than dividing it between the warlords and the government."[62] One positive area of development in this context is the United States support of building a national army,[63] which would weaken warlord's legitimacy in the long run. In the meantime however, Americans must bring about certain amendments in their current policy.

If the United States continues to play the cold war game of "containment" and "encirclement" against the neighbouring countries of Afghanistan, then no cooperation will be forthcoming for any Washington sponsored regional peace initiative. If at all nations cooperate, that would be only superficial, and at best half-hearted, and that the real hidden agenda would be different. The time-to-time American official statements about Afghanistan's neighbours in this context are not very encouraging. Iranians feel insecure and fear US encirclement due to the presence of American bases in Central Asia and Turkey. They also feel threatened about the current US policy on Iraq, and American stand on their nuclear program as well as the possible presence of Al Qaeda operatives in their territory. The insufficiently Islamic nature of the present Afghan regime also makes the Iranians nervous. Similarly, Washington is not ready to accommodate the traditional Russian interests in Central Asia and Afghanistan, which makes Moscow too much apprehensive and vigilant about the U.S. presence in Central Asia. China, Pakistan and Afghanistan's Central Asian neighbours are not without remonstrations against the United States policy towards the region. Since containment of terrorism is the main objective, the United States must look at the problem in terms of domino impact of American policy. Afghanistan cannot be a self-determining problem. It is part of the entire strategic landscape of the whole region.

With the increasing American attention in Iraq, lawlessness and factional fighting increased in Afghanistan. Almost daily attacks on civilians, peacekeepers or government targets by insurgent groups, criminal elements and rogue warlords created a climate of fear; impeding the country's rehabilitation and development.[64] One of the suitable steps Washington could initiate at his juncture is the expansion of the International Security Assistance Force (ISAF). Many people working on the ground in Afghanistan believe that the NATO's agreement to assume control of peacekeeping operations from August 2003 presents a fresh and ideal opportunity to expand security across the country. In a recent statement, the NGO's urged the UN and NATO "to expand the ISAF to locations and transport routes beyond Kabul," and "to provide support for a comprehensive program of disarmament, demobilization and reintegration of militia forces outside the control of the government and the accelerated recruitment and training of an Afghan national army and police force."[65] The NGO's also feel that the interim administration of Hamid Karzai needs much more support and resources to maintain peace and security. "Unless there are dramatic security improvements in Afghanistan, reconstruction efforts will be stymied, the Bonn peace process risks collapse, free and fair elections may never be realized and a return to anarchy and civil war become increasingly likely," warned the International Rescue Commitee President George Rupp.[66] But Washington, so far, is wary about the expansion of the ISAF beyond Kabul.[67] A serious review of present American policy and active cooperation of the United States is, however, required to make the proposed arrangements effective and functional.

United States can also contribute towards the economic developments of the region both by pushing the poverty-stricken economies through moderate aid programs as well as giving and implementing ideas, as poverty and illiteracy are among the several chronic types of problems interlinked with terrorism. Expansion of trade ties among the nation is one option, especially in terms of Central Asia's huge oil and gas resources. Such an arrangement would involve the participation of so many countries and international financial institution (like the World Bank and Asian Development Bank) simultaneously, and help restore the economy in the region. This would also benefit the United States. Some U.S. officials are, of late debating about Central Asia's untapped "southern option—a network of roads, railroads and pipelines to markets of Pakistan and India, and access to the global markets through the Indian Ocean."[68] Afghanistan as the transit country can be benefited without much of its won investment and financial risk. But Washington has not come forward with any specific proposal in this regard.

Finally, the United States must contribute generously to the poverty-stricken Afghan economy. Washington has also to bear responsibility to organise among other rich nations to come forward with moderate financial assistance for the on-going reconstruction process. The international community must understand that the problems of terrorism cannot be solved unless Afghanistan's war-ravaged economy is stabilized. The United States has come under severe criticism for its very low-level and marginal aid program in Afghanistan as its focus was shifted to Iraq. The recent announcement by the Bush administration to propose $1 billion aid package aimed at bolstering the Hamid Karzai government and countering international criticism that America is not doing more, is a step in right direction. According to senior US officials, the current aid package is designed to fund projects that can be completed within a year to have maximum impact on the lives of the Afghan people before the scheduled democratic elections in October 2004.[69]

After nearly two years since 9/11, though the United States liberated Afghanistan from the clutches of the ultra-fundamentalist Taliban rule and dismantled the Al Qaeda terrorist's camps and infrastructure, Washington has not done much to bring about a qualitative change in the Afghan life, society, and economy. So far, Afghans live on only "hopes," and "promises" from the United States. Narrating the American thinking about his country after a trip to Washington in March 2003, President Karzai said, "When I went to Washington earlier this month, the President and all government departments spoke strongly of continuing support for Afghanistan. But whether it will have as much time devoted to it as one year ago, three months ago, or even one day ago... well, you can draw your own conclusions."[70]

From the above analysis, and all indications, it may be inferred that the United States is not going to go back from Afghanistan any time soon.[71] It may face a low-intensity guerrilla war, may have to encounter traditional Afghan resentment against the "occupying forces," or may be criticised for a low-level aid program for the reconstruction efforts, etc. etc., but Washington wouldn't be in a position to backtrack from its current Afghan commitments. Also, Americans will not leave the country because of their own "strategic reasons" in terms of maintaining their hold and supremacy in the region in the name of their indefinite search for terrorists. Ultimately, American presence will have a very chilling prospect not only for the Afghans themselves, but also for the entire region. Hence, Afghanistan's neighbours' must learn to live with an arrogant superpower at their own backyards. It may be worrisome for many people in the periphery, but there is no choice. Afghanistan will remain within the United States' global strategy of what a Neo-Conservative in Washington would tacitly concede as a part of Pax Americana. The superpower is here for an enduring engagement.

Notes and References

1. As available in the "Joint Statement between the United States of America and Afghanistan," *Weekly Compilation of Presidential Documents,* Washington D.C., March 3, 2003.
2. J.N. Dixit, *India's Foreign Policy Challenge of Terrorism,* Gyan Publishing House, New Delhi, 2002, p. 102.
3. Stephen Biddle, "Afghanistan and the Future of Warfare," *Foreign Affairs,* Vol. 82, No. 2, March/April 2003, p. 32.
4. *Ibid,* p. 35.
5. Dexter Filkins and Carlotta Gall, "A Nation Challenged: The Siege; Pakistanis again said to Evacuate Allies of Taliban," *The New York Times,* November 24, 2001.
6. *Ibid.*
7. *Ibid.*
8. Ariel Cohen, "Washing Fears for Karzai's Future," *eurasianet.org* September 4, 2002.
9. Ahmed Rashid "Taliban Stepping up Attacks against Targets in Afghanistan," *Eurasianet.org,* July 28, 2003.
10. Quoted in Ahmed Rashid, "Pakistan closes its Embassy in Afghanistan amid escalating diplomatic tension," *eurasianet.org* July 8, 2003.
11. Simon Denyer, "Off US radar, Afghanistan slipping back into chaos," *The Indian Express,* April 4, 2003.
12. As quoted in *Ibid.*
13. Ahmed Rashid, "United States faces fault lines in building Afghan Army," *eurasianet.org* July 29, 2002.
14. As cited in *Ibid.*
15. As per the estimate in *Ibid.*
16. As quoted in *Ibid.*
17. *Ibid.*
18. *Ibid.*
19. It may be noted that several NGO's, various women's groups, leading Afghan personalities, outgoing commander of the ISAF German General Norbert van Heyst, United Nations, and above all Afghan President Hamid Karzai, support for the expansion of the 31-nation 5,000 strong International Security Assistance Force, the command of which is now being taken over by the most powerful military alliance of the world, the North Atlantic Treaty Organisation (NATO) on 11th of August 2003. Ironically, nobody talks about any expansion or any increasing role for the presently deployed more than 8,500 American troops in a coalition of 11,500 multi-national forces to hunt down the remnants of the Taliban/Al Qaeda elements.
20. For a details discussion of the American support to the warlords and its larger implications, see the previous chapter.

21. Sohail Abdul Nasir, "Afghanistan: The more it changes..." *Bulletin of the Atomic Scientists*, Chicago, March/April 2003.
22. Ahmed Rashid, "American Commander alters military strategy in Afghanistan," *eurasianet.org* January 13, 2003.
23. *Ibid.*
24. *Ibid.*
25. *Ibid.*
26. As quoted in Ahmed Rashid, "Team Approach Spreads in Afghanistan, But Security Worries Remain," *eurasianet.org* August 7, 2003.
27. *Ibid.* The North Atlantic Treaty Organisation (NATO) began its first operation outside Europe in its 54-year history when it took command of peacekeepers in the Afghan capital on August 11, 2003. Germany and the Netherlands had held that joint command of the ISAF until Lieutenant General Norbert van Heyst, outgoing commander transferred command to another German three-star General Goetz Gliemeroth, from NATO command. For more details, see "NATO takes over command in Afghanistan," *The Times of India*, August 12, 2003. Also see, Ron Synovitz, "Afghanistan: NATO takes over ISAF command amid calls for expansion," *eurasianet.org* August 12, 2003.
28. Ahmed Rashid, *Ibid.*
29. As reported in *Ibid.*
30. *Weekly Compilation of Presidential Documents*, U.S. Government Printing Office, Washington D.C., March 12, 2002.
31. "Hundreds of Al-Qaida men killed," *The Times of India*, March 7, 2002.
32. *Ibid.*
33. See the testimony of General Tommy Franks, the overall commander of U.S. and coalition forces in Afghanistan, to a Senate Committee on 31 July 2002. Text: "U.S. Commander Says Much Remains to be done in Afghanistan," is available in *Washington File*, International Information Programs, U.S. Department of State, Washington D.C., August 1, 2002.
34. *Ibid.*
35. Ahmed Rashid, "Taliban Stepping up Attacks against Targets in Afghanistan," *eurasianet.org* July 28, 2003.
36. *Ibid.*
37. Ahmed Rashid, "Jockeying for Influence, Neighbours undermine Afghan Pact," *eurasianet.org* January 15, 2003.
38. "Kabul sees anti-US protest," *The Times of India*, May 7, 2003.
39. *Ibid.*
40. Traditionally, shabnamas or night letters have played a very influential role in the beginning of resistance movements in Afghanistan. On the eve of the communist revolution in 1978 and the Soviet invasion of the country in 1979, shabnamas had a crucial role in instigating and organising people for resistance movements against the communists and the Soviets. For earlier role of shabnamas in Afghanistan, see Henry S. Bradsher, *Afghanistan and*

the Soviet Union, Duke University Press, Durham, N.C., 1983, pp. 106, 208, 214, 233, 247, 268 and 291.

41. As quoted in Sohail Abdul Nasir, "Afghanistan: The more it changes..." *Bulletin of the Atomic Scientists,* Chicago, March/April 2003.
42. For the alliance between Hezb-i-Islami leader Gulbuddin Hekmatyar and Taliban leader Mullah Omar, see *Ibid.*
43. Ahmed Rashid, "Taliban Stepping up Attacks against Targets in Afghanistan," *eurasianet.org* July 28, 2003.
44. *Ibid.*
45. "US forces kill four Taliban attackers," *The Times of India,* August 2, 2003.
46. Simon Denyer, "Off US radar, Afghanistan slipping back into chaos," *The Indian Express,* April 4, 2003.
47. Ahmed Rashid, "Jockeying for Influence, Neighbours undermine Afghan Pact," *eurasianet.org* January 15, 2003.
48. As quoted in Jyoti Malhotra, "Face off: Crossing the (Durand) Line," *The Indian Express,* July 24, 2003.
49. Ahmed Rashid, "Kabul to Islamabad: you have hurt, pained us," *The Indian Express,* July 26, 2003.
50. Owais Tohid, "Taliban Fighters Infiltrating back into Afghanistan from Pakistan," *eurasianet.org* May 5, 2003.
51. "Experts Blames Afghan Instability on Pakistani and American Support to Warlords," *eurasianet.org,* June 10, 2003.
52. *Ibid.*
53. Mark Berniker, "Can Afghan Reconstruction Surge After Latest Violence?" *eurasianet.org* August 16, 2003.
54. *Ibid.*
55. Quoted in "Concern in Kabul," *The Indian Express,* July 26, 2003.
56. For example, see the quoted statement of US Joint Chiefs of Staff Chairman Richard Myers on December 21, 2002, in Ahmed Rashid, "Jockeying for Influence, Neighbours undermine Afghan Pact," *eurasianet.org* January 15, 2003.
57. Jim Hoagland, "Fools Gold in Pakistan," *The Washington Post,* June 30, 2003.
58. "Drafting of New Afghan Constitution may be 'Meaningless Exercise' Without Greater Security-Expert," *eurasianet.org* April 11, 2003.
59. Ariel Cohen, "Washington Fears for Karzai's Future," *eurasianetnet.org* September 4, 2002.
60. "Dostum is regarded by the U.S. as a close ally, his power depended less on the allegiance of his fellow Uzbeks than on American taxpayers' money. More Radovan Karadzic than Lech Walesa, he belongs at a courtroom in the Hague rather than in a palace at Sheberghan." See Masood Farivar, "Let's not forget Afghanistan yet," *The Indian Express,* November 20, 2002.
61. Ahmed Rashid, "Karzai Mounts Anti-Warlord Campaign in Afghanistan," *eurasianet.org* March 1, 2003.

62. *Ibid.*
63. So far, the Ministry of Defence has procrastinated in this task, as only 2,000 soldiers have received training for serving in a 70,000-slot army. See Ahmed Rashid, "Karzai Mounts Anti-Warlord Campaign in Afghanistan," *eurasianet.org* March 1, 2003.
64. For the latest killings in bomb attacks and border firings involving Taliban/Al Qaeda cadres and government forces, see "36 dead in Afghan violence," *The Times of India,* August 14, 2003.
65. "International Aid, Advocacy Groups Urge Expanded NATO Role to Stabilize Afghanistan," *eurasianet.org* June 18, 2003. Nearly 80 humanitarian, human rights and conflict prevention groups in a statement, "Afghanistan: A Call for Security," urged NATO Secretary General Lord Robertson and U.N. Secretary General Kofi Annan for an expanded role for NATO in Afghanistan. The complete text of the statement is available on the IRC's web site, *www.theIRC.org*
66. *Ibid.*
67. For a details discussion on the American indifference about the expansion of the ISAF, see the previous chapter.
68. Ariel Cohen, "Washington Fears for Karzai's Future," *eurasianetnet.org* September 4, 2002.
69. "US proposes $1bn aid package for Afghanistan." *The Times of India,* July 28, 2003.
70. Christina Lamb, "Reconstruction still a far cry here," *The Times of India,* March 25, 2003.
71. For the post-war U.S. policy towards Afghanistan, see, Matthew Riemer, "Post-war Patterns in Afghanistan and Iraq, *eurasianet.org* August 14, 2003.

Appendix A
Text: Afghan Agreement on Broad-Based, Multi-Ethnic Government

(Interim Authority to be established December 22, 2001) (3290)
Following is the full text of the agreement signed December 4 by Afghan representatives meeting in Bonn, Germany, aimed at establishing a stable, representative government in Afghanistan following 23 years of war.

AGREEMENT ON PROVISIONAL ARRANGEMENTS IN AFGHANISTAN PENDING THE RE-ESTABLISHMENT OF PERMANENT GOVERNMENT INSTITUTIONS

The participants in the UN Talks on Afghanistan,

In the presence of the Special Representative of the Secretary-General for Afghanistan,

Determined to end the tragic conflict in Afghanistan and promote national reconciliation, lasting peace, stability and respect for human rights in the country,

Reaffirming the independence, national sovereignty and territorial integrity of Afghanistan,

Acknowledging the right of the people of Afghanistan to freely determine their own political future in accordance with the principles of Islam, democracy, pluralism and social justice,

Expressing their appreciation to the Afghan mujahidin who, over the years, have defended the independence, territorial integrity and national unity of the country and have played a major role in the struggle against terrorism and oppression, and whose sacrifice has now made them both heroes of jihad and champions of peace, stability and reconstruction of their beloved homeland, Afghanistan,

Aware that the unstable situation in Afghanistan requires the implementation of emergency interim arrangements and expressing their deep appreciation to His Excellency Professor Burhanuddin Rabbani for his readiness to transfer power to an interim authority which is to be established pursuant to this agreement,

Recognizing the need to ensure broad representation in these interim arrangements of all segments of the Afghan population, including groups that have not been adequately represented at the UN Talks on Afghanistan.

Noting that these interim arrangements are intended as a first step toward the establishment of a broad-based, gender-sensitive, multi-ethnic and fully representative government, and are not intended to remain in place beyond the specified period of time,

Recognizing that some time may be required for a new Afghan security force to be fully constituted and functional and that therefore other security provisions detailed in Annex I to this agreement must meanwhile be put in place,

Considering that the United Nations, as the internationally recognized impartial institution, has a particularly important role to play, detailed in Annex II to this agreement, in the period prior to the establishment of permanent institutions in Afghanistan,

Have agreed as follows:

THE INTERIM AUTHORITY

I. General provisions

1. An Interim Authority shall be established upon the official transfer of power on 22 December 2001.
2. The Interim Authority shall consist of an Interim Administration presided over by a Chairman, a Special Independent Commission for the Convening of the Emergency Loya Jirga, and a Supreme Court of Afghanistan, as well as such other courts as may be established by the Interim Administration. The composition, functions and governing procedures for the Interim Administration and the Special Independent Commission are set forth in this agreement.
3. Upon the official transfer of power, the Interim Authority shall be the repository of Afghan sovereignty, with immediate effect. As such, it shall, throughout the interim period, represent Afghanistan in its external relations and shall occupy the seat of Afghanistan at the United Nations and in its specialized agencies, as well as in other international institutions and conferences.
4. An Emergency Loya Jirga shall be convened within six months of the establishment of the Interim Authority. The Emergency Loya Jirga will be opened by His Majesty Mohammed Zaher, the former King of Afghanistan. The Emergency Loya Jirga shall decide on a transitional Authority, including a broad-based transitional administration, to lead Afghanistan until such time as a fully representative government can be elected through free and fair elections to be held no later than two years from the date of the convening of the Emergency Loya Jirga.
5. The Interim Authority shall cease to exist once the Transitional Authority has been established by the Emergency Loya Jirga.
6. A Constitutional Loya Jirga shall be convened within eighteen months of the establishment of the Transitional Authority, in order to adopt a new constitution for Afghanistan. In order to assist the Constitutional Loya Jirga prepare the proposed Constitution, the Transitional Administration shall, within two months of its commencement and with the assistance of the United

Nations, establish a Constitutional Commission.

II. Legal framework and judicial system

1. The following legal framework shall be applicable on an interim basis until the adoption of the new Constitution referred to above:
   (i) The Constitution of 1964, a/ to the extent that its provisions are not inconsistent with those contained in this agreement, and b/ with the exception of those provisions relating to the monarchy and to the executive and legislative bodies provided in the Constitution; and
   (ii) existing laws and regulations, to the extent that they are not inconsistent with this agreement or with international legal obligations to which Afghanistan is a party, or with those applicable provisions contained in the Constitution of 1964, provided that the Interim Authority shall have the power to repeal or amend those laws and regulations.
2. The judicial power of Afghanistan shall be independent and shall be vested in a Supreme Court of Afghanistan, and such other courts as may be established by the Interim Administration. The Interim Administration shall establish, with the assistance of the United Nations, a Judicial Commission to rebuild the domestic justice system in accordance with Islamic principles, international standards, the rule of law and Afghan legal traditions.

III. Interim Administration

A. Composition

1. The Interim Administration shall be composed of a Chairman, five Vice Chairmen and 24 other members. Each member, except the Chairman, may head a department of the Interim Administration.
2. The participants in the UN Talks on Afghanistan have invited His Majesty Mohammed Zaher, the former King of Afghanistan, to chair the Interim Administration. His Majesty has indicated that he would prefer that a suitable candidate acceptable to the participants be selected as the Chair of the Interim Administration.
3. The Chairman, the Vice Chairmen and other members of the Interim Administration have been selected by the participants in the UN Talks on Afghanistan, as listed in Annex IV to this agreement. The selection has been made on the basis of professional competence and personal integrity from lists submitted by the participants in the UN Talks, with due regard to the ethnic, geographic and religious composition of Afghanistan and to the importance of the participation of women.
4. No person serving as a member of the Interim Administration may simultaneously hold membership of the Special Independent Commission for the Convening of the Emergency Loya Jirga.

B. Procedures

1. The Chairman of the Interim Administration, or in his/her absence one of the Vice Chairmen, shall call and chair meetings and propose the agenda for these meetings.

2. The Interim Administration shall endeavour to reach its decisions by consensus. In order for any decision to be taken, at least 22 members must be in attendance. If a vote becomes necessary, decisions shall be taken by a majority of the members present and voting, unless otherwise stipulated in this agreement. The Chairman shall cast the deciding vote in the event that the members are divided equally.

C. Functions

1. The Interim Administration shall be entrusted with the day-to-day conduct of the affairs of state, and shall have the right to issue decrees for the peace, order and good government of Afghanistan.
2. The Chairman of the Interim Administration or, in his/her absence, one of the Vice Chairmen, shall represent the Interim Administration as appropriate.
3. Those members responsible for the administration of individual departments shall also be responsible for implementing the policies of the Interim Administration within their areas of responsibility.
4. Upon the official transfer of power, the Interim Administration shall have full jurisdiction over the printing and delivery of the national currency and special drawing rights from international financial institutions. The Interim Administration shall establish, with the assistance of the United Nations, a Central Bank of Afghanistan that will regulate the money supply of the country through transparent and accountable procedures.
5. The Interim Administration shall establish, with the assistance of the United Nations, an independent Civil Service Commission to provide the Interim Authority and the future Transitional Authority with shortlists of candidates for key posts in the administrative departments, as well as those of governors and uluswals, in order to ensure their competence and integrity.
6. The Interim Administration shall, with the assistance of the United Nations, establish an independent Human Rights Commission, whose responsibilities will include human rights monitoring, investigation of violations of human rights, and development of domestic human rights institutions. The Interim Administration may, with the assistance of the United Nations, also establish any other commissions to review matters not covered in this agreement.
7. The members of the Interim Administration shall abide by a Code of Conduct elaborated in accordance with international standards.
8. Failure by a member of the Interim Administration to abide by the provisions of the Code of Conduct shall lead to his/her suspension from that body. The decision to suspend a member shall be taken by a two-thirds majority of the membership of the Interim Administration on the proposal of its Chairman or any of its Vice Chairmen.
9. The functions and powers of members of the Interim Administration will be further elaborated, as appropriate, with the assistance of the United Nations.

IV. The Special Independent Commission for the Convening of the Emergency Loya Jirga

1. The Special Independent Commission for the Convening of the Emergency Loya Jirga shall be established within one month of the establishment of the Interim Authority. The Special Independent Commission will consist of twenty-one members, a number of whom should have expertise in constitutional or customary law. The members will be selected from lists of candidates submitted by participants in the UN Talks on Afghanistan as well as Afghan professional and civil society groups. The United Nations will assist with the establishment and functioning of the commission and of a substantial secretariat.
2. The Special Independent Commission will have the final authority for determining the procedures for and the number of people who will participate in the emergency Loya Jirga. The Special Independent Commission will draft rules and procedures specifying (i) criteria for allocation of seats to the settled and nomadic population residing in the country; (ii) criteria for allocation of seats to the Afghan refugees living in Iran, Pakistan, and elsewhere, and Afghans from the diaspora; (iii) criteria for inclusion of civil society organizations and prominent individuals, including Islamic scholars, intellectuals, and traders, both within the country and in the diaspora. The Special Independent Commission will ensure that due attention is paid to the representation in the Emergency Loya Jirga of a significant number of women as well as all other segments of the Afghan population.
3. The Special Independent Commission will publish and disseminate the rules and procedures for the convening of the Emergency Loya Jirga at least ten weeks before the Emergency Loya Jirga convenes, together with the date the date for its commencement and its suggested location and duration.
4. The Special Independent Commission will adopt and implement procedures for monitoring the process of nomination of individuals to the Emergency Loya Jirga to ensure that the process of indirect election or selection is transparent and fair. To pre-empt conflict over nominations, the Special Independent Commission will specify mechanisms for filing of grievances and rules for arbitration of disputes.
5. The Emergency Loya Jirga will elect a Head of the State for the Transitional Administration and will approve proposals for the structure and key personnel of the Transitional Administration.

V. Final provisions

1. Upon the official transfer of power, all mujahidin, Afghan armed forces and armed groups in the country shall come under the command and control of the Interim Authority, and be reorganized according to the requirements of the new Afghan security and armed forces.
2. The Interim Authority and the Emergency Loya Jirga shall act in accordance with basic principles and provisions contained in international instruments on human rights and international humanitarian law to which Afghanistan is a party.
3. The Interim Authority shall cooperate with the international community in

the fight against terrorism, drugs and organized crime. It shall commit itself to respect international law and maintain peaceful and friendly relations with neighbouring countries and the rest of the international community.

4. The Interim Authority and the Special Independent Commission for the Convening of the Emergency Loya Jirga will ensure the participation of women as well as the equitable representation of all ethnic and religious communities in the Interim Administration and the Emergency Loya Jirga.
5. All actions taken by the Interim Authority shall be consistent with Security Council resolution 1378 (14 November 2001) and other relevant Security Council resolutions relating to Afghanistan.
6. Rules of procedure for the organs established under the Interim Authority will be elaborated as appropriate with the assistance of the United Nations.

This agreement, of which the annexes constitute an integral part, done in Bonn on this 5th day of December 2001 in the English language, shall be the authentic text, in a single copy which shall remain deposited in the archives of the United Nations. Official texts shall be provided in Dari and Pashto, and such other languages as the Special Representative of the Secretary-General may designate. The Special Representative of the Secretary-General shall send certified copies in English, Dari and Pashto to each of the participants.

For the participants in the UN Talks on Afghanistan:

Ms. Amena Afzali Mr. S. Hussain Anwari Mr. Hedayat Amin Arsala Mr. Sayed Hamed Gailani Mr. Rahmatullah Mousa Ghazi Eng. Abdul Hakim Mr. Houmayoun Jareer Mr. Abbas Karimi Mr. Mustafa Kazimi Dr. Azizullah Ludin Mr. Ahmad Wali Massoud Mr. Hafizullah Asif Mohseni Prof. Mohammad Ishaq Nadiri Mr. Mohammad Natiqi Mr. Aref Noorzay Mr. Yunus Qanooni Dr. Zalmai Rassoul Mr. H. Mirwais Sadeq Dr. Mohammad Jalil Shams Prof. Abdul Sattar Sirat Mr. Humayun Tandar Mrs. Sima Wali General Abdul Rahim Wardak Mr. Azizullah Wasefi Mr. Pacha Khan Zadran

Witnessed for the United Nations by:

Mr. Lakhdar Brahimi Special Representative of the Secretary-General for Afghanistan

ANNEX I

INTERNATIONAL SECURITY FORCE

1. The participants in the UN Talks on Afghanistan recognize that the responsibility for providing security and law and order throughout the country resides with the Afghans themselves. To this end, they pledge their commitment to do all within their means and influence to ensure such security, including for all United Nations and other personnel of international governmental and non-governmental organizations deployed in Afghanistan.
2. With this objective in mind, the participants request the assistance of the international community in helping the new Afghan authorities in the establishment and training of new Afghan security and armed forces.

3. Conscious that some time may be required for the new Afghan security and armed forces to be fully constituted and functioning, the participants in the UN Talks on Afghanistan request the United Nations Security Council to consider authorizing the early deployment to Afghanistan of a United Nations mandated force. This force will assist in the maintenance of security for Kabul and its surrounding areas. Such a force could, as appropriate, be progressively expanded to other urban centers and other areas.
4. The participants in the UN Talks on Afghanistan pledge to withdraw all military units from Kabul and other urban centers or other areas in which the UN mandated force is deployed. It would also be desirable if such a force were to assist in the rehabilitation of Afghanistan's infrastructure.

ANNEX II

ROLE OF THE UNITED NATIONS DURING THE INTERIM PERIOD

1. The Special Representative of the Secretary-General will be responsible for all aspects of the United Nations' work in Afghanistan.
2. The Special Representative shall monitor and assist in the implementation of all aspects of this agreement.
3. The United Nations shall advise the Interim Authority in establishing a politically neutral environment conducive to the holding of the Emergency Loya Jirga in free and fair conditions. The United Nations shall pay special attention to the conduct of those bodies and administrative departments which could directly influence the convening and outcome of the Emergency Loya Jirga.
4. The Special Representative of the Secretary-General or his/her delegate may be invited to attend the meetings of the Interim Administration and the Special Independent Commission on the Convening of the Emergency Loya Jirga.
5. If for whatever reason the Interim Administration or the Special Independent Commission were actively prevented from meeting or unable to reach a decision on a matter related to the convening of the Emergency Loya Jirga, the Special Representative of the Secretary-General shall, taking into account the views expressed in the Interim Administration or in the Special Independent Commission, use his/her good offices with a view to facilitating a resolution to the impasse or a decision.
6. The United Nations shall have the right to investigate human rights violations and, where necessary, recommend corrective action. It will also be responsible for the development and implementation of a programme of human rights education to promote respect for and understanding of human rights.

ANNEX III

REQUEST TO THE UNITED NATIONS BY THE PARTICIPANTS AT THE UN TALKS ON AFGHANISTAN

The participants in the UN Talks on Afghanistan hereby

1. Request that the United Nations and the international community take the

necessary measures to guarantee the national sovereignty, territorial integrity and unity of Afghanistan as well as the non-interference by foreign countries in Afghanistan's internal affairs;

2. Urge the United Nations, the international community, particularly donor countries and multilateral institutions, to reaffirm, strengthen and implement their commitment to assist with the rehabilitation, recovery and reconstruction of Afghanistan, in coordination with the Interim Authority;
3. Request the United Nations to conduct as soon as possible (i) a registration of voters in advance of the general elections that will be held upon the adoption of the new constitution by the constitutional Loya Jirga and (ii) a census of the population of Afghanistan;
4. Urge the United Nations and the international community, in recognition of the heroic role played by the mujahidin in protecting the independence of Afghanistan and the dignity of its people, to take the necessary measures, in coordination with the Interim Authority, to assist in the reintegration of the mujahidin into the new Afghan security and armed forces;
5. Invite the United Nations and the international community to create a fund to assist the families and other dependents of martyrs and victims of the war, as well as the war disabled;
6. Strongly urge that the United Nations, the international community and regional organizations cooperate with the Interim Authority to combat international terrorism, cultivation and trafficking of illicit drugs and provide Afghan farmers with financial, material and technical resources for alternative crop production.

ANNEX IV
COMPOSITION OF THE INTERIM ADMINISTRATION

Chairman:........................... Mr. Hamid Karzai

Membership (of whom 5 will be Vice-Chairs) Department of Defence: Department of Finance: Department of Foreign Affairs: Department of the Interior: Department of Planning: Department of Commerce: Department of Mines and Industries: Department of Small Industries: Department of Information and Culture: Department of Communication: Department of Labour and Social Affairs: Department of Hajj & Auqaf: Department of Martyrs & Disabled: Department of Education: Department of Higher Education: Department of Public Health: Department of Public Works: Department of Rural Development: Department of Urban Development: Department of Reconstruction: Department of Transport: Department of Water and Electricity: Department for the Return of Refugees: Department of Agriculture: Department of Irrigation: Department of Justice: Department of Air Transport & Tourism: Department of Border Affairs: Department of Women's Affairs.

Appendix B
Chronology of Important Events in the Anglo-American Relations with Afghanistan: 1839-2003

1839: First Anglo-Afghan War: Results in British puppet, Shah Shuja, on Afghan throne.

1872: Anglo-Russian agreement on Afghan independence.

1873: Great Britain and Russia agreed that Afghanistan lay outside the Russian sphere of influence.

1878: Russia refused to help Afghanistan against Great Britain in Second Anglo-Afghan War.

1879: Second Anglo-Afghan War: Great Britain invades Afghanistan fearing Russian dominance in Kabul.

1879: Treaty of Gandamak gives British control of Khyber Pass.

1893: Durand Line demarcated by Great Britain as Afghan-British Indian boundary divides ethnic Pushtuns into both sides of the border.

1895: The Wakhan Corridor annexed by Afghanistan with British support to separate Russian and British empires.

1907: British-Russian Convention of St. Petersburg declares Afghanistan a buffer state within the British sphere of influence.

1914: World War I breaks out: Afghanistan remains neutral.

1919: Third Anglo-Afghan War: Afghanistan becomes an independent and sovereign state after gaining control of its own foreign affairs from Great Britain.

1921: Great Britain recognizes Afghan independence.

1922: Great Britain sends its first ambassador to Kabul.

1934: United States accords diplomatic recognition to Afghanistan: Appoints minister in Teheran as nonresident envoy.

1941: Both British and Russians demanded nondiplomatic Axis personnel to leave Afghanistan. Afghanistan declares neutrality in World War II.

1942: United States opened its legation in Kabul.

1945: The government of Afghanistan begins negotiations with the United States construction company—Morrison-Knudsen—for extensive irrigation and agricultural development of Helmond Valley river systems. This becomes one of the major American foreign aid projects in the country through the 1970s.

1947: Partition of Indian subcontinent and the beginning of the Pushtunistan issue. Afghanistan protests Pakistan's entry in the United Nations because of dispute over their mutual border in Pushtun tribal area.

1948: United States legation upgraded to embassy.

1953: US Vice President Richard Nixon visits Kabul to pursue Afghan leaders to join western alliance.

1954: United States decides to supply arms and military aids to Pakistan.

1954: Pakistan joins the South East Asia Treaty Organization (SEATO), the US sponsored military alliance to encircle the communist USSR and China. Afghanistan views this as threat to its security.

1955: Pakistan joins the Baghdad Pact, (later the Central Treaty Organization, CENTO).

1959: United States signs bilateral security arrangements with Pakistan.

1959: President Dwight D. Eisenhower visits Kabul in 1959, which helped establish a cordial relationship between the two countries.

1961: United States offers to mediate on Pak-Afghan border disputes, without success.

1963: American funding of Afghan road, energy, and agricultural projects expands.

1963: King Zahir Shah visits the United States: More aids forthcoming.

1971: Afghanistan suffers a devastating famine in the northern and central region of the country. American food aid program "Operation Help" carried to the worst affected areas earned a good image for the United States.

1975: Encouraged by the United States, Iran signs agreement with Afghanistan to provide aid and technical assistance up to US$2 billion.

1978: "Saur Revolution" takes place in Kabul. The United States pursued a policy of "watchful waiting," but American aid continued to the new (communist?) regime.

1979: American ambassador Adolph Dubs is kidnapped by a militant organization called Sitam-i-Melli in Kabul. Both Dubs and his captors are killed in suspicious shoot-out between kidnappers and government security services.

1979: U.S. embassy seized in Teheran. Islamic government abrogates 1959 bilateral security agreement with United States.

1979: Soviet Union invades Afghanistan.

1980: Refugee exodus accelerates from Afghanistan to Pakistan and Iran.

1980: President Jimmy Carter authorizes supply of weapons to Afghan resistance through Pakistan to fight the Soviet troops in Afghanistan.

1980: In the State of the Union address, President Carter announces that any attempt by outside force to control the Persian Gulf region would be treated as an assault on the U.S. vital interests and subject to U.S. intervention, including military force (Carter Doctrine).

1980: American media starts highlighting the plight of the Afghans to generate sympathy and public awareness.

1980: United Nations General Assembly adopts resolution calling for the "immediate withdrawal of foreign troops from Afghanistan."

1981: Javier Perez de Cuellar appointed as special representative of the U.N. Secretary General to promote Afghan peace talks.

1981: United States signs agreement with Pakistan to supply military and economic aid, including forty F-16 fighters over the next six years, totaling US$3.2 billion.

1981: Diego Cordovez, UN under secretary for political affairs is designated as the personal representative of the newly elected Secretary General Perez de Cuellar to promote Afghan peace talks. The Geneva talks begin.

1982: U.S. Congress forms bipartisan Afghanistan Task Force to pressurize the Reagan administration to supply effective aid to Afghan mujahiddin. The Task Force headed by staunch supporters of the resistance like Senator Paul Tsongas and Senator Gordon Humphrey.

1982: Soviet President Leonid Brezhnev dies, and succeeded by Yuri Andropov who stresses Soviet willingness for a political settlement of the Afghan conflict.

1983: Andropov agrees to second round of Geneva talks. Cordovez announces settlement to be 95 percent complete.

1983: Influential American lawmakers call for supply of effective military aid to Afghan mujahiddin.

1984: CIA targets Soviet Central Asia through Islamic propaganda missions.

1984: Andropov dies and replaced by Konstantin Chernenko.

1984: U.S. Congress passes the Tsongas-Ritter resolution calling for the Reagan administration to "render effective military aid to the freedom fighters."

1985: Chernenko dies and Mikhail Gorbachev takes over as the President and the general secretary of the Soviet communist party.

1985: President Ronald Reagan signs National Security Decision Directive (NSDD) 166, increasing aid to Afghan mujahiddin with goal of forcing Soviet withdrawal from the country.

1985: Fundamentalist mujahiddin leader Gulbuddin Hekmatyar, representing the resistance alliance at the United Nations, refuses to meet President Reagan.

1985: Reagan-Gorbachev Summit at Geneva.

1986: In his State of the Union address to the joint seating of US Congress, President Reagan pronounces his famous "roll back policy," later dubbed as Reagan Doctrine.

1986: Gorbachev describes Afghanistan as "bleeding wound."

1986: President Reagan meets Afghan "freedom fighters" in the Oval Office, promises more aid.

1986: United States decides to supply the resistance with surface-to-air Stinger missiles.

1987: United States annual assistance to the Afghan resistance rises to more than US$630 million.

1987: President Reagan honors head of Afghan resistance in the White House.

1987: U.S.-supplied Stinger missiles show spectacular success in destroying Soviet and Afghan aircrafts.

1988: On 14 April, Geneva Accords are signed between Pakistan and Afghanistan as two signatories and United States and Soviet Union as two guarantors. United States declares to continue arms supply to the resistance as long as the Soviets do the same to the communist regime in Kabul, described as "negative symmetry."

1988: The mujahiddin forms the Afghan Interim Government in Peshawar.

1988: President Zia-ul-Haq along with U.S. ambassador to Pakistan Arnold Raphel and other American and Pakistani officials killed in air sabotage.

1989: Soviet Union completes troop withdrawal from Afghanistan as per Geneva accords.

1990: United States continues to insist on the change of Najibullah regime in Kabul.

1990: Cold War between United States and Soviet Union ends, and Afghanistan reduces to a low priority area in the American thinking.

1991: United States and Soviet Union agree to stop all military aid to their respective Afghan clients by the end of the year, described as "positive symmetry" accord.

1992: Afghan President Najibullah appeals to the United States for help in checking the spread of Islamic fundamentalism in Central Asia.

1992: President Najibullah resigns.

1992: U.S. delegation visits Kabul to discuss diplomatic relations between the two countries.

1992: Afghanistan enters into a phase of civil war.

1992: Petroleum companies of the United States and Uzbekistan signs agreement on a fifty-fifty joint venture to develop Mingbulak oil field in Ferghana valley over a twenty-eight-year period.

1993: Americans realize that bombing of the World Trade Center, killing six people and injuring 100, is the work of terrorists with an Afghan background.

1993: Washington urges Islamabad to expel 'Arab Afghans' from Pakistan.

1994: Armed Afghan/Pakistan students, emerge as Taliban, capture Afghan territory and head north toward the capital Kabul.

1994: United States sends a State Department delegation to Kabul, Islamabad and Rome (to consult former king Zahir Shah).

1995: Taliban advance to the outskirts of Kabul.

1995: United States sends envoy to Jalalabad and Mazar-i-Sharif.

1996: United States Senator Hank Brown organizes conference on Afghanistan in Washington D.C.

1996: Senator Hank Brown visits Kabul.

1996: Under U.S. and Saudi pressure, Osama bin Laden is expelled from Sudan, and moves to Afghanistan.

1996: Former President Najibullah taken from United Nations compounds and hanged by Taliban in a Kabul light outpost.

1997: Taliban delegation, headed by Mullah Wakil Ahmed, visiting the United States, meets with Assistant Secretary of State, Robin Raphel and other officials.

1997: Osama bin Laden claims through a CNN interview that his disciples were behind the killing of 18 American soldiers in Somalia in 1993.

1997: Taliban declare to award natural gas pipeline contract to whomever gives greater concessions to Afghanistan. The interested parties are UNOCAL (USA) and Bridas (Argentina).

1998: Terrorist attacks on the American embassies in Kenya and Tanzania, killing over 250 people, including 12 Americans, and wounding more than 5000, traces to Osama bin Ladin's network Al Qaeda headquartered in Afghanistan.

1998: United States launches 75 Tomahawk cruise missiles against terrorist bases and camps in eastern Afghanistan killing only 20 militants.

1999: United States imposed economic sanctions against Afghanistan, barring Americans from trading with or investing in the country.

2000: United States traces Al Qaeda for bombing of *USS Cole*, which claims 17 lives.

2001: United States traces Al Qaeda for terrorist attacks in New York and Washington D.C. killing more than three thousand people.

2001: America declares war against Taliban regime, and hunts for Bin Laden, Al Qaeda, Mullah Omar, and associates.

2001: Bush administration successfully maneuvers the Security Council resolution 1373 and then centers around formation of a coalition against its "war on terrorism."

2001: United States claims that 48 countries' support for the military campaign in Afghanistan.

2001: NATO declares its full support to the American war efforts, by involving article 5 of the North Atlantic Treaty: an attack on one is an attack on all.

2001: Kabul falls to American backed Northern Alliance.

2001: United States detalibanizes the country and help set up an interim government under Hamid Karzai.

2001: Afghan representatives meet in Bonn, Germany, to establish a stable representative government in Afghanistan following 23 years of war.

2002: U.S. President George W. Bush and British Prime Minister Tony Blair declare that the war on Afghanistan was won, Al Qaeda defeated and the international anti-terrorist coalition victorious.

2002: After heavy American casualties during Operation Anaconda in Eastern Afghanistan, United States asks Britain to help with more British troops.

2002: A noted Pakistani weekly comes out with a proof about involvement of regular Pakistani army and ISI with Taliban even after the September 11 attacks in the United States.

2003: U.S. warplanes launch heavy air strikes against Taliban targets near Spin Boldak. A-10, Harrier, and B-1 aircrafts as well as AC-130 gunship and Apache helicopters participate in the air strike.

2003: Afghan President Hamid Karzai meets President Bush in the White House. American support to Karzai continues.

2003: About 300 Afghans, including government employees and students chanted anti-American slogans in Kabul in the first such protest since U.S. forces invaded Afghanistan to topple the fundamentalist Taliban in late 2001.

2003: 3 German peacekeepers are killed in Kabul car bomb attack.

2003: In a major battle since the end of Taliban regime, 40 Taliban militia and 9 government fighters are killed in Spin Boldak province near Pak-Afghan border.

2003: Afghan resentment against the American "occupying forces" increases.

Appendix C
The White House Washington
Special Coordination Committee Meeting
Monday, January 14, 1980

Time and Place : 10:00 am—12:00 Noon
White House Situation Room

SUBJECT: SCC Meeting on US Strategy for South West Asia and Persian Gulf

PARTICIPANTS

State
Under Secretary for Political Affairs, David Newsom
Assistant Secretary Harold Saunders

Energy
Secretary Charles Duncan

White House
Zbigniew Brzezinski
David Aaron

Defence
Deputy Secretary W. Graham Claytor
Mr. Robert Murray

JCS
Chairman, General David Jones; Lt. General John Pustay

NSC
Colonel William E. Odom
Colonel Leslie Denend
Henry Owen
Thomas Thornton
Robert Hunter
Fritz Ermarth

CIA
Director Stansfield Turner

SUMMARY OF CONCLUSIONS

Dr. Brzezinski opened the meeting with an overview of what is happening and what is at stake in the region. The results of this meeting, he said, are to provide a basis for a National Security Council meeting with the President later this week. We must deal with the continued deterioration of the US position in the region. Whatever the Soviet motives for their actions in Afghanistan, they have created an objective threat and a dynamic development in the area as serious for our security and vital interests as Soviet actions in Greece in 1947. We must provide the President with a basis for responding adequately to this change, specifically what we should do about Pakistan and about the larger Persian Gulf region. The President believes that there will be lasting strategic consequences. He wants to reaffirm that there will be no zig-zag in US-Soviet relations on our side. No warm up is to be expected soon. The mistake in 1968 after the Soviet action in Czechoslovakia was, in the President's view, to ease up on Moscow too early.

The President spoke with Aga Shahi over the weekend and reaffirmed our commitment to the agreement of 1959. The problem is how to define the US commitment under the agreement. If there is major Soviet aggression, the US will respond within the limits of our Constitutional authority. The US will not, however, become involved in border skirmishes. We want our support to help Pakistan to take a firm stand against Soviet forces in the region even if they are faced by a Moscow/Kabul/New Delhi axis. In that case, the US will develop a US/Saudi Arabian/PRC/Pakistan/and eventually Iran axis as a counter.

Dr. Brzezinski next declared that the task before us is how to translate this basic stand by the President into:

— effective military relations with Pakistan and other countries in the region;
— economic assistance to Pakistan in a way that supports our broader purposes;
— a regional web of political relations to counter effectively the threat created by Soviet moves in Afghanistan.

We cannot duplicate NATO in this region; a more eclectic mix of bilateral, multilateral, and informal arrangements must suffice.

There was a brief discussion of the implications of Dr. Brzezinski's framing of the overall context and the tasks to be accomplished. State asked if the US guarantee to Pakistan against aggression was for only a Soviet attack or also an Indian attack, adding that this would be a major problem in our relations with India if it included both. Defense insisted that it must include both because the Pakistanis cannot shift forces between their western and eastern frontiers to meet the Soviet aggression without a guarantee in the east as well as against the Soviets in the west. State accepted this argument by Dr. Brzezinski and Defense that sooner or later we would have to face up to Pakistan's security problem with India. Dr. Brzezinski said that the US commitment was only against a threat from the north. Dr. Brzezinski asked at this point if there were disagreements with his analysis of the situation because it carries a number of assumptions which are key for further decisions. No dissenting views were expressed. Defense strongly supported the analysis. State added that we must include the nuclear issue within this policy context. State also pointed out that we must anticipate the criticism that we are merely restoring a 'cold war alliance' with the rebuttal that such an alliance is inadequate for the contemporary political and military realities in the region. Dr. Brzezinski accepted both points, especially that we have in mind something more than a cold war alliance as we build a new regional security system.

The meeting next turned to specific issues for decision.

I. Military Assistance to Pakistan

In discussion of the fighter aircraft issue, Graham Claytor reported that the Pakistanis did not request specific U.S. aircraft but rather asked the United States to provide what is necessary for them to defend themselves against the new Soviet threat which includes MIG-23s and MIG-25s. There was discussion of the value of A-7 fighters for close air support along the western borders, the extent to which helicopter gunships could perform the same mission, and whether the A-7s were meant for an air defense role also.

General Jones agreed that helicopters would be useful but added that A-7s would provide much greater air ground capability. All agreed that we should encourage the Pakistanis to use the French Mirage fighter for the larger air defense problem against the Soviet Union.

Tasking. State was asked to :

(1) determine whether the Mirages will in fact suffice to meet the threat;

(2) clarify with the French their willingness to provide Mirages;

(3) With Defense, consider A-7s for Pakistan, about 30.

II. Bases, Political Assurances to Host Nations, and Increased RDF

Bases. Dr. Brzezinski raised the question of a base in Pakistan. General Jones said 'facilities' ('bases' have a poor political connotation, it was observed) for air and naval deployments to Pakistan would be a significant advantage. Others pointed out that such U.S. facilities in Pakistan would drive India into closer cooperation with Moscow against Pakistan. Most all agreed that this is possible, but there were differing views on whether we should take the step and the risks it involves. Dr. Brzezinski added that we should consider it but not overload our relations with India by taking the step now.

Tasking. State and Defense will develop a paper on US military 'facilities' in Pakistan, describing their purpose, possible Indian reaction, and what those reactions would entail for the United States.

Military Consortium for Pakistan. State reported that George Vest and Peter Constable will be going to Europe for discussions about British, French, and Saudi Arabian participation in the military consortium. Dr. Brzezinski added that the Japanese should also be asked to participate. Newsom and others were less enthusiastic about bringing the Japanese in. It would be a new step for them. Newsom and Owen suggested we emphasize greater Japanese economic aid to Pakistan in forms that will release Pakistan domestic funds for military purposes. There was some question about the Japanese laws permitting financing of direct military aid to Pakistan. Dr. Brzezinski argued that the Japanese have greater interests in the area than the US. Thirty years after the war, when they are economically powerful, surely they can contribute to the security of the Persian Gulf. We should raise the issue with them even if they do not accept our proposal.

Tasking. State will check what the Japanese law permits. Defense will produce a paper outlining a specific division of labour among the members of the military consortium, integrating each country's contribution to meet the overall Pakistani military needs in the most efficient fashion possible.

Political Assurances to Host Nations. Defense made clear that the technical survey teams can proceed to Oman and Somalia without providing their hosts with "political assurances" on what the US will give for the bases. Work is presently under way to produce a military-economic aid package for each host country with appropriate "political assurances."

Tasking. State will provide a paper which sets forth the assurances for each country, the form in which the assurances should be given, and what consultations with Congress are appropriate.

Diego Garcia. It was recommended that we expand the runways and the storage facilities on Diego Garcia. Conservationists may lobby against this construction. When Dr. Brzezinski asked whether we actually need this expansion in light of acquisition of bases in Oman and Somalia, State and Defense pointed out that it is much better to have a larger number of small bases to absorb minor setbacks if we must abandon some bases in the future.

Tasking. None.

Improved RDF Capabilities. General Jones made a presentation at this point in which he pointed out that Soviet military deployments into Afghanistan will fundamentally change the military threat to our allies on the Persian Gulf:

— Soviet fighter aircraft based in Afghanistan will be able to reach the Gulf of Hormuz, a wholly new development.

— Soviet armored ground forces could reach the waters of the Arabian Sea through Baluchistan in 10 to 12 days if unopposed.

— Preferred Soviet land routes to Tehran probably still remain those from the caucasus. Soviet heavy military ground forces on this route could reach the oil field regions in the vicinity of Kuwait in 10 to 12 days.

— Using sealift from the Black Sea, the Soviets could project forces through the Suez Canal to the Persian Gulf in about 21 days.

— One Soviet airborne division, about 8,000 troops, with organic armor vehicles, could land anywhere in the vicinity of the Persian Gulf in two to three days if all Soviet airlift is employed.

General Jones outlined our options for rapid short-term measures to meet this changed Soviet threat by early spring this year:

1. Our *naval presence* in the Arabian Sea will eventually have to be reduced to one aircraft carrier battle group. We do not have sustaining power for the two there at present.
2. *Tactical air power* projected into Egyptian and Jordanian basis can improve our air projection capability. We should also request that the Saudis "over build" their air-fields, something we can do privately with no political costs, but something which will greatly enhance their capability to support "fly in" of US fighter formations.
3. *Prepositioning of heavy equipment and supplies* backed up by a significant

increase in our sealift capability can give us a much larger and earlier force projection capability into the region. To achieve this in the next two or three months, General Jones proposes the following package:

(a) Purchase two RO/RO ships which will hold the prepositioned equipment for one mechanised brigade and ground support equipment for three fighter squadrons.

(b) Lease three cargo ships to be prepositioned with dry cargo supplies, ammunition, water, and fuels.

(c) Followup supply from the US can be moved through the Suez Canal in 11 days by SL-7 class sea-land ships. General Jones proposed to lease a fleet of eight SL-7s, six of which would be kept in use and two of which would be under conversion to a RO/RO capability.

(d) The overall costs for this package is estimated at $450 million.

The advantages of this proposal are :

— The deployment time for getting heavy ground forces through the region would be cut from roughly 25/28 days to 5/8 days through prepositioning.

— For the first time we would have a followup sealift supply capability in the SL-7s which travel at 33 knots, a difficult speed for an enemy to locate and intercept.

— This capability could be exercised for demonstration in the region by late spring or early summer.

Tasking. Defense is to submit the proposal in detail to OMB and have the results available for the NSC meeting.

Exercises. Dr. Brzczinski insisted that we need ground force exercises in the area soon in order to improve the local sense of confidence about American commitment to the region. General Jones agreed that he could speed up the deployment of two marine units, one from the Eastern Mediterranean and one from the Pacific to exercise in Oman and Somalia by March. Airlift of ground forces from the United States would be extremely expensive. General Jones prefers not to take that step but rather only exercise the Marines now. General Jones argued that more importantly, if we purchase the two RO/RO, which are ready for immediate delivery and loading, we can use them for exercises in March or April, exercises that will have a much greater psychological effect for a lesser cost than projecting airborne units with no armor from the US.

Tasking. State will give us a paper by Thursday on the political effects that exercises would have. Defense will provide a paper recommending specific exercises.

III. Security Consultations with India and Pakistan

There was debate about the sequence and timing of the upcoming missions to Pakistan and India. Dr. Brzezinski pointed out that the Clifford mission to New Delhi would find the climate all the more hostile if at the same time the Christopher mission is in Pakistan. He argued that it is better to have the mission to India completed in advance so that we can take the results into consideration in preparing the Christopher mission for Pakistan. State agreed to reconsider and suggested that the Clifford mission might best depart on January 20, at the same time that the Defense military technical mission goes to Pakistan to discuss details of military assistance. Five days later the Christopher 'political' mission can go to Pakistan, providing a decent interval to take into account the results of the Clifford mission.

IV. Consultations with North Yemen

The danger of an imminent union between North and South Yemen was discussed. An NSC working group recommended that we pursue a two-track strategy, US demarches to President Salih in North Yemen and a Saudi Arabian demarche to Salih. Most argued this is an unpromising course of action. Dr. Brzezinski pointed out that we should consider a much more fundamental political change in South Yemen. It is clear that US interests in the area could be greatly damaged by a union of South and North Yemen. Egypt and Jordan interests would be similarly hurt, not to speak of Saudi Arabia's concern. We should, therefore, consider a joint action to bring about a fundamental political change in South Yemen. A discussion followed on Saudi capabilities to do this, which were judged wholly inadequate, and the difficulties of getting Egyptian and Jordanian cooperation.

Tasking. State and CIA are to consult on preparing a high level mission to North Yemen to make Salih aware of the depths of our opposition to a union of the two Yemens. Dr. Brzezinski suggested that Frank Carlucci might be an appropriate person to head such a mission. A NSC-chaired working group will prepare a paper on the Yemen problem.

V. Refugees

The discussion next turned to ways to provide aid other than through the UNHCR. Dr. Brzezinski pointed out that citizens from the Soviet bloc may be officials in the UNHCR. They could use their positions to make it difficult for refugee camps to support the insurgency in Afghanistan. State argued that it is US policy to avoid bilateral transfers of funds for refugees. Others pointed out that this is not always our policy. We do make bilateral contributions to certain countries in Africa.

Tasking. State will examine the alternative ways of supporting refugees in Pakistan other than through the UNHCR so that the UNHCR cannot, if it chooses, interfere seriously with refugee camps supporting the insurgency.

VI. ASEAN, the PRC, and non-Friendly Countries Support for US Policy

Dr. Brzezinski asked about the possibility of getting ASEAN countries to help us reduce India's resistance to our policy toward Pakistan. Most believe ASEAN is unlikely to help. Dr. Brzezinski mentioned that some non-friendly states, might change their policies toward the US in the region in light of the recent Soviet actions. State suggested that relaxing our sanctions on Mozambique might produce a change in that country's policy towards us. It was agreed that we should send messages to a group of non-friendly states, Angola, Cuba, Vietnam, Ethiopia, Syria and Iraq.

Tasking. State will produce for the next SCC a list of presidential messages or demarches to ASEAN, some African countries, and non-friendly countries for consideration in light of the above discussion.

VII. The PLO and Mid East Peace Process

Dr. Brzezinski pointed out that it is very important to accelerate the peace process in light of the Soviet action in Afghanistan. Would a public statement by the President on this matter be useful at this time? State and others pointed out the old dilemma that if we want progress for the PLO then we do not talk about it. If there is a lot of public support for the PLO, it might prevent progress in the negotiations by frightening Israel. Newsom pointed out that we might get the Israelis to back down on some of their recent actions in the East Bank.

VIII. A Public Communique on Aid to Pakistan

State offered a public US statement to be released on what we have offered in the way of aid to Pakistan. This was prepared in response to an earlier tasking. It was agreed that events have changed the circumstances so that such a statement is inappropriate.

The White House Washington
Special Coordination Committee Meeting
Monday, January 14, 1980

MEMORANDUM FOR THE SECRETARY OF STATE

SUBJECT : Presidential Decisions on Pakistan, Afghanistan and India (S)

The following decisions were made by the President as a result of the PRC Meeting of December 27 and the NSC Meeting of December 28 and should be implemented:

Afghanistan

1. Our ultimate goal is the withdrawal of Soviet troops from Afghanistan. Even if this is not attainable, we should make Soviet involvement as costly as possible and should use the events in Afghanistan as a rallying point for our policies in the area.
2. We should push these objectives vigorously, going to the United Nations if necessary. It would be preferable, however, for other countries to take the lead in the UN.
3. Messages should be sent to our NATO Allies, China and key leaders in the UN and Non-Aligned Movement, drawing their attention to the events in Afghanistan and calling for appropriate responses.
4. We will not link the Soviet action in Afghanistan to SALT. At the same time, however, we will not permit our interest in SALT to deter us from speaking and acting forcefully.

5. We will send public and private messages to the Soviets, citing the unacceptability of their behaviour, the threat to the peace posed by their actions, and their violation of the principles of behaviour we agreed to in 1972. (TS)

Pakistan

1. We are prepared to send a high-level mission to Pakistan, headed by Deputy Secretary Christopher, to consult on the new situation in the region.
2. Military sales will be resumed and facilitated.
3. We shall ask the Saudis to assist on financing military purchases by Pakistan.
4. Two Gearing-class destroyers will be provided to Pakistan expeditiously.
5. We shall move promptly in providing $40 million in PL-480 assistance.
6. Additional assistance will be provided to help Pakistan deal with the Afghan refugee problem.
7. We will reaffirm our nuclear policy towards Pakistan and make clear the legislative restrictions. We will, however, urge the Pakistanis to put the problem aside for solution later while we deal with the Soviet-Afghan problem. (S)

India

1. A high-level mission will be sent to India following the Indian elections.
2. Ambassador Gerard Smith should provide a memorandum to the President before we move to approve the pending license for supply of fuel to the Tarapur reactor or submit the second Indian request to the NRC. (S)

Zbigniew Brzezinski

cc: The Secretary of Defense
The Director of Central Intelligence.

Bibliography

Department of State, Bureau of Public Affairs, "Developing a Co-operative Security

—— Framework," Current Policy, no.152, Washington D.C. March 24,1980.

—— "Afghanistan: Two years of Occupation," Special Report No. 91, Washington DC, December 1981.

—— "Afghanistan: Four years of Occupation," Special Report No. 112, Washington DC, December 1983.

—— "Afghanistan: Five years of Tragedy," Current Policy No. 636, Washington DC, November 14, 1984.

—— "Afghanistan: Seven years of Soviet Occupation," Special Report No. 155, Washington DC, December 1986.

—— "Afghanistan: Eight years of Soviet Occupation," Special Report No. 179, Washington DC, December 1988.

—— "Assistance to and Trade with Afghanistan," US Department of State Dispatch, Vol. 3, No. 41, October 12, 1992.

Department of State Bulletin, "South Asia: Situation in Afghanistan," Vol. 79, No. 2033, December 1979.

—— "Interview with US News and World Report," Vol. 80, No. 2043, October 1980.

—— "Political Feuding in Afghanistan: A Dilemma for the Soviets," Vol. 80, No. 2040, July 1980.

—— "Afghanistan: 3 Years of Occupation," Vol. 83, No. 2071, February 1983.

—— "Call for Soviet Withdrawal from Afghanistan," Vol. 83, No. 2070, January 1983.

—— "Afghanistan: 4 Years of Occupation," Vol. 84, No. 2082, January 1984.

—— "Afghanistan and Afghan Attacks on Pakistan," Vol. 84, No. 2091, October 1984.

—— "Afghanistan: Five Years of Occupation," Vol. 85, No. 2095, February 1985.

—— "Afghanistan under the Soviets: Five Years of Tragedy," Vol. 85, No. 2094, January 1985.

—— "Afghanistan Struggle for Freedom," Vol. 86, No. 2107, February 1986.

—— "UN calls on Soviet Union to withdraw from Afghanistan," Vol. 88, No. 2130, January 1988.

—— "South Asia and the United States: An evolving partnership," Vol. 87, No. 2124, July 1987.

—— "Afghanistan: Soviet Occupation and Withdrawal," Vol. 89, No. 2144, March 1989.

Foreign Broadcast Information Service, Daily Report, Middle East and North Africa (covering Afghanistan and the Indian Sub-continent up to 1 April 1980), Washington DC.

—— Report, South Asia (covering Afghanistan and the Indian Sub-continent from April 1, 1980), Washington DC.

—— Daily Report, Soviet Union, Washington DC.

U.S. Congress, House Committee on Foreign Affairs, Sub-committee on Asian and Pacific Affairs, Crisis in the Sub-continent: Afghanistan and Pakistan," 96th Congress, 1st session, May 15, and September 26, 1979, U.S. Government Printing Office, Washington DC, 1980.

—— House Committee on Foreign Affairs, Sub-committee on Europe and the Middle East, East-West Relations in the Aftermath of Soviet Invasion of Afghanistan," 97th Congress, 2nd session, January 24 and 30, U.S. Government Printing Office, Washington DC, 1980.

—— House Committee on Foreign Affairs, Sub-committee on Europe and the Middle East, "U.S. interests in and policies towards the Persian Gulf, 1980," 96th Congress, 2nd session, U.S. Government Printing Office, Washington DC, 1980.

—— Senate Committee on Banking, Housing and Urban Affairs, "Suspension of United States Exports of High Technology and Grain to the Soviet Union," 96th Congress, 2nd session, August 19, 1980, U.S. Government Printing Office, Washington DC, 1980.

—— Senate Committee on Foreign Relations, Sub-committee on Near Eastern and South Asian Affairs, "U.S. Security Interests and Policies in Southwest Asia," 96th Congress, 2nd session, U.S. Government Printing Office, Washington DC, 1980.

—— House Committee on Foreign Affairs, and the Committee on Security and Cooperation in Europe, Sub-committee on Human Rights and International Organizations, "Soviet Violation of Helsinki Act: Invasion of Afghanistan," 97th Congress, 1st session, U.S. Government Printing Office, Washington DC, 1981.

—— House Committee on Foreign Affairs, and Sub-committee on Europe and the Middle East, "An Assessment of the Afghanistan Sanctions: Implications for Trade and Diplomacy in the 1980's," 97th Congress, 1st session, U.S. Government Printing Office, Washington DC, 1981.

—— Senate Committee on Foreign Relations, "Situation in Afghanistan," 97th Congress, 2nd session, U.S. Government Printing Office, Washington DC, 1982.

—— Senate Committee on Foreign Relations, A Staff Report, "Hidden War: The Struggle for Afghanistan," 98th Congress, 2nd session, U.S. Government Printing Office, Washington DC, 1984.

—— House Committee on Foreign Affairs, and Sub-committee on Asia and Pacific Affairs, "The Situation in Afghanistan," 99th Congress, 2nd session, U.S. Government Printing Office, Washington DC, 1986.

—— House Committee on Foreign Affairs, and Sub-committee on Asia and Pacific Affairs, "The Geneva Accords on Afghanistan," 100th Congress, 2nd session, U.S. Government Printing Office, Washington DC, 1989.

—— House Committee on Foreign Affairs, and Sub-committee on Asia and Pacific Affairs, "Developments in Afghanistan, February 1988," 100th Congress, 2nd session, U.S. Government Printing Office, Washington DC, 1989.

—— House Committee on Foreign Affairs, and Sub-committee on Asia and Pacific Affairs, "Developments in Afghanistan and their Implications for U.S. Policy," 101st Congress, 2nd session, U.S. Government Printing Office, Washington DC, 1990.

—— Senate Committee on Foreign Relations, A Report by Senator Claiborne Pell, "Stalemate in Afghanistan, Democracy in Pakistan," October 1, 1989, U.S. Government Printing Office, Washington DC, 1990.

—— House Committee on Foreign Affairs, Sub-committee on Europe and the Middle East, "United States Policy towards Afghanistan," 101st Congress, 2nd session, U.S. Government Printing Office, Washington DC, 1990.

—— House Committee on Foreign Affairs, Sub-committee on Asia and Pacific Affairs, "Recent Developments in U.S. Policy towards Afghanistan," June 20, 1991, U.S. Government Printing Office, Washington DC, 1993.

—— House Committee on International Relations, "U.S. Assistance for Afghanistan," November 1, 2001. U.S. Government Printing Office, Washington DC, November 01, 2001.

—— Senate Committee on Foreign Relations, Sub-committee on Near Eastern and South Asian Affairs, "Humanitarian Crisis in Afghanistan," U.S. Government Printing Office, Washington DC, November 11, 2001.

Weekly Compilation of Presidential Documents (from 1978 to 1989) Washington DC.

Books

Adamec, Ludwig W., *Afghanistan's Foreign Affairs to the Mid-Twentieth Century: Relations with the USSR, Germany and Britain,* University of Arizona Press, Tucson, 1974.

—— *Afghanistan, 1900 – 1923: A Diplomatic History,* University of California Press, Berkeley, 1967.

Adelman, Jonathan R., *Super Powers and Revolution,* Praeger, New York, 1986.

Amstutz, J. Bruce, *Afghanistan: The First Five Years of Soviet Occupation,* National Defence University, Washington DC, 1986.

Arnold, Anthony, *Afghanistan: The Soviet Invasion in Perspective*, The Hoover Institution Press, Stanford, 1985.

—— *Afghanistan's Two Party Communism: Parcham and Khalq*, The Hoover Institution Press, Stanford, 1985.

Berman, Larry, ed., *Looking Back on the Reagan Presidency*, The Johns Hopkins University Press, Baltimore, 1990.

Bowker, Mike, and Williams, Phil., *Superpower Détente: A Reappraisal*, Sage, London, 1988.

Bradsher, Henry S., *Afghanistan and the Soviet Union*, Duke Press, Durham, 1983.

Brown, Seyom, *The Faces of Power: Constancy and Change in United States Foreign Policy from Truman to Reagan*, Columbia University Press, New York, 1983.

Brzezinski, Zbigniew, *Power and Principle: Memoirs of the National Security Adviser, 1977-1981*, Farrar, Straus, Giroux, 1983.

Carter, Jimmy, *Keeping Faith: Memoirs of a President*, New York, Bantam Books, 1982.

Chadda, Maya, *Paradox of Power: The United States in South West Asia, 1973-1984*, ABC-CLIO, Barbara, 1986.

Chopra, V.D. ed., *Global Challenge of Terrorism*, Gyan Publishing House, New Delhi, 2002.

Cooley, John K., *Unholy Wars: Afghanistan, America and International Terrorism*, Pluto Press, London, 1999.

Dixit, J. N., *India's Foreign Policy: Challenge of Terrorism*, Gyan Publishing House, New Delhi, 2002.

Dupree, Louis, *Afghanistan*, Princeton University Press, Princeton, 1973.

Eliot Jr, Theodore L., and Robert L. Jr, Pfaltzgraff, ed. *The Red Army on Pakistan's Border: Policy Implications for the United States*, Pergomon, Washington DC, 1886.

—— *Gorbachev's Afghan Gambit*, National Security Papers, Institute for Foreign Policy Analysis, Washington DC, 1988.

Emadi, Hafizullah, *State, Revolution and Superpowers in Afghanistan*, Greenhood Press, Greenhood, 1990.

Emerson, Steven, *Secret Warriors: Inside the Covert Military Operations of the Reagan Era*, G.P. Putnam's Sons, New York, 1988.

Ewans, Martin, *Afghanistan: A New History*, Curzon Press, Richmond, 2001.

Farr, Grant M., and Merriam, John G., ed. *Afghan Resistance: The Politics of Survival*, Westview Press, Boulder, 1987.

Fraser Tytler, Sir William K., *Afghanistan: A Study of Political Developments in Central and Southern Asia*, London, 1967.

Girardet, Edward R., *Afghanistan: The Soviet War*, St. Martin's Press, New York, 1985.

Glaus, Abdul Samad, *The Fall of Afghanistan*, Pergamon-Brassey's, Washington DC, 1987.

Griffiths, John C., *Afghanistan: Key to a Continent*, Westview Press, Boulder, 1981.

Hass, Richard N., *Conflicts Unending: The United States and the Regional Disputes*, Yale University Press, New Haven, 1990.

Hamilton, Edward K., ed. *America's Global Interests; a New Agenda*, W.W. Norton & Company, New York, 1989.

Hammond, Thomas T., *Red Flag Over Afghanistan: The Communist Coup, the Soviet Invasion, and the Consequences*, Westview Press, Boulder, 1984.

Hauner, Milan & Canfield, Robert I., ed. *Afghanistan and the Soviet Union: Collision and Transformation*, Westview Press, Boulder, 1989.

Horelick, Arnold L., ed. *US – Soviet Relations: The Next Phase*, Cornell University Press, Ithaca, & London, 1986.

Hsiung, James C., & Chai, Winberg, ed. *Asia and US Foreign Policy*, Praeger, New York, 1981.

Hyland, William G., *Mortal Rivals: Superpower Relations from Nixon to Reagan*, Random House, New York, 1987.

Khalilzad, Zalmay, *The Return of the Great Game: Superpower Rivalry and Domestic Turmoil in Afghanistan, Iran, Pakistan, and Turkey*, California Seminar on International Security and Foreign Policy, Discussion Paper No.88, Santa Monica, September 1980.

Khan, Riaz M., *Untying the Afghan Knot: Negotiating Soviet Withdrawal*, An Institute of the Study of Diplomacy Book, Duke, 1991.

Klass, Rosanne, ed., *Afghanistan: The Great Game Revisited*, Freedom House, New York, 1987.

Krickus, Richard J., *The Superpowers in Crisis: Implications of Domestic Discord*, Pergamon – Brassey, Washington, 1987.

Lavrentyev, Alexander, *USA and Asia*, Sterling, New Delhi, 1982.

Magnus, Ralph, ed. *Afghanistan Alternatives: Issues, Options and Policies*, Transaction Books, Oxford, 1985.

Magnus, Ralph H., and Naby, Eden, *Afghanistan: Mullah, Marx, and Mujahid*, Westview Press, Boulder, 1998.

Maley, William, ed., *Fundamentalism Reborn? Afghanistan and the Taliban*, Hurst & Co., London, 1998.

Myers, R.H., ed. *U.S. Foreign Policy for Asia: The 1980s and Beyond*, Hoover Institution Press, Stanford, 1982.

Newell, Nancy Peabody, and Newell, Richard S., *The Struggle for Afghanistan*, Cornell University Press, Ithaca, 1981.

O'balance, Edgar, *Afghan Wars: What Britain Gave up and the Soviet Union Lost*, Brasseys, Mcmillan, 1991.

Oberdorfer, Don, *From the Cold War to a New Era: The United States and the Soviet Union 1983-1990*, Poseidon Press. New York, 1991.

Orman, John, *Comparing Presidential Behaviour: Carter, Reagan, and the macho Presidential Style*, Greenwood, New York, 1987.

Payne, Keith B., *Nuclear Deterrence in US – Soviet Relations,* Westview Press, Boulder, 1982.

Poullada, Leon B., and Poullada, Leila D.J., *The Kingdom of Afghanistan and the United States: 1828-1973,* Center for Afghanistan Studies at the University of Nebraska at Omaha, 1995.

Rais, Rasul Bakhsh, *War Without Winners: Afghanistan's Uncertain Transition after the Cold War,* Oxford University Press, Oxford, 1994.

Raymond, L. Garthoff, *Détente and Confrontation: American – Soviet Relations from Nixon to Reagan,* The Brookings Institution, Washington DC, 1985.

Reagan, Ronald, *An American Life,* Simon and Schuster, New York, 1990.

Rodman, Peter W., *More Precious than Peace: The Cold War and the Struggle for the Third World,* Charles Scribner's Sons, New York, 1994.

Rubinstein, Alvin Z., ed. *The Great Game: Rivalry in the Persian Gulf and South Asia,* Praeger, New York, 1983.

Schweizer, Peter, *Victory: The Reagan Administration's Secret Strategy that Hastened the Collapse of the Soviet Union,* The Atlantic Monthly Press, New York, 1994.

Sengupta, Bhabani, *Afghan Syndrome: How to Live with Soviet Power,* Vikas, New Delhi, 1982.

—— *Afghanistan: Politics, Economics and Society, Revolution, Resistance, Intervention,* Francis Printer, London, 1986.

Shultz, George P., *Turmoil and Triumph: My Years as Secretary of State,* Charles Scribner's Sons, New York, 1993.

Turner, Stansfield, *Secrecy and Democracy,* Houghton Mifflin Company, Boston, 1985.

Vance, Cyrus, *Hard Choices: Critical Years in America's Foreign Policy,* Simon and Schuster, New York, 1983.

Weinbaum, Marvin G., *Pakistan and Afghanistan: Resistance and Reconstruction,* Westview Press, Boulder, 1994.

White, Ralph K., *Fearful Warriors: A Psychological Profile US – Soviet Relations,* The Free Press, New York, 1984.

Woodward, Bob, *Veil: The Secret Wars of the CIA 1981 – 1987,* Simon and Schuster, New York, 1987.

Yousaf, Mohammad, and Adkin, Mark, *The Bear Trap: Afghanistan's Untold Story,* Jung Publishers, Lahore, 1992.

Articles

Ahady, Anwar-ul-Haq, "The Decline of the Pashtuns in Afghanistan," *Asian Survey,* Vol. 35, No. 7, July 1995.

Allan, Nigel J R, "Rethinking Governance in Afghanistan," *Journal of International Affairs,* Vol. 56, No. 2, Spring 2003.

Allan, P., and Stahel, A.A., "Tribal Guerrilla Warfare against a Colonial Power: Analyzing the War in Afghanistan," *Journal of Conflict Resolution,* Vol. 27, December 1983.

Ayoob, Mohammed, "South-west Asia after the Taliban," *Survival,* Vol. 44, No. 1, Spring 2002.

Azmi, M. Raziullah, "Afghanistan: Moscow's "Vietnam?" *Pakistan Journal of American Studies,* Vol. 7, No. 1, March 1989.

Barfield, Thomas, "The Afghan Morass," *Current History,* January 1996.

Bearden, Milton, "Afghanistan, Graveyard of Empires," *Foreign Affairs,* Vol. 80, No. 6, November/December 2001.

Bennigsen, A., "Mullahs, Mujahiddin and Soviet Muslims," *Problems of Communism,* Vol. 33, November/December 1984.

Berkowitz, Bruce, "The New Protracted Conflict: Intelligence and the War on Terrorism," *Orbis,* Spring 2002.

—— "Confessions of a Soviet Muslim Rebel," *Orbis,* Vol. 32, Summer 1988.

Biddle, Stephen, "Afghanistan and the Future of Warfare," *Foreign Affairs,* Vol. 82, No. 2, March/April 2003.

Boade, William R., "The Reagan Doctrine," *Strategic Review,* Winter 1986.

Braddock, L., "Moral Unequivalence: Afghanistan is not Soviet's Vietnam," *Policy Review,* No. 45, Summer 1988.

Brown, Horald, "U.S. Security Policy in South West Asia: A case study in complexity," *Occasional Paper,* School of Advanced International Studies, Foreign Policy Institute, John Hopkins University, Washington DC, 1981.

Campbell, Kurt M., "Globalization's First War?" *The Washington Quarterly,* Winter 2002.

Chanda, N., "Reagan's Responses," *Far Eastern Economic Review,* Vol. 133, July 3, 1986.

Carpenter, Ted Galen, "The Unintended Consequences of Afghanistan," *World Policy Journal,* Vol. 11, No. 1, Spring 1994.

Cohen, S.P., "South Asia after Afghanistan," *Problems of Communism,* Vol. 34, January/February 1986.

Coldren, L.O., "Afghanistan in 1984: the fifty year of the Russo – Afghan War," *Asian Survey,* Vol. 25, February 1985.

—— "Afghanistan in 1985: the sixth year of the Russo – Afghan War, *Asian Survey,* Vol. 26, February 1986.

Copson, Raymond W., and Cronin, Richard P., "The Reagan Doctrine and its prospects," *Survival,* January/February 1987.

Craffetz, D., "Afghanistan in Turmoil," *International Affairs,* Vol. 56, January 1980.

Cronin, R.P., "Afghanistan in 1988: A year of decision?" *Asian Survey,* Vol. 29, February 1989.

—— "U.S. Interests, Objects and Policy Options in South West Asia," *Occasional Paper,* Strategic Studies Institute, U.S. Army War College,

Carlisle Barracks, 15 January 1982.

—— "Afghanistan: Soviet Invasion and U.S. Response," *Congressional Research Service (CRS),* The Library of Congress, Washington DC, January 10, 1980.

—— "Afghanistan after five years: Status of the conflict, the Afghan resistance and the U.S. role, *CRS,* The Library of Congress, Washington DC, January 1985.

—— "The United States, Pakistan, and the Soviet threat to Southern Asia: Options for Congress," *CRS,* The Library of Congress, Washington DC, September 1985.

—— ""Military Effectiveness of the Afghan Resistance," Testimony before the Congressional Task Force on Afghanistan, *CRS,* The Library of Congress, Washington DC, August 13, 1986.

—— "Afghanistan: Issues for U.S. Policy," in Contra Aid and the Reagan Doctrine, A major issue forum, *CRS,* Vol. 8, No. 3, March 1987.

—— "Afghanistan after the Soviet withdrawal: Contenders for powers," *CRS,* The Library of Congress, Washington DC, March 2, 1989.

—— and Miko, Francis T., "Afghanistan: Status, U.S. role, and implications of a Soviet withdrawal," *CRS,* The Library of Congress, Washington DC, April 20, 1988.

Daley, T., "Afghanistan and Gorbachev's global foreign policy," *Asian Survey,* Vol. 29, May 1989.

Davison Jr., Kenneth L., "The Geopolitics of the Soviet Withdrawal from Afghanistan," *Strategic Review,* Vol. 18, No. 1, 1990.

Delpech, Therese, "The Imbalance of Terror," *The Washington Quarterly,* Winter 2002.

Denman, D., "Afghanistan: Buffer Disappears," *Far Eastern Economic Review,* Vol. 107, January 11, 1980.

—— "Win in the Great Game," *Far Eastern Economic Review,* Vol. 110, November 14, 1980.

Dorronsoro, Gilles, "Afghanistan's Civil War," *Current History,* January 1995.

Dunbar, C., "Afghanistan in 1986: the balance endures," *Asian Survey,* Asian Survey, Vol. 27, February 1987.

—— "Afghanistan in 1987: a year of decision?" *Asian Survey,* Vol. 28, February 1988.

Dunn, Keith, "Soviet Constraints on South West Asia," *Occasional Paper,* Strategic Studies Institute, U.S. Army War College, Washington DC, December 7, 1981.

Dupree, L., "Afghanistan in 1983: and still no solution," *Asian Survey,* Vol. 24, February 1984.

—— "The Soviet Union and Afghanistan in 1987," *Current History,* Vol. 86, No. 522, October 1987.

—— "Afghanistan's Big Gamble: Part I, Historical Background of Afghan –

Russian Relations," *American Universities Field Staff Reports (AUSF)*, Vol. IV, No. 3, April 29, 1960.

—— "Afghanistan's Big Gamble: Part II, The Economic and Strategic Aspects of the Soviet Aid," *AUFS*, Vol. IV, No. 4, May 2, 1960.

—— "Afghanistan's Big Gamble: Part III, Economic Competition in Afghanistan, *AUFS*, Vol. IV, No. 5, May 9, 1960.

—— "The Mountains go to Mohammed Zahir: Observations on Afghanistan's Reactions to visits from Nixon, Bulganian-Khrushchev, Eisenhower and Khrushchev," *AUFS*, Vol. IV, No. 6, May 20, 1960.

—— "The Bamboo Curtain in Kabul: An American Finds Communication with the Chinese Embassy close to him," *AUFS*, Vol. IV, No. 7, July 31, 1960.

—— "American Private Enterprise in Afghanistan: The Investment Climate, Particularly as it relates to one company," *AUFS*, Vol. IV, No. 9, December 1, 1960.

—— "Pushtunistan: The Problems and its Larger Implications, Part I, The Complex Interrelationships of Regional Disputes," *AUFS*, Vol. V, No. 2, November 1961.

—— "Pushtunistan: The Problems and its Larger Implications, Part II, The Effects of the Afghan – Pakistan Border Closure," *AUFS*, Vol. V, No. 3, November 1961.

—— "Toward Representative Government in Afghanistan," Part II, *AUFS*, No. 14, 1978.

—— "The Democratic Republic of Afghanistan, 1979," *AUFS*, No. 32, 1979.

—— "Red Flag Over the Hindu Kush, Part V: Repressions or Security through terror purges," *AUFS*, No. 28, 1980.

—— "Red Flag Over the Hindu Kush, Part VI: Repressions or Security through terror," *AUFS*, No. 29, 1980.

—— "Red Flag Over the Hindu Kush, Part III: Rhetoric and Reforms, or Promises, Promises," *AUFS*, No. 23, 1980.

Eliot, T.L., "Afghanistan in 1989: stalemate," *Asian Survey*, Vol. 30, February 1990.

—— "Afghanistan in 1990: Groping towards peace," *Asian Survey*, Vol. 31, No. 2, February 1991.

Felton, J., "Afghanistan, human rights: Reagan, Gorbachev agree on little more than good will," *Congressional Quarterly Weekly Report*, Vol. 45, December 12, 1987.

Fromkin, Devid, "The Great Game in Asia," *Foreign Affairs*, Vol. 58, Spring 1980.

Fullerton, J., "Call to Rebellion," *Far Eastern Economic Review*, Vol. 113, September 11, 1981.

• Ganguly, Sumit, "India and Pakistan in the Shadow of Afghanistan," *Current History*, April 2002.

—— "Putting South Asia Back Together Again," *Current History*, December 2001.

Garfinkle, Adam, "Afghanistanding," *Orbis*, Vol. 43, No.3, Summer 1999.

Ghufran, Nasreen, "The Taliban and the Civil War Entanglement in Afghanistan," *Asian Survey,* Vol. 41, No. 3, May/June 2001.

Gibbs, Devid, "The Peasant as Counter – Revolutionary: The Rural Origin of the Afghan Insurgency," *Studies in Comparative International Development,* Vol. XXI, No. 1, Spring 1986.

—— "Does the USSR have a 'grand strategy,'" reinterpreting the invasion of Afghanistan," *Journal of Peace Resolution,* Vol. 24, December 1987.

Haendel, Dan, "The Persian Gulf: Geopolitics Revisited," *International Security Review,* Vol. VI, No. 1, Spring 1981.

Helliday, F., "War and Revolution in Afghanistan," *New Left Review,* No. 119, January 1980.

Hannah, N.B., "Afghanistan: The Great Gamble," *Asian Affairs,* Vol. VI, No. 3, January/February 1979.

Haqqani, H., "The Unseen Soviet Hand," *Far Eastern Economic Review,* Vol. 38, October 29, 1987.

Harrison, S.S., "Nightmare in Baluchistan," *Foreign Policy,* No. 32, Fall 1978.

—— "Dateline Afghanistan: Exit Through Finland?" *Foreign Policy,* No. 41, Winter 1980/81.

—— "Breakthrough in Afghanistan?" *Foreign Policy,* No. 51, Summer 1983.

—— "Inside the Afghan Talks," *Foreign Policy,* No. 72, Fall 1988.

Hauner, Milan, "Forum: The War in Afghanistan," *Orbis,* Vol. 29, Spring 1985.

Hersh, Seymour M., "Watching the Warheads," *The New Yorker,* November 5, 2001.

Hoffmann, Stanley, "Reflections on Present Danger," *The New York Review,* March 6, 1980.

Hyman, A., "Invaders with a sweet tooth," *New Statesman,* Vol. 100, August 8, 1980.

Islam, Mohammad, "April 1978 Coup in Kabul and the US Response," *Pakistan Journal of American Studies (PJAS),* Vol. V, No. 1, March 1987.

—— "US and the Afghan Issue," *PJAS,* Vol. VI, No. 2, September 1988.

—— "US – Afghanistan Relations: A Historical Perspective," *PJAS,* Vol. IX, No. 1 & 2, Spring/Fall 1991.

Johns, M., "The Lessons of Afghanistan: bipartisan support for freedom fighters pays off," *Policy Review,* No. 40, Spring 1987.

Judah, Tim, "The Taliban Papers," *Survival,* Vol. 44, No. 1, Spring 2002.

Kamrany, Nake M., "Afghanistan under Soviet occupation," *Current History,* Vol. 81, No. 475, May 1982.

—— "The Continuing war in Afghanistan," *Current History,* Vol. 85, No. 513, October 1986.

Karp, C.M., "The War in Afghanistan," *Foreign Affairs,* Vol. 64, Summer 1986.

Katz, Mark N., "Anti-Soviet Insurgencies: Growing Trend or Passing Phase?" *Orbis,* Vol.30, No.2, 1986.

Khalilzad, Z., "Soviet Occupied Afghanistan," *Problems of Communism,* Vol. 29, November 1980.

—— "The Soviet Dilemma in Afghanistan," *Current History,* Vol. 84, No. 509, October 1985.

—— "Moscow's Afghan War," *Problems of Communism,* Vol. 35, January/ February 1986.

—— "Afghanistan in 1993: Abandoned but Surviving," *Asian Survey,* Vol. 34, No. 2, February 1994.

—— "Afghanistan in 1994: Civil War and Disintegration," *Asian Survey,* Vol. 35, No. 2, February 1995.

—— "Afghanistan in 1995: Civil War and a Mini-Great Game," *Asian Survey,* Vol. 34, No. 2, February 1996.

—— "Anarchy in Afghanistan," *Journal of International Affairs,* Vol. 51, No. 1, Summer 1997.

Kirkpatrick, J.J., "Afghanistan: Implications for peace and security," *World Affairs,* Vol. 144, Winter 1981/82.

Klass, R.T., "The Tragedy of Afghanistan," *Asian Affairs,* Vol. 7, September/October 1979.

—— "Afghanistan: The Accords," *Foreign Affairs,* Vol. 66, Summer 1988.

Krakowski, Elie D., "Defining success in Afghanistan," *Washington Quarterly,* Vol. 8, No. 2, Spring 1985.

Kurth, James, "The New Protracted Conflict: The War and the West," *Orbis,* Spring 2002.

Levy, Walter J., "Oil: An Agenda for the 1980's," *Foreign Affairs,* Vol. 59, Summer 1981.

Lifschultz, Lawrence, "Afghanistan: The not-so-new rebellion," *Far Eastern Economic Review,* January 30, 1981.

Magnus, Ralph H., and Naby, Eden, "Afghanistan and Central Asia: Mirrors and Models," *Asian Survey,* Vol. 35, No. 7, July 1995.

Magnus, Ralph H., "Afghanistan in 1997: The War Moves North," *Asian Survey,* Vol. 38, No. 2, February 1998.

Maitre, H. Joachim, "Ask the Afghans," *Strategic Review,* Vol. 17, No. 1, 1989.

Malhuret, C., "Report from Afghanistan," *Foreign Affairs,* Vol. 62, Winter 1983/ 84.

Mehta, Jagat S., "A neutral solution," *Foreign Policy,* No. 47, Summer 1982.

Menges, Constantine, "The Diplomacy of Defeat: Are we losing Nicaragua, Angola, and Afghanistan Again?" *Policy Review,* No. 46, Fall 1988.

Miller, Steven, E., "The End of Unilateralism or Unilateralism Redux?" *The Washington Quarterly,* Winter 2002.

Mohan, C. Raja, "Geo-Politics and Energy Security," *Strategic Analysis,* Vol. 19, No. 9, December 1996.

Moss, Robert, "What Russia Wants," *The New Republic,* January 19, 1980.

Naby, E., "Ethnic Factor in Soviet – Afghan Relations," *Asian Survey,* Vol. 20,

March 1980.
Nasir, A., "New Soviet Game Plan," *Far Eastern Economic Review,* Vol. 134, November 27, 1986.
Nasir, Sohail Abdul, "Afghanistan: The more it changes. . ." *Bulletin of Atomic Scientists,* Vol. 59, No. 2, March/April 2003.
Nagaran, Hannah, "Afghanistan: A Marxist Regime in a Muslim Society," *Current History,* Vol. 76, No. 446, April 1979.
—— "Afghan coup of April 1978: revolution and international security," *Orbis,* Vol. 23, Spring 1979.
Newell, R.S., "International Response to the Afghan Crisis," *World Today,* Vol. 37, May 1981,
—— "Post – Soviet Afghanistan: the position of the minorities," *Asian Survey,* Vol. 29, November 1989.
Newman, J., "The future of northern Afghanistan," *Asian Survey,* Vol. 28, July 1988.
Overholt, W.H., "The Geopolitics of the Afghan War," *Asian Affairs,* Vol. 7, No. 4, March/April 1980.
Peake, Gordon, "From warlords to peacelords?" *Journal of International Affairs.* Vol. 56, No. 2, Spring 2003.
Pipes, Daniel, "Who is the Enemy," *Commentary,* January 2002.
Pope, R.R., "Afghanistan and the Influence of Public Opinion on Soviet Foreign Policy," *Asian Affairs,* Vol. 8, July/August 1981.
Poullada, L.B., "Afghanistan and the United States: the crucial years," *Middle East Journal,* Vol. 35, Spring 1981.
—— Failure of American Diplomacy in Afghanistan," *World Affairs,* Vol. 145, Winter 1982/83.
Radu, Michael, "Terrorism After the Cold War: Trends and Challenges," *Orbis,* Spring 2002.
Rais, R.B., "Afghanistan after the Soviet withdrawal," *Current History,* Vol. 91, No. 563, March 1992.
Ram, M., "Causes of a coup," *Far Eastern Economic Review,* Vol. 107, January 11, 1980.
Ramazani, R.K., "Comments," *Orbis,* Vol. 30, Winter 1987.
Rashid, Abdul, "An Afghan Resistance Commander Looks at the War and Its Strategic Implications," *Strategic Review,* Vol. 13, No. 1, 1985.
Rashid, Ahmed, "Afghanistan: Friend of the people," *Far Eastern Economic Review,* July 20, 1995.
—— "Afghanistan: Heart of Darkness," *Far Eastern Economic Review.* August 5, 1999.
—— "The Taliban: Exporting Extremism," *Foreign Affairs.* Vol. 78, No. 6, November/December 1999.
—— "Afghanistan: Ending the Policy Quagmire," *Journal of International Affairs,* Vol. 54, No. 2, Spring 2001.
Rubin, Barnett R., "Afghanistan: Back to Feudalism," *Current History,* Vol. 88,

No. 542, December 1989.

—— "Afghanistan: the next round," *Orbis*, Vol. 33, Winter 1989.

—— "The Fragmentation of Afghanistan," *Foreign Affairs*, Winter 1989/90.

—— "Afghanistan under the Taliban," *Current History*, February 1999.

—— "Women and pipelines: Afghanistan's proxy wars," *International Affairs*, Vol. 73, No. 2, April 1997.

Rubin, Michael, "The Teheran Temptation," *Commentary*, January 2002.

Rubinstein, Alvin Z., "Soviet Imperialism in Afghanistan," *Current History*, Vol. 79, No. 459, October 1980.

—— "Afghanistan: embraced by the bear," *Orbis*, Vol. 26, Spring 1982.

—— "The Soviet Union and Afghanistan," *Current History*, Vol. 82, No. 486, October 1983.

—— "Afghanistan at War," *Current History*, Vol. 85, No. 509, March 1986.

—— "Speculation on a National Tragedy," *Orbis*, Vol. 30, Winter 1987.

—— "The Soviet Withdrawal from Afghanistan," *Current History*, Vol. 87, No. 531, October 1988.

Rumsfeld, Donald H., "Transforming the Military," *Foreign Affairs*, Vol. 81, No. 3, May/June 2002.

Saikal, Amin, "Afghanistan's Ethnic Conflict," *Survival*, Vol. 40, No. 2, Summer 1998.

—— "The Role of outside actors in Afghanistan," *Middle East Policy*, Vol. 7, No. 4, October 2000.

Schultheis, Rob, "In Afghanistan: Peace Must Wait," *New York Times Magazine*, December 29, 1991.

Sheel, Ram Rahul, "Afghanistan in International Perspective," *International Studies*, Vol. 22, No. 2, April/June 1985.

Shultz, George P., "New Realities and New Ways of Thinking," *Foreign Affairs*, Vol. 63, No. 4, Spring 1985.

Smolansky, O.M., "Soviet Policy in Iran and Afghanistan," *Current History*, Vol. 80, No. 468, October 1981.

Steel, Ronald, "Afghanistan doesn't matter," *The New Republic*, February 1980.

Stern, Jessica, "Pakistan's Jihad Culture," *Foreign Affairs*, Vol. 79, No. 6, November/December 2000.

Stobdan, P., "War in Afghanistan," *Asian Strategic Review 1996-97*, Institute for Defence Studies and Analysis (IDSA), New Delhi.

—— "Backing Away From Afghanistan," *Strategic Analysis*, Vol. 19, No. 9, December 1996.

—— "The Afghan Conflict and Regional Security," *Strategic Analysis*, Vol. 23, No. 5, August 1999.

Strmecki, Marin, "Can the Afghan Rebels Win?" *National Review*, Vol. 38, No. 12, July 4, 1986.

Talbott, Otrobo, "Afghanistan: In the Capital of a Quagmire," *Time*, October 26, 1981.

Tarzi, Shah M., "Afghanistan in 1991: A Glimmer of Hope," *Asian Survey,* Vol. 32, No. 2, February 1992.

—— "Afghanistan in 1992: A Hobbesian State of Nature," *Asian Survey,* Vol. 33, No. 2, February 1993.

Thapar, K., "Now its up to Reagan," *New Statesman,* Vol. 111, May 30, 1986.

Tomsen, Peter, "A Chance for Peace in Afghanistan: The Taliban's Days Are Numbered," *Foreign Affairs,* Vol. 79, No. 1, January/February, 2000.

—— "Untying the Afghan Knot," *Fletcher Forum,* Vol. 25, Winter 2001.

Valenta, J., "Soviet invasion of Afghanistan: the difficulty of knowing where to stop," *Orbis,* Vol. 24, Summer 1980.

—— "From Prague to Kabul," *International Security,* Fall, 1980.

Wafadar, K., "Afghanistan in 1980: the struggle continues," *Asian Survey,* Vol. 21, February 1981.

—— "Afghanistan in 1981: the struggle intensifies," *Asian Survey,* Vol. 22, February 1982.

Wallop, Malcolm, "U.S. Covert Action: Policy Tool or Policy Hedge?" *Strategic Review,* Vol. 12, No. 3, Summer 1984.

Weinbaum, M.G., and Gautam Sen, "Pakistan Enters the Middle East," *Orbis,* Vol. 22, 1978.

Weinbaum, M.G., "Pakistan and Afghanistan: The Strategic Relationship," *Asian Survey,* Vol. 31, No. 6, June 1991.

Westad, Odd Arne, "Afghanistan: Perspective on the Soviet War," *Bulletin of Peace Proposal,* Vol. 20, No. 3, 1989.

Wright, C., "Winnable Wars," *New Statesman,* Vol. 111, March 14, 1986.

Yadav, Sanjay, "Prospects of a Non-aligned Afghanistan," *Strategic Analysis,* Vol. 12, October/March 1988/89.

Zonis, M., "Middle East Responses," *Orbis,* Vol.30, Winter 1987.

Index